TOOLS FOR PREACHING & TEACHING THE BIBLE

SECOND EDITION

Stewart Custer

STEWART CUSTER

Bob Jones University Press, Greenville, South Carolina 29614

John 5:39

Library of Congress Cataloging-in-Publication Data

Custer, Stewart, 1931–
    Tools for preaching and teaching the Bible / Stewart Custer. —
2nd ed.
      p.   cm.
    Includes bibliographical references and index.
    ISBN 0-89084-764-9
    1. Bible—Study and teaching—Bibliography. 2. Bible—
Bibliography. I. Title.
Z7770.C97 1998
[BS600.2]
220'.071—dc21
                                         97–36578
                                            CIP

NOTE:
The fact that materials produced by other publishers are referred to in this volume does not constitute an endorsement by Bob Jones University Press of the content or theological position of materials produced by such publishers. The position of Bob Jones University Press, and the University itself, is well known. Any references and ancillary materials are listed as an aid to the reader and in an attempt to maintain the accepted academic standards of the publishing industry.

Tools for Preaching and Teaching the Bible
Second Edition
by Stewart Custer

Designed by Chris Hartzler
Project Editor: Don Harrelson

©1998 Bob Jones University Press
Greenville, South Carolina 29614
First Edition ©1979 Bob Jones University Press

ISBN 0-89084-764-9

15 14 13 12 11 10 9 8 7 6 5 4 3 2 1

To the most dedicated and faithful men I know—
my colleagues in the Division of Bible of
Bob Jones University

The modern preacher in his study is a man with his tools. If he does not have the right tools upon his desk, he cannot produce rapid results and as high grade work as he otherwise may. . . . One can usually tell the quality of a preacher's work by looking at the books in his library.

—A. T. Robertson

If a man can purchase but very few books, my first advice to him would be, let him purchase the very best. If he cannot spend much, let him spend well. The best will always be the cheapest. . . . The next rule I shall lay down is, master those books you have. Read them thoroughly. Bathe in them until they saturate you.

—C. H. Spurgeon

CONTENTS

PREFACE

The person who wishes to master the content of Scripture so that its content may master him will be greatly helped by the right study tools. This book helps him select tools that will make his study more beneficial and rewarding. A pastor or Bible teacher cannot afford to be uninformed—or ill-informed—for a task as important as unfolding the Word of God for his people.

A portion of this material is adapted from a series of articles in *Biblical Viewpoint,* a semiannual journal for serious students of the Bible published by the Bob Jones University School of Religion. The bibliographies are highly selective rather than exhaustive. They are intended to suggest new vistas rather than to limit investigation. The listing of books in this volume does not necessarily mean they are available since books come into and go out of print. The reader should consult used-book dealers.

The author's special thanks goes to Dr. Ronald Horton, whose many thoughtful suggestions have added greatly to the value of this book. Dr. Mark Sidwell has also provided significant help and contributed the chapter on tools for studying church history.

The work is sent forth with the prayer that it may help to many of God's faithful servants as they seek to expound the inexhaustible treasures of God's Word. May their use of tools be attended with eternal blessing.

INTRODUCTION
THE INSPIRATION AND USE OF THE BIBLE

Conservative Christians affirm that the Bible is inspired and without error. Liberals often ask, "Why do you conservatives defend such an obscure doctrine as the inspiration of the Bible?" There is a good reason that conservative Christians emphasize this doctrine: *the Bible teaches* that it is inspired and without error. If it did not teach this, conservatives certainly would not waste their time defending this doctrine.

It is important that conservatives know what the Bible teaches on this subject and what its meaning is for their lives. When the apostle Paul describes the armor of believers, it is significant that the only offensive weapon that the believer has is the sword of the Spirit, the Word of God (Eph. 6:17). Just as it would be foolish for a soldier in an earthly army to neglect the only weapon he is issued, so it is foolish for the Christian to neglect the mastery of the one weapon at his disposal.

The Inspiration of the Bible

A vital verse on which this doctrine is based is John 10:35. When the Lord Jesus Christ was debating another subject with His opponents, He said in an aside, "The scripture cannot be broken." This is in contradistinction from the word of men. It is easy to prove the word of men to be fallible, but the Word of God, the Scripture, "cannot be broken"; that is, it cannot be loosed from its power and force in life. If the believer will take his stand on the Word of God, he will discover that the Scriptures will never fail to accomplish in his life what the Scriptures promise to do. God is not mistaken.

1

When He promises something in His Word, it shall be fulfilled. It is impossible for the Scriptures to be broken.

Someone will say, "Haven't the critics attacked portions of Scripture?" Yes, countless times, but they have not diminished its power at all. It has been proven true in the lives of multiplied millions of believers in all ages of God's dealing with men. The Bible is the power of God, for it conveys to us the revelation of the living God.

Another passage of great importance on this subject is found in the high priestly prayer of the Lord Jesus in John 17. He prayed to the Father, "Sanctify them through thy truth: thy word is truth" (John 17:17). How much error can the truth have and still be true? When the Lord Jesus said that the Word of God is truth, He did not say that it contained the truth. Liberals sometimes admit that much. The Lord said that it *is* the truth. The Word of God is made up only of the truth. It cannot have lies or falsehoods in it and still be the truth. When the believer reads the Bible, he is not reading merely the words of wise men, but the Word of the living God. Granted, we are reading words of David, Isaiah, Paul, John, and others; but God moved on the hearts of these men and breathed into this Book, the Bible, the message for the ages. The Bible is therefore the Word of God and is the Truth, not in part but in whole.

One passage in Scripture that is striking in its comparison of the human and divine elements is Acts 1:16. In the early church, Peter explained that they must seek a replacement for Judas Iscariot, who had betrayed the Lord. Peter said, "Men and brethren, this scripture must needs have been fulfilled, which the Holy Ghost by the mouth of David spake before concerning Judas, which was guide to them that took Jesus." Here, on the one hand, we see the active agent of inspiration, the Holy Spirit. The Spirit is the one who pronounced this Word, but it was foretold through the mouth of David. On the other hand, we see the human author, David, the king, who set down words filled with meaning for himself at the same time he was uttering words that the Holy Spirit was moving him to pronounce. David was the spokesman for the living God. David would be the last person in the world to take credit for Psalm 23, or any of the other seventy-three psalms that bear his name. He was indeed the human author, but he was not setting forth his own opinions or ideas: he was recording the Word of God.

Thus, while it can be said that every part of the Bible is the word of man by a human author, it must also be added that there is a divine Author: in every part it is the *Word of God*. The Holy Spirit was moving upon the hearts of these men of God, drawing out of their vocabulary, style, and experiences those expressions that would best convey His exact meaning for mankind.

When the believer reads the Bible, he must remember that he is not reading a mere book of ancient history that deals with obsolete ideas; he is reading a message designed to provide the help he needs today. The Scriptures have always shown that they can provide strength, comfort, encouragement, and power for service in every age. They are sharper than any two-edged sword. The believer will often be surprised at how convincing the Word can be. The Holy Spirit of God still illumines the Word for believers and still applies it to their hearts.

When the apostle Paul touches upon this subject, he says, "Which things also we speak, not in the words which man's wisdom teacheth, but which the Holy Ghost teacheth; comparing spiritual things with spiritual" (I Cor. 2:13). The great apostle disclaims his own wisdom. Paul does not set forth his opinions in his epistles: he sets forth the Word of the Holy Spirit. The Holy Spirit empowered him and conveyed to him the words that he recorded for all ages. Paul was not just an unusually shrewd man; he was the recipient of divine wisdom, spiritual illumination such as only God could provide. With this wisdom Paul proclaimed the infallible Word of God.

In another passage, Paul demonstrates his confidence in God's Word. He refers to a promise given to the patriarch Abraham long before, saying, "Now to Abraham and his seed were the promises made. He saith not, And to seeds, as of many; but as of one, And to thy seed, which is Christ" (Gal. 3:16). The word *seed,* Paul emphasizes, is singular rather than plural. Therefore, he argues, it must refer to Christ. There can hardly be a more minute doctrine of inspiration than this. Paul is basing his whole argument on the presence of a single word in the Old Testament text. If only the general thought in Scripture is inspired by God, and one cannot reason on the basis of the exact, individual words, Paul's argument means nothing. Paul is reasoning that the word is singular; God must have made it singular; therefore, that word must refer to one person, the Christ. The promises of God are summed up in Him. That is an analytical doctrine of inspiration. Not just the words of Scripture are inspired; even their very form is inspired.

Paul returns to the subject when he says, "All scripture is given by inspiration of God [God-breathed], and is profitable for doctrine, for reproof, for correction, for instruction in righteousness: that the man of God may be perfect, throughly furnished unto all good works" (II Tim. 3:16-17). "All Scripture" means every part of the Bible. Everything from Genesis to Revelation is "God-breathed and profitable." It does not mean that God merely breathed into the Bible some vague flavor of inspiration but rather that God breathed forth the content of the Bible. Inspiration is not merely an atmosphere in which the prophets labored; it was God's activity in communicating the content of the Scriptures. This action of God did not destroy their personalities or styles of writing but secured for us the exact message of the Word of the living God. The Word of God is profitable for everything we need in the Christian life. It is profitable for teaching: if we do not know what the will of God is for our lives, the Word of God can make known to us this very thing. It is profitable for reproof: when the believer does wrong, the reading of the Bible convicts him of that disobedience. It corrects the believer so that he may have "straight," or "orthodox," doctrine. It is not just children who need training; all believers need training in righteousness. The Word of God provides all this that the man of God may be "perfect"—perfect in the sense that the believer lacks nothing for God's service or for obedience to God's will. God, through His Word, can equip the believer so that he may be a good soulwinner, a good witness, and a consistent testimony in his community. The Bible can make the believer all this if he will use it.

The apostle Peter adds a solemn word to the subject. He says, "For the prophecy came not in old time by the will of man: but holy men of God spake as they were moved [literally, being borne along] by the Holy Ghost" (II Pet. 1:21). No part of the Bible ever originated because some man decided that such and such was a good idea; every part of the Bible is here because God moved these men to write it. No ancient prophet ever penned his own bright ideas into Scripture. The Holy Spirit moved men to set down the content of Scripture. These prophets are said to speak from God, "being borne along by the Holy Spirit." The word translated "being borne along" is the same vocabulary word used in the account of Paul's shipwreck. The great storm is described as it caught the apostle's party on the way to Rome. The sailors struggled with the sails and found that they could not bear up against the wind, so they furled the sails and were "being borne along" by the wind (Acts 27:15). They were not able to bear up against the wind and hence were driven along before the wind. This is the word used by Peter concerning these men of God who were "being borne along" by the Spirit. The prophets were not giving their opinions or their ideas; they were controlled by the Spirit of God. The message they gave was the Word of the living God.

The Use of the Bible

A person who believes in the Bible cannot benefit from it if he does not use it. When a man truly believes in something, he acts upon it. If a man believes in the public bus system, he will stand on the street corner, expecting to get a ride. If a person believes that the Bible can provide the guidance and strength that he needs, he must act upon this belief and apply himself to the use of the Word. There are several ways in which the Bible must be used if the believer is to have a strong Christian testimony.

The believer must use the Bible *against temptation.* Any believer who tries to stand for the Lord will find that he has an active foe, the Devil, who will try to destroy his testimony for Christ. Satan is always glad to send some of his emissaries to make life hard for the believer. The Devil's henchmen are always ready to try to turn to turn the believer from the path of God's will for his life. The best scriptural example of the use of the Bible against temptation is found in the life of our Lord when the Devil came to tempt him. Many believers consider that, since Christ was the great God-man incarnate, somehow His temptation was less trying than ours. Believers must not forget that He was human as surely as any ordinary believer is. Granted, He was much more than merely human, but He was truly human. He experienced the sharp cutting edge of temptation as certainly as any believer ever does. In Matthew 4:1-10, the Lord Jesus shows believers what to do about temptation. Christ does not draw upon His innate deity in order to conquer Satan's temptation; He surely could have cast the Devil down to the infernal regions if He had so desired. Instead He chose to defend Himself with the same weapon that every believer has at his disposal: the Word of God, the Sword of the Spirit.

After the Lord Jesus had fasted for forty days and forty nights, the Tempter came to Him. He suggested to the Lord that since He was the Son of God, He ought to command that the stones be made bread. The Lord was certainly hungry. The first temptation was an appeal to the physical nature. There is nothing wrong in eating; it is one of the natural acts of life. But the Devil chose hunger to sway the Lord from the path of God's will for His life. The Lord responded to this temptation by saying, "It is written, Man shall not live by bread alone, but by every word that proceedeth out of the mouth of God" (Matt. 4:4). Man cannot sustain his life by food alone; man's life is sustained by the grace of God. Vitamins and special diets cannot sustain a life one second beyond God's appointed time for that life. The Lord Jesus quoted Deuteronomy 8:3 to show that the Devil was trying to get Him to do something apart from the will of God. He used the Bible to destroy the effect of the temptation. The Lord had the power to make the stones bread, but He would not use this power selfishly—He chose instead to use the same weapon that every believer has. The Lord would not be induced into eating a wholesome meal if this meant departing from God's will.

The second temptation is the one concerning the world. The Devil brought the Lord into Jerusalem and set Him on the pinnacle of the temple and said, "If thou be the Son of God, cast thyself down: for it is written, He shall give his angels charge concerning thee: and in their hands they shall bear thee up, lest at any time thou dash thy foot against a stone" (Matt. 4:5-6). If the Lord would just cast Himself down in this public place alongside the temple, the multitudes would surely see Him and acclaim Him as the Messiah. The temptation to achieve worldly success is strong indeed. Had not Christ come to raise up God's people? What better way of gaining success in His ministry than this spectacular feat of casting Himself down before the worshiping multitudes? The Devil was not tempting the Lord to do evil; he was tempting Him to do the will of God by the wrong method. What makes the temptation even more forceful is that the Devil quotes Scripture for his suggestion. But when he quoted Psalm 91:11-12, he left out a phrase—the verses actually read, "For he shall give his angels charge over thee, to keep thee *in all thy ways*. They shall bear thee up in their hands, lest thou dash thy foot against a stone." The Devil did not want to remind the Lord that it is God's way that man must follow. Often the temptation is not to do something violent and evil but simply to set your path differently from God's path for your life. It is ultimately the choice of "my way" instead of God's way.

The Lord takes the sword of the Spirit in hand and says, "It is written again, Thou shalt not tempt the Lord thy God" (Matt. 4:7). He quoted another verse of Scripture to show that the Devil was misquoting Scripture. The Devil twists Scripture to give it his own meaning. Many times in our day the Devil's followers use the Bible to pervert its meaning. Men do not turn to the Scriptures to learn what it says but to gain support for their own selfish purposes. Liberal preachers often quote Scripture to give their false teaching an aura of piousness. Believers must learn to perceive when these false teachers are using the Bible improperly. When liberal critics tell believers not to take the Bible so seriously but just to take a few verses here and there as having meaning, the believer must be quick to disagree and to affirm the full validity of the Scriptures.

The Devil does not give up easily; he now tempts the Lord to submit to his own infernal person. "Again, the devil taketh him up into an exceeding high mountain, and sheweth him all the kingdoms of the world, and the glory of them; and saith unto him, All these things will I give thee, if thou wilt fall down and worship me" (Matt. 4:8-9). Christ came to establish the kingdom of God. It is the will of God that ultimately Christ should take the kingdoms of this world and rule over them in righteousness and holiness. The time for this, however, must be God's time. The Second Advent is the time prophesied for the triumphant rule; the First Advent was not the time. The Devil offered Christ the kingdoms of this world. He has usurped them. He could deliver them. It is no accident that the political governments of this world are opposed to God. The Devil is the prince of the power of the air; he is the god of this age. He controls governments and men who are blind to his influence. The force of the Devil's temptation is that if Christ would worship him, he would make it easy for Christ to rule. The Devil is still offering the easy path rather than the hard and narrow way.

Again the Lord takes the sword of the Spirit and says, "Get thee hence, Satan: for it is written, Thou shalt worship the Lord thy God, and him only shalt thou serve" (Matt. 4:10). Three times the Lord, faced with the harshest of temptations, used this holy Book, the Bible, to crush the temptations. This is exactly what the believer must do. When the Devil's henchmen come and start whispering, "Spare yourself," remember that the Bible provides the antidote for that kind of poison. The believer must know the Bible, meditate on its truth, and let its power grip his heart. He must feed on the Word daily to attain the strength that he needs. When the temptations come, the believer must remember that the Bible is more than adequate to meet them. The Lord Jesus Christ proved that. But when most Christians are tempted, they do not turn to the Bible. Instead they worry about whatever is tempting them and concentrate on the temptation rather than on the means of deliverance. How much better to dwell on the Scriptures and realize the strength that God has provided for poor, tempted mankind! Obviously, the believer knows the Bible, the easier it will be to wield it against the temptations of the Devil.

In the second place, the believer must use the Bible *against false doctrine*. During the last week of our Lord's earthly ministry, various groups of His opponents came to Him with difficult questions, seeking to ensnare Him in His talk. The Sadducees were one of these groups—they presented the strange story of the woman who married seven brothers in succession, all of whom died. Then they asked, "Therefore in the resurrection whose wife shall she be of the seven?" (Matt. 22:28). They had chosen this story because they did not believe in the resurrection of the dead and thought that they had a problem too complicated to solve. But the Lord Jesus responded, "Ye do err, not knowing the scriptures, nor the power of God" (Matt. 22:29). Two things are necessary. The believer must know the Scriptures, and he must experience the power of God. If a person reads the Bible without understanding it and without asking the Holy Spirit to illuminate it for him, he is not going to benefit from such reading of mere words. The believer must carefully study the Bible and seek God's help in understanding it. If the believer has correct understanding of the Bible and accepts the guidance of the Spirit in his study, he will know what correct doctrine is.

The Sadducees were teaching false doctrine because they did not understand the Scriptures and had not experienced the illuminating power of the Spirit. The Lord corrected their doctrine by saying, "For in the resurrection they neither marry, nor are given in marriage, but are as the angels of God in heaven. But as touching the resurrection of the dead, have ye not read that which was spoken unto you by God, saying, I am the God of Abraham, and the God of Isaac, and the God of Jacob? God is not the God of the dead, but of the living" (Matt. 22:30-32). The doctrine of the resurrection was implicit in the words of the Old Testament. God certainly would not call Himself the God of the dead who no longer exist; He was instead the God of the patriarchs who were very much alive. These patriarchs will one day stand on the earth in resurrection glory to bring added honor to God. This is plain in the Old Testament—if a person understands the Scriptures.

The believer must also use the Bible *for guidance*. Every believer faces many choices in his life. The path of God's will often seems to have forks in it. The believer can find help in making his decisions if he turns to the Scriptures. The psalmist often mentions this quality of the Word of God. "The law of the Lord is perfect, converting the soul: the testimony of the Lord is sure, making wise the simple" (Ps. 19:7). The Bible can impart wisdom. There is no better source of guidance for the believer than the precious Word.

The longest chapter in the Old Testament, Psalm 119, is devoted to this very theme. The psalmist claims, "I have more understanding than all my teachers: for thy testimonies are my meditation. I understand more than the ancients, because I keep thy precepts" (Ps. 119:99-100). We must remember that this was an Oriental speaking. He had profound reverence for the elders, the teachers. Throughout the Orient the aged are especially revered. Yet the psalmist states bluntly that he has more insight than his teachers and more understanding than the ancients. Was this arrogance? Was he speaking in disrespect to the elders? On the contrary, the only reason he would speak thus was that the testimonies of God had been his meditation. The Scriptures provide an insight that no mere human being could give him. He was showing the unique power of the Scriptures to give guidance and insight. The Bible is still the one Book that can provide the supernatural guidance and insight that the believer needs.

The psalmist also says, "Through thy precepts I get understanding: therefore I hate every false way" (Ps. 119:104). In order for the believer to detect which path is the true one and which is false, he must read the Word of God. Continued reading of the Word makes the believer hate the false way. The psalmist adds, "Thy word is a lamp unto my feet, and a light unto my path" (Ps. 119:105). If the believer does not use the Word, it cannot illuminate the pathway. If the believer does hold the Word up before his life, he will find that the Word sheds a light on his path and provides answers for the many questions that arise. The believer desperately needs this kind of illumination concerning God's will for his life.

The believer must also use the Bible *for soulwinning*. When Philip discovered the Ethiopian eunuch in his chariot reading the Scriptures, he was ready to guide him because Philip knew the Scriptures. When the believer speaks to a person about getting right with God, many verses should leap to mind to meet the problems that the inquiring soul may raise. The Bible provides the exact answers to the spiritual problems that man faces. The better the believer knows the Bible, the better he will be able to meet the needs of inquiring souls. God's Holy Spirit illumines the mind of the believer to enable him to meet the needs of the lost. Philip began at the very passage the eunuch was reading and expounded to him the Lord Jesus Christ in the Scriptures. Modern believers must use the same method to lead others to Christ.

It is not enough for the believer to have a cold, orthodox doctrine of the inspiration of the Bible. He must beware of saying that he believes the inspiration of the Bible and not conforming his practice to it. If the believer wholeheartedly trusts that the Bible is the Word of the living God, inspired, inerrant, and infallible, he will then use it to the utmost. He will exert every effort to master the content of Scripture and let its content master him.

PART I
THE IMPORTANCE
OF TOOLS

CHAPTER I
WHY STUDY THE BIBLE?

Every believer knows that the Bible is a good book and that he ought to study it. Many Christians, however, have no definite program of Bible study that provides spiritual help. All faithful pastors and Christian workers know that ninety-nine out of a hundred persons who come forward in invitations seeking spiritual help have no daily Bible study. They have not sought daily help from God's ordained Source, the Bible. If the average Christian were asked why he should study the Bible, he would be hard-pressed to give scriptural answers. Therefore, let us consider the reasons the Bible gives for the study of Itself.

To Gain Spiritual Food

The apostle Peter tells believers that "as newborn babes" they should "desire the sincere milk of the word" that they "may grow thereby" (I Pet. 2:2). A newborn baby that will not drink milk is in critical condition. All normal babies cry for milk. The newborn convert needs spiritual food just as much as his physical counterpart needs milk. Without daily food from God's Word, the new Christian is in critical condition spiritually. The Bible provides not only milk for new converts but also solid meat for mature believers (Heb. 5:12-14). No Christian ever gets to a point at which he does not need spiritual food. What would we think of a person who ate a big Sunday dinner and decided that it would last him until the next Sunday? Everyone knows that by Saturday he would be so weak that he would hardly be able to walk. What some believers do, however, is just as foolish. They attend church on Sunday and think the sermon will last them until the next Sunday. Daily feeding on the Word of God is just as necessary as three square meals a day.

No one can ever exhaust the Bible; it is an infinite book. The believer can study God's Word all his life and find it continually growing richer and fuller in meaning and strength-imparting power. The psalmist exclaims, "How sweet are thy words unto my taste! yea, sweeter than honey to my mouth!" (Ps. 119:103). The longer the Bible is studied, the sweeter it tastes to the believer.

To Gain Spiritual Cleansing

The Bible is necessary not only for spiritual growth but also for spiritual cleansing. When the apostle Paul discusses the relationship between husbands and wives, he uses this relationship to set forth the relationship between Christ and His church. "Husbands, love your wives, even as Christ also loved the church, and gave himself for it; that he might sanctify and cleanse it with the washing of water by the word" (Eph. 5:25-26). The Word of God is God's appointed means of cleansing His church from the defilements of the world, the flesh, and the Devil. There must be daily cleansing of the life if there is to be a good testimony. A person who concludes that since he had a bath last week or last month he does not need one today is uncivilized. If he persists in this practice, everyone will be able to tell when he is coming. There is also an unpleasant aroma emanating from someone who will not use God's appointed means of cleansing. He contaminates the atmosphere. Every time he comes near, one can expect complaining, backbiting, and selfish attitudes. Other more mature believers who treasure their daily opportunities of cleansing sweeten the atmosphere with the aroma of the presence of the Lord Jesus Christ. What a pity that some believers neglect that daily cleansing and thus harm their testimony for Christ. The old saying is still true: Either the Bible will keep you from sin, or sin will keep you from the Bible.

To Gain Spiritual Wisdom

The apostle Paul, writing to his son in the faith, Timothy, says, "But continue thou in the things which thou hast learned and has been assured of, knowing of whom thou hast learned them; and that from a child thou hast known the holy scriptures, which are able to make thee wise unto salvation through faith which is in Christ Jesus" (II Tim. 3:14-15). The Bible is the only book in the world that can impart divine wisdom. The Bible is a divinely inspired book (II Tim. 3:16). Only the Bible is "God-breathed." The Bible shows man that true faith in Christ as Savior and Lord produces salvation; all other religions deceive. Every other world religion teaches a salvation by works; the Bible alone teaches salvation by grace through faith in God's Son, the Lord Jesus Christ. The believer who holds fast the faithful Word will find that he has sound doctrine and will be able to refute those who contradict the Word (Titus 1:9). The believer must surely be on his guard against the false teachings of the cults and sects and the false interpretations of unbelieving theologians like Karl Barth and Paul Tillich. The believer who daily studies God's Word will be able to detect the errors of false teachers. God imparts His wisdom through the Word. Every believer should avail himself daily of the divine wisdom in Scripture.

To Gain Spiritual Guidance

The psalmist says, "Thy word is a lamp unto my feet, and a light unto my path" (Ps. 119:105). In biblical times a small oil lamp, no bigger than the palm of the hand, provided light for traveling about at night. The lamp would provide just enough illumination to show the path for the next step. In the same way, the Bible illuminates the spiritual path of the believer. Every believer is faced with many forks in the road, many difficult decisions to make daily. The Bible provides the help necessary to make such decisions. Believers should read the Bible devotionally, looking for guidance. The believer should pray every time he reads the Bible that God will guide him and show him the passage that will provide the insight that he needs. Believers should look for principles in Scripture that they can apply to their specific situations. They should look for examples to follow or to avoid. The Bible can provide guidance such as no earthly counselor can give. The psalmist claimed, "I have more understanding than all my teachers: for thy testimonies are my meditation" (Ps. 119:99). The psalmist was not proud; he was rejoicing in the divine guidance that the Word of the living God alone can impart.

To Increase Faith

A believer, by definition, is one who has faith. Faith in what? His faith is in God's revelation. The apostle Paul says, "So then faith cometh by hearing, and hearing by the word of God" (Rom. 10:17). A follower of Islam may have faith; a follower of the Jehovah's Witnesses may have faith. But it is only faith in God's Word that can bring life and salvation. A person becomes a Christian by faith in the Lord Jesus Christ portrayed in the Scriptures. The Christian life not only is begun with faith but also is maintained by faith. A man is saved by believing the promises in God's Word about the salvation in Christ; he then must increase his faith by continuing to read the Scriptures. One of the glories of the Berean Christians was that "they received the word with all readiness of mind, and searched the scriptures daily, whether those things were so." The result was that "many of them believed" (Acts 17:11-12*a*). Their faithful reading of the Scriptures produced faith in their hearts. Christians who desire to make progress in the Christian life must believe that God has a blessing for them in the study of His Word. In discovering this blessing, they will also discover that God has a blessing for them in the fellowship of prayer and in the service of witnessing for Him. As they continue studying God's Word, all of God's blessings will be realized in their lives.

To Be Transformed into His Image

What a person continues looking at will sooner or later change his appearance. Everyone has seen photographs in the newspaper of murderers and other criminals and been struck by the hardness of their faces. This hardness is not accidental. Young people sometimes think that they can let their minds dwell on dirty books or pictures and no one will ever know, but such practices leave scars on the faces of those who do such things. The apostle Paul holds before us a glorious possibility: "But we all, with open face beholding as in a glass the glory of the Lord, are changed into the same image from glory to glory, even as by the Spirit of the Lord" (II Cor. 3:18). As a believer meditates on the portrait of the Lord Jesus Christ in the Bible, the Holy Spirit of God conforms him to the image of Christ, making him more like his blessed Lord. The Spirit of God is continually forming the character of the Lord Jesus Christ within the believer. As the believer continues in the Word, his very appearance is changed. That is why some of the saints who have walked with the Lord for a generation have such beatific countenances. The presence of the Lord can be seen in them. No greater blessing can be imparted to believers.

To Gain the Knowledge of God

The apostle Paul continues, "For God, who commanded the light to shine out of darkness, hath shined in our hearts, to give the light of the knowledge of the glory of God in the face of Jesus Christ" (II Cor. 4:6). The more a believer studies the portrait of the Lord Jesus Christ in the Scriptures, the more true knowledge of God he obtains. This knowledge is not mere information about God, such as theological definitions or the attributes of God. The term *knowledge* in Scripture regularly implies real fellowship and unity with the person known. Believers know God in the sense of obeying Him, living for Him, and seeking to please Him. The most striking instance of this usage is the euphemistic use of the word *know* for a husband's sexual relations with his wife—the most intimate and unifying aspect of marriage (Gen. 4:1; Matt. 1:24-25). The biblical word *know* implies a fellowship and a unity that vastly transcends mere information. The believer who lets his mind dwell on the portrait of the Lord Jesus Christ in Scripture will come to know God in the sense of manifesting oneness with God in obedience to His will. People will be able to tell that he has been with Jesus (Acts 4:13).

To Impart the Blessing of the Word

Every believer must "be ready always to give an answer to every man that asketh [him] a reason of the hope that is in [him]" (I Pet. 3:15). The best answer that a believer can give to the world is the Word, upon which his hope is based. One of the qualifications of the bishop is that he be "apt to teach" (I Tim. 3:2). It is clear that what he must teach is the Word of God. Paul plainly commands, "Preach the word" (II Tim. 4:2). There is no surer way to impart blessing to others than to be able to give them the truth of the precious Word of God that the believer cherishes. To be able to share the Faith with others is a high privilege. The believer has a ministry of reconciliation and is an ambassador for Christ (II Cor. 5:18-20). Sharing blessings with others never diminishes them for the believer: the believer is like a flowing stream of blessing and is never stronger than when he is the instrument of blessing to others.

Daily prayerful reading of God's Word is necessary not only for the ministry of preachers but also for the spiritual prosperity of every born-again Christian. Today the believer is surrounded by so many temptations to waste his time and by so many false teachings of cults and sects that he must maintain his daily devotional study of God's Word to keep from being swallowed up in the world's activities and deceptions. There has never been an age in which the quiet time with God and His Word was more needed in the believer's life than it is now. He should meditate daily on God's Word, praying over every verse that God would show him His will and impart to him His blessing and the strength that he needs for the day.

The Scriptures contain many instructive examples of Bible study for students today. When Moses mentioned the possibility that the Israelites would have a king over them one day, he gave strict commands for the king to be a Bible student: "And it shall be, when he sitteth upon the throne of his kingdom, that he shall write him a copy of this law in a book out of that which is before the priests the Levites: and it shall be with him, and he shall read therein all the days of his life: that he may learn to fear the Lord his God, to keep all the words of this law and these statutes, to do them" (Deut. 17:18-19). It is certainly no less suitable for every believer to have his personal copy of the Bible and to study it daily all his life.

In Psalm 119 the psalmist speaks continually of his benefit from studying and meditating upon the Word of God: "O how love I thy law! it is my meditation all the day. . . . I have more understanding than all my teachers: for thy testimonies are my meditation"(Ps. 119:97, 99). He speaks of the pleasure this study has given him: "How sweet are thy words unto my taste! yea, sweeter than honey to my mouth!" (Ps. 119:103). He speaks also of the guidance he has received from his study: "Thy word is a lamp unto my feet, and a light unto my path" (Ps. 119:105). The believer today, like the psalmist, ought to meditate on the Scriptures; he can find understanding, guidance, and joy by his personal study of God's Word.

The prophet Daniel explained the benefits of his personal study of the Scriptures: "In the first year of his reign I Daniel understood by books the number of the years, whereof the word of the Lord came to Jeremiah the prophet, that he would accomplish seventy years in the desolations of Jerusalem" (Dan. 9:2). Even though Daniel was an inspired prophet himself, he studied the writings of another prophet, Jeremiah, and learned through his study that God would banish Israel from its land for seventy years. If an inspired prophet felt the need of studying other Scriptures, it is certainly fitting for believers today to study the Bible with diligence to learn God's purpose for themselves.

When the Israelites had returned from their captivity, Ezra the scribe instructed them in the Scriptures systematically: "So they read in the book in the law of God distinctly, and gave the sense, and caused them to understand the reading" (Neh. 8:8). Since the Israelites by that time were speaking Aramaic, they would have had some difficulty understanding Hebrew text. Ezra interpreted the text for them and caused them to understand it. That is a standing challenge to preachers to this day. It is a solemn responsibility to cause a congregation to understand the Word of the living God in our time. Far too often the congregation does not understand the text that is read and the preacher does not take the time to explain it.

The Lord Jesus Christ was Himself an example of a biblical expositor. He placed no premium on ignorance. When He appeared to the disciples in the upper room after His resurrection, He caused them to understand the Scriptures about Himself: "Then opened he their understanding, that they might understand the scriptures" (Luke 24:45). He then went on to explain to them the meaning of the messianic prophecies. If they were going to have a gospel to preach, they would have to understand the meaning of Scripture. It is still our responsibility to seek the illumination of the Lord in understanding His Word. The apostle Peter explained the Scriptures and expounded a text from Joel on the day of Pentecost (Acts 2:14-21). He was obviously explaining what he had heard his Lord explain. He was also inaugurating the New Testament style of preaching: taking a text and explaining it. For almost twenty centuries this style has been common in both textual and expository preaching.

In a striking passage, believers who study the Bible are represented as more noble than others: "These were more noble than those in Thessalonica, in that they received the word with all readiness of mind, and searched the scriptures daily, whether those things were so" (Acts 17:11). Their example should encourage all believers to undertake a systematic and diligent study of God's Word. The daily searching or examining of the Scriptures in the will of God still forms nobility of character.

One of the most moving scenes in the Bible is that in which the apostle Paul in prison writes to his son in the faith, Timothy, saying, "The cloke that I left at Troas with Carpus, when thou comest, bring with thee, and the books, but especially the parchments" (II Tim. 4:13). The apostle Paul, at the end of a long and arduous ministry, was still diligently studying the Holy Scriptures, the parchments, and other books, no doubt about the Scriptures. He did not presume upon his divine inspiration to relieve himself of the necessity of studying God's Word with all the tools at his disposal. Until his death he was a student of the Word. His conscientious study surely convicts all believers of their own personal responsibility of a continuing and determined study of God's Holy word.

CHAPTER 2
WHY STUDY WITH TOOLS?

Why is it that many people study the Bible without seeming to gain any benefit from it? Young people often ask pastors, "How can I study the Bible so that it will really help me? I study it, but it doesn't seem to mean anything." People do not get the right answers from their Bible study because they have not learned to ask the right questions. Let us ask some questions that will help us improve our study of the Bible.

What Is Bible Study Supposed to Do?

If one were to ask a class of serious Bible students what they expected to get out of Bible study, their answers would no doubt include (1) gaining spiritual benefit, (2) finding out what is there, (3) preserving from error, and (4) equipping to teach others. Certainly Bible study should accomplish these purposes.

How Are Its Purposes Accomplished?

The Lord Jesus Christ said, "*Search* the scriptures; for in them ye think ye have eternal life: and they are they which testify of me" (John 5:39). The word *search* means "examine," "investigate," or "trace out." It implies a diligent and systematic search. A physician may examine a wound. An explorer may map the countryside. The context of the verse indicates, however, that the audience was a very hostile one, which had refused to believe in Christ. The Lord adds, "And ye will not come to me, that ye might have life" (John 5:40). This tells us that the true benefit of Bible study is found in Christ. No matter how diligent the search, it will not be of benefit unless there is faith in Christ. The student must be prepared to believe what he finds in Scripture and must submit to the authority of Christ. The writer to the Hebrews warns, "The word preached did not profit them, not being mixed with faith in them that heard it" (Heb. 4:2). We must search the Scriptures with submission to the Lord Jesus Christ to gain spiritual benefit.

After His resurrection, the risen Lord appeared to the disciples on the road to Emmaus, "and beginning at Moses and all the prophets, he *expounded* unto them in all the scriptures the things concerning himself" (Luke 24:27). The word *expounded* means "explained," "interpreted," or "translated." The Lord called to their attention the messianic prophecies concerning Himself and caused them to understand their meaning. The disciples had no doubt read those passages before but without understanding them. Now they found out what was really there. No wonder the psalmist prays, "Open thou mine eyes, that I may behold wondrous things out of thy law" (Ps. 119:18). We all need that spiritual insight, that illumination to understand the Word of God. Explaining, expounding, and interpreting imply a use of proper principles of interpretation. But proper principles of interpretation do not rule out the need for humble dependence on the illumination of the Holy Spirit of God. We must find out what is there by reverent study and prayer.

When the Sadducees came to Jesus with their tricky question about the woman who had married seven husbands, He gave them a sharp answer: "Ye do err, not *knowing* the scriptures, nor the power of God" (Matt. 22:29). The word translated "knowing" refers to intuitive knowledge, "having insight into." The Sadducees had become heretical because they did not have insight into the real meaning of Scripture. The apostle Paul prays that believers be "enriched by him, in all utterance, and in all knowledge" (I Cor. 1:5). If we are to be preserved from error, we must gain insight into the Scriptures so that we can detect at once any deviation from the standard of Scripture. Our stand must be based on a clear knowledge of the Scriptures and an experience of the power of God in our lives.

The apostle Paul wrote to Timothy and charged him, "The things that thou hast heard of me among many witnesses, the same commit thou to faithful men, who shall be able to teach others also" (II Tim. 2:2). The phrase translated "able to teach" conveys the idea of being "sufficient for teaching." Men who are faithful to the things they have learned from the Scriptures will be sufficient to the task of training others to stand fast. Paul also exhorted Timothy, "Take heed unto thyself, and unto the doctrine; continue in them: for in doing this thou shalt both save thyself, and them that hear thee" (I Tim. 4:16, one of the famous 4:16's in Scripture: cf. II Cor. 4:16; I Thess. 4:16; Heb. 4:16). If we are going to be able to teach others the truth, we must have that faithful dedication to the Word of God that characterized Timothy.

Where Do I Start?

The first method of Bible study must be the study of the Bible as a whole. The believer must not forget that, even though he is studying one passage, his goal is the mastery of the whole Book. No part of Scripture should be interpreted without considering the overall teaching of the Bible on that subject. It is useful to pursue two methods of study at the same time to accomplish this. The student should be engaged in a rapid survey of the whole Bible, reading it through to gain a "bird's-eye view" of the whole of revelation. At the same time it is well to concentrate on a specific passage, analyzing every phrase and word in it. As he continues adding one short passage to another, his thorough knowledge will begin to supplement his survey of the Book. If the student has not read through the Bible twenty-five times, he should take steps to correct that. Of course, he certainly will not want to stop then.

The bird's-eye view of Scripture, considered by itself, is called *synthesis.* This method seeks to relate any given passage to the teaching of the entire Scriptures. It tries to explain Scripture by Scripture. Cross-references are often a great help in explaining Scripture. In the Gospels the parallel passages can shed much light on different subjects. One whole book devoted to this method of study is James M. Gray's *Synthetic Bible Studies.*

Analysis is the opposite method of study. It seeks to take apart and examine everything in a passage or book of the Bible. The outlining, defining, and explaining of the contents of a passage is analysis. An example of this method is G. Campbell Morgan's *Analyzed Bible.* These two methods should not be regarded as opposed to one another but should be used together in order that both analysis and synthesis may add their parts to the student's understanding of a passage.

How Can I Do It?

If a believer has merely read the Bible but never really studied it, he may not know where to start in his analysis of a passage. It is important to ask the right questions. One should ask the following questions of every passage of Scripture that he studies. The usefulness of tools in answering these questions will become obvious.

What is the main theme? The main theme or proposition is what the passage is all about. The best way to perceive the theme is to settle down with the passage and to read it over and over and over again until an impression of the main idea begins to form in the mind. When it becomes clear, it is time to write it down. It should be no more than a single phrase or a short sentence. The theme of the passage will be the theme of an expositional message on that passage. Concerning sermon preparation, the famous preacher John Henry Jowett once wrote, "I have a conviction that no sermon is ready for preaching . . . until we can express its theme in a short, pregnant sentence as clear as crystal. I find the getting of that sentence is the hardest, the most exacting, and the most fruitful labour in my study" (*The Preacher, His Life and Work,* p. 133). That is good advice from a master-craftsman of sermons. Once one knows what the passage is all about, it is time to ask another question.

What is a good outline? The need for an outline should not send one to a book of sermons or a commentary to steal someone else's outline. Instead, one should go back to the passage and start reading it over again. Now it is time to look for the natural divisions in the passage. Certain tools can be a help. Good reference editions of the Bible and, of course, the Greek Testament will show at once what the natural paragraph divisions of the passage are. Now one should take each division and read it over until he can state its meaning in a short phrase, trying to keep the phrases parallel in form. The points of the outline should prove the main theme. If the outline and the theme do not agree, either the outline is illogical or the theme is inaccurate. One should work on both until the points of the outline logically prove the theme, step by step. The number of points in the outline is not important, but their logical relationship is vital. One homiletician has divided all sermons into the vertebrate and the molluscan types (Lenski, *The Sermon,* p. 76). The vertebrate type is far better. Once one has a clear theme and a logical outline, it is time to ask further questions.

What is the background? Here a whole series of questions leaps to mind. Who wrote the passage? When did he write it? To whom did he write it? What are the conditions of that time? From this point on, the tools used become increasingly important. A good Bible dictionary (*International Standard Bible Encyclopedia* [ISBE] or *Zondervan Pictorial Encyclopedia of the Bible* [ZPEB]) can provide much help. It is well to consult a good Old Testament introduction (Archer or Young) or New Testament introduction (Thiessen or Guthrie). With the right tools, the answers to these questions are readily attainable.

Where are the geographical places mentioned? One should never guess but, instead, reach for a good Bible atlas that has clear maps. A geography of the Bible can be a real help at this point, for not only the cities but also the terrain may be important for interpretation. The natural geography sometimes makes a place important. Jericho became important because of its location. Megiddo, because of its geographical situation, has figured in every invasion that has passed through Palestine and will figure in the future battle of Armageddon. Geography must influence any exposition of the Exodus or the wilderness wanderings, the exile, or the journeys of Paul. The highways linking countries and cities often figure in the events described in Scripture. It is important to determine what religious significance the places have had.

Who are the people mentioned? How are their characters manifested elsewhere in the Scripture? ISBE has very strong articles on biblical persons. Books on Bible biography can be a help as well.

The Bible is filled with accounts of persons; they are all there for a purpose.

What do the sentences of the text mean? The student should think through every sentence to be sure that he understands the meaning. He should pray that God's Holy Spirit will illuminate his mind to perceive what is important about the statement. It is well to consult several commentaries. If they disagree on interpretation, one should determine why and seek the best interpretation. If the student is fortunate enough to know Greek or Hebrew, grammatical meaning will often settle the interpretation.

What do the words mean? The sentences cannot be interpreted correctly if the words are not understood as well. Every serious Bible student should have an analytical concordance to the Bible, such as Young's or Strong's. He can then trace down every occurrence of a word used in the Bible, which is sometimes necessary before a meaning can be determined in the immediate context. If there is any uncertainty about the meaning of the English words, they should be looked up in an English dictionary. If the student knows Greek or Hebrew, the words of the text should be looked up in appropriate lexicons. Studies in synonyms, such as Girdlestone on the Old Testament and Trench and Custer on the New Testament, add much to the understanding of words. The better commentaries will often give very valuable help in word studies.

What doctrines are taught? When the meaning of the words and sentences is established, the student should think through the text again to perceive the different doctrines that are taught or implied by the statements of the text. He should consult books on theology to determine the best definitions of doctrines and to discover where those doctrines are dealt with elsewhere in Scripture. If the student discovers that these doctrines are under attack by unbelievers, he should pray over them and study them with special care so that he may strengthen his own faith and the faith of those to whom he ministers.

What parallels can be found? A good reference Bible can provide great help by its marginal references and notes. Nestle's

Greek Testament suggests some of the most apt parallels of any work. A harmony of the Gospels (a work that weaves the different Gospel accounts together) is often the quickest way to see parallels in the Gospels.

What topics appear in the text? It is well for the student to keep a record of the major topics that appear in the text. Some of them may arouse his interest so much that he will start a study of the topic through the whole book he is studying or even throughout all of Scripture.

What principles can be formulated from the text? Does the text teach certain principles of God's dealing with men? Or does it teach principles of Christian conduct? Does the text reveal the evil workings of sin or the methods of temptation of the Devil? Does it deal with principles of prayer or of faithfulness?

How does the context influence the passage? The student should always look carefully at the passages that precede and follow the one that he is currently studying. No interpretation can be correct if it contradicts the context. The study of the context will often preserve one from making an inaccurate interpretation.

What is the purpose of the passage? It is important to consider the larger context of the whole book in which the given passage is found. How does this passage fit into the logical structure of the whole book? What did the author intend this passage to say? There are times when the student must raise the question to an even higher step. What does the divine Author intend men to see in this passage in the context of His Word?

Other Methods of Bible Study

There are other methods of Bible study available in addition to studying specific passages in depth. Often the study of a passage will create an interest in another area. For example, during a study of Jesus' arrest in the garden, the Bible student might become interested in Peter's action of cutting off the servant's ear and decide to trace the life of Peter through the New Testament.

One of the most helpful methods of Bible study is the study of whole books of the Bible. ***Biblical Viewpoint*** is devoted to this kind of study in all the regular issues.* The Bible student should select his favorite book of the Bible and determine to master it. He should read the book through over and over to determine its main theme and to outline its contents. Then he should read each chapter and give headings for each chapter. He will find that the chapter division regularly corresponds to the larger division of the outline. Then he should apply the preceding questions to each paragraph or subsection in the book, one after another. He should learn who every person is who is mentioned in it, what and where every place is, and what every doctrine means that is found in it. In doing so he will consult books on Bible biography, Bible atlases, books on theology, and other sources. As he continues making one exposition after another, his skill of analysis and outlining will increase. He should be careful to spend much time in prayer to determine the meaning of the text and to apply its meaning to himself. He should try to get a group of commentaries on the book that he is working on and to read them all in conjunction with the text as he studies. If the student has only one commentary on a given book of the Bible, he may be following the private interpretations of the commentator without being aware of it. If he reads several commentaries, he will be able to see the points at which they all agree, and the others at which private interpretations are advanced.

When he finishes studying the book as a whole, it can be divided into paragraphs (in addition to chapters and verses) to be studied in depth. By this time the organic unity of the book and an amazing quantity of factual and devotional teaching will be clear. When the student has thoroughly mastered that book of the Bible and has let its truth master him, he has only sixty-five more to go! The amazing

---

Biblical Viewpoint is a journal for Bible study published biannually by Bob Jones University. For information write
Biblical Viewpoint
Bob Jones University
Greenville, SC 29614

thing about this kind of careful Bible study is that the Bible student can come back to a book after twenty years and work through it again with even greater blessing and benefit because his abilities have increased over the years so that he can now see much more in the Word than he could see before. The Bible is an infinite book and can never be exhausted in its meaning or blessing no matter how carefully it is studied. There is always more there than the expositor has yet seen.

After a study of specific books, chapters, paragraphs, verses, and even words, there are still many avenues of study. Topical study, for example, has been continually popular. Great topics such as grace, prayer, faith, the deity of Christ, the love of God, the coming judgment, heaven, and hell have been the object of much study and the source of great blessing to multitudes. This method was the favorite of D. L. Moody; he often encouraged it, as he did in his book *Pleasure and Profit in Bible Study.* Here again the student needs a good concordance to trace out the references to such subjects. An inexpensive aid is the *New Topical Textbook.* R. A. Torrey's *What the Bible Teaches* and the latest edition of Jerome Smith's *Treasury of Scripture Knowledge* may also help.

Another similar method is the biblical theological method of Bible study. In this method a subject is studied by the chronological order of the passage in which it is revealed in the Bible. It is thrilling to see a great doctrine unfold through the writings of Moses, the histories and prophets, the Gospels, the Epistles, and finally the Book of Revelation. Such a study shows how a doctrine is revealed in germ form, grows, expands, and becomes clearer and more detailed. Ideal subjects are the doctrines of God, Christ, the Holy Spirit, salvation, prophecy, sin, and the kingdom.

One of the most interesting methods is the biographical study. The study of Bible characters is rich in instruction and inspiration. It is necessary to search out the entire scriptural teaching on a person; it is not enough to take only one passage or event. An amazing amount of truth and blessing can be found in the lives of Jacob, David, Thomas, Stephen, Timothy, and others. The lives of men like Abraham and Paul lend themselves to whole series of sermons. The preacher who was most famous for his biographical sermons was Alexander Whyte, whose messages were collected into a six-volume set entitled *Bible Characters.*

A fascinating but rarely used method is the study of biblical geography. Many locations mentioned in Scripture make perfect subjects for messages. It is exciting to watch the drama of the ages unfold in a particular place as one traces through the Bible the references to cities such as Bethlehem or Hebron, mountains such as Olivet or Sinai, valleys such as Jehoshaphat, and rivers such as the Arnon, Jordan, and Euphrates. Whole series of sermons could be delivered on the significance of the holy city Jerusalem in Scripture. The geographical subjects are inexhaustible. For this study it is essential that the expositor have the best in Bible atlases, geographies, and dictionaries.

Another area rich in truth is the study of types and symbols. A type is a divinely authorized illustration of a scriptural doctrine. If Scripture does not make such an identification, it may be an illustration but not a type. One of the richest areas for the study of types is the tabernacle with all its furniture and ministry. The ark with the mercy seat, the lampstand, the altar, the laver, and the other articles all illustrate the ministry of the Lord Jesus Christ. The different kinds of sacrificial offerings are another type study. Persons such as Melchizedek, Abraham, Aaron, and Adam are also types. In this study a concordance is necessary to find the New Testament antitype for the fulfilled reality of the type. One of the most helpful books on this subject is Patrick Fairbairn's *Typology of Scripture.*

One of the most important methods is the theological study. This method seeks to find and unfold the doctrines in a passage of Scripture. These doctrines must always be interpreted in the light of the overall teaching of Scripture. Many sections in the New Testament Epistles are filled with doctrinal passages that are themselves the basis of systematic theology. These passages should never be studied in a coldly technical manner, but rather the student should recognize that these passages are the Word of the living God, filled with spiritual truth that he needs for his own Christian life.

A method absolutely necessary to the success of the others is the devotional study. The student should never come to Scripture with the idea of finding truth that applies only to someone else. He must come to the Bible looking for a personal blessing for himself. When he finds it, it will surely be worth sharing with others. As the old expositor J. A. Bengel said, "Apply thyself wholly to the text; apply the text wholly to thyself." We must always be alert to find a promise we can claim, a prayer we can echo, an error we must avoid, and an example we can follow. Your study must meet your spiritual need; if it does not bless your heart, it cannot bless others.

The Bible student should record his results in studying the Bible in a notebook or in the pages of a reference Bible. He should not hesitate in marking his reference Bible. The old saints used to regularly mark "railways" in their Bibles, linking a common theme over a chapter or several chapters. (See chart on railways, p. 34.) The *Thompson Chain Reference Bible* recommends a color-coded marking system (App. 4315). The *International Inductive Study Bible* gives several pages of examples of Bible marking (pp. IISB-15b–IISB-19, IISB-21). However it is done, the results of study should be recorded.

Once in a while one hears a sincere but self-assured preacher say, "I don't need all those commentaries and books about the Bible. All I need is my Bible and God the Holy Spirit!" Now there is no doubt that God the Holy Spirit can and does make up for defective preparation resulting from unavoidable circumstances. There may be abundant compensation. But God will not make up for a willful refusal to utilize providentially provided aids and helps. The angel made the chains fall off Peter's hands and the great iron gate swing noiselessly open but would not stoop to tie Peter's sandal thongs (Acts 12:7-10). The Holy Spirit may well bring to a preacher's mind a verse of Scripture during the course of a sermon or may cause certain verses in Scripture to come to his attention as though they were written in letters of fire, but He will not memorize the Scripture for the preacher, nor will He study the Bible for him. If

ST. JOHN 15, 16

The true Vine

4 Abide *c*in me, and I in you. As the branch cannot bear fruit of itself, except it abide in the vine; no more can ye, except ye abide in me.

5 I am the vine, ye *are* the branches: He that abideth in me, and I in him, the same bringeth forth much *d*fruit: for ¹without me ye can do nothing.

6 If a *e*man abide not in me, he is cast forth as a branch, and is withered; and men gather them, and cast *them* into the fire, and they are burned.

7 If ye abide in me, and my words abide in you, ye shall ask what ye will and it shall be done unto you.

8 Herein *f*is my Father glorified, that ye bear much fruit; so shall ye be my disciples.

9 As the Father hath loved me, so have I loved you: continue ye in my love.

10 If ye keep my commandments, ye shall abide in my love; even as I have kept my Father's commandments, and abide in his love.

11 These things have I spoken unto you, that my joy might remain in you, and *g*that your joy might be full.

12 This *h*is my commandment, That ye love one another, as I have loved you.

13 Greater *i*love hath no man than this, that a man lay down his life for his friends.

14 Ye are my friends, if ye do whatsoever I command you.

15 Henceforth I call you not servants; for the servant knoweth not what his lord doeth: but I have called you friends; *j*for all things that I have heard of my Father I have made known unto you.

16 Ye *k*have not chosen me, but I have chosen you, and *l*ordained you, that ye should go and bring forth fruit, and *that* your fruit should remain: that

whatsoever ye shall ask of the Father in my name, he may give you.

17 These things I command you, that ye love one another.

18 If *m*the world hate you, ye know that it hated me before *it hated you.*

19 If *n*ye were of the world, the world would love his own: *o*but because ye are not of the world, but I have chosen you out of the world, therefore the world hateth you.

20 Remember the word that I said unto you, The servant is not greater than his lord. If they have persecuted me, they will also persecute you; if they have kept my saying, they will keep yours also.

21 But all these things will they do unto you for my name's sake, because they know not him that sent me.

22 If *q*I had not come and spoken unto them, they had not had sin: but *r*now they have no ²cloke for their sin.

23 He *g*that hateth me hateth my Father also.

24 If I had not done among them the works which none other man did, they had not had sin: but now have they both seen and hated both me and my Father.

25 But *this cometh to pass*, that the word might be fulfilled that is written in their law, *t*They hated me without cause.

26 But *u*when the Comforter is come, whom I will send unto you from the Father, *even* the Spirit of truth, which proceedeth from the Father, *v*he shall testify of me:

27 And *w*ye also shall bear witness because *x*ye have been with me from the beginning.

CHAPTER 16

THESE things have I spoken unto you, that ye should not be offended.

d Pro. 11.30.
Hosea 14.8.
Luke 13.6-9.
Gal. 5.22.
Phil. 4.13.

1 Or, severed from me.

e Matt. 3.10.
Heb. 6.4-6.

f Matt. 5.16.
Phil. 1.11.

g ch. 16.24.
1 John 1.4.
h 1 Thes. 4.9.
1 Pet. 4.8.

i Rom. 5.7.
Eph. 5.2.
j Gen. 18.17-19.
Matt. 13.11.
Acts 20.27
Rom. 16.25, 26.
k 1 John 4.10.
l Mark 16.15.
m 1 John 3.13.
n 1 John 4.5.
o ch. 17.14.
p Eze. 3.7.
q Gen. 9.41.
r Rom. 1.20.
2 Or, excuse.
s 1 John 2.23.
t Ps. 35.19.
Ps. 69.4.
u ch. 14.26.
Acts 1.4.
v 1 John 5.6.
w Acts 1.8.
1 Pet. 5.1.
2 Pet. 1.16.
x Luke 1.2.

CHAP. 16

a Acts 1.8.
b Rom. 10.2.
1 Cor. 2.8.
1 Tim. 1.13.
c Acts 2.33.
Eph. 4.8.
1 Or, convince.
d Acts 2.22.
Rom. 3.9.
Gal. 3.22.
e Isa. 42.6, 21.
Dan. 9.24.
Acts 2.32.
1 Cor. 1.30.
Gal. 5.5.
f Matt. 12.18, 36.
Acts 10.42.
1 Cor. 4.5.
Heb. 6.2.
Rev. 1.7.
g Luke 10.18.
ch. 12.31.
Eph. 2.2.

it be true that we do not need anything but the Bible, then we do not need the preacher's interpretation either. We may take our Bible and go home and read it. But the arrogant preacher did not intend that. What he really intended was that people listen to his explanation of the Bible and to no other. This is arrogant piosity.

Tools are no substitute for diligent firsthand study of the Bible in humble dependence on the guidance of the Holy Spirit. But the student should use all the helps he can find. God has commanded that believers not forsake the assembling of themselves together (Heb. 10:25) because they need the help of one another. The church is a fellowship, not just a collection of individuals. Likewise, the experiences and insights of others can be a real help to students of the Bible. The commentaries of Charles Hodge, who taught the Pauline Epistles for fifty years, greatly illuminate the books of Romans and I and II Corinthians. The godly and faithful explanations of many other devout men can be a rich blessing and a source of true insight into the meaning of Scripture.

There are several good biblical reasons for using tools in Bible study. First, tools are needed to avoid the arrogance of self-sufficiency. We are reminded of the words of Job to his heartless "comforters": "No doubt but ye are the people, and wisdom shall die with you" (Job 12:2). When a man gets the idea that he has a private supply of divine wisdom, he becomes a harsh man and a very poor interpreter of God's Word. We do not disparage the idea of personal Bible study; we encourage it. But we do disparage the idea that a student should seek no help from others for his understanding of the Bible. Second, use tools in Bible study to add the illumination of other spiritual minds to yours. When Apollos went to the believers at Corinth, he "helped them much" (Acts 18:27). The spoken or written words of a godly man can be a great help in Bible study and in the discipline of living what is learned. When the average Bible student has studied a given passage carefully and then turns to four or five good commentaries on the passage, he is usually astonished to see all that he has overlooked in the passage. The apostle Paul longed to see the Roman believers and desired to impart spiritual blessing to them (Rom. 1:11, 15). How much poorer we would all be if the apostle had not shared his thoughts, but it is also true that he had thought long and deeply upon the Old Testament revelation concerning Abraham (Gal. 3:6-7), David (Rom. 4:6-8), the patriarchs (Rom. 9:9-15), and Isaiah (Rom. 9:27-29). No wonder believers flocked to listen to him and even listened all night (Acts 20:7-11).

Tools are not an end in themselves; they are the means to an end. The use of tools is vitally important. It is possible for a farmer to break up ground with his bare hand to plant seed; it is possible to pull weeds with the fingers, but it is much easier and efficient to do it with a hoe and a rake. A far greater harvest can be gained by using a modern tractor and commercial sowers and harvesters. The application to Bible study is obvious. When the Bible student draws upon commentaries and reference works, he is drawing upon the results of thousands of years of Bible study. He can see so much because he is standing upon the shoulders of generation after generation of dedicated students of the Bible who have shared the benefits of their study of God's Word with others. "Get thy tools ready; God will provide the work."

PART II
THE USE
OF TOOLS

CHAPTER 3
PRINCIPLES OF INTERPRETATION

If everything in the Bible were always simple and clear, there would be no need for interpreting it. Although many passages are clear and simple, there are some passages that even the biblical writers themselves admit are "hard to be understood" (II Pet. 3:16). Furthermore, the Bible is an infinite book with a profundity of meaning that no scholar can exhaust. The scholars call the study of how to understand the Scriptures *hermeneutics:* the branch of theology that determines rules for the interpretation of Scripture. If a person comes to the Bible with liberal presuppositions and a set of liberal hermeneutical principles, he will surely leave with a liberal theology and a very destructive interpretation of the Bible. The fact that men like Rudolf Bultmann and Ernst Fuchs have torn the Bible into little pieces trying to "demythologize" it should surprise no one. They began as radical liberal form critics, and their liberal interpretation logically followed. If a person comes to the Bible with conservative presuppositions and a set of conservative hermeneutical principles, he will end with a conservative theology and a constructive interpretation of the Bible. It should surprise no one that men like Leon Morris and Edmond Hiebert write books that are constructive and genuinely helpful to Bible students. As conservative scholars, they have applied conservative principles to the understanding of the Bible.

An interpreter of the Bible must be spiritually qualified. He must be a born-again believer in order to have spiritual perception (John 3:3). He must be a surrendered and obedient believer in order to know the truth (John 7:17). He must be taught by the Holy Spirit of God (I Cor. 2:10-16). He must be a man of prayer to attain wisdom (James 1:5). He must be honest in order that the truth, not prejudice, may dominate his thinking (Acts 20:26-27). He must be diligent if he is to profit much (Acts 17:11-12).

Real exegesis is the unfolding of the true meaning of Scripture so that persons can understand it and benefit from it. Eisegesis, the reading of one's own opinions into Scripture, is the reverse of true interpretation. Let us consider some general principles of interpretation that will aid our understanding of the Bible.

Divine-Human Authorship

An interpreter should not ignore either the divine or the human character of Scripture. The Bible ought not to be interpreted merely as a human book with principles of interpretation that would apply equally well to Shakespeare or Herodotus. The Bible is a unique revelation from God and should be interpreted accordingly. The importance of this truth, however, is no justification for ignoring the human factor. Human authors of a specific period and cultural background manifest their differing styles, vocabularies, and situations in the various books of the Bible. Both natures of Scripture must be taken into account.

Interpret reverentially. The Scripture is the Word of the living God. Students of the Bible should come to it with awe and humility, seeking God's message for their souls. There must be submission to the will of the divine Author. The student ought to be prepared to obey what he understands in Scripture. It has been often said that no man can judge the Bible; the Bible judges men. *In many ways this is the master principle of all biblical studies.* If it is true that the Bible is the verbally inspired and infallible Word of God, the student should treat it with a reverence that is not proper for any other book. This reverence is not at the expense of a concern for the grammar and history of the Bible but in addition to it.

The biblical writers encourage a profound reverence for the Word of God. The psalmist says, "For ever, O Lord, thy word is settled in heaven" (Ps. 119:89). Isaiah promises that the Lord will pay special attention to the person who "trembleth at my word" (Isa. 66:2). The Lord Jesus Christ assured men that His Word was identical with the truth: "If ye continue in my word, then are ye my disciples indeed; and ye shall know the truth, and the truth shall make you free" (John 8:31-32). The apostle Paul reminds Timothy, "that from a child thou hast known the holy scriptures, which are able to make thee wise unto salvation through faith which is in Christ Jesus" (II Tim. 3:15). The holy Scriptures alone are able to impart salvation. There is never any hint in Scripture that the Word of God might be mistaken. The apostle Paul commends believers for receiving his preaching by saying, "For this cause also thank we God without ceasing, because, when ye received the word of God which ye heard of us, ye received it not as the word of men, but as it is in truth, the word of God, which effectually worketh also in you that believe" (I Thess. 2:13). The student of the Bible must have the conviction that he is studying the Word of God if he is truly to benefit from the study.

Interpret grammatically. Since the Bible is the verbally inspired Word of God, a student should study every word in it to gain the complete and accurate revelation of God. Since divine revelation uses the medium of human language, a knowledge of the rules of language (and especially of the biblical languages) will illuminate the truths of Scripture. The sentence structure and meaning of the words determine the interpretation of every passage in Scripture. The interpreter who knows Greek or Hebrew has a distinct advantage in determining the meaning of Scripture. If the student of the Bible does not know the original languages, he must consult the more technical commentaries in order to see the grammatical relationships of the words of a given passage. A knowledge of English grammar, current idioms, logic, and rhetorical techniques all contribute to an understanding of the Scriptures. The study of etymology and the tracing of biblical words through extrabiblical literature shed much light on the meaning of Scripture. The well-equipped interpreter should use grammar, lexicons, word studies, and other aids freely.

It is significant that God prepared Daniel for his ministry as a prophet by causing him to be instructed in Babylonian science and "the learning and the tongue of the Chaldeans" (Dan. 1:4). Clearly the study of grammar is a good preparation for interpreting God's Word. The apostle Paul did not hesitate to argue from the grammatical construction of words of Scripture (Gal. 3:16). In the mystery of the inspiration of Scripture, the words of devout men became the Word of the living God. Although the words of Isaiah are always Isaiah's, he was not voicing a private opinion when he cried out, "Hear the word of the Lord" (Isa. 1:10) but was delivering faithfully the Word of God. The better the interpreter's grammatical understanding, the more fully his spiritual understanding can illuminate the Scriptures.

Interpret historically. It is not inconsistent with belief in the divine authorship and plenary verbal inspiration of the Scriptures to recognize that the biblical writers were often influenced by local and temporal factors. Consequently, the cultural and social background of the times is important for interpretation. Political and religious conditions often dominated the thinking of the biblical writers. The better the interpreter knows the biblical background, the easier it is for him to correctly interpret Scripture. A study of the ancient history of biblical lands can shed great light on many passages in Scripture. The study of archaeology can illuminate many passages of Scripture. Traveling to the Holy Land to examine the actual sites and locations often brings astonishing insight into the meaning of Scripture that will influence a man's preaching ever after.

Why did King David choose Jerusalem as his capital city, and why is Millo important (II Sam. 5:9)? What is the significance of the bank that Joab made (II Sam. 20:15)? Why did King Solomon build a high place for false gods (I Kings 11:7)? Why did Elisha ask for a double portion of Elijah's spirit (II Kings 2:9)? What does the word *virgin* denote (Matt. 1:23)? What does *Raca* mean (Matt. 5:22)? How could a baby "wrapped in swaddling clothes, lying in a manger" be a sign (Luke 2:12)? What is the significance of the dogs that licked Lazarus's sores (Luke 16:21)? Why did the Lord Jesus sit "on the well" (John 4:6)? Why did Peter mention the "name" by which we must be saved (Acts 4:12)? What did the animals in the great sheet mean to Peter (Acts 10:11-13)? What was a "judgment seat" (II Cor. 5:10)? What heathen writer does Paul quote (Titus 1:12)? What is the meaning of the "white stone" (Rev. 2:17)? Why are "dogs" excluded from the heavenly city (Rev. 22:15)? The historical background provides answers to all these questions and many more in Scripture. The interpreter ignores such help only to his own loss. The better commentaries and historical studies are rich sources of help for the interpreter.

Interpret according to literary form. Do not interpret poetry as though it were prose. It was Marcus Dods who cried out in anguish, "How long, O Lord, must thy poetry suffer from those who can only treat it as prose?" The student must recognize different literary forms and treat them with appropriate methods. Poetry forms a much larger body of Scripture than most Bible students realize. (See Chart 1.) Some poems are acrostics, in which each line begins with a different letter of the Hebrew alphabet (Pss. 25, 34, 111; Lam. 1, 2, 3). The most famous of these acrostics, Psalm 119, is usually identified as such even in English translations. The Book of Job is in the form of a drama. Many books of the Bible are histories: Samuel, Kings, Acts, and so on. The four Gospels are a unique form of biography. Many of the New Testament books are epistles, or letters: Romans; Philemon; James; I, II, III John; and so on. The stories of Ruth and Jonah are beautifully shaped narratives.

Chart 1

Old Testament Poetry

1. The "Poetic" Books:
   Job, Psalms, Proverbs, Ecclesiastes, Song of Solomon, Lamentations

2. Other books written predominantly in poetry:
   Isaiah, Jeremiah, Hosea, Joel, Micah, Nahum, Habakkuk, Zephaniah

3. Poems found in other OT Books:
   "The Song of the Sword" (Gen. 4:23-24)
   Noah's curse (Gen. 9:25-27)
   Jacob's blessing (Gen. 49:1-27)
   "The Song of Moses" or "Song of the Horse and Rider" (Exod. 15:1-21)
   "The Song of the Well" (Num. 21:17-18)
   "The Song of Victory" (Num. 21:27-30)
   "The Song of Moses" (Deut. 32:1-43)
   The blessing of Moses (Deut. 33:1-29)
   "The Song of Deborah and Barak" (Judg. 5:1-31)
   "The Lament of David" (II Sam. 1:17-27)
   The parable of the vine (Ezek. 15:1-8)

The parable of the eagles (Ezek. 17:1-24)
"The Lament for the Princes of Israel" (Ezek. 19:1-14)
Judgment of Tyre (Ezek. 26:2-14, 17-18)
Lament for Tyre (Ezek. 27:3-10, 26-36)
Lament for the prince and king of Tyre (Ezek. 28:2-23)
The prayer of Jonah (Jon. 2:2-9)
Prophecy of the Messiah and the end (Zech. 9:9–11:3)

It is important to recognize figures of speech in Scripture. To construe a figure of speech as a literal statement leads to grave misinterpretation. (For a brief sampling of biblical figures of speech with examples from both the Old and New Testaments, see Chart 2, p. 50.) The interpreter must also recognize biblical types, prayers, parables, and prophecies and interpret each one accordingly.

Unity

If the Bible is a divine-human Book, the expositor should expect to find a unity and consistency in its content. The idea of coherence, the widest possible consistency with the truth, is an important element of man's thinking processes. Unbelievers have frequently attacked Scripture for being full of contradictions. Upon careful study and reflection, most of these alleged "contradictions" appear surprisingly shallow and as misinformed conjectures. The old critic Julius Wellhausen attacked the Mosaic authorship of the Pentateuch because he thought writing was unknown at that time. It has since been discovered that writing was ancient in Mosaic times. Bauer and other critics attacked the accuracy of the Book of Acts, until the discoveries of Sir William Ramsay proved its exact precision (cf. Acts 14:6). The interpreter should bring to Scripture a sincere faith in God's Word and should expound its meaning constructively.

Interpret according to the harmony of the Scripture. This is the application of the principle of coherence. No passage of Scripture should be interpreted so as to contradict another passage. All the Bible should be considered as the context of any given passage. The old expositors used to speak of "the analogy of faith," meaning that there is only one system of doctrine to be found in Scripture. The Roman Catholic Church applies the term to the system of doctrine it holds to, but Protestants apply it to the consistency of scriptural doctrine. Since God inspired the Bible, there is an organic unity to all the teaching of Scripture.

Some liberal commentators think that Paul and James contradict one another on the matter of faith and works. They fail to perceive that Paul is writing about a genuine faith that can transform the life (Rom. 3:28; 12:1-2), whereas James is writing about a false faith that can neither change the life nor save the soul (James 2:14-26). The apostle Peter sets forth the scriptural principles: "Knowing this first, that no prophecy of the scripture is of any private interpretation. For the prophecy came not in old time by the will of man: but holy men of God spake as they were moved by the Holy Ghost" (II Pet. 1:20-21). The Bible is not the product of man's opinions but of the inspiration of the Holy Spirit. No paragraph, therefore, should be taken out of context and given a private interpretation according to the whim of an expositor. Every part of the Bible must be interpreted as part of a unified whole: the Word of God. Its interpretation must be consistent with the meaning of all other passages of Scripture.

Interpret according to local context. This is a more specific application of the preceding principle. The interpreter must pay special attention to the paragraphs immediately before and after the text he is studying. It is important to do this in order to determine accurately the main theme of the passage and to prevent the interpreter from mistaking the meaning of the passage. Preachers violate this principle more than any other, largely because they assume that they know the context when in reality they do not. Few conservative preachers would deliberately take a text out of context and use it as a springboard for their own opinions, but some accidentally do so by ignoring the context.

Preachers are not the only ones who err in this way. There is a widely advertised two-piece medallion designed for lovers. When the pieces are put together, the inscription reads, "The Lord watch between me and thee, when we are absent one from another" (Gen. 31:49). The verse sounds beautifully appropriate for two lovers until its context is considered. It turns out to be the suspicious words of Laban to Jacob, warning him not to try to rob him blind when his back is turned! This kind of grievous mistake can be avoided by simply making it a habit to examine the context. It is also beneficial to notice the place of the passage in the whole structure of the book in which it is found. This practice often reveals the intention of the author and helps to make an exposition logically consistent with the immediate context.

Interpret in the light of progressive revelation. Although there is a real unity to the teaching of all of Scripture, it is not all equally complex or complete. Scripture introduces a doctrine in elementary form. A number of important ideas may be there, but they are in condensed, cryptic form. As the interpreter traces the doctrine through the Scriptures in chronological order of its appearances, the interpreter can perceive the doctrine being expanded, clarified, and thoroughly developed into a unified whole. The last chronological occurrences of the doctrine are usually the most detailed and complete. There are several important corollaries to this principle. The law of first mention stresses that the first time a subject is introduced is often a key to the understanding of the later development of the doctrine. A careful study of that first passage will give insight into later references. Also, in at least one passage in Scripture, the doctrine will be fully discussed and explained. The interpreter should search for such a key passage. Finally, the last references to a subject often have parallels with the first mention.

For example, the subject "justification by faith" is first mentioned in Genesis 15:6-7, and this passage strongly influences later teaching on the subject. Romans 3 and 4 fully expound the subject of justification by faith and specifically refer to Genesis 15:6-7. The last references to justification bring the doctrine to a fitting climax (Rev. 15:3; 19:11; 22:11). The great doctrine of the person of Christ begins in Genesis 3:15 with a cryptic reference to the seed of the woman; there are key passages in the New Testament that shed floods of light on the doctrine (Matt. 1:23; Gal. 4:4 ff.); the doctrine comes to a complex end in the final book (Rev. 12:1-5; 22:13). Most of the biblical doctrines follow this form of presentation. God has revealed the doctrines in "germ" form at the beginning, expanded and clarified them by succeeding revelation, and finally brought them to a consummation at the close of His revelation. The expositor should not expect to find the most complex and detailed presentation of a doctrine at the chronological beginning of its revelation.

The method of progressive revelation must be sharply distinguished from the liberal hypothesis of the evolutionary development of religion. Liberals suppose that mankind started out in animism and slowly developed first into polytheism, then on to monolatry, and finally into monotheism. This supposition contradicts the Genesis record as well as the clear teaching of the New Testament (Gen. 4:4; Rom. 1:21-23).

Perspicuity

Not only is there a unity in Scripture but there is also a clarity in its contents. God gave the Scriptures not to obscure the truth but to make it manifest. The Word of God does not merely contain the truth; it is Truth (John 17:17). Although some religious groups believe that believers must have a priesthood over them to interpret the Bible to them properly, it has been the position of Protestants since the Reformation that the Scriptures are perspicuous; that is, they are clear enough to be understood by the average layman without the explanations of a priest. The priesthood of all believers is a tenet of faith for Protestants. The believer can come to the Bible with the faith that God will illuminate his understanding so that he will be able to comprehend the teaching that he needs from Scripture. He should pray to that end (Ps. 119:18).

Interpret literally. In contrast to the allegorizing methods of the Roman Catholics, Protestants from Luther on have stressed the necessity of interpreting Scripture literally. *Literal* means taking words in their normal, customary meaning rather than in a figurative or symbolic sense. It does not imply a blind refusal to see any figurative meanings in Scripture. The maxim of Horatius Bonar is apt: "Literal, if possible." If something in the context indicates that a figurative sense is expected, then the passage should be taken in that sense. However, the expositor should not first seek a figurative sense. David L. Cooper has well said, "When the plain sense of

Scripture makes common sense, seek no other sense." If the Bible is indeed verbally inspired, its words ought to be taken at face value and not transposed into some other, more figurative meaning at the subjective whim of the expositor.

When the apostle John reports that the soldiers did not break the legs of the Lord because He was already dead but instead pierced His side (John 19:33-34), he goes on to argue that this was the fulfillment of an Old Testament prophecy (John 19:36). He interprets the text in a literal, not an allegorical, manner. On the other hand, the Book of Revelation describes a woman clothed with the sun and expressly terms the description a "great wonder" (Greek *semeion,* "sign"). Thus there is justification in the text for giving the description a symbolical sense (Rev. 12:1 ff.). In the same context, the great red dragon is also called a wonder or sign and hence is not to be interpreted as a member of the reptilian family but as a symbol of "that old serpent, called the Devil, and Satan" (Rev. 12:3, 9).

Interpret in one way only. A given passage has only one true interpretation, though it may have many applications to the life of the believer. When the scholastics of the Middle Ages gave a fourfold interpretation of Scripture, it was assumed that a priest would have to explain it to the laity. Such methods led only to confusion. In the medieval church the term *Jerusalem* would be given four different meanings in any text of Scripture. Literally it referred to the city; allegorically it meant the church; morally it meant the human soul; and analogically it referred to the heavenly city. No wonder a priest was needed to explain it! It is much clearer to take *Jerusalem* as the earthly city (Acts 1:8) unless there is something in the context to indicate that additional meaning is implied (Rev. 21:2).

A good illustration of the importance of this principle is what interpreters have done with the account of the healing of the lame man at the Beautiful Gate of the temple (Acts 3:1-8). The proper interpretation of the account is that the incident is a demonstration of the power of the Lord Jesus Christ in a spectacular miracle (Acts 3:16). But many applications have been exalted by expositors into the primary position of the interpretation: the lame man is like a sinner sitting at the gate of religion but powerless to enter in; although he may have been an authority on ankle bones, he could not use his own, and so on. Rather than choosing a text that requires such allegorizing methods, it is better to choose one that contains in its main theme the exact literal meaning on which the expositor desires to preach. If the expositor desires to preach a salvation message, how much better it is to choose a text that tells exactly what one must do to be saved (Acts 16:23-33).

Interpret according to the simplest and clearest meaning. The expositor should not make an interpretation more complicated than is necessary to explain a passage. This principle of economy is often termed *Occam's Razor* because of the famous saying of William of Occam: "The number of entities should not be increased unnecessarily." The doctrinal expositions of some preachers remind one of an inverted pyramid: a vast structure delicately balanced on a single proof text. If the verse were interpreted more simply and naturally, the entire structure would come crashing down. A doctrinal exposition is much more satisfactory and convincing when it rests on a broad basis of coherent exposition of all related Scripture passages and is in agreement with the historic fundamentals of the Faith. Like a pyramid with broad foundations, it is not easily shaken.

This principle does not mean that the difficult interpretation is invariably wrong, but a complex interpretation should be used only when genuinely necessary. This principle of economy gets rid of such strange interpretations as the early fathers were fond of: that Adam was bisexual and that the "side" that the Lord took was his feminine structure. On the other hand, a verse such as "This is my blood of the new testament, which is shed for many" (Mark 14:24) is justly interpreted in the light of the doctrine of the vicarious, substitutionary death of the Lord Jesus Christ because of the vast body of teaching elsewhere in the New Testament that does set forth this great truth (Rom. 3:21-26; I Cor. 15:3-4; Gal. 2:20-21; etc.). All obscure passages should be interpreted in the light of clear ones.

Chart 2

Figures of Speech

1. Simile is a stated comparison using *like* or *as.*
   "Is not my word like as a fire?" (Jer. 23:29)
   "As the lightning . . . so also shall the coming . . . be." (Matt. 24:27)

2. Metaphor is an implied comparison in which one thing is said to be another.
   "Judah is a lion's whelp." (Gen. 49:9)
   "Ye are the salt of the earth." (Matt. 5:13)

3. Metonymy is using one noun for another because it may suggest the other.
   "Take you a lamb . . . and kill the passover." (Exod. 12:21)
   "They have Moses and the prophets." (Luke 16:29)

4. Synecdoche is using a part for a whole or a whole for a part.
   "Jephthah the Gileadite . . . was buried in one of the cities of Gilead." (Judg. 12:7)
   "We were all in the ship two hundred threescore and sixteen souls." (Acts 27:37)

5. Personification portrays a thing or idea as a person.
   "The mountains and the hills shall break forth before you into singing, and all the trees of the fields shall clap their hands." (Isa. 55:12)
   "The morrow shall take thought for the things of itself." (Matt. 6:34)

6. Apostrophe addresses a thing or idea as a person.
   "Be not afraid, ye beasts of the field." (Joel 2:22)
   "O death, where is thy sting?" (I Cor. 15:55)

7. Ellipses purposely omit part of the thought of a sentence.
   "He feared to say [she is] my wife; lest [said he] the men . . . kill me." (Gen. 26:7)
   "Thou bearest not the root, but the root thee." (Rom. 11:18)

8. Aposiopesis suppresses part of a sentence because of emotion.
   "If thou wilt forgive their sin—; and if not, blot me, I pray thee, out." (Exod. 32:32)
   "If we shall say, Of men; they feared the people." (Mark 11:32)

9. Zeugma is the yoking of one verb to two subjects which require different verbs.
   "The people saw the thunderings, and the lightnings, and the noise." (Exod. 20:18)
   "Forbidding to marry, [and commanding] to abstain from meats" (I Tim. 4:3)

10. Euphemism is substituting a less offensive word for a more accurate one.
    "Thou shalt be buried in a good old age." (Gen. 15:15)
    "When he had said this, he fell asleep." (Acts 7:60)

11. Litotes affirms something by denying its opposite.
    "A broken and a contrite heart, O God, thou wilt not despise." (Ps. 51:17)
    "Jews who . . . persecuted us; and . . . please not God" (I Thess. 2:14, 15)

12. Meiosis is deliberate understatement to magnify something else.
    "I . . . speak unto the Lord, which am but dust and ashes." (Gen. 18:27)
    "He shook off the beast . . . and felt no harm." (Acts 28:5)

13. Hyperbole is deliberate overstatement.
    "I will multiply thy seed as the stars of the heaven." (Gen. 22:17)
    "Even the world itself could not contain the books." (John 21:25)

14. Irony conveys disapproval under the cover of apparent approval.
    "Micaiah . . . answered him. Go, and prosper." (I Kings 22:15)
    "Ye have reigned as kings without us." (I Cor. 4:8-10)

15. Epizeuxis repeats the same word with the same meaning for emphasis.
    "Comfort ye, comfort ye my people, saith your God." (Isa. 40:1)
    "Holy, holy, holy, Lord God Almighty" (Rev. 4:8)

16. Rhetorical questions are not meant to learn something but to provoke thought.
    "Where wast thou when I laid the foundations of the earth?" (Job 38:4)
    "Shall we continue in sin, that grace may abound?" (Rom. 6:1)

17. Anabasis and katabasis: ascending and descending climax, respectively.
    "I have pursued . . . overtaken . . . wounded them [my enemies]." (Ps. 18:37-38)
    "Took upon him the form of a servant . . . humbled himself . . . unto death" (Phil. 2:6-8)

18. Anadiplosis is a linking device by which the last word of one statement is the first of the next.
    "God created the heaven and the earth. And the earth was . . ." (Gen. 1:1-2)

19. Anaphora is the repeating of the same word at the beginning of successive sentences.
    "Blessed, cursed" (Deut. 28:3-6, 16-19)
    "Blessed" (Matt. 5:3-11)

20. Epistrophe is the ending of successive sentences with the same word or phrase.
    "King of glory"; "for His mercy endureth forever" (Ps. 24:10; Ps. 136)
    "Still" (Rev. 22:11)

21. Repetition is the use of the same word over and over in a paragraph.
    "You," "your" (Ezek. 36:23-29)
    "I," "you" (John 14:1-14)

22. Paranomasia is the repetition of words similar in sound but not in sense.
    "Seth, appointed" (Gen. 4:25)
    "Always having all sufficiency in all things" (II Cor. 9:8)

23. Chiasmus is an inverted correspondence in which the first member is parallel to the fourth and the second to the third.
    "The man, thou, thou, the man" (Gen. 43:3-5)
    "Love, faith, toward the Lord Jesus, toward all saints" (Philem. 5)

24. Hendiadys is the use of two words for one item.
    "The king had burned the roll, and the words which Baruch wrote." (Jer. 36:27)
    "That he may take part of this ministry and apostleship, from which Judas" (Acts 1:25)

25. Enigma is a riddle, a truth expressed in ambiguous language.
    "Out of the eater came forth meat, and out of the strong came forth sweetness." (Judg. 14:14)
    "Numbered . . . weighed . . . divided" (Dan. 5:25-28)

26. Ambiguity is the use of an expression that has two different meanings.
    "Go in peace" to Naaman. (II Kings 5:19)
    "In all things ye are too superstitious." (Acts 17:22)

27. Oxymoron is the use of apparently contrary expressions to convey striking truth (literally a "wise-foolish" statement).
    "The tender mercies of the wicked are cruel." (Prov. 12:10)
    "Whosoever will save his life shall lose it: and whosoever will lose his life for my sake shall find it." (Matt. 16:25)

28. Anthropomorphism is the attribution of human or bodily characteristics to God.
    "The Lord smelled a sweet savour." (Gen. 8:21)
    "The eyes of the Lord run to and fro." (II Chron. 16:9)
    "The eyes of the Lord are upon the righteous, and his ears are open unto their cry." (Ps. 34:15)
    "No man is able to pluck them out of my Father's hand." (John 10:29)

CHAPTER 4
HOW TO USE
GREEK OR HEBREW

Up to this point the methods discussed can be used by anyone, but what about ministers who have had Greek or Hebrew in a seminary and now wish to use their biblical languages? If the language is still fresh in the mind, it is easy to gain great benefit from it; but if it has been some years since it was studied, the Hebrew is often a lost cause, and the Greek is difficult to use. Still, it is worthwhile to try to gain some of the rich treasures to be found in a study of the original languages.

The method advocated here is designed for the busy pastor, not the seminary student. The seminary student is trying to learn a language and trying to learn to translate it properly. He must work on the text "cold" (without using translations) in order to gain an adequate command of the language. The busy pastor is not trying to learn to translate; he has translations before him. He is trying to perceive treasures of meaning from the text to set before his people so as to bring illumination and blessing to their hearts.

While the pastor is searching for the main theme and the outline for his text, he will have before him the King James Version and some will also desire a good modern language version, such as the New American Standard Bible. Instead of turning to paraphrases or liberal translations, he should take out the Greek text for a New Testament passage or the Hebrew text for an Old Testament passage. The purpose is not to make a new translation, but to be sure of what the text says and to be able to shed light on the meaning of that text for a congregation. The pastor who tries to make a new translation will spend so much time on it that he may become discouraged and abandon the use of biblical languages altogether. The following is a definite procedure that does not consume much time but brings great benefit.

Look over the text. Compare the text with the translations. Find the main verb in the text; identify the other verbs, participles, infinitives, and main nouns in the sentence. If it is the New Testament, some of these words should be familiar.

Locate (parse) the main verb. Record the tense, voice, and mood of the verb. Notice how these facts influence the translations.

Locate (parse) the secondary verbs, participles, and infinitives. Record their tense, voice, and so on. Watch for changes in tense especially. Note how these elements influence the logic of the sentence.

Locate (parse) the major nouns. Notice the case relations and prepositions. Notice also whether any of the nouns have theological significance.

Study the important words. Look up the meaning in lexicons such as Arndt and Gingrich. Search for parallels in Moulton and Geden's concordance. Note the doctrinal and practical light that these word studies shed on the text.

Distinguish between synonyms. Notice words that are close in meaning and be sure that you understand why one word and not another is used in the text. Consult the index in Trench's or Custer's book on synonyms.

Consult the technical commentaries. Thorough commentaries that use the grammatical-historical method of expounding the meaning of the text will be especially helpful. Do not bother with the little devotional works that tell you what you already know.

Record your findings. Always take the time to record in a notebook the grammatical and lexical information that the study has uncovered. Some later year you may come back to this text and rejoice that you have done such careful work.

Finish the sermon. Incorporate into the sermon outline all the rich treasures that your study has uncovered. Organize the material with care. Make it practical and helpful for your people.

Pray it hot. Do not offer to your people dry, cold grammatical or historical material. Pray over the treasures you have found until they begin to flame with spiritual power. Your purpose is not to communicate more information but to proclaim, "Thus saith the Lord."

If the busy pastor makes this method of study a lifetime habit, he will always have the ability to use the biblical languages that he studied in seminary, and he will always have fresh and powerful truth to set forth to his people. His words will have the ring of authority because he knows what the text really says. His messages will be filled with treasures that can be found only in the biblical text.

(For specific tools to use in the study of Greek and Hebrew, see Chapters 33 and 34.)

CHAPTER 5
HOW TO EVALUATE CONFLICTING INTERPRETATIONS

What does the expositor do when commentaries disagree? The decision must not be left to mere whim or prejudice. Believers are commanded: "Prove all things; hold fast that which is good" (I Thess. 5:21). Believers must continually test all things, reject what is unworthy, and continue holding what is evident as "the good." Scripture tells us that a spiritual man is able to judge all things (I Cor. 2:15). The expositor must depend on the Holy Spirit of God to impart spiritual discernment to him. Scripture also tells us that continual use enables believers to discern between good and evil (Heb. 5:14). The longer one studies the Bible, the sharper his powers of discernment will become.

In the meantime, a firm grasp of certain principles and an awareness of certain pitfalls will help the Bible student to distinguish good interpretations from poor ones. Of course, all the principles of interpretation and criteria for judging interpretations are discussed in Chapter 3. The following, however, deserve special emphasis.

I. General Principles

Choose the interpretation that accounts for the most details. Usually this interpretation will be the one that provides the most exact analysis. Some expositors briefly summarize verses without explaining the details. A thorough commentary will try to account for as many of the details of a passage as possible. It is interesting for the student to compare a commentary on the whole Bible that summarizes a half dozen verses in less than a page to a very careful exposition such as Philip E. Hughes's comments on II Corinthians 5:1—seven pages of closely reasoned exegesis (pp. 160-67). Charles Hodge discusses the Reformed, the Romanist, and the Lutheran interpretations of I Corinthians 10:16 for five pages (pp. 185-90). John Broadus examines Matthew 16:18-19 in seven pages of careful and thoughtful exposition (pp. 355-62). As the expositor gets used to reading this kind of commentary, the inferior ones begin to become obvious. It is extremely important for the expositor to get the best commentaries and to use them with diligence so that his sense of good exposition will be constantly sharpened. He must beware of counterfeits of good commentaries. There are some expositors who will say the obvious about a verse—and say it, and say it, over many pages. Yet when the student has finished reading all these pages, he has learned nothing about the passage that he did not know when he first opened the book! Only firsthand acquaintance will make the student realize the valuelessness of such books. Do not waste space on a shelf for such.

Choose the interpretation that agrees with the widest range of truth (that has the most thorough coherence). One cannot read commentaries by Broadus, Hodge, Hughes, and men of that caliber without recognizing the breadth of their study and the thoroughness of their preparation for writing. The best commentators are aware that their readers will check the author's interpretations against the context, the harmony of Scripture, the statements of creeds, previous commentaries, philosophic thought, facts of science, principles of logic, English grammar, and ultimately, knowledge of all of life itself. The interpretations that are most consistent with the widest range of truth will be treasured and quoted generation after generation. That is one reason the best commentaries are reprinted even a century after they were written. At times, even a good commentary will violate this principle of consistency, and hence the expositor must always be on his guard. The knowledge of the physical universe increases every year. An old commentary such as Lange's on Genesis may become dated because of this increase. In 1864, Lange did not know of the Mendelian laws of genetics and, because of this fact, suggests that Jacob's colored rods may have actually caused the offspring of the sheep to be spotted in color (p. 537). Woe to the expositor who ignorantly quotes such interpretations today. The context makes it clear that the color variations were an act of God in vindicating Jacob (Gen. 31:8-12).

A good liberal arts education in a Christian school is the best place for a preacher to begin his preparation for the ministry. The more he can learn about all of life, the better equipped he will be to interpret the Scriptures accurately. This claim presupposes a thorough study of the Bible that will last a lifetime. A limited education does not equip one to detect the fallacious interpretations in commentaries.

II. Choice of Books

The expositor must learn to recognize the best books for his study. This raises the question of what makes a useful book. What qualities should an expositor look for in books he is considering for his study?

Spiritual perception. If the expositor is considering two different commentaries on a book of the Bible, one by a liberal unbeliever and one by a conservative believer, he should choose the one by the believer (unless he can purchase both). The presence of the Spirit of God in the heart of the believer communicates a perception that the unbeliever does not share (I Cor. 2:14-16). It is not to be inferred from this that the expositor is never to buy a book by an unbeliever. Some unbelievers study the Bible with diligence; some do indeed recognize what it teaches and set it forth honestly. Some liberal works, especially in the field of background and historical studies, have real value. Still, such exceptions do not invalidate the general principle that the expositor should require faith and spiritual perception in the books he intends to use.

Accuracy. Accuracy first entails fidelity to the Word of God. If a commentary tries to substitute liberal humanism for the message of the Bible, it ought to be categorically rejected. A work dealing with the Bible ought to let the Bible say what it says. Works like those of Bultmann that substitute philosophical existentialism for the truth of the Bible are worthless to the expositor. He should not clutter his shelf with such books. Second, accuracy implies factuality: correspondence to the truth of history, grammar, and the physical universe. Unfortunately, there are some books by good men who are true to the Bible yet who manifest great ignorance of history, grammar, and the world at large. Sometimes the expositor is confronted with a choice between such a book and a work by a liberal that manifests a much more accurate knowledge of history, grammar, and so on. There are some books of the Bible upon which no entirely satisfactory commentary has yet been written. In this case one must try to get several books to supplement one another.

Comprehensiveness. A devotional commentary that makes no attempt to grapple with the problems of the text or to provide answers for the difficulties in it is vastly inferior to a work that does intend to provide answers and give a serious evaluation of different interpretations. G. Campbell Morgan used to say, "I would rather have on my study shelf one book of scholarly exegesis than forty volumes of devotional exposition" (*Preaching,* p. 64). He would prefer Westcott's commentary on John to all the devotional volumes written on John. There are exceptions to this rule as well. Sometimes a small volume like Davidson's commentary on Hebrews is valuable far beyond its size. The expositor should consult solid, thorough expositions that truly provide answers to the questions he has about the text.

Specific content. Some works provide much more factual information and detailed analysis than others. The biographical articles in *The International Standard Bible Encyclopedia* are unusually thorough in their presentation of scriptural background. The Scripture references covered are so numerous and complete that each article is practically a concordance on that biblical biography. The commentaries by Westcott are unusually thorough and analytical in their phrase-by-phrase exegesis; but, in addition, Westcott has extended notes on a number of important topics, such as the meaning of the tabernacle (pp. 233 ff.), the words for redemption (pp. 295 ff.), and the Christology of Hebrews (pp. 424 ff.). Once the expositor becomes acquainted with such works, he realizes that some books provide much more help than others that may sell for the same price.

Spiritual fervor. Most commentaries tend in either a technical or a devotional direction. Only a few combine real scholarship with devotional warmth. The commentary on Romans by H.C.G. Moule is one, as are Nicholson's exposition of Colossians and Candlish's exposition of I John. Such books are extremely rare and should be digested and absorbed by every faithful expositor. At times a work may make up in fervency what it lacks in scholarship. Examples of this kind of commentary are Spurgeon's **Treasury of David** (Psalms), George Reith's **Gospel of John,** and Seiss's **Apocalypse.**

Practicality. The expositor who consults A. T. Robertson's massive grammar for expository help soon learns that it was not designed for easy reference. Some of the old Puritan divines wrote volume after volume on small books of the Bible. The busy pastor of today usually does not have time to spend reading pages upon pages of what others have put more succinctly. Some commentaries have no references on each page; thus, the expositor cannot find where he is in the book unless he looks at the table of contents to see on what page a certain chapter begins. The expositor should look for books that are concise, clearly organized, and in other ways easy to use.

Readability. Some works provide rich content, but their style is so forbidding that few expositors dare to use them. When one thinks of the studies in dogmatics by G. C. Berkouwer, the word *dry* inevitably comes to mind. One of the greatest conservative theologians, Geerhardus Vos, has written a number of richly helpful books (e.g., **Biblical Theology, The Self-Disclosure of Jesus**), but his style is so difficult that few pastors take the time and trouble to read him. This is unfortunate.

Currency of information. A fine exposition that thoroughly unfolds the text is a blessing to preachers for generations. But of two good commentaries, the one closer to the present time will naturally be more aware of present issues and theological problems. The great commentary on Mark by J. A. Alexander is generally reprinted today in the 1864 edition. It is a tribute to the commentator that it is valuable after all these years. When Edmond Hiebert wrote his fine commentary on Mark in 1974 (revised 1994), he had an advantage of 110 years over Alexander. Hiebert's commentary addresses itself to the problems that expositors face in our time and succeeds in providing many answers to biblical problems. Only a few great commentaries effectively resist the ravages of time. As long as men study the Bible, they will study Luther on Galatians and Calvin on Romans, which have had powerful influence for centuries.

III. Specific Warnings

Once the student gets the preceding principles in mind, it will become easier for him to detect what is inferior within the commentaries. To aid the student in sharpening his perception, it is not out of place to examine some concrete examples of misinterpretation.

Watch for heresy. When Rudolf Bultmann in his commentary on the Gospel of John claims that the Bible is just like Gnostic mythology (p. 28) and refers to the "legend" of the virgin birth of Christ (pp. 62-63), the expositor ought to recognize the voice of liberal unbelief. Bultmann offers no help at all to a reverent expositor. The preacher ought to preach his faith, not his doubts. If a preacher has no more faith than Bultmann, he does not belong in the pulpit. In *Dake's Annotated Reference Bible* one may find in place of the true doctrine of the Trinity a denial of the unity of the Trinity and the claim that Jesus Christ was not as great as His Father (p. 281 in the NT). The expositor must be able to detect works that are not sound in the faith.

Look for private interpretations. It is always dangerous for the student to consult only one commentary on a given passage. He may not recognize that the commentator is giving merely a personal opinion. When the student consults several commentaries, he will be able to distinguish at once between the individual opinions and the substantial interpretations. Even well-known commentators such as Arthur W. Pink in *An Exposition of the Sermon on the Mount* give peculiar interpretations. Pink uses the phrase "Give not that which is holy unto the dogs" to launch into a tirade against the literal four-footed animals (p. 293)!

Beware of riding a hobby. It is all too easy for a commentator to become so interested in certain doctrines that he can see little else in Scripture. The charge that Fundamentalists preach only salvation, separation, and stewardship is unfortunately true in the case of some. No one would argue that these doctrines are unworthy of emphasis, but there are scores of other doctrines that are also vital to the believer's life in Christ. The apostle Paul kept back nothing that was profitable for his converts but declared to them all the counsel of God (Acts 20:20, 27). Even first-rate commentators err on this score. An expositor as worthy as Herbert C. Leupold manifests some denominational bias when he discusses the sacraments in his commentary on Genesis (p. 120). It takes some scholarly ingenuity even for a Lutheran to find the sacraments in Genesis.

Be mindful of logical fallacies. There are commentators who argue from the silence of Scripture. Some conclude that since Matthias, chosen to take Judas's place in Acts 1, is not mentioned again in Scripture, God must have disapproved of the choice. Most of the apostles, however, are not mentioned after Acts 1. It is unjust of commentators to assume that this silence implies disfavor.

Certain commentaries argue that Paul was out of the will of God to go to Jerusalem after Agabus had warned him, "Thus saith the Holy Ghost, So shall the Jews at Jerusalem bind the man that owneth this girdle, and shall deliver him into the hands of the Gentiles" (Acts 21:11). But the vast majority of commentators explain this statement as a warning that would prepare Paul for the persecution that was coming. This explanation is much more in keeping with the context and with the character of the apostle as it is revealed in Scripture (Acts 20:22-23; 21:13; 23:1, 11). It is wrong to infer a command from a statement. A whole cult of "snake handlers" has risen because a few people interpret the statement "They shall take up serpents" (Mark 16:18) as a command. A better interpretation is the accidental example of Paul on Malta (Acts 28:3-5). In the same way, some people infer a command from an example. Some maintain that since the early church fasted (Acts 13:3), all believers are obligated to fast. This does not follow.

Few works are strong in all of the points mentioned. Those works that do excel in a number of categories are marked with an asterisk in the following bibliographies. The expositor should have those books in his library at all costs. It is also wise for the student to have more than one work on a specific subject since the recommended works often complement one another. Checking more than one source preserves one from idiosyncratic interpretations of even good commentators. The following bibliographies are designed to call to the attention of Bible students the most useful tools available on a wide variety of subjects. With the study of such works will come greater discrimination for further choices of tools.

PART III
THE CHOICE OF TOOLS

Note: Some of the following books are by liberals; their inclusion in the present work is not to be taken as endorsement of their whole content or position, but rather as a recognition that they supply help or information on a specific segment of the study of the Bible. Some books by New Evangelicals are also listed. This should not be construed as an endorsement of their blindness toward the doctrine of separation. There are times when the believer must reject a writer's theological position, while still realizing that he can gain factual information from him on specific areas of biblical geography, archaeology, and so on. The scriptural admonition is always "prove all things; hold fast that which is good" (I Thess. 5:21).

CHAPTER 6
REFERENCE BIBLES

The serious Bible student should have more than one kind of reference Bible so that his thought will not always be channeled into the same mold by the same notes. Many times different reference Bibles will supplement one another. The cross references, notes, maps, outlines, and other helps in a good reference Bible will add a great deal to any believer's understanding of the Word of God. There are times, however, when the believer will need to turn to a text Bible—that is, a Bible with just the English text before him, with no notes or references in it at all. This almost always gives him new ideas and fresh insights into the meaning of the Word. But there is no denying that a good reference Bible is one of the most useful tools that a serious Bible student can have. The following list suggests some of the most helpful reference Bibles.

The International Inductive Study Bible (Eugene, Ore.: Harvest House, 1992, 1993. 2,262 pp.) is perhaps the most delightful reference Bible to use that is now available. There is a detailed introduction that explains how to use the Bible, providing color examples of Bible marking (IISB-15 ff.), beautiful illustrations of the tabernacle and temples (IISB-34 ff.), and a time line chronology (IISB-42 ff.). Every biblical book begins with an introduction, and every chapter begins with a blank line on which the reader may write his theme for the chapter. The margins are wide enough for outlines and notes. Every book concludes with a blank page on which to record the theme, author, date, purpose, key words, and a chapter-by-chapter outline of the book. It is absolutely thrilling to study the Bible and to fill in the outlines and special studies from your personal study.

There are notes listing some of the gods of Egypt (p. 101) and offering insights on the tabernacle (pp. 129 ff.). Other notes describe the placement of the tabernacle furniture (pp. 189, 1984), the Jewish calendar (p. 200), the feasts of Israel (pp. 214-15), David's family tree (p. 516), Solomon's temple (p. 561), and prophetic points of history (p. 1094). The editors explain the tribes, the prince's portion, the city, and the sanctuary (p. 1397). They outline world kingdoms from Daniel's time on (p. 1411), a prophetic overview of Daniel (p. 1432), and Herod's family tree (pp. 1561, 1658). Illustrations offer views inside Herod's temple (p. 1614) and detailed maps of the missionary journeys (pp. 1787, 1794, 1800). After the Book of Revelation, the reader finds many blank pages on which to record Jesus' messages to the churches; what Revelation teaches about God, Jesus, and the Holy Spirit; the seven seals, trumpets, and bowls; and the nature of "Babylon" and the day of the Lord (pp. 2068-82). It concludes with notes on understanding the value of God's Word (pp. 2085 ff.), historical and grammatical information (pp. 2089 ff.), and a NASB concordance (pp. 2119-206). This is surely one of the most fruitful editions of Scripture published in this century.

The Scofield Reference Bible (New York: Oxford University Press, 1909. 1,362 pp.) is one of the most popular and most valuable of the reference Bibles. Some feel that it is so dispensational that it is of little value, but this is an unjust estimate. Many of the notes are simply explanatory and have nothing to do with prophecy. Regardless of the reader's prophetic position, such notes can be extremely helpful. Of course, many of the notes are strongly premillennial, and adherents to this prophetic position will therefore value it all the more highly, but even Bible students who do not share this view can profit from the paragraph headings found throughout the Bible and the parallel-passage references provided in the Gospels and in Kings and Chronicles. Some of the notes should be questioned (no man is infallible), but here is still a most valuable aid to the understanding of Scripture.

The *New Scofield Reference Bible* (New York: Oxford University Press, 1967. 1,392 pp.) is a great improvement over the original work.

Changes in attitude. Although the present editors still hold to the extreme dispensational distinction between the "Kingdom of God" and the "Kingdom of Heaven," they have softened their phraseology considerably (see Matt. 3:2 and 6:33). A more irenic tone replaces the dogmatic statements of the older Scofield (notice the cautious advocacy of trichotomy in I Thess. 5:23). Often an impartial list of interpretations accompanies controversial passages, with no one view vigorously advocated. Whereas the old Scofield Bible argued a single interpretation of the famous "apostasy" passage in Hebrews 6:4, the new Scofield impartially lists four interpretations. The New Scofield has removed the critical bias of the old against the Sermon on the Mount: whereas the old Scofield relegated the Sermon on the Mount to the millennium, the new stresses that it is profitable "for the redeemed of all ages" (p. 997). The old bluntly dismissed the Lord's Prayer as "legal ground" (p. 1002); the new gives a much more careful and sensible interpretation, relating it to the present age (pp. 1000-1001).

Changes in text. There is a consistent practice of modernizing archaic words and phrases. "Holy Ghost" is changed to "Holy Spirit," "devils" to "demons," "publican" to "tax collector," "husbandman" to "farmer," "one who has a familiar spirit" to "medium," "wineskin" to "bottle," and others. Although the vast majority of these changes are undoubtedly for the better, there are a few questionable ones. To change "south" to "Negev" (Gen. 12:9) and then put a footnote saying it means "south" is peculiarly pedantic.

The editors tend toward the better manuscript reading generally. In I Corinthians 9:20, they insert an entire clause into the text because the better manuscripts have it. But they are not consistent; for John 5:3 they stress the better manuscript reading, but for John 7:53–8:11 they argue against it.

Changes in the notes. There are many more notes in the new edition, and many of the old ones have been expanded or modified.

The note on the Pentateuch (p. xvi) has been enlarged to include an attack against those who regard portions of the Bible as "myths." Exodus 17:14 has a note attacking the documentary hypothesis. There are new notes on archaeological subjects: the Code of Hammurabi (Gen. 21:13), the Nuzi excavations (Gen. 31:30), and others. Some scientific objections to Scripture (II Cor. 12:2) are answered, and much historical background (Acts 19:28) has been added. Many new notes are designed simply to give more help on difficult passages (I Cor. 15:29; Col. 1:15).

The most striking change connected with the seven dispensations is in terminology. The dispensation of grace is now called that of the church (Gen. 1:28). Perhaps the weakest note in the old Scofield was the one on grace (John 1:17). Although Scofield did not teach this concept elsewhere, he seemed here to teach that a person was saved by keeping the law in the Old Testament but now is saved by grace! The new notes soften the phraseology and make it clear that men are saved through faith in all ages (p. 1124). Some pains are taken to defend the premillennial position more carefully (see the note on the church, Acts 2:1). There are new notes defending against amillennial arguments (John 18:36) and against posttribulation arguments (I Thess. 5:4), and other notes are sharpened (Rev. 19:19; I Thess. 4:17).

The note on inspiration is greatly improved and strongly defends verbal inerrancy (II Tim. 3:16). The note on the Holy Spirit is finally completed (Acts 2:4). Although the New Covenant is still referred primarily to the Jews, the editors admit that believers in the present age also have their place in the Covenant (Jer. 31:31). The editors have also dropped an overemphasis on typology (Eph. 5:32) by removing Asenath and Zipporah from the types of the church. There is a very interesting new note on Nahum 1:12 that stresses the providential preservation of the biblical text. One of the finest aids in the entire edition is the identification of the speakers in Song of Solomon (pp. 705-10), making an otherwise obscure book clear to the lay reader. The new note on the imprecatory psalms is also very helpful (Ps. 109:1).

Although the new edition is often impartial on controversial interpretations, it is not invariably so. The dispensational view of some of the parables is still given without mentioning that some good interpreters disagree. The parables of the mustard seed and the leaven are among the most obvious of these (Matt. 13:31, 33). The old note on the resurrection that taught that Old Testament believers are raised with the church is now replaced by a note that favors the resurrection of the Old Testament believers after the tribulation period and the church before (I Cor. 15:52). The note on Daniel 12:2 advocates this view without mentioning an alternative. This view ignores the progressive nature of God's revelation by making an Old Testament passage teach a more minute chronological distinction than the New Testament teaches.

The most serious flaw that remains is the note on the gospel (Rev. 14:6). The old Scofield listed four different gospels. The new at least combines "Paul's Gospel" with the "Gospel of the Grace of God," reducing the total to three. Most conservatives see only one gospel in Scripture. It is pitiable exegesis to make the "everlasting gospel" good for only seven years.

All in all, the improvements outweigh the defects. The New Scofield is a powerful tool for the pastor.

Another great help is the *New Chain-Reference Bible* (Indianapolis: Kirkbride, 1934. 1,566 pp.) edited by Dr. Frank Charles Thompson. The paragraph headings are in the margins, along with an immense number of subject listings, which can be found classified in the 293-page "Cyclopedia of Topics and Texts" in the back of the Bible. The "Cyclopedia" provides diagrams of the journeys of Paul and aids on literally thousands of other thought-provoking subjects. There are analyses of every book in Scripture, giving the key text and major topics for each. This Bible will repay careful use.

The Master Study Bible (Nashville: Holman, 1981. 2,384 pp.) is a very helpful edition of the Bible. The publishers wished to have an accurate, scholarly text, so they chose the NASB with all its marginal references. They wished to provide significant study aids, and they have done so with over a thousand pages of helps. There are special articles by men such as F. F. Bruce and William F. Albright; the volume includes a complete harmony of the Gospels (pp. 1313-455), a topical collection of the teachings of Jesus (pp. 1456-513), a topical encyclopedia of over seven hundred pages, special articles on how to study the Bible and how to read it through, and articles on many other subjects. Each book of the Bible begins with an outline, a survey of its content and leading ideas, and a brief discussion of the authorship. Although the editors mention liberal opinions on authorship, they do defend traditional biblical authorship: see the comments on Daniel (p. 896), II Peter (p. 1275), and Revelation (p. 1291). The typeface is clear, and each page seems to be well laid out so that it is a pleasure to use this Bible. There are no notes on individual pages to solve difficulties; all notes follow page 1309. *The Master Study Bible* is helpful enough to deserve a place in every serious Bible student's library.

The Life Application Bible (Wheaton, Ill.: Tyndale House, 1986-89. 2,388 pp.) is one of the most practical and helpful Bibles for personal study. The publishers advertise that there are ten thousand practical applications in the footnotes. Most seem to be conservative and devotional in content. Each book of the Bible begins with a time line, vital statistics, a blueprint, megathemes, and key places. There are also major biographical notes: Adam, Eve, Abel, and so on (pp. 11, 13, 17, etc.). It is impressive to find conservative dates for the Exodus (p. 107) and a defense of the miraculous nature of the Exodus (p. 132). The notes give a sober and careful interpretation of Saul and the witch of Endor (p. 531), outline the five books of the Psalms (p. 950), provide a strong interpretation of the Song of Solomon (p. 1143), defend the virgin birth of Christ (pp. 1549-50), stress the unique features of John's Gospel (p. 1792), emphasize the incarnation and preexistence of Christ (p. 2087), show that James refers to the teaching of the Lord Jesus (p. 2191), give four different interpretations of the book of Revelation without favoring any (p. 2239), and list the three millennial views without favoring any (p. 2268).

A work that should be better known is the *New Analytical Bible* (Chicago: Dickson, 1950). Each book of the Bible is prefaced with a chart of its contents and followed with an outline and notes on special subjects in the book. One of the distinctive features of this Bible is its placement of references; they are not marginal but printed in the text in smaller type immediately after the verse they illustrate. Thus, the reader can see at a glance the references for a given verse. In the back of the Bible are a number of tables and indexes on the lives of famous Bible personalities, miracles, prayers, and prophecies.

Nave's Topical Bible (Nashville: Nelson, 1979. 1,632 pp.) by Orville J. Nave claims to have over twenty thousand topics and over one hundred thousand Scripture references. He tends to have broader subjects with numerous subtopics: "Afflictions" (pp. 20-48), with subtopics "Forsaken by friends in," "Unclassified Scriptures relating to," "Benefits of," "Consolation in," "Deliverance from," "Design of," "Despondency in," "From Satan," "As a judgment," "Murmuring in," "Prayer in," "Resignation in," and so on. Likewise "Blessing" (pp. 120-34) contains many subtopics—"Responsive blessings of the law," "Divine, contingent upon obedience," "Spiritual, from God," "Temporal, from God," "Temporal, prayer for," and so forth. The entry "Death" (pp. 280-94) has subtopics such as "Miscellaneous subjects," "Unclassified Scriptures relating to," "Preparation for," "Of the righteous," "Scenes of," "Of the wicked," "Spiritual," and "Second Death." Many of his topics are a spiritual challenge: "Faith" (pp. 356-73), "God" (pp. 427-515), "Jesus, the Christ" (pp. 654-746), and "Psalms" (pp. 1019-87). This work is a rich source of ideas for sermonic themes.

The purpose of Joseph Bryant Rotherham's *Emphasized Bible* (Grand Rapids: Kregel, 1959) is to give a literal translation of the Greek and Hebrew texts and to indicate the grammatical emphasis in every verse by the use of diacritical marks. Although the translation is so literal as to be stilted English in some passages, the ease with which the emphasized words can be spotted in a passage is a great help in perceiving where the stress in a sermon should fall for a given passage. For the pastor whose Greek and Hebrew are only a dim memory of student days, this version can bring to his mind the grammatical emphasis that only a critical knowledge of Greek and Hebrew can provide.

It is well known that the *Companion Bible* (London: Lamp Press, n.d.) was edited by E. W. Bullinger, the dispensationalist, although his name is not on the title page. On many pages the notes are more extensive than the text. Although most notes are simple explanations, many of the notes give grammatical facts. Every paragraph is outlined separately, often by introversion or alternation. A very valuable part of this edition of the Bible is the great amount of material in the 198 appendixes at the back. There are word studies, maps, charts, and a wide variety of topical studies.

The Holy Bible: Easy-to-Read Version or *English Version for the Deaf* (Grand Rapids: Baker, 1978) is a Bible with two formats, but only one translation. It is a careful, literal translation in the thought patterns of the deaf. Long or complex sentences are broken up into short sentences: "No man has ever seen God. But the only. Son (Jesus) is God. He is very close to the Father (God). And the Son has shown us what God is like" (John 1:18). They translate the *dragon* as a "giant snake" (Rev. 12:3). They interpret "who walks disorderly" as "who refuses to work" (II Thess. 3:6). This is a conservative translation that is a great help for the hearing-impaired and the learning-impaired.

The International Children's Version: New Testament (Fort Worth: Sweet Publishing, 1978, 1981. 584 pp.) is a new translation from the Greek edited by English experts to enable children of the third grade and up to read it with understanding. It follows the oldest Greek text (omitting I John 5:7, etc.), bringing out the true meaning of Titus 2:13 ("our great God and Saviour Jesus Christ") and of other texts (I John 3:1). The first feature that is noticeable in this new work is the way in which it breaks up long sentences into shorter ones. "And people don't hide a light under a bowl. They put the light on a lampstand. Then the light shines for all the people in the house" (Matt. 5:15). They are very precise in doctrinal passages. "The virgin will be pregnant and will give birth to a son. They will name him Immanuel. (Immanuel means, 'God with us.')" (Matt. 1:23). There is a footnote explaining that a virgin is "a pure girl who is not married." Other verses are also translated with care. "I do not live anymore—it is Christ living in me. I still live in my body, but I live by faith in the Son of God. He loved me and gave himself to save me" (Gal. 2:20). If there is a slight bias in interpretation, it is probably on baptismal regeneration. "That water is like baptism that now saves you. Baptism is not the washing of dirt from the body. It is the promise made to God from a good heart. It saves you because Jesus Christ was raised from death" (I Pet. 3:21). Some verses are made transparently clear. "Jesus is the way our sins are taken away. And Jesus is the way that all people can have their sins taken away, too" (I John 2:2). A third grader could indeed read this version with profit.

The *New American Standard Bible* (La Habra, Calif.: The Lockman Foundation, 1971.) appears in a Reference Edition. It is a strongly conservative translation; no liberal version would translate Isaiah 7:14 "Therefore the Lord Himself will give you a sign: Behold, a virgin will be with child and bear a son, and she will call His name Immanuel." The translators pay special attention to the grammatical structure of the Hebrew. In Isaiah 9:6 the titles of the Lord Messiah are given in four groups of two each: "And His name will be called Wonderful Counselor, Mighty God, Eternal Father, Prince of Peace."

The editors have a policy of capitalizing pronouns that refer to deity. In the account of Babel the text reads, "Come, let Us go down there and confuse their language" (Gen. 11:7). (In rendering the same phrase in Genesis 1:26, however, the editors seem to have forgotten their policy.) The passage recounting Abraham's visitation by God reads, "And He took him outside and said, 'Now look toward the heavens, and count the stars, if you are able to count them.' And He said to him, 'So shall your descendants be' " (Gen. 15:5). The latter passage also illustrates their practice of putting direct speech in quotation marks.

In many passages there is no essential difference from the King James Version.

> Bless the LORD, O my soul;
> And all that is within me, bless His holy name.
> Bless the LORD, O my soul,
> And forget none of His benefits;
> Who pardons all your iniquities;
> Who heals all your diseases. (Ps. 103:1-3)

The only changes are in verse 1 the capitalizing of "His," referring to the Lord; in verse 2 the changing of "not all" to "none," which is logically better; and in verse 3 the changing of "forgiveth" and "healeth" to "pardons" and "heals." The Psalms, like the other poetry of the Scriptures, are shown as poetry. This is especially helpful in the Prophets, the poetry of which is treated by most translations as prose (e.g., Isa. 40).

The great majority of changes consists of the modernization of archaic or obsolete words. A sampling of the types of changes includes "slime" to "tar" (Gen. 11:3); "shoe" to "sandal" (Gen. 14:23); "dreadful" to "awesome" (Gen. 28:17); "Leah was tender eyed" to "Leah's eyes were weak" (Gen. 29:17); "images" to "household idols" (Gen. 31:19); "Thou shall not kill" to "You shall not murder" (Exod. 20:13); "a woman that hath a familiar spirit" to "a woman who is a medium" (I Sam. 28:7); "Go near, and fall upon him" to "Go, cut him down" (II Sam. 1:15); "The house of the women" to "the harem" (Esther 2:9); "the chief prince of Meshech, and Tubal" to "the prince of Rosh, Meshech, and Tubal" (Ezek. 38:2); "that ye would gain the time" to "that you are bargaining for time" (Dan. 2:8).

Some of the changes are examples of interpretation. The King James translates literally Abraham's action in weighing out "four hundred shekels of silver, current money with the merchant" (Gen. 23:16); the New American Standard changes this to "four hundred shekels of silver, commercial standard." Likewise, where the King James translates literally, "no stranger" shall offer incense, the New American Standard says "no layman" should do so (Num. 16:40). A person familiar with the King James finds it strange for the New American Standard to have the people respond to Elijah by saying,

"That is a good idea" (I Kings 18:24). The "still small voice" Elijah heard has become "a sound of gentle blowing" (I Kings 19:12). "Kiss the Son" has become "Do homage to the Son" (Ps. 2:12); "he leadeth me" has become "He guides me" (Ps. 23:3); "desert" has become "Arabah" (Isa. 35:1), which certainly forces the layman to consult a dictionary. The famous verse in the King James "and though after my skin worms destroy this body, yet in my flesh shall I see God" (Job 19:26) reads in the New American Standard "Even after my skin is flayed, yet without my flesh shall I see God." This change demands at least a marginal note by the translators explaining what they have done.

At times their interpretations come close to changing the text. In one example, the New American Standard has "Now again the anger of the LORD burned against Israel, and it incited David against them" (II Sam. 24:1), whereas the King James reads "he moved David against them," agreeing with the normal reading of the commentators, who hold that the subject of the verb must be "Jehovah" (Keil, Kirkpatrick, and others). In a very cryptic verse the editors do not hesitate to supply words to make better sense: "Saul was *forty* years old when he began to reign, and he reigned thirty-two years over Israel" (I Sam. 13:1). Again, their change deserves a marginal note of explanation.

All the messianic prophecies from the woman's seed (Gen. 3:15) and Shiloh (Gen. 49:10) to the Branch (Zech. 6:12-13) are faithfully translated.

The New Testament translation of the New American Standard Bible is an even more accurate translation. It has a good, readable English style. The prodigal son asks, "Father, give me the share of the estate that falls to me" (Luke 15:12). In key passages in the New Testament, the New American Standard Bible translates in such a way as to emphasize the deity of Christ: "Whose are the fathers, and from whom is the Christ according to the flesh, who is over all, God blessed forever. Amen" (Rom. 9:5). Many liberal translations try to remove the deity of Christ from this passage by splitting the verse into two parts. Another important passage reads "For God so loved the world, that He gave His only begotten Son, that whoever believes in Him should not perish, but have eternal life" (John 3:16). The key translation "only begotten" is clearly there. In Titus 2:13 the New American Standard Bible correctly ascribes deity to the Lord Jesus Christ: "Looking for the blessed hope and the appearing of the glory of our great God and Savior, Christ Jesus." Many other translations incorrectly make this passage sound as though God were a different person from the Savior.

Many of the changes are beneficial, giving a more modern meaning and more accurate translation. Some of the changes may not be necessary. It is the best English translation produced in the twentieth century.

The New Open Bible, Study Edition (Nashville: Nelson, 1990. 2,011 pp.) is a very valuable help, especially for one who is beginning Bible study. The introduction has articles on "How to Study the Bible" (pp. 17 ff.), "The Christian's Guide to the New Life" (pp. 23 ff.), and a thorough topical index to the Bible (pp. 33-343). Every biblical book has an introduction: that on Genesis defends Mosaic authorship (p. 1); that on Exodus gives a conservative date for the Exodus (1445-1405 B.C.; p. 64). Perhaps the most helpful feature is the multitude of boxes explaining the text: "The Garden of Eden" (p. 7), "Noah's Ark" (p. 13), "The Tower of Babel" (p. 17), "Birthright" (with pictures of lentils; p. 34), "Ark of the Testimony" (p. 95), "The Tabernacle" (pp. 112-13), "Casting of Lots," (p. 188), "Mountains of the Bible" (p. 241), "Old Testament Women" (p. 314), "Israel and the Hittites" (p. 360), "Sheol and Gehenna" (p. 374), "The Temple" (pp. 496-97), "Hezekiah's Water Tunnel" (p. 522), "Types of Psalms" (p. 614), "The Remnant" (p. 761), "Major Messianic Passages" (p. 801), "The Day of the Lord" (p. 978), "Sodom and Gomorrah" (p. 987), "The City of Bethlehem" (p. 1008), "The Lord's Prayer" (p. 1088), "The Sermon on the Mount" (p. 1090), "Pharisees and Sadducees" (p. 1111), "The Synagogue" (p. 1164), "The Kingdom of God" (p. 1205), "Titles of Christ" (p. 1211), "The Two Paracletes" (p. 1225), "Overseers, Presbyters, Deacons" (p. 1270), "Roman Roads in Paul's Time" (p. 1282), "The City of Rome" (pp. 1288-89), "Justification" (p. 1296), "Love" (p. 1323), "Salvation and Redemption" (p. 1336), "Grace and Mercy" (p. 1345), "Laying on of Hands" (p. 1395), "Sanctification" (p. 1445), "Jesus Is Lord" (pp. 1478-79), "The Seven Churches" (p. 1485), "Names for Satan" (p. 1494), and "The Millennium" (giving the three views; p. 1504). It concludes with a harmony of the Gospels, prophecies of the Messiah fulfilled in Jesus Christ, prayers of the Bible, archaeological discoveries, and other notes and maps. It is very easy to use. It can be obtained with either the KJV or the NASB texts.

The Ryrie Study Bible (Chicago: Moody, 1976, 1978. 2,006 pp.) by Charles Caldwell Ryrie is a very helpful reference Bible. He gives introductions to each book of the Bible. He defends the Mosaic authorship of Genesis (p. 5), provides footnotes explaining the text (see Gen. 3:15), argues for the conservative date for the Exodus (p. 90), teaches the premillennial position (Dan. 9:24-27; Matt. 24:15; I Thess. 4:16-17), strongly defends the deity of Christ (John 1:1; 8:58), and provides a harmony of the Gospels (pp. 1817 ff.). Perhaps the strongest part of this Bible is the synopsis of Bible doctrine that covers the Scriptures, God, Christ, the Holy Spirit, angels, Satan, demons, man, sin, salvation, the church, and future things (pp. 1825-46). He concludes with a thorough index of principal subjects in the notes (pp. 1883-2006). It can be obtained with either the KJV or the NASB texts.

The Holy Bible, New King James Version (Nashville: Nelson, 1979, 1982. 1,236 pp.) is another attempt to modernize the KJV without abandoning its wording completely. The preface makes clear that the editors dislike the ancient Greek text (which they refer to as the "Alexandrian Text") and imply that only two, the Sinaitic and the Vatican manuscripts are important (p. vii). They ignore the fact that there are seventeen Uncials and the vast majority of the ninety-seven papyri that agree with the ancient text. All Greek manuscripts before the fourth century agree with the ancient text. The NKJV largely substitutes synonyms: the serpent was "more cunning" rather than "more subtil" (KJV); God promised the land "to you and your descendants" (NKJV, Gen. 13:15), with footnote 23 admitting, "Literally *seed,* and so throughout the book." Since the apostle Paul makes a great point of that verse meaning *seed,* singular, referring to Christ Himself, and not to plural *descendants,* which they correctly translate in Galatians 3:16, they have introduced a contradiction into the text. They often adopt a dry and pedantic style: for "I speak of the things which I have made touching the king" (Ps. 45:1) they substitute "I recite my composition concerning the King" (NKJV). They repeat a typographical error in Jeremiah 34:16, "whom he had set at liberty," whereas the Hebrew text reads "whom ye had set at liberty" (see any Cambridge Bible). At times it no longer reminds one of the KJV at all: "And why beholdest thou the mote that is in thy brother's eye, but considerest not the beam that is in thine own eye?" (Matt. 7:3, KJV) becomes "And why do you look at the speck in your brother's eye, but do not consider the plank in your own eye?" (NKJV). The Lord's words "Verily, verily, I say unto you, I am the door of the sheep" (John 10:7, KJV) become "Most assuredly, I say to you, I am the door of the sheep" (NKJV). Why not a literal translation, "Truly, truly"? They fill the footnotes with references to the NU-Text (Acts 4:25), which refers to the ancient text, and the M Text (Acts 5:25), which refers to the more recent Majority text. Thus in hundreds of references, problems of textual criticism are foisted upon the readers, who may have no source of help. This is not a kindness. Why are not the footnotes filled with spiritual explanation and helps for believers, instead of the dry bones of textual criticism? They do not hesitate to add *Abraham* to a verse (Acts 7:5). They do, however, correct one verse so that it attributes deity to the Lord Jesus Christ (Titus 2:13). The NKJV as a whole is not a liberal translation, just a commonplace one. The glory and beauty of the King James Version is missing.

The Word in Life Study Bible, New Testament Edition (Nashville: Nelson, 1993. 1,013 pp.) is a new edition of the NKJV that seeks to correct its inadequacies. Listing the Lord Jesus Christ as merely one of twenty-five important figures in the New Testament is a blasphemous way to begin (pp. xxvii ff.). The introduction to each book is printed in giant type, which makes it appear that their comments are more important than the text of Scripture (pp. 1 ff., 125, etc.). The idea that Matthew is a "Christian Torah" was advanced by the liberal Lohse years ago (p. 5). The note on the kingdom does not evaluate the different meanings of the term in different contexts (pp. 18-19); another note devotes a whole page to a prayer of St. Francis (p. 46); other notes have no explanation of the prophetic meaning of the Olivet Discourse (pp. 101-6) or any prophetic help on the interpretation of the Book of Revelation (pp. 873-931). They do try to make their edition "relevant": there are notes, for example, on Jesus and Ethnicity and on Leprosy and AIDS (pp. 156, 229, etc.). Some notes dominate the page so that the text looks small ("Scribes," pp. 294-95); other notes fill double page spreads so that there is no room for the text at all (pp. 304-5, 342-43, 384-85). Perhaps the text of NKJV is small and unimportant to the editors.

The Believer's Study Bible, formerly *The Criswell Study Bible* (Nashville: Nelson, 1979, 1991. 1,968 pp.) is another Bible now limited to the NKJV text. Although there is every reason for the separated Fundamentalist to be leery of this work (Criswell's name, Billy Graham's recommendation, etc.), it must be admitted that this is an excellent reference Bible. Dr. Criswell has gone through the entire Bible giving solutions to every problem or difficulty imaginable. His note on Christ in John 1:1 is a theological masterpiece. One may question whether the believer would be blessed by the discussion of the Synoptic Problem and the two-source and four-source solutions (pp. 1326-27). But it is a pity that he has linked his Bible to an inferior translation.

The NIV Study Bible (Grand Rapids: Zondervan, 1985. 1,950 pp.), edited by Kenneth Barker, is not one of the grand succession of reference Bibles designed for the Bible-believing Fundamentalist. It is the Bible for the New Evangelical. It not only has an inferior translation (the New International Version) but also systematically manifests an unbelieving attitude toward the passages it is supposed to explain. The Genesis 5:5 note leaves open whether the great age of the patriarchs is to be taken literally or as conventional fiction (p. 13). On Genesis 6:17 it actually encourages belief in a local rather than universal flood. The cross-reference to II Peter 3:6 continues the argument there. The reference to the city of Dan in

Genesis 14:14 is taken as evidence for a later editor revising the text of Moses (p. 27). Conservative commentaries such as Keil and Delitzsch and Leupold regularly identify the city with Dan-Jaan without tampering with the text. In the note on Exodus 14:2 the NIV interprets the Red Sea as the Sea of Reeds and actually identifies it with Lake Menzaleh in the north of Egypt (p. 107). The biblical text makes very clear that the Lord led Israel to the Red Sea, not to the way of the Philistines in the north (Exod. 13:17-18). The exact Hebrew phrase is identified as the place from which Solomon launched his navy (I Kings 9:26). Since the fleet brought back apes and peacocks, it is certain that they sailed south in the Red Sea and not northward into the Mediterranean Sea. The arrows on the map that illustrates the note do not even give the possibility of crossing the Red Sea (p. 106).

Over and over the *NIV Study Bible* balances liberal and conservative interpretations against one another. Concerning Joshua's long day, they comment that some believe that God extended the hours of daylight; others, they say, suggest that God provided a cool day in which to fight (Josh. 10:13; p. 305). The editors remain theologically neutral. In the scene of Saul and the witch of Endor they leave open the possibilities of what happened, even though the text says, "Samuel said to Saul" (I Sam. 28:15; p. 417). All that they will say about the sunlight on the steps of Ahaz is "perhaps the miracle involved the refraction of light" (Isa. 38:8; p. 1069). In the note on the Day of the Lord in Joel 2:22, they remove all eschatological meaning from the phrase, interpreting it as merely a "locust infestation" (p. 1340). In a similar way they interpret the abomination of desolation to refer merely to Antiochus Epiphanes, although they admit that "some" hold to a prophetic fulfillment (Matt. 24:15; pp. 1477-78). They remove the term "only begotten" from John 1:18 (p. 1593).

One of the most serious examples of their changing the text of Scripture can be found in I Corinthians 7:36-38. Both in the wording of the text and in their notes they change the interpretation from a father and his virgin daughter to a man and his fiancée (p. 1743). This involves inserting phrases into the text ("the virgin he is engaged to") and changing the translation of Greek words from "to give in marriage" to "to marry." Such interpretations can be found only in liberal commentaries and the NRSV and do not belong in the text of Scripture.

Thus all Bible-believing Fundamentalists should beware. The *NIV Study Bible* is not a reliable reference Bible. It is a sounding board for the New Evangelical interpretation of the Bible. Many interpretations are simply liberal and unworthy of a believer's notice.

The Holy Bible, New Revised Standard Version (New York: Oxford University Press, 1989. 1,280 pp.) is the Bible of liberalism. Conservatives opposed the old RSV (1946, 1952) and will oppose this new revision on the same grounds. Yet the editorial policies changed significantly in the new version. The translators are politically correct at all costs. They translate Genesis 1:26 as follows: "Then God said, 'Let us make humankind in our image.' " The grossness of this uncouth translation does not bother them as much as their fear of the feminist movement. After I Samuel 10:27 they interpolate eleven lines that are not in the Masoretic Text (p. 281). Instead of the KJV "they pierced my hands and my feet" (Ps. 22:16), they translate "My hands and feet have shriveled," admitting that the meaning of the Hebrew is uncertain. Of course they translate Isaiah 7:14 as "the young woman is with child," whereas Matthew 1:23 they translate as "the virgin shall conceive." The old RSV removed the deity of Christ from Romans 9:5 by putting a period in the midst of the verse: "to them belong the patriarchs, and of their race, according to the flesh, is the Christ. God who is over all be blessed forever. Amen." The NRSV puts a conservative translation in the text and relegates the liberal interpretation to a footnote: "to them belong the patriarchs, and from them, according to the flesh, comes the Messiah, who is over all, God blessed forever. Amen." Apparently the editors intend to make the NRSV a genuinely ecumenical Bible. The familiar word *brethren,* in the sense of "fellow believers," has been customary for centuries. Now the NRSV translates it "brothers and sisters," interpolating the "and sisters" into all the New Testament references (Rom. 12:1; 14:10,

15, 21; 15:14, 30; 16:14, 17; I Cor. 4:6; 5:11, etc.). The translators change the word *virgin* in I Corinthians 7:36-38 to "fiancée," a liberal interpretation that changes the text. The NRSV is not recommended.

The New Jerusalem Bible, Reader's Edition (New York: Doubleday, 1985, 1990. 1,433 pp.) is one of the leading new Roman Catholic Bibles. Of course, all the Apocrypha is printed with it. It is a sophisticated and, at times, eloquent translation. Psalm 23 is a good example:

> Yahweh is my shepherd, I lack nothing.
> In grassy meadows he lets me lie.
> By tranquil streams he leads me.

The angel says to Mary, "Mary, do not be afraid; you have won God's favour" (Luke 1:30). That phraseology has a Catholic ring to it. Baptismal regeneration is clearly taught in I Peter 3:21. The New Jerusalem Bible is not recommended.

CHAPTER 7
BOOKS ON BIBLE STUDY

Brooks, Keith L. *The Summarized Bible.* 1919. Reprint, Grand Rapids: Baker, 1965. 305 pp. An old classic. The author provides a daily calendar for Bible reading (pp. 11-12); lists the key thought, verse, date, and so on for every book of the Bible (pp. 13, 23, etc.); gives a brief summary of the contents of every chapter in the Bible with a key word, well-known verses, and any teaching about Christ; and has indexes of biblical events and biblical promises (pp. 299 ff.).

Gray, James M. *Synthetic Bible Studies.* 1906. Reprint, New York: Revell, n.d. 186 pp. Gray presents a study of the Bible as a whole. He provides outline studies of every book of the Bible and explains how to study: read a section repeatedly, at a single sitting, prayerfully, and so on (pp. 7-8). He gives premillennial interpretations (p. 149)..

Jensen, Irving, L. *Independent Bible Study.* Chicago: Moody, 1963. 179 pp. This book gives an application of the inductive method to Bible study. The author emphasizes the use of analytical charts in studying the Bible. He has a good illustration in "The Student, the Fish, and Agassiz" (pp. 173-78).

Job, John B. *How to Study the Bible.* Downers Grove, Ill.: Inter-Varsity, 1972. 110 pp. This book is a compendium of New Evangelical advice on Bible study. The author recommends reading the Bible through, keeping a notebook (pp. 12-13); studying it by books (pp. 24 ff.); finding the main theme, divisions, links, key words, illustrations, and so on (pp. 36 ff.); studying Bible characters (pp. 46 ff.) and words (pp. 54 ff.); learning Greek and using concordances, and so on. He applies his methods of studying to the issue of abortion (pp. 86 ff.).

Menzies, Mrs. Stephen. *How to Mark Your Bible.* 1917. Reprint, Westwood, N.J.: Revell, 1959. 174 pp. The author gives practical suggestions for underlining words and connecting them by railways (diagonal lines). The whole book is devoted to "railway connections" and marginal references; a good example is Titus 1:9, 13 and 2:1-2, 8 on "sound doctrine."

Perry, Lloyd M., and Robert D. Culver. *How to Search the Scriptures.* Grand Rapids: Baker, 1967. 276 pp. In this general introduction to Bible study, the authors give the testimonies of famous men on the value of the Bible (pp. 26-33); defend the inspiration of the Bible (pp. 58-71); give testimonies by Christian leaders of how they study the Bible (pp. 83-110); discuss studies of Bible books (pp. 111 ff.), chapters, paragraphs (pp. 141 ff.), words (p. 164), figures of speech (pp. 167 ff.), names (pp. 173-74), doctrine (pp. 174 ff.), biographies (pp. 180 ff.), prayers, miracles, parables (pp. 185 ff.), and poetry (pp. 203 ff.); and recommend comparing liberal translations for study: Moffatt, Goodspeed, the RSV (pp. 223 ff.).

Pierson, Arthur T. *Keys to the Word.* Grand Rapids: Zondervan, n.d. 163 pp. The author presents a brief study of the content of each book of the Bible. He urges believers to search, meditate on, and compare the Scriptures (pp. 4-7); provides key words and key verses for every book of the Bible (pp. 17, 19, 22, etc.); and includes a brief outline of every book.

————. *Knowing the Scriptures.* 1910. Reprint, Grand Rapids: Zondervan, n.d. 317 pp. This book is one of the most interesting and practical helps available. Pierson gives fifty different methods and ideas for study: biblical names, similar terms, dominant words, analysis and synthesis, poetic parallelism, legal standards, figures of speech, typology, dispensations, the humorous element in Scripture, and so on. He observes both the literal and spiritual aspects of Scripture (p. 15).

Smith, Jerome H. *The New Treasury of Scripture Knowledge.* Nashville: Nelson, 1992. 1,680 pp. This book is the most exhaustive and inspirational gathering of cross-references in the literature. It is like the marginal references in a study Bible expanded to fill the pages of the whole Bible. Whatever verse in the Bible one picks, there is an astonishing array of cross-references. There are special symbols that help as well: an * before a reference denotes an especially clear reference; a ✓ denotes a very significant reference; a || denotes a strict parallel passage, as in the Gospels. In any study of the Bible it is a special blessing to use this treasury of spiritual truth.

Smith, Wilbur M. *Profitable Bible Study.* Boston: Wilde, 1939, 1953. 227 pp. In this helpful work, Smith, a famous bibliographer, explains what Bible study will do for the believer (pp. 11 ff.); gives eight methods of devotional Bible study (pp. 26 ff.); cites the Bible-reading habits of John Quincy Adams, Robert E. Lee, and other famous Americans (pp. 75 ff.); and lists one hundred books for the Bible student's library (pp. 94 ff.). His recommendations are very discriminating and helpful.

Thomas, W. H. Griffith. *Methods of Bible Study.* Philadelphia: Sunday School Times, 1926. 120 pp. The author presents brief studies with many seed thoughts. He urges study of the Bible as a whole (pp. 1 ff.); surveys the Old Testament and New Testament (pp. 10 ff.); and gives helpful ideas on Bible book studies (pp. 22 ff.), the study of special topics (pp. 51 ff.) and Christ in the Old Testament (pp. 64 ff.), and the study of verses and words (pp. 90 ff.). He concludes by recommending the use of two Bibles: one for knowledge and one for power (pp. 112 ff.).

Torrey, R. A. *How to Study the Bible.* New York: Revell, 1896. 121 pp. The author gives a brief introduction to the study of the Bible. He explains and emphasizes how to study the Bible book by book (pp. 14 ff.); gives methods of studying topics (pp. 57 ff.), Bible biographies (pp. 79 ff.), and types (pp. 82 ff.); compares the study of the Bible in the printed order with its study in chronological order (pp. 85 ff.); and urges daily study (p. 117) and memorization (p. 119).

CHAPTER 8
BIBLE CONCORDANCES

In addition to a reference edition of Scripture, the most helpful single book for the expositor is a good Bible concordance. There is no more frustrating experience than to think of a fitting text for a sermon and then not be able to find it in Scripture. Every serious Bible student should have on his desk at all times the finest concordance he can afford.

The most helpful concordance is probably Robert Young's *Analytical Concordance to the Bible* (1880; reprint, Grand Rapids: Eerdmans, n.d.). Here is listed every word in the Bible and, with a few accidental exceptions, every reference in which it occurs (311,000 in all). An excellent feature of this work is its practice of dividing up the references according to the original Hebrew and Greek words. Thus, under the English *good* are listed fourteen Hebrew and Greek words with their meanings and references. Anytime a number of different words in the original languages are all given the same English translation, it is well to note their distinctions. If the pastor knows only a single word of his text and has patience, he can find the passage by consulting Young's concordance.

Another work of almost equal value is James Strong's *Exhaustive Concordance of the Bible* (1890; reprint, New York: Abingdon-Cokesbury, n.d.). It also claims to give all words and all passages in which they are used. Unlike Young, Strong lists all English words under one heading (such as *good*) with no distinctions among the differing Hebrew or Greek words (as in the Greek *kalos, agathos,* and others). There are numbers, however, opposite each reference, and if the expositor takes the trouble to look these up in the back of the concordance, he can find which Hebrew or Greek words were translated thus. This is an extra troublesome step, but some will not mind it.

For the pastor whose Greek is still active, the most accurate of these tools is *A Concordance to the Greek Testament* by William Fiddian Moulton and Alfred Shenington Geden (Edinburgh: Clark, 1897). It gives every Greek word and every reference, using as a basis the great Westcott and Hort Greek Testament. In passages that quote the Old Testament, it also gives the Hebrew parallels. One of the most beneficial studies a pastor can make is to determine exactly how a particular Greek word is used throughout the Greek Testament.

A more popular work on the Old Testament is Aaron Pick's *English and Hebrew Bible Student's Concordance* (n.d.; reprint, Bible Study Classics, n.d.). Here is a list of all the English words in the Old Testament with all the Hebrew words that they translate and their "literal" meanings. No attempt is made to list all the references.

Another specialized work for the pastor who likes to study the Greek Old Testament is *A Concordance to the Septuagint,* 2 vols., (Oxford: Clarendon, 1897) by Edwin Hatch and Henry A. Redpath. All references to proper names are omitted.

Since some Bible students are still attached to the American Standard Version of 1901, they may wish to use Marshall Custiss Hazard's *Complete Concordance to the American Standard Version* (New York: Nelson, 1922). Many will be glad to get the *New American Standard Exhaustive Concordance of the Bible,* edited by Robert Thomas (Nashville: Broadman-Holman, 1981). Some may wish to use *Nelson's Complete Concordance of the Revised Standard Version Bible,* edited by John W. Ellison (New York: Nelson, 1957) or *The NIV Exhaustive Concordance,* edited by Goodrick and Kohlenberger (Grand Rapids: Zondervan, 1990). Likewise useful is *The Complete Concordance to the Bible, New King James Version* (Nashville: Nelson, 1983).

Nelson's Concordance of Bible Phrases (Nashville: Nelson, 1992) is a new and welcome help for finding familiar phrases throughout the Bible. It can be time consuming to run down phrases in a regular concordance, but this work gives a direct list of such phrases as "Abide in Him" (p. 1), "Bless the Lord" (pp. 57-58), "Day of the Lord" (p. 131), "Grace of God" (pp. 232-33), "I am the Lord" (pp. 286-89), "Kingdom of God" (pp. 339-41), "Power of God" (p. 478), "Seek the Lord" (p. 534), "Son of God" (pp. 559-60), and "Your sin will find you out" (p. 685).

An excellent example of the profitable use of the concordance is Harold K. Moulton's *Challenge of the Concordance* (London: Bagster, 1977, 288 pp.). He provides over eighty devotional and scholarly studies in New Testament words and phrases: "The Seeing of Jesus" (pp. 8 ff.), "Authority" (pp. 30 ff.), "The People of God" (pp. 51 ff.), "Thy Will Be Done" (pp. 137 ff.), "Fruit" (pp. 144 ff.), "Abiding" (pp. 190 ff.), "Causes of Stumbling" (pp. 207 ff.), and so on. He urges students to let the concordance teach them what the Bible has to say about a given subject (pp. xiii-xiv).

The conclusion is that the Bible student, with either Young's or Strong's concordance and, if his Greek merits it, Moulton and Geden's concordance, has made a good start toward acquiring the tools he needs for exposition.

A well-known, though much inferior, work is *Cruden's Concordance* by Alexander Cruden. It has been reprinted often since 1737, but it omits so many references that it is inadequate for serious study.

CHAPTER 9
BIBLE DICTIONARIES: SETS

Next to a reference edition of the Bible and a concordance, the most important tool for Bible study is a good Bible dictionary. Since there are so many, we will consider the major sets first and the one-volume dictionaries in the next chapter. If the student of the Scriptures hopes to become a competent expositor, he must cultivate the habit of looking up every person, place, and subject with which he is unfamiliar. Even though this practice is time consuming, it is most profitable.

A set that is perhaps too old to be of great importance for today's Bible student is William Smith's *Dictionary of the Bible,* 4 vols., (New York: Hurd and Houghten, 1868, revised from the Cambridge edition of 1863. 3,667 pp.). Though there are articles of lasting value, such as the one by B. F. Westcott on the "Canon of Scripture" (39 cols.) and others on "Antichrist" (21 cols.), "Chronology" (40 cols.), "David" (30 cols.), "Jerusalem" (140 cols.), "Jesus Christ" (80 cols.), and many more, the student needs a more up-to-date work.

Another older set that retains its value is Patrick Fairbairn's *Imperial Bible Dictionary,* 6 vols., (London: Blackie, 1889). It is particularly good on biblical biography with thorough articles on "Adam" (12 cols.), "Abraham" (11 cols.), "David" (21 cols.), "Jacob" (16 cols.), "Paul the Apostle" (25 cols.), and others. There are also helpful articles on "Arms, Armour" (17 cols., with many drawings), "Atonement" (16 cols.), "Creation" (19 cols.), "Inspiration" (22 cols.), "Jerusalem" (69 cols.), "Money" (21 cols., with many drawings), "Priest" (36 cols.), and "Tabernacles" (13 cols., with many drawings). Any work that has contributors such as Franz Delitzsch, A. B. Davidson, Robert B. Girdlestone, and George Smeaton will be of permanent help.

The Cyclopedia of Biblical, Theological and Ecclesiastical Literature, 10 vols. (New York: Harper, 1867-81), edited by John McClintock and James Strong, is a monumental work (with two supplementary volumes, 1890), averaging more than one thousand pages per volume. Although there are some articles of doubtful value, contributors such as Philip Schaff, Charles Hodge, A. A. Hodge, and others insure a generally high quality. This work is very strong on historical and geographical subjects: "Alexandria" (10 cols.), "Arabia" (23 cols.), "Ararat" (7 cols.), "Assyria" (24 cols.), "Babylon" (15 cols.), "Damascus" (10 cols.), "Egypt" (64 cols.), "Jerusalem" (52 cols.), "Maccabee" (18 cols.), "Nineveh" (40 cols.), "Palestine" (64 cols.), "Red Sea" (22 cols.), "Tabernacle" (35 cols.), "Tyre" (17 cols.), and many others. There are also interesting articles on "Antichrist" (14 cols.), "Atonement" (23 cols.), "Baptism" (28 cols.), "Blood" (9 cols.), "Calendar" (11 cols.), "Divination" (20 cols.), "Faith" (31 cols.), "Hell" (17 cols.), "Jesus Christ" (56 cols.), "Marriage" (76 cols.), "Paul" (70 cols.), "Septuagint" (31 cols.), "Wine" (13 cols.), and others. Although the article on "Christology" is sixteen columns in length, many other subjects that are considered very important today receive brief treatment: "Biblical Theology" (2 cols.), "Hermeneutics" ($1\frac{1}{2}$ cols.), "Salvation" ($1\frac{1}{2}$ cols.), "Soteriology" (1 col.). It seems strange to devote only eleven columns to the "Holy Spirit" and eighteen columns to "Preadamite."

Another very thorough work is James Hastings's *Dictionary of the Bible,* 4 vols. (1898-1904; reprint, Peabody, Mass.: Hendrickson, 1988), with each volume averaging nine hundred pages. Although some articles are dry and technical, and some are by liberals, many are genuinely interesting and helpful. There are many notable contributors, such as A. B. Bruce, B. B. Warfield, James Candlish, F. C. Conybeare, and Geerhardus Vos. Some of the thorough articles are "Apocrypha" (26 cols.), "Chronology of the Old Testament" (12 cols.), "Chronology of the New Testament" (44 cols.), "Eschatology" (44 cols.), "Ethics" (25 cols.), "Faith" (24 cols.), "Galatia" (16 cols. by W. M. Ramsay), "God" (39 cols.: A. B. Davidson on the Old Testament, W. Sanday on the New Testament), "Holy Spirit" (18 cols. by H. W. Swete), "Jesus Christ" (102 cols. by W. Sanday), "Kingdom of God" (25 cols. by J. Orr), "Law," (37 cols.: E. R. Driver on the Old Testament, J. Denney on the New Testament), "Miracle" (33 cols. by J. H. Bernard), "Paul the Apostle" (67 cols. by G. G. Findlay), "Peter, Simon" (47 cols.), "Predestination" (32 cols. by B. B. Warfield), "Priests and Levites" (60 cols.), "Prophecy and Prophets" (41 cols. by A. B. Davidson), "Salvation, Savior" (33 cols.), "Son of God" (18 cols. by W. Sanday), "Tabernacle" (30 cols., illustrated), "Temple" (42 cols., illustrated), and "Writing" (27 cols. by F. G. Kenyon). It is interesting that there are no articles on biblical theology or hermeneutics.

One of the most exhaustive works in the field is the *New Schaff-Herzog Encyclopedia of Religious Knowledge,* 12 vols. (New York: Funk and Wagnalls, 1908), edited by Samuel M. Jackson, with each volume averaging well over five hundred pages. It covers much more than biblical subjects, and many of the discussions of other areas are helpful to the Bible student. There are biographical articles: "Augustine, St." (16 cols.), "Huss, John" (11 cols.), "Luther, Martin" (20 cols.), "Wesley, John" (only 8 cols.), "Wycliff, John" (26 cols.); there are also articles on theological and historical subjects: "Buddhism" (7 cols.), "Catechisms" (13 cols.), "Comparative Religion" (25 cols.), "Hellenistic Greek" (8 cols. by A. Deissmann), "Mohammed" (13 cols.), "New England Theology" (20 cols.), "Talmud" (18 cols.), and "Zoroaster" (26 cols.). B. B. Warfield has some great contributions: "Apologetics" (12 cols.), "Atonement" (14 cols.), "Calvinism" (11 cols.), "Imputation" (6 cols.), and "Renewal" (2 cols.), to name a few. There are articles by liberals like Harnack and Johannes Weiss, which are not helpful, but a great many of the discussions are useful: "Angel" (7 cols.), "Apocrypha" (34 cols.), "Bible Versions" (84 cols.), "Canon of Scripture" (24 cols. by T. Zahn), "Christology" (a great contribution of 34 cols. by Philip Schaff), "Conscience" (5 cols.), "Ethics" (20 cols.), "Inspiration" (14 cols.), "Lord's Supper" (34 cols.),

"Messiah" (14 cols. by von Orelli), "Paul the Apostle" (34 cols. by T. Zahn and others, with an excellent bibliography), "Preaching, History of" (62 cols.), "The Reformation" (17 cols. by Philip Schaff), "Virgin Birth" (26 cols.), "Will, Freedom of the" (15 cols.), and many others. There does seem to be a strange imbalance favoring nonbiblical subjects. For instance, why should there be nine columns on "Bernard of Clairvaux" and only one on "Son of God"? Why are 103 columns devoted to "Theological Seminaries" and only one to "Love"? Yet there are helpful articles on some important modern subjects such as "Biblical Theology" (5 cols. by Martin Kaehler), "Exegesis or Hermeneutics" (22 cols.), "Soteriology" (4 cols.), and "Theology As a Science" (10 cols.). There are also some unusual subjects: "Bibles, Annotated" (13 cols.), "Colors in the Bible" (4 cols.), "Numbers, Sacred" (4 cols.), "Serpent in Worship, Mythology, and Symbolism" (16 cols.), "Stars" (5 cols.), and others.

Baker Encyclopedia of the Bible, 2 vols. (Grand Rapids: Baker, 1988), edited by Walter A. Elwell, is not as thorough as the larger sets can be, but some articles are significant: "Animals" (pp. 91-115), a survey from adder to worm; "Archaeology" (pp. 148-56); "Armageddon" (p. 171) does not settle whether it is literal or figurative; "Bible, Inspiration of" (pp. 306-8) says that inspiration is plenary and verbal and that the Bible is infallible but does not use the word *inerrant;* "Biblical Theology" (pp. 339-46); "Birds" (pp. 348-59) from bittern to water hen; "Christology" (pp. 434-39); "Coins" (pp. 485-94), with three pages of drawings; "Daniel, Book of" (pp. 572-77) does not identify the author of Chapters 1-6 and gives a bibliography limited to liberal and amillennial works; "Demythologization" (pp. 612-14) gives a mild evaluation of Bultmann; "Exodus, the" (pp. 742-46) does not settle the date; "Flood, the" (pp. 796-98) does not settle the extent; "Isaiah, Book of" (pp. 1047-53) defends the unity of the book; "Jerusalem" (pp. 1123-35), with eleven photos; "Jesus Christ, Life and Teaching of" (pp. 1141-63); "Joel, Book of" (pp. 1174-78) gives an amillennial interpretation; "Peter, Second Letter of" (pp. 1657-59) holds that the epistle is posthumous (p. 1657); "Quotations of the Old Testament in the New

Testament" (pp. 1808-13); "Trades and Occupations" (pp. 2083-93) from ambassador to writer; and "Woman, Doctrine of" (pp. 2156-59).

An overwhelmingly liberal contrast to the *ISBE* is *The Interpreter's Dictionary of the Bible,* 4 vol. (New York: Abingdon, 1962), edited by George A. Buttrick; each volume averages almost a thousand pages. Here the reader is ambushed by unbelief on almost every page. When he can find a conservative article (e.g., "Trinity" by F. F. Bruce), it is only a half column long. There are thorough articles on the most up-to-date subjects: "Biblical Theology, Contemporary" (28 cols. by K. Stendahl), "Biblical Theology, History of" (11 cols.), "Church, Idea of" (19 cols. by P. S. Minear), "Dead Sea Scrolls" (23 cols.), "Interpretation" (11 cols.), "Myth in the New Testament" (5 cols. by E. Dinkler), "Time" (13 cols.), and many others. Some of the major articles are "Assyria and Babylonia" (82 cols.), "Holy Spirit" (25 cols. by G.W.H. Lampe), "Jerusalem" (48 cols. by M. Burrows), "Jesus Christ" (55 cols. by F. C. Grant), "Paul the Apostle" (46 cols. by A. C. Purdy), "Resurrection in the New Testament" (20 cols. by J.A.T. Robinson, who wrote *Honest to God*), "Salvation" (27 cols. by Alan Richardson), "Sermon on the Mount" (19 cols.), "Temple, Jerusalem" (53 cols.), and "Versions, Ancient" (23 cols. by B. M. Metzger). The help is not worth the effort to sift out the unbelief.

The Anchor Bible Dictionary, 6 vols. (New York: Doubleday, 1992.), edited by David Noel Freedman, expresses the hard-line liberal position. The editors are interested in relevant subjects such as "Abortion in Antiquity" (1:31-35). No pictures are provided except for unusual articles, e.g., "Art and Architecture" (1:401-61, forty-eight illustrations), "Dan, the Place" (2:12-17, six photos of the site), and "Megiddo" (4:666-79, five illustrations). The dictionary casts doubt on the historical accuracy of Scripture: "Daniel, Book of" (2:29-37) states bluntly that "Daniel is not a historical person but a figure of legend" (p. 30) and goes on to add that the "one like a son of man" probably refers to "the archangel Michael" (p. 35); the article "Demons" (2:138-42) does not decide whether they actually exist or are merely a psychological problem (p. 142);

"Flood" (2:798-803) argues that the Flood is disproved by archaeology; and "Exodus, the" (2:700-708) throws out the conservative
date of 1446 B.C. (p. 702). It asserts destructive higher critical
views: "Elohist" (2:478-82) supports the documentary hypothesis;
"Isaiah, Book of" (3:472-507) discusses the alleged collections of
First, Second, and Third Isaiah; "Jesus, Quest for the Historical"
(3:796-802) discusses all the radical opinions; "John, Epistles of"
(3:901-12) sees no common authorship with the Gospel (p. 907);
"John, the Gospel of" (3:912-31) concludes about the author that
"he (or she) was a prominent and respected figure in the Johannine
community" (p. 920); "Paul" (5:186-201) considers II Corinthians
and Philippians to be merely fragments, the pastoral Epistles non-
Pauline; "Peter" (5:251-63) holds that I and II Peter are not genuine
(p. 262); "Q (Gospel Source)" (5:567-72); and "Revelation, Book
of" (5:694-708) thinks that the author is a person named John
"otherwise unknown" (p. 702). "Wrath of God (OT)" (6:989-96)
holds that there is no uniform Old Testament answer on how to be
delivered from wrath (p. 995).

The Encyclopedia of Religion, 16 vols. (New York: Macmillan,
1987), edited by Mircea Eliade, is by the "History-of-Religions"
school, for whom everything is relative and Christ is just one of
many "saviors." They provide sympathetic and thorough presenta-
tions of "Buddhism" (2:334-560), "Judaism" (8:127-205), and so
on but do not expect such sympathy toward biblical subjects:
"Abraham" (1:13) says that the patriarch was not a historical person
and that the whole account of Genesis 14 "is historically impossible," and "Incarnation" (7:156-61) sees parallels between Christ's
incarnation and those of persons in Greek (Gnosticism), Indian
(Vishnu, Buddha), and Iranian (Mithra) religions. The article "Jesus" (8:15-28), a Jesuit survey, holds that "the starting point for
Christology was Christ's existence after death" (8:19) and encourages a Christology "from below" (8:22).

The most helpful and practical work for the average Bible
student is the *International Standard Bible Encyclopaedia,* 5 vols.
(Grand Rapids: Eerdmans, 1939. 3,541 pp. in addition to maps and
photographs), edited by James Orr. If a pastor has this one work,

he will probably need no other in this field. Not only is the *ISBE* dominantly conservative, but many of the articles are outstanding contributions by the greatest scholars of their generation: "Acts of the Apostles" (18 cols. by A. T. Robertson), "Adam in the New Testament" (3 cols. by Griffith Thomas), "Apocalyptic Literature" (35 cols. by J.E.H. Thomson), "Apocrypha" (10 cols. by T. W. Davies), "Archaeology" (14 cols. by M. G. Kyle), "Ascension" (6 cols. by Griffith Thomas), "Astronomy" (31 cols. by the great astronomer E. W. Maunder), "Bible" (20 cols. by J. Orr), "Biblical Theology" (6 cols. by J. Lindsay).

There are also articles entitled "Canon of the Old Testament" (18 cols. by George L. Robinson), "Christianity" (12 cols. by J. Orr and J. Dickie), "Chronology of Old Testament" (23 cols. by Edward Mack), "Chronology of New Testament" (12 cols. by W. P. Armstrong), "Commentaries" (9 cols. by J. Orr), "Daniel, Book of" (9 cols. by R. Dick Wilson), "David" (18 cols. by George L. Robinson), "Dictionaries" (9 cols.), "Egypt" (20 cols. by Sir Flinders Petrie), "Eschatology of the Old Testament" (15 cols. by J. Orr), "Eschatology of the New Testament" (28 cols. by the amillennialist Geerhardus Vos), "Essenes" (16 cols. by J.E.H. Thomson), "Ethics" (26 cols. by Archibald Alexander), "Evolution, the Theory Disproved" (16 cols. by J. R. Straton), "God" (29 cols.), "Hittites" (25 cols. by John Garstang).

Other articles include "Holy Spirit" (23 cols. by E. Y. Mullins), "Imputation" (7 cols. by C. W. Hodge), "Inspiration" (21 cols. by B. B. Warfield), "Israel, History of the People" (34 cols. by von Orelli), "Jerusalem" (53 cols.), "Jesus Christ" (87 cols. by J. Orr), "Johannine Theology" (22 cols. by R. Law), "Kingdom of God" (6 cols. by James Stalker), "Logos" (12 cols. by Archibald Alexander), "Moses" (15 cols. by M. G. Kyle), "Palestine" (29 cols.), "Paul the Apostle" (49 cols. by A. T. Robertson), "Pauline Theology" (12 cols. by J. H. Webster), "Pentateuch" (39 cols. by H. M. Wiener and M. G. Kyle), "Person of Christ" (20 cols. by B. B. Warfield), "Prophecy" (14 cols. by von Orelli), "Resurrection" (17 cols. by B. B. Warfield), "Roman Empire and Christianity" (27 cols. by S. Angus), "Sacrifice" (40 cols.), "Son of God" (5 cols. by James

Stalker), "Tabernacle" (21 cols. by T. Whitelaw), "Temple" (25 cols.), "Trinity" (20 cols. by B. B. Warfield), "Virgin Birth" (11 cols. by L. M. Sweet), and "Writing" (24 cols. by E. C. Richardson). This is an impressive list, both in terms of quantity and quality. Any Bible student will benefit greatly from a systematic reading of such articles.

The International Standard Bible Encyclopedia, rev. ed., 4 vols. (Grand Rapids: Eerdmans, 1979-88.), edited by G. W. Bromiley is greatly improved by newer illustrations and photographs. Many articles are strengthened; some, weakened. "Acts of the Apostles" (1:33-47) has a strong explanation by F. F. Bruce; "Archaeology" (1:235-83) covers Arabia to the Indus Valley, with twenty-one color plates and text by LaSor, Van Elderen, and others; "Art" (1:299-306); "Astronomy" (1:344-48) is weaker than Maunder's article in the original edition; "Babylon, Babylonia" (1:384-402) by authority D. J. Wiseman; "Biblical Theology, History of, Nature of" (1:498-509) by G. E. Ladd; "Christology" (1:663-66) with precise definitions by Bromiley; "Daniel, Book of" (1:859-66) by R. K. Harrison attacks the idea of a Maccabean date (p. 861); "Dead Sea Scrolls" (1:883-97) by LaSor has a strong bibliography.

The reader will also find "English Versions" (2:83-102), with illustrations of many Bibles, by W. M. Smith and Bromiley; "Eschatology" (2:130-43) with a whole column of bibliography but only about four premillennialists; "Ethics" (2:164-93) covering Old Testament, New Testament, and philosophical ethics by Hubbard, Verhey, Bromiley; "Exodus, Date of the" (2:230-38) argues for a fifteenth-century B.C. date; "Flood" (2:316-21) attacks a Flood geology (p. 318); "Genealogy of Jesus" (2:428-31) suggests that the two genealogies are probably attempts "to historicize traditional motifs in the Gospel material" (p. 430); "Holy Spirit" (2:730-46) by Tappeiner and Bromiley; "Infallibility" (2:821-22) defends "infallibility," attacks "inerrancy"; "Inspiration" (2:839-49) is the old article by Warfield; "Inspiration, History of the Doctrine of" (2:849-54) is the new view by Bromiley; "Isaiah" (2:885-904) argues that Isaiah is an anthology (p. 898).

Articles also include "Jesus Christ" (2:1034-49), with a bibliography that lists one strong conservative, F. F. Bruce; "Kingdom of God" (3:23-29) by Ladd; "Library" (3:122-27) by LaSor; "Literature, the Bible as" (3:143-46); "Messiah" (3:330-38) by O. A. Piper; "Millennium" (3:356-61), a very fair survey of the different views, with adequate coverage of individual authors; "Palace" (3:629-32), with photos of Herod's palaces at Jericho and Jerusalem; "Parousia" (3:664-70) by L. Morris is another article that offers neutral appraisal of the different views; "Pastoral Epistles" (3:679-87), by D. Guthrie, defends Pauline authorship; "Paul the Apostle" (3:696-720) by F. F. Bruce; "Person of Christ" (3:781-801) by C. Brown, with a very strong bibliography; "Q" (4:1-4) by R. P. Martin admits that "Q" is a hypothetical document; "Quotations in the NT" (4:18-25) by E. E. Ellis; "Religions of the Biblical World" (4:79-129), covering areas such as Asia Minor and Assyria, cultures such as Canaanite, Egyptian, Greco-Roman, and Judaism; "Revelation, Book of" (4:171-77) by Ladd leaves open the question of authorship; "Sanctification" (4:321-31); "Science and Christianity" (4:351-56) argues for science and theology complementing one another; "Seal" (4:369-75) with many illustrations; "Stones, Precious" (4:623-30) covers agate to turquoise; "Temple" (4:759-76); "Virgin Birth of Jesus Christ" (4:990-93) shrunk to two and a half pages from the first edition; "Woman" (4:1089-97); "Women in Church Leadership" (4:1098-1100) promotes women in leadership; and "Worship" (4:1117-33).

Another major reference work is now available for the expositor: the ***Zondervan Pictorial Encyclopedia of the Bible,*** 5 vols. (Grand Rapids: Zondervan, 1975. 1,056; 854; 1,015; 965; 1,094 pp.; 17 maps), edited by Merrill C. Tenney. The *ZPEB* is a strange combination of competent and incompetent scholarship. Some articles are excellent; others are pitiable. A work with 241 different contributors is bound to be of uneven quality. Oddly enough, at times, the same contributor has produced superior and inferior articles. R. K. Harrison wrote the "Dead Sea Scrolls" (11:53-68), an excellent, factual article with good illustrations, providing a ground plan of the Qumran community and a helpful bibliography.

He also authored "Demon, Demoniac, Demonology" (11:92-101), which discusses most demon possession as mental illness and gives a useless bibliography of out-of-print books and German titles and his own articles in *The Interpreter's Dictionary of the Bible*! He also wrote a one-column article, "Devil" (11:117), which utterly confuses the Devil with demons and omits the vast bibliography of contemporary works on the subject. We would expect the area of archaeology to be lavishly illustrated from the wealth of recent discoveries. Scattered throughout the set are photographs that illustrate much of interest: photos of Ai (1:91), the winged bull from Assyria (1:373), and Athens (1:402-7); sixteen pages of color plates in Volume I and eight pages of color photos in each of the other volumes. The article "Archaeology" (1:258-86) by Blaiklock is disappointing, however, because of the few illustrations and the fact that most of the article (pp. 266-77) is an unillustrated list of dates and persons important to the field. One could hope that a pictorial encyclopedia would provide illustrations of every important site and excavator in such a major article.

The article "Astronomy" (1:394-99) is a disaster. Not only does it reprint a diagram by the liberal S. H. Hooke, illustrating the alleged primitive opinion of the Hebrews that the universe was a three-decked design with literal pillars holding up a solid dome of the firmament (p. 365), but it also demonstrates that the author of the article, D. C. Morton, is a thoroughgoing evolutionist. He argues that the solar system is 4.7 billion years old. Apparently Morton prefers Gammow's "big bang" theory to Hoyle's "steady state" theory as an adequate explanation of the existence of the universe. It is sad that such an article was printed at all. This is not the only example of evolutionary bias in the encyclopedia. The article "Stones" (5:520-24) by D. R. Bowes suggests that there are granite rocks in Palestine 3.4 billion years old (p. 523) and states bluntly that there are Precambrian rocks of the Arabo-Nubian Massif that are 600 million years old (p. 520). Wolf's article "Earth, Circle of the" (2:177) denies that the Old Testament can be interpreted so that the earth may be thought of as a sphere. The same liberal diagram that was in the article "Astronomy" also appears in the article "Firmament" (2:540), this time without an explanation. Several illustrations are duplicated: a photo of the Baal of Lightning appears twice (3:6, 244) and a photo of a leper is repeated (2:139; 4:160).

There are some very strong, thorough articles. J. B. Payne has an article on "Jerusalem" (3:459-95) with fine illustrations. Payne also contributes a helpful article on the "Chronology of the Old Testament" (1:829-45); Thompson matches it with one on the "Chronology of the New Testament" (1:816-29). Thompson also had helpful articles on "Israel, History of" (3:335-54) and "Israel, Religion of" (3:354-73). This latter article has a peculiar illustration of Solomon's temple (p. 363) that looks more like Ezekiel's temple (5:635). Kelso has a helpful article on "Occupations, Trades, and Professions in Palestine" (4:486-503). Stigers has a good article on "Temple, Jerusalem" (5:622-56). Huey has a helpful article on "Weights and Measures" (5:913-22).

Perhaps the best articles in the set are on very technical subjects. There is precise information in White's articles "Greek Language" (2:826-34) and "Writing" (5:995-1015) with good illustrations, and in Archer's article "Hebrew Language" (3:66-76). There are good articles on "Text and Manuscripts of the Old Testament" by Mac-Rae (5:683-97) and on "Text and Manuscripts of the New Testament" by Greenlee (5:697-713), although one could hope for better illustrations in them. Greenlee soundly attacks the authority of the Textus Receptus (pp. 710-11).

On the other side of the ledger there are some articles that manifest a high degree of inadequacy. It is incredible that Smick could dispatch "Yahweh" (5:102) with only eight lines and not even a cross-reference to Kuhn's article "God, Names of" (2:760-66), where some additional material can be found. Cole's article "Christology" (1:805-9) deals merely with the titles of the Lord and leaves whole continents of major information untouched. Wolf has an article on "E (Elohist)" explaining the liberal critical theory and does not even mention one argument against the documentary hypothesis (2:175). In the article "Imprecatory Psalms" (2:265), S. J. Schultz treats these psalms so perfunctorily that he omits mentioning Psalms 35, 52, and 58 and does not give any real defense to their existence in the Old Testament. Drumwright's article "Interpretation" (3:297-305) deals almost entirely with the history of interpretation; there is only a page or so that actually gives practical principles. The article "Marriage" (4:92-102) could have been written by a Jew, for it deals almost entirely with Rabbinic and Talmudic interpretations of marriage. The vitally important New Testament teaching on marriage is dispatched in only nine lines (pp. 94-95). Petersen's article "Matthew, Gospel of" (4:120-38) gives a backhanded defense of the ascribed authorship by saying that "the traditional view of Matthaean authorship of the First Gospel should not be entirely excluded" (p. 124). Dayton's article "Teaching of Jesus" (5:607-11) devotes less than one page to the actual content of Jesus' teaching. C.F.H. Henry covers the "Trinity" (5:822-24) in about four columns. *Mediocre* is the most merciful word that can be applied to the article; one cannot help thinking of B. B. Warfield's magnificent article "Trinity" in the ***International Standard Bible Encyclopaedia*** (5:3012-22).

Some of the strongest articles were contributed by Guthrie: "Canon of the New Testament" (1:731-45), "Bible" (1:554-66), "Jesus Christ" (3:497-583), "Johannine Theology" (3:623-36), and "New Testament" (4:418-28). Prophetic subjects are covered well. Walvoord has articles on "Antichrist" (1:178-81), "Premillennialism" (4:845-48), and "Second Coming" (5:325-28), clearly teaching the Rapture (p. 327). Hiebert urges the doctrine of imminency in his article "Parousia" (4:600-602), whereas Jewett omits any mention of the pretribulation rapture in his article "Eschatology" (2:342-58). There is some imbalance when Horne treats "Thessalonians, Second Epistle" (5:725-27) in just three columns and Hagner devotes seven pages to "Tobit, Book of" (5:761-66).

The *ZPEB* is a work of mixed quality. At many points it suffers by comparison with *ISBE*. A number of the contributors seem more concerned with proving themselves scholars than with providing practical biblical help for the average Bible student. Worse still, the work manifests the new evangelical susceptibility to liberal opinions. The *ZPEB* is an important reference source but a flawed one.

One of the best one-volume Bible dictionaries has been revised and expanded into a three-volume set. *The New Bible Dictionary* is now available as *The Illustrated Bible Dictionary,* 3 vols. (Wheaton, Ill.: Tyndale House, 1980, 1,728 pp.), edited by J. D. Douglas. It uses the RSV text and has many illustrations. "Abraham" (1:5-8) lists only one commentary on Genesis, one by Speiser, a liberal; "Animals" (1:52-68) offers a photograph of a Syrian rock hyrax (p. 60); "City" (1:292-98) shows a model of Megiddo; "Daniel, Book of" (1:360-63) defends the authenticity of the book; "Herbs and Spices" (2:636-39) has color photos of mint, dill, and so on; "Jerusalem" displays an aerial view and other photos; "Jewels and Precious Stones" (2:781-88) gives color views of lapis lazuli, cornelian, turquoise, and so on; "Music and Musical Instruments" (2:1031-40) contains many illustrations; "Plants" offers color photographs of mustard, poppy, and so on; "Stars" (3:1485-86) holds that the star of Bethlehem was a supernova, with no comment on the miraculous; and "Virgin Birth" defends the miracle. The illustrations are a welcome addition, but the text of the articles has not been made thorough enough to be the equal of *ISBE* or *ZPEB*.

For the pastor, then, the best works to choose from are the *Zondervan Pictorial Encyclopedia of the Bible* and the revised edition of the *International Standard Bible Encyclopedia.* They both have their strong points, and both have weaknesses. In addition, the old edition of *ISBE* is still being kept in print, and since it is at a much reduced price, it is still a serious contender. Systematically consulting any of these will provide great help for a serious preacher.

CHAPTER 10
BIBLE DICTIONARIES: ONE-VOLUME

Although the Bible dictionary sets are almost always to be preferred to single-volume works because of their greater thoroughness, there are some small Bible dictionaries that are worthwhile. Four of these smaller dictionaries are edited by avowed conservatives: Fausset, Unger, Tenney, and Douglas.

The *Bible Cyclopedia* (Hartford, Conn.: Scranton, 1910), edited by Andrew Robert Fausset, is too old to be of great help to the Bible student. Although it is 753 pages long, many of the articles are too short: "Atonement" (1 p.) and "Justification" (less than a page). He does defend the Mosaic authorship of the Pentateuch ($2\frac{1}{2}$ pp.), verbal inspiration (2 pp.), and the premillennial interpretation of Scripture under "Dispensations" ($\frac{1}{3}$ p.) and "Thousand Years" (2 pp.). In "Creation" (4 pp.) he advocates the "long day" theory. The Bible teacher needs a more up-to-date work.

Another conservative work, *The New Unger's Bible Dictionary,* rev. ed. (Chicago: Moody, 1988), edited by Merrill F. Unger and R. K. Harrison, is a more substantial work of about fourteen hundred pages. Part of the material has been drawn from *People's Bible Encyclopedia* edited by Charles Randall Barnes. The part by Unger and Harrison is more modern and helpful. Since Unger is a strong premillennialist, there are good articles on "Day of the Lord" (18 lines), "Millennium" (1 col.), "Jerusalem, New" ($\frac{1}{2}$ col.), "Abomination of Desolation" ($\frac{1}{2}$ col.), and "The False Prophet" ($\frac{1}{2}$ col.). The article on "The Judgments" (2 cols.) is one of the clearest from the premillennial view. There are also excellent articles on "Dead Sea Scrolls" (5 cols.), "Festivals" (27 cols.), "Tabernacle of Israel" (13 cols.), "Familiar Spirit" ($\frac{1}{2}$ col.), and "Magic" (9 cols.). Some articles, however, are far too short: "Eschatology" (1 col.), "Kingdom of God" (1 col.), "Righteousness" (less than $\frac{1}{2}$ col.), and, even though he calls it "of immense importance" (p. 527), Unger devotes only five columns to "Inspiration." The color illustrations and diagrams, and the revisions and additions have made Unger's work one of the most helpful: "Gospels, the Four" (20 cols.), "Jesus Christ" (10 cols.), "Paul" (25 cols.), "Temple" (12 cols.), and others.

The *Zondervan Pictorial Bible Dictionary* (Grand Rapids: Zondervan, 1963. 942 pp. and 22 color maps), edited by Merrill C. Tenney, is a large work, well illustrated and attractive in format. Some of the major articles are extremely helpful: "Archaeologist" (19 cols., 16 illus.) by practicing archaeologist J. P. Free; "Babylon" (8 $\frac{1}{2}$ cols., 5 photos); "Christ, Jesus" (13 cols.) by Everett F. Harrison; "Dead Sea Scrolls" (8 cols., 7 photos); "Demons" (2 cols.) by Merrill F. Unger; "Flood" (5 cols.), which defends a universal Flood; "Herod" (8 cols., 4 photos); "Israel" (15 cols., 6 photos) by J. Barton Payne; "Jerusalem" ($21\frac{1}{2}$ cols., 16 illus.) by Wilbur M. Smith, with a superb bibliography; "Money" (10 cols.), with photographs of ten biblical coins and American coins to illustrate their sizes; "Prophets" ($9\frac{1}{2}$ cols.) by E. J. Young; "Resurrection of Jesus Christ" (10 cols., 4 illus.); and "Temple" (12 cols., 11 illus.). The articles are of uneven value; in "Creation" (2 cols.) Allan A. MacRae gives very moderate comments, favoring the "long day" view; in "Ecumenism" (2 cols.) G. W. Bromley advocates a form of it; "Inspiration" (2 cols.) defends the inerrancy of the autographs; and in "Miracles" (5 cols.) J. A. Buswell Jr. defends the miraculous in the Bible. Some discussions of major subjects are altogether too brief: it is impossible to do justice in one and a half columns to such themes as "Holy Spirit," "Justification," "Salvation," and "Son of Man." There are no articles on interpretation or biblical theology. This work also groups together a great number of entries under "Animals of the Bible" (13 cols.), "Insects of the Bible" ($8\frac{1}{2}$ cols.), "Minerals of the Bible" (17 cols.), and "Plants of the Bible" (18 cols.). These articles would be easier to find under regular alphabetical order. Although there are defects, there is a great amount of valuable help in this work.

The New International Dictionary of the Bible Pictorial Edition, rev. ed. (Grand Rapids: Zondervan, 1963, 1987. 1,178 pp.), edited by Merrill Tenney and revised by J. D. Douglas, is from the *Zondervan Pictorial Bible Dictionary* and adapted to the NIV. It has black-and-white photographs of Acco (p. 11), the altar at Megiddo (p. 36), conies (p. 48), Baalbek (p. 115), Corinth (p. 234), and the mud-brick gate at Dan (p. 250). There are separate articles on Caesarea Maritima and Caesarea Philippi (pp. 179-80); "Christ, Jesus" (pp. 203-10) defends His deity and humanity; "Daniel, Book of" (pp. 253-54) gives a strong defense of its authenticity; "Flood, the" (pp. 354-57) discusses different interpretations but does not decide between them; "Isaiah" (pp. 471-74) defends the unity of the book; there are sixteen pages of color plates between pages 554-55; "Occupations and Professions" (pp. 716-27) from apothecary to writer; "Pastoral Letters" (pp. 752-55) defends Pauline authorship; "Peter, Second Letter of" (pp. 774-75) defends genuineness; "Son of God" (p. 957) defends Christ's deity; "Temple" (pp. 990-97) with ten photographs and illustrations; and "Weights and Measures" (pp. 1060-63) has a photograph of Hebrew weights.

The Revell Bible Dictionary (Grand Rapids: Revell, 1990. 1,156 pp.), edited by Lawrence Richards, is a colorful source of information. There are articles on "Abraham" (pp. 8-12) with a chart of his life and New Testament parallels (p. 12); "Acts of the Apostles" (pp. 18-21) with a chapter-by-chapter outline of Acts; "Altar" (pp. 50-52) with illustrations of seven different altars; and "Archaeology" (pp. 84-87) with a photograph of Laish-Dan. "Art" (pp. 95-97) gives examples of art in the Bible. The dictionary has a color drawing of the high priest's breastplate (p. 171). "Caesarea" (p. 183) is limited to Caesarea Maritima; Caesarea Philippi is just mentioned. (The map index lists it on map XI, but it is on XII.) "Chronology of the Bible" (pp. 214-19) gives a conservative date for the Exodus, 1446 B.C. (p. 216); "Daniel, Book of" (pp. 276-78) defends the authenticity of the book; "Flood" (pp. 389-91) defends the traditional view of the Deluge; "Galilee, Sea of" (pp. 413-15) has a photograph of the Galilee boat and a drawing of how it looked; "Housing" (pp. 502-6) has ground plans and photographs of fourteen places; "Isaiah, Book of" (pp. 523-27) defends the unity of the book; "Jerusalem" (pp. 551-55) has a reconstruction of Jerusalem in the time of Jesus; "Jesus Christ" (pp. 556-65) defends His deity; "Revelation, the Book of" (pp. 861-64) gives both futurist and historicist interpretations; "Star of Bethlehem" (p. 946) argues that the star was a miracle; and "Weights and Measures" (pp. 1019-20) has not only a table of such but also photographs of different kinds. The dictionary concludes with indexes of people, places, and maps (pp. 1049 ff.).

Perhaps the most useful one-volume Bible dictionary is *The New Bible Dictionary,* rev. ed. (Grand Rapids: Eerdmans, 1962, 1982), edited by J. D. Douglas. There are 1,391 pages in addition to plates and maps. The help available here is impressive. "Abraham" ($4\frac{1}{2}$ cols. and a map) defends the early date and historicity of the patriarch; "Acts, Book of the" ($5\frac{1}{2}$ cols.) by F. F. Bruce defends the historical character of Acts (though half of the books he recommends are liberal); "Angel" (3 cols.) by R. A. Stewart holds that the "sons of God" in Genesis 6 are fallen angels; "Archaeology" (23 cols.) has a five-page chart of the principal excavated sites in Palestine; "Atonement" (6 cols.) by L. L. Morris defends the substitutionary work of Christ; "Babylonia" ($10\frac{1}{2}$ cols.) has a three-page chart of excavated sites; "Chronology of the Old Testament" (12 cols.) has a five-page chronological outline of the Old Testament; "Chronology of the New Testament" ($9\frac{1}{2}$ cols.) has a chronological outline; "Covenant" (7 cols.) by John Murray divides the unilateral covenant into six aspects; "Daniel, Book of" (6 cols.) defends the authorship; "Dead Sea Scrolls" ($4\frac{1}{2}$ cols.) by F. F. Bruce gives a brief, accurate survey; "Dress" (3 cols.) has two pages with twenty-eight illustrations; "Eden, Garden of" ($3\frac{1}{2}$ cols.) defends the reality of the garden; "Egypt" (32 cols.) is very thorough; "Eschatology" (10 cols.) by G. E. Ladd covers the major topics, all millennial views; "Ethics, Biblical" (7 cols.) by John Murray presents the biblical teaching; "Fall" (3 cols.) by P. E. Hughes defends the biblical account and attacks evolution; "God" (6 cols.)

denies the universal fatherhood of God; "Grace" ($3\frac{1}{2}$ cols.) is a brief survey in the method of biblical theology; "Incarnation" ($7\frac{1}{2}$ cols.) by J. I. Packer defends the absolute deity and humanity of Christ; "Inspiration" (5 cols.) by J. I. Packer defends verbal inspiration but does not mention inerrancy; "Interpretation, Biblical" ($3\frac{1}{2}$ cols.) by F. F. Bruce gives a brief history of interpretation. There are articles on "Holy Spirit" (7 cols.), "Israel" ($20\frac{1}{2}$ cols.), "Jerusalem" (11 cols.), "Jesus Christ, Life of" (9 cols.), and "Jesus Christ, Teaching of" ($10\frac{1}{2}$ cols.). "Justification" (7 cols.) by J. I. Packer harmonizes Paul and James; "Kingdom of God" (7 cols.) by H. Ridderbos distinguishes present and future aspects but does not discuss millennialism; "Messiah" (14 cols.) by F. F. Bruce and J. A. Motyer gives a thorough survey of the doctrine; "Money" ($9\frac{1}{2}$ cols.) includes a dozen illustrations; "Paul" ($24\frac{1}{2}$ cols.) by E. E. Ellis carefully surveys his life and teaching; "Pentateuch" ($13\frac{1}{2}$ cols.) maintains the unity but concedes that Moses may not have written all of it; "Potter, Pottery" (3 cols. and 82 illus.) shows the exact differences between pottery of different periods; "Prophecy, Prophets" ($18\frac{1}{2}$ cols.) by J. A. Motyer discusses inspiration, the writing prophets, and worship in Israel; "Sacrifice and Offering" (20 cols.) describes in detail kinds of sacrifices, altars, and New Testament sacrifices; and "Salvation" occupies seven columns and "Temple" fourteen columns. Some of the articles are disappointing: "Creation" (9 cols.) holds that a six-day creation "does not agree with the facts of geology"; "Exodus" (1 col. and map) tries to show that the route of the Exodus does not cross the Red Sea; "Gospels" ($8\frac{1}{2}$ cols.) by F. F. Bruce advocates the existence of "Q"; and "Plants" ($4\frac{1}{2}$ cols.) names only a few. But in spite of these flaws the work is quite valuable.

The remaining works are liberal. One of the best of these liberal works is *Hastings' Dictionary of the Bible* (New York: Scribner's, 1963. 1,059 pp.), revised by F. C. Grant and H. H. Rowley. "Abraham" (2 cols.) is riddled with the documentary hypothesis; "Amos" ($2\frac{1}{2}$ cols.) by John Bright waxes eloquent on the theology of Amos; "Assyria and Babylon" (20 cols.) gives much historical background; "Atonement" ($3\frac{1}{2}$ cols.) by James Barr gives a clear, brief survey; "Biblical Theology" (1 col.) tells of the method from 1650 to the present; "Christology" (26 cols.) is one of the best articles in any dictionary, although it admits the possible coexistence of legends with reliable information in the New Testament; "Chronology of the New Testament" (10 cols.) by F. C. Grant shows the difficulty of determining exact dates; "Expiation" (5 cols.) denies a limited expiation; "God" (10½ cols.) by James Barr discusses the names of God and other topics; "Holy Spirit" (11½ cols.) by G.W.H. Lampe identifies the Holy Spirit as "the mysterious, creative power of God"; "Inspire, Inspiration" (2 cols.) by Bruce M. Metzger holds to verbal inspiration but not to inerrancy; "Israel" occupies forty and one-half columns; "Jesus Christ" (38 cols.) refers to the transfiguration as a "puzzling pericope"; "Justification" (4 cols.) harmonizes Paul and James; "Messiah (18 cols.) by James Barr discusses the key passages; "Paul's Theology" (13 cols.) by G. B. Caird centers on salvation; and "Temple" (14 cols.) has a clear diagram of Herod's temple. There is genuine value here if the reader is always on guard against the unbelief.

The Lion Encyclopedia of the Bible, rev. ed. (Tring, England: Lion, 1978, 1986. 352 pp.), edited by Pat Alexander, is organized by major topics rather than alphabetically. He begins with the "Land of the Bible," covering the geography, major plants, animals, birds, and so on (pp. 9-26); then follows "Archaeology and the Bible" (pp. 27-66), with photographs of Tel Beer Sheba (p. 27), Jericho (p. 43), Lachish (p. 57), Ephesus (p. 59), and Masada (p. 62). The "Story of the Bible" (pp. 67-84) argues that the more ancient manuscripts are the more accurate (p. 71), and "Understanding the Bible" (pp. 85-112) surveys the books of the Bible, favoring a date of 165 B.C. for Daniel (p. 96) and suggesting that John and Revelation may not be by the same author (p. 107). "Religion and Worship in the Bible" (pp. 113-40) features a Jew blowing a shofar (p. 113); "Key Teaching of the Bible" (pp. 141-58) covers atonement, faith, God, Holy Spirit, and Jesus Christ (defending the deity, p. 150); "Home and Family Life" (pp. 159-92); "People of the Bible" (pp. 193-216) is selective, not exhaustive (Jemima, Zeruiah are missing); "Work and Society in the Bible" (pp. 217-52); "Places of the Bible" (pp. 253-78); "Nations and Peoples of the Bible" (pp.

279-310); and concludes with an "Atlas of Bible History" (pp. 311-45). It is brief and popular.

The Holman Bible Dictionary (Nashville: Holman, 1991. 1,450 pp.), edited by Trent C. Butler, is a very thorough, critical dictionary. It begins with a time line history dating the Exodus at 1280 B.C. There are beautiful photographs of the Acropolis (p. 1), Haifa (p. 12), a shepherd and sheep (p. 55), the Pantheon (p. 95), the waterfall at Engedi (p. 419), and more. There are many significant articles: "Accountability, Age of" (p. 13) contains Pelagian overtones; "Archaeology and Bible Study" (pp. 83-93) gives valuable insights; "Christ, Christology" (pp. 250-52) by Ralph P. Martin sets forth a Christology "from below"; "Daniel, Book of" (pp. 336-37) gives conservative and liberal views without deciding between them; "Eschatology" (pp. 432-36) gives arguments for and against universalism; "Gates of Jerusalem" (p. 532) has four photographs; "Homosexuality" (pp. 663-64) sternly condemns the sin; "Inspiration of Scripture" (pp. 703-4) holds that there are truths and weaknesses in all the views; "Isaiah" (pp. 716-20) favors the existence of three Isaiahs; "Jericho" (pp. 759-64) has six photographs and a drawing; "2 Peter" (p. 1101) defends the epistle as canonical; "Plants in the Bible" (pp. 1116-20) has two interesting photographs; "Revelation, the Book of" (pp. 1183-91) commends authorship by John the Apostle and gives amillennial and premillennial interpretations; "Temple of Jerusalem" (pp. 1325-31) has thorough diagrams and drawings of Herod's temple; "Virgin, Virgin Birth" (pp. 1394-96) states that *almah* occurs seven times in the Old Testament, when it actually occurs nine times.

Another liberal work is the *Westminster Dictionary of the Bible* (Philadelphia: Westminster, 1944. 658 pp. and 16 color maps), edited by John D. Davis and Henry S. Gehman. This is the old *Davis Bible Dictionary* (1898, last revised 1924), revised and transformed by liberal editors. Although the old edition is badly outdated, it is still being reprinted by Baker Book House. Gehman's influence has removed most of the conservatism of the old edition: "Abraham" (4 cols.) leaves open the possibility that the name may be that of a tribe rather than of a person; "Canon" ($5\frac{1}{2}$ cols.) gives liberal dates for the formation of the Old Testament canon; "Daniel" ($7\frac{1}{2}$ cols.) does not decide the date; "Flood" (5 cols.) argues for a limited flood; and "Isaiah" (7 cols.) holds to the Trito-Isaiah theory of authorship. There are, however, some helpful articles: "Creation" ($3\frac{1}{2}$ cols.) holds to literal twenty-four-hour days and denies a conflict between the Bible and science; "Ezekiel" (5 cols.) has a remarkably accurate plan of Ezekiel's temple (p. 177); "God" (3 cols.) is by B. B. Warfield; "High Priest" (6 cols.) includes the line of the high priests; "Inspiration" ($1\frac{1}{2}$ cols.) by Warfield has been revised by Gehman. There are no articles on such important subjects as the virgin birth, salvation, interpretation, and biblical theology; and some other subjects are dispatched with regrettable brevity, such as "Atonement" (13 ll.) and "Sin" (7 ll.). The Bible expositor needs something better.

Harper's Bible Dictionary (New York: Harper, 1952. 854 pp. and about 500 illus.), edited by Madeleine S. Miller and J. Lane Miller, is no better. The usual liberal dates are given for the time of Abraham (p. 3), the fall of Jericho (p. 100), the Book of Daniel (p. 127), the Exodus (p. 178), and other disputed periods and incidents. There are some good articles on neutral subjects: "Archaeology" (15 cols.) with a good list of excavated sites in Bible lands; "Scrolls, the Dead Sea" (4 cols.); and other articles of historical interest. But most of the work is filled with liberalism: it advocates the documentary hypothesis (p. 219), explains away miracles (p. 329), denies the future fulfillment of the Book of Revelation (p. 615), and contradicts the biblical doctrine of Satan (p. 648). It is a selective dictionary, deliberately omitting hundreds of minor names: Abaddon, Abagtha, Abdeel, Abel-Beth-Maachah, and others. Since identification of obscure names is often the reason a person reaches for a dictionary, this is not the dictionary a person should reach for.

An even more selective dictionary is the ***Pictorial Biblical Encyclopedia*** (New York: Macmillan, 1964), edited by Gaalyahu Cornfeld. It is thoroughly Jewish. One may discern something of the selectivity of this 720-page work by a glance at the first six articles: "Aaron" (4 cols.); "Acts of the Apostles" ($10\frac{1}{2}$ cols. in addition to 8 photos and 2 maps), which favors a date of A.D. 80-90;

"Aegean Civilization" ($4\frac{1}{2}$ cols. and 10 illus.); "Agriculture" (16 cols. and 32 illus.); "Alphabet and Writing" (10 cols. and 29 illus.); and "Amarna Letters, Tel el" ($2\frac{1}{2}$ cols. and 3 illus.). Though what is included is thoroughly discussed and illustrated, a great number of subjects are omitted. Other important articles are "Ancient Cities, Excavated Sites, Biblical Archaeology" (pp. 44-107, 109 illus.); "Canaan, Gods and Idols, Cult" ($13\frac{1}{2}$ cols. and 31 illus.); "Cities, Israelite, Building and Houses" ($7\frac{1}{2}$ cols. and 15 illus.); "Epistles, Pauline" (15 cols.), which favors a date of A.D. 90-100 for the pastoral Epistles; "Exodus, the" ($6\frac{1}{2}$ cols. and 7 illus.), which denies the biblical number of the people in the Exodus; "Genesis" (11 cols. and 8 illus.), which speaks of the myths in Genesis; "Jesus of Nazareth" ($13\frac{1}{2}$ cols. and 7 illus.), which calls the death and resurrection of Jesus a mystery and lists the Jewish legends of Jesus' illegitimacy, His learning magic in Egypt, and other blasphemous notions; and "Paul" (10 cols.), which presumes that the apostle had never fully endorsed orthodox Pharisaic Judaism, the testimony of the New Testament notwithstanding.

The Illustrated Dictionary and Concordance of the Bible (Jerusalem: G. G. The Jerusalem Publishing House [Reader's Digest Association], 1986. 1,070 pp.), general editor Geoffrey Wigoder, is a work with Jewish emphasis in Old Testament texts and Roman Catholic emphasis in New Testament texts. There are many beautiful photographs: a farmer plowing (p. 15); "Altar" (p. 59) with three photographs; "Animals" (pp. 77-93) covering ant to worm, with fifty illustrations; "Corinth" (pp. 242-44) with four photographs; and "Plants" (pp. 798-811) with seventy-nine photographs. The article "Baptism" (p. 153) teaches baptismal regeneration; "Church" (pp. 233-35) refers to the eucharistic body of Christ; "Daniel, Book of" (pp. 260-63) attacks the authenticity of the book and dates it in the time of the Maccabees; "Isaiah" (pp. 474-77) teaches the existence of two Isaiahs; "John, Gospel of" (pp. 550-52) doubts that "John" is the son of Zebedee; "Mary" (p. 662) is mentioned as "the Virgin Mother of God"; and "Peter (Simon)" (pp. 778-79) refers to Peter as the "leader" of the apostles and has a photograph of the Church of the Primacy of Peter.

Among the older works, *Funk and Wagnalls New Standard Bible Dictionary,* 3rd ed. (Philadelphia: Blakiston, 1936), edited by M. W. Jacobus, Elbert Lane, and A. C. Zenos, is of unequal value. Its contributors are mostly liberal, ranging from the conservative A. T. Robertson to the liberal James Moffatt. Some of the more interesting articles are "Antichrist, the Man of Sin" (4 cols.) by George Milligan; "Babylonia" (7 cols. and 2 full-page maps) by James F. McCurdy; "Conscience" (3 cols.); "Eschatology" (12 cols.), a liberal survey by Zenos; "Israel, Religion of" (27 cols.); "Jerusalem" (18 cols. and 2 full-page maps); and "Jesus Christ" (37 cols.) by James Denney. There is an interesting ground plan of Ezekiel's temple (p. 896).

The editor's choice among all the Bible dictionaries remains the *International Standard Bible Encyclopaedia,* the five-volume set mentioned in Chapter 9. Among the one-volume works, the most helpful is probably Douglas's *New Bible Dictionary,* although Tenney's *Zondervan Pictorial Bible Dictionary* is close to it in usefulness.

CHAPTER 11
BIBLE HANDBOOKS

Bible handbooks are intended to aid the reader in understanding the Bible as a whole, book by book, and in its individual passages. They regularly supply a great amount of historical and archaeological background. They are organized the way the Bible is, book-by-book, chapter-by-chapter, from Genesis to Revelation.

Halley's Bible Handbook, 24th rev. ed. (Grand Rapids: Zondervan, 1965), by Henry H. Halley, is the old classic among handbooks. (By its fifty-eighth printing in 1986, over four and a half million copies were in print.) Halley begins with notable sayings about the Bible (pp. 18 f.), followed by sections on Christ as the center and heart of the Bible (pp. 20 f.), the Bible as God's Word (pp. 22 f.), and the leading thought of each biblical book (pp. 28 f.). He provides geographical background (pp. 36 ff.) and archaeological discoveries (pp. 42-57). Halley then gives the chapter-by-chapter content of Genesis (pp. 58-108) and proceeds through the other books of the Bible. He has photos of Egyptian temples and kings (pp. 114 ff.), the Moabite Stone (p. 202), Sargon's palace (p. 289), a section on "Between the Testaments" (pp. 402-12), and a detailed treatment of New Testament books (pp. 413 ff.). He argues that the Bethlehem star was a miracle (p. 419), urges believers to memorize the Sermon on the Mount (p. 433), speaks fervently of the reality of heaven and hell (p. 515), declares that Jesus was called God (p. 528), gives a list of the miracles in Acts (pp. 563 f.), teaches the universal church (pp. 614 f.), and gives the different interpretations of Revelation (pp. 684 f.). He concludes with "How We Got the Bible" (pp. 741 ff.) and a survey of church history (pp. 757 ff.). He urges the habit of Bible reading (pp. 805 ff.)

and encourages each church to have a congregational plan of Bible reading (p. 814).

Unger's Bible Handbook (Chicago: Moody, 1966. 952 pp.), by Merrill F. Unger, is another small handbook (7" x 4 $\frac{1}{2}$") that is packed with information. He starts with "What the Bible Is" (pp. 1 f.); "Christ, the Unifying Theme of the Bible" (p. 6); and "The Bible and Archaeology" (pp. 18-33). Unger then surveys the Bible from Genesis to Revelation (pp. 36 ff.). He defends the universal Flood (p. 49), has photos from Ur and Mt. Nebo (pp. 60, 153), shows the shepherd anointing the sheep (p. 277), gives a helpful synopsis of the Song of Solomon (pp. 299 ff.), defends the unity of Isaiah (pp. 306 f.), identifies Ezekiel's temple as millennial (pp. 379 ff.), treats Joel 2 as eschatological (p. 404), supplies material on "Between the Testaments" (pp. 450 ff.), has photos of the Church of the Nativity and the Theater at Caesarea (pp. 515, 574), defends Pauline authorship of Ephesians and the pastoral Epistles (pp. 671, 715), and teaches premillennialism (p. 875). He concludes with "How the Bible Came to Us" (pp. 882 ff.) and "Outline of Church History" (pp. 898 ff.).

Eerdmans' Handbook to the Bible (Grand Rapids: Eerdmans, 1973. 680 pp.), edited by David and Pat Alexander, is a larger work in lavish color. The editors begin with the Bible and its environment (pp. 10 ff.), its geography (pp. 17 ff.), world religions (pp. 24 ff.), the unique power of the Bible (pp. 32 ff.), and Jesus Christ and the Bible (pp. 37 ff.). They show how to understand the Bible (pp. 58 ff.) and then discuss different texts and versions (pp. 69 ff.); the findings of archaeology (pp. 81 ff.); plants and animals of the Bible (pp. 97 ff.); and weights, measures, and money (pp. 104 ff.). The bulk of the handbook is a survey of the books of the Bible from Genesis to Revelation (pp. 127 ff.). It includes photos of the Ziggurat at Ur (p. 135), a locust (p. 159), and a model of the high priest (p. 169). John Wenham discusses the large numbers in the Old Testament and seems to "debunk" most of them (pp. 191-92). There are photos of mud-brick villages (pp. 216-17), reapers harvesting grain (p. 227), a model of Solomon's temple (p. 256), ancient ships (pp. 260-61), a harp (p. 349), a watchtower in the hills (p. 453), five loaves and two small fish (p. 505), the Egnatian Road (p. 561), and the Colosseum (p. 587). The editors defend the Pauline authorship of the pastoral Epistles (p. 618) and give an amillennial interpretation of Revelation (pp. 645-56). They conclude with key themes of the Bible (pp. 657 ff.), a "who's who" in the Bible (pp. 662 ff.), and a gazetteer of places (pp. 670 ff.).

Abingdon Bible Handbook (Nashville: Abingdon, 1975. 511 pp.), edited by Edward P. Blair, is a liberal contrast to the other handbooks. It has few pictures, and most of these are black and white, except for a few color maps and pictures between pages 256-57. He commends the Documentary Hypothesis ("J," "E," "D," etc.) and refers to it frequently (pp. 23, 84-92, 102, etc.). He dates the Exodus at 1280 B.C. (p. 99); denies the unity of Isaiah (p. 150); dates Daniel at about 165 B.C. (p. 164); summarizes all the books of the Apocrypha as well (pp. 195 ff.); commends "Q" and gives a five-source origin for the Gospels (pp. 214-17); denies John's authorship of his Gospel, Epistles, and Revelation (pp. 245 f., 337, 348); and denies that Peter wrote I and II Peter (pp. 329, 332).

The Bible Almanac (Nashville: Nelson, 1980. 765 pp.), edited by Packer, Tenney, and White, is one of the larger books of background for Bible study. The editors cover Bible history (pp. 26 ff.); chronology (pp. 44 ff.); texts and translations (pp. 65 f.); archaeology (pp. 85 ff.); and pagan religions and cultures, including Egypt (pp. 118 ff.), Babylon (pp. 129 ff.), Ugarit (pp. 138 ff.), Persia (pp. 148 ff.), Greece (pp. 162 ff.), and Rome (pp. 175 ff.). They treat a wide variety of subjects: geography (pp. 187 ff.), minerals and gems (pp. 214 ff.), animals and plants (pp. 223 ff.), trade (pp. 280 ff.), warfare (pp. 302 ff.), writing (pp. 340 ff.), literature and poetry (pp. 348 ff.), family (pp. 411 ff.), women (pp. 420 ff.), food (pp. 465 ff.), architecture (pp. 487 ff.), Jesus Christ (pp. 511 ff.), and Paul (pp. 547 ff.). They conclude with "Outline of the Books of the Bible" (pp. 559 f.), "All the People of the Bible" (pp. 602 ff.), and "All the Places of the Bible" (pp. 678 ff.).

The Victor Handbook of Bible Knowledge (Wheaton, Ill.: Victor Books, 1981. 640 pp.), edited by V. Gilbert Beers, is a beautiful supply of background information on the historical portions of Scripture, covering almost three hundred passages from Genesis to Acts. There is not much on the Old Testament prophets or the New Testament Epistles. There are brilliant color photos of camels at a well (pp. 10-11), black goats and white sheep (p. 54), Hazor (p. 140), the interior of Samuel's tomb (p. 202), Hebron (p. 206), Jerusalem (p. 226), the Hinnom Valley (p. 283), the Dome of the Rock (pp. 312-13), Nazareth (p. 336), Capernaum (pp. 360-61), Nain (pp. 394-95), Bethsaida (pp. 426-27), a shepherd and his sheep at Beersheba (pp. 440-41), the Via Dolorosa (p. 514), Gordon's Tomb (p. 521), Berea (p. 587), and the Appian Way (p. 613). There are also many drawings, maps, and other illustrations.

World's Bible Handbook, (Iowa Falls, Iowa: World Bible, 1991. 799 pp.), by Robert T. Boyd, is a very conservative work with good outlines and some black-and-white pictures and maps. The author defends the doctrine of inspiration and attacks the interpretations of Neo-Evangelicals, liberals, and so on (pp. 21-22); he also defends the unity of Isaiah (p. 267), the authenticity of Daniel (p. 307), and the virgin birth of Christ (p. 386).

Holman Bible Handbook (Nashville: Holman, 1992. 896 pp.), edited by David S. Dockery, is another professional work filled with charts, maps, and illustrations. The editor argues for verbal inspiration but hedges slightly on inerrancy (pp. 5-11). The book gives archaeological finds (pp. 66-77), covers how to understand the Bible (pp. 88 ff.), discusses differences in Bible manuscripts (pp. 104-7), and commends a universal Flood (p. 125). The book has beautiful color photos of the Sphinx (p. 143), Mount Sinai (p. 149), Jericho (p. 199), the Wailing Wall (p. 296), Mount Hermon (p. 348), Petra (p. 476), the theater at Ephesus (p. 717), and Patmos (p. 788). The work traces the route of the Exodus through the Red Sea (p. 169); shows an illuminated manuscript (p. 327), provides intertestamental history (pp. 505-35), defends Pauline authorship of the pastoral Epistles (pp. 736 f.), defends Peter as author of II Peter (p. 768), gives the differences in millennial interpretation in the book of Revelation (pp. 793-95), and concludes with notes on the Bible and Christian faith (pp. 805-94). Some beautiful reconstructions of the city of David (pp. 238-39), Herod's temple (p. 523),

Herod's palace (p. 557), and Jerusalem in the time of Jesus (pp. 602-3) are also pictured.

Holman Book of Biblical Charts, Maps, and Reconstructions (Nashville: Broadman and Holman, 1993. 176 pp.), edited by Marsha A. E. Smith, is a selection of materials from the Holman Bible Handbook enlarged to $8\frac{1}{2}$" x 11" for use in Bible classes. The charts include a fifty-two-week Bible reading plan (p. 13), prayers of the Bible (p. 27), a table of weights and measures (pp. 30-31), characteristics of God in the Psalms (pp. 46-47), discourses of Jesus (p. 73), and parables of Jesus (pp. 96-97). Then follow twenty-one colorful maps. The real delight of the book is the reconstructions: the ark of the covenant (p. 139); an eighth-century Israelite house (p. 140); Jerusalem, city of David (p. 141); Solomon's temple (p. 142); the tabernacle (p. 144); Caesarea Maritima (p. 149); a first-century Israelite house (p. 150); a synagogue (p. 151); Herod's temple (p. 153); New Testament Jericho (p. 157); the pool of Bethesda (p. 160); and the temple of Diana (p. 163).

The combination of the last two works probably is the most helpful source for Bible and Sunday school classes. Churches would do well to get them for church libraries; pastors, for pastoral libraries. They provide answers to a great many questions.

CHAPTER 12
BIBLE ATLASES

If the Bible expositor is to make the scriptural accounts real and vivid to his hearers, he must form within his own mind a clear perception of the location of the biblical places he mentions in his teaching. He must determine never to pass over a single place name without taking the trouble to look it up in a Bible atlas. Eventually the locations mentioned in the Bible will become clearly established in his understanding and memory.

Perhaps the greatest single aid to the expositor in identifying place names is the *Westminster Historical Atlas to the Bible,* rev. ed. (Philadelphia: Westminster, 1956), edited by George Ernest Wright and Floyd Vivian Filson. This is a large volume (about 11" x 16") of 114 pages, containing eighteen magnificent color maps and seventy-seven illustrations. The maps and the map index are so detailed and comprehensive that the expositor will find in this work many places that are left unidentified or even unmentioned by other works. But when an event has a genuinely uncertain location, this atlas is quick to state just that (e.g., p. 86). The text is liberal in its theology but still reverent and helpful in geographical and historical information.

The most striking and lavish of these geographical aids is L. H. Grollenberg's *Atlas of the Bible* (New York: Nelson, 1956), edited and translated by J.M.H. Reid and H. H. Rowley. This is a Roman Catholic work of 166 pages containing 35 beautiful color maps, 2 large maps on the endpapers, and 408 illustrations, some full page (pp. 101, 128, 137, etc.). The illustrations include remarkable photographs of ancient art (pp. 37, 86, 112, etc.) and many ground plans of palaces, temples, cities, and harbors (pp. 71, 102-3, etc.). Though liberal (note the reference to the discrepancies among the

Gospels, p. 122), the work gives much factual, historical information.

Another useful work is the **Rand-McNally Bible Atlas** (New York: Rand-McNally, 1956), edited by Emil G. Kraeling. The text is more extensive than that of the works cited above (487 pp.), and there are 22 color maps, 136 numbered photographs, and many other photographs, maps, diagrams, plans of buildings, and the like. Although this work gives a good survey of the geography of the land as well as a thorough historical survey of biblical places and events, it is liberal in its theology. Kraeling refers to the Tower of Babel as a "charming" tradition (p. 53), cites Joshua 1-12 as an example of material put together centuries after the events (p. 132), and calls the feeding of the five thousand "clearly" another version of the feeding of the four thousand (p. 386).

Another valuable help for the expositor is the **Macmillan Bible Atlas,** 2nd ed. (New York: Macmillan, 1968, 1977), edited by Yohanan Aharoni and Michael Avi-Yonah. This is a Jewish work of 184 pages, including 264 maps and a great number of photographs and illustrations. The format is different: there is no continuing text; each page describes its own maps and illustrations. The book has a map for most of the events in Scripture: the "Travel of the Spies" (p. 41), the "War of Deborah" (p. 46), the "Campaign of Tiglath-Pileser III" (p. 94), the "Dead Sea Sect" (p. 141), "Paul's Voyage to Rome" (p. 155). These editors make their Jewish position clear by their language: "According to Christian belief, Jesus rose from the dead on the third day after crucifixion" (p. 150). All things considered, there is a great amount of help in this work.

There is more help in Jan. H. Negenman's **New Atlas of the Bible** (Garden City, N.Y.: Doubleday, 1969), edited by H. H. Rowley. It is a lavishly illustrated work with a theologically liberal text of 208 pages. It gives a chart showing *Homo sapiens* at 50,000 B.C. (pp. 22-23). It has aerial photographs of Mari (p. 44) and color photographs of Wadi en-Nar (p. 57), the Arnon (p. 60), Hebron (p. 110), Qumran (p. 135), Petra (pp. 140-41), and Ba'albek (p. 190). There are sketches of different types of city gates (p. 68), of types of houses (p. 81), of the ground plan of Qumran (p. 134), and of the reconstruction of the synagogue at Capernaum (p. 166). The author declares that the history of salvation found in Scripture is "faulty and far from comprehensive" (p. 111). The work provides useful background information but with a very liberal text.

Another large, valuable work is *The Atlas of the Bible* (New York: Facts on File Publications, 1985), edited by John Rogerson. It surveys the Bible and its literature (pp. 13 ff.), with photographs of Codex Sinaiticus and St. Catherine's Monastery (pp. 18 f.), and traces different routes for the Exodus, leaving the matter unsettled (pp. 26-27). There is a beautiful section on "The Bible in Art" (pp. 43-56). The atlas divides the Holy Land into twelve regions and surveys each one (pp. 70 ff.). There are beautiful color photographs of Dor (p. 78), Caesarea (pp. 82-83), Lachish (pp. 88-91), Bethlehem (pp. 100-101), Masada (pp. 110-11), Arad (pp. 118-19), Beersheba (pp. 120-21), Dan (p. 128), Hazor (pp. 134-35), Jerusalem (pp. 162-91), and Jericho (pp. 196-99). It concludes with "Empires Surrounding Israel" (pp. 214-24).

From a more conservative background, *Baker's Bible Atlas* (Grand Rapids: Baker, 1961. 333 pp.), edited by Charles F. Pfeiffer, meets a real need for a longer text surveying the geography of Palestine and the Near East and providing a thorough discussion of all the periods of biblical history. There are twenty-six color maps, seventeen black-and-white maps, and seventy-six illustrations. There are also interesting chapters on "Bible Lands Today" and "Biblical Archaeology in the Twentieth Century." The latter includes a map of excavated sites in Bible lands and an illustration of what the different strata of an excavation will yield to the spade (pp. 260-61).

The Student Map Manual (Jerusalem: Pictorial Archive [Near Eastern History], 1979) is the most exhaustive and minute atlas of the Bible available. It surveys the archaeological periods—Chalcolithic, Early, Middle, Late Bronze, Iron Age I and II, Persian, Hellenistic, Herodian, and Late Roman—and shows excavations from each period. The atlas then surveys the periods of Israel's history: Canaanite, Conquest, Judges, United Monarchy, Divided Kingdom, Persian, Hellenistic, Herodian, and Late Roman. It discusses the archaeology of Jerusalem and shows all the major cities inhabited in these periods. There is a master index listing every city and a grid showing every period for which evidence for that city's habitation exists. This is a unique work. The maps are superior and the historical study impressive, but there are no illustrations.

The Moody Atlas of Bible Lands (Chicago: Moody Press, 1985. 234 pp.), by Barry J. Beitzel, surveys the physical and historical geography of the lands of the Bible from an avowedly "evangelical Christian standpoint" (p. xvi). The text and the photographs reveal the author to be a traveler in the Holy Land (fig. 1, etc.). There are many colorful maps showing the borders of the Promised Land, Old Testament districts, New Testament districts, and so on (pp. 9, 17, 19). There are helpful diagrams to explain the Jordan rift, the Jabbok Gorge, and so on (pp. 28-29). There are also relief maps showing the elevation of the land (p. 32) and other maps showing the geologic formations in the land (p. 43), the mountains and rivers (p. 47), the rainfall (p. 50), the cities (pp. 56-59), the archaeological sites (pp. 60-63), and the roads (p. 68). There is a brief biblical history with maps illustrating the text. It is a shame that some of these maps give only liberal interpretations. The map portraying the route of the Exodus gives three alternative routes, none of them conservative. The northernmost route along the Mediterranean the author admits is not biblical (p. 88); the middle route that he recommends (p. 90) is the regular road to Beersheba, crossing a canal only; the southern route clearly avoids the Red Sea. In an "evangelical" book, why is the conservative view not even mentioned? Whether one translates the Hebrew phrase "the Red Sea" or the "Reed Sea," it was not marsh if Solomon could launch his navy there (I Kings 9:26). To Beitzel the real miracle was not the depth of the water but that so many Israelites could cross a canal so quickly (p. 90). His interpretation of the miracle at Gibeon in which the "sun stood still" is that it was not a miracle of time at all, but one of shade for the attacking Israelites. The Lord sent "much needed cloud cover" so that Israel could continue fighting during the heat of the day (pp. 96-97). The Lord also managed to work in a hailstorm to help them. Although the maps are helpful and the photographs often beautiful, the text leaves much to be desired from a conservative viewpoint. If "evangelical" Christians use this work, they should do so with their guard up.

The *Oxford Bible Atlas,* 2nd ed. (London: Oxford University Press, 1962, 1974. 144 pp.), edited by Herbert G. May, is a smaller work, but it is lavishly illustrated with twenty-six full-color maps and seventy-seven illustrations. There are helpful relief maps as well as maps showing the vegetation and rainfall in biblical lands. Conservatives will object to the plotting of the route of the Exodus through Lake Menzaleh, near the Mediterranean Sea, instead of toward the south (pp. 58-59). There are also some tables of dates from the tenth century B.C. to the first century A.D. (pp. 16-17, 35).

The Atlas of the Bible Lands (Maplewood, N.J.: Hammond, 1959. 32 pp., 35 color maps, gravure illustrations, without text) is too short to be of great help. *A Bible Atlas* (New York: Rand-McNally, 1910), edited by Jesse Lyman Hurlbut, is too old, though there is still much help in its 168 pages. The physical map of Palestine is worth study (p. 12), as are the map of Jerusalem (pp. 68-73) and the diagrams of Herod's temple (pp. 138-40).

In conclusion, the most helpful atlas for the expositor is probably the *Westminster Historical Atlas to the Bible,* if one is aware of the liberal opinions in the text. *The Student Map Manual* and the *Macmillan Bible Atlas* are close behind. The best conservative atlas is *Baker's Bible Atlas.*

CHAPTER 13
BIBLE GEOGRAPHY

One of the constant problems the pastor must face is how to make the scriptural accounts real to his people. Perhaps the reason that this remains a problem is that the accounts are not real to the pastor. But several recent works on Bible background can help Scripture come alive in the pastor's mind and, hence, become vivid for his people too.

The Wycliffe Historical Geography of Bible Lands (Chicago: Moody, 1967), by Charles F. Pfeiffer and Howard F. Vos, is a marvelously helpful work that makes the Bible lands vivid to the Bible student. There are 459 illustrations, many of them full-page photographs (e.g., Petra, p. 94; Baalbek, p. 214; Corinth, p. 406). There are forty-five small maps scattered throughout the text as well as nine full-color maps in the back. Although the route of the Exodus will be disputed by most conservatives (map 2, p. 590), all the maps do help fix in one's mind the relation between the places mentioned in the Scriptures.

The work deals with the ten major areas of biblical influence in the chronological order of their prominence in the Scriptures: Mesopotamia, Egypt, Palestine, Phoenicia, Syria, biblical Iran, Cyprus, Asia Minor, Greece, and Rome. In each section are surveys of the geographical features of the area, accounts of the historical events that took place there, a city-by-city description of the historical and archaeological discoveries in the area, and a helpful bibliography. There are very careful descriptions of Ur (pp. 14-20), Babylon (pp. 21-32), Megiddo (pp. 117-22), Ephesus (pp. 357-95), Athens (pp. 460-75), Corinth (pp. 478-87), and Rome (pp. 538-50), as well as brief descriptions of practically every biblical site. The regional surveys of Palestine are well done, describing the coastal plain, the Shephelah, the valley of Esdraelon, Galilee, Samaria, the hill country of Judah, the Jordan valley, and other important geographical features (pp. 99-181). Although the authors are almost always strictly factual, once in a while they give a naturalistic explanation of a miraculous biblical event, such as their observation that it was merely a thunderstorm that enabled Barak to defeat Sisera (p. 117). All things considered, it is an immensely helpful work that should be on the expositor's bookshelf.

In contrast, Yohanan Aharoni's *Land of the Bible* (Philadelphia: Westminster, 1967, 1979. 481 pp.) is a historical geography for the scholar. Although there are thirty-five maps in the work, there is not a single illustration. The text is quite technical and has a definite Jewish flavor, since Aharoni is an archaeologist from the Hebrew University of Jerusalem. Some of its maps are helpful, such as "The Main Roads of Palestine" (p. 40) and the "Archaeological Excavation" (p. 90). But it does not make the land come alive for the reader.

The land does become living and vibrant in the National Geographic Society's *Everyday Life in Bible Times* (Washington, D.C.: National Geographic Society, 1967). There are 412 full-color illustrations of the kind that has made the *National Geographic* periodical famous. The photographs of the treasures from Ur (pp. 48-49), King Tutankhamen's treasures (pp. 118-19), the Dome of the Rock—outside view (pp. 226-27) and inside view (pp. 228-29), Mount Ararat (p. 264), Gethsemane (p. 363), and the Cilician Gates (p. 407) are good examples of these superlative skills. There are many other illustrations and maps. Some of the artists' reproductions are also very helpful, such as the drawings of an Egyptian temple (pp. 172-73), Solomon's temple, and the brazen sea (pp. 221-23). Other drawings, however, are inconsistent. One portrays desert dwellers (pp. 64-65) as half naked. Any people who live in the heat of the desert know better than that. Another which shows baby lions in front of Solomon's throne is ludicrous (pp. 230-31). Conservatives will not appreciate the naturalistic explanations of the miraculous crossing of the Red Sea (p. 183). But a student does not turn to a volume like this for theology and biblical interpretation. As a source of background information, it is not only greatly helpful but also so fascinating that the reader can hardly put it down. In a pocket at the back of the volume is the large map "Lands of the Bible Today."

Another vividly helpful work is David Alexander's *Lion Photoguide to the Bible* (Tring, Herts, England: Lion Publishing, 1972, 1973, 1983). A systematic presentation of photographic background from Genesis to Revelation, the book begins with the Eden-like springs of Dan (pp. 10-11) and continues to the ruins of Laodicea (pp. 282-83). There are color photos of Hebron (p. 19), the Dead Sea (p. 22), the Sinai Desert (pp. 31, 36-37), Jericho (p. 48), Mount Tabor (p. 54), En Gedi (p. 66), Jezreel (pp. 84-85), Masada (p. 107), the pool of Gibeon (p. 129), Nazareth (pp. 148-49), Lake Galilee (pp. 174-75), and more. Every page is a visual education.

The following list is merely a sampling of the many helps available in the field of biblical geography. These works are recommended not for their theology but for their illustrations, maps, and lucid descriptions of the geographical features of the Holy Land.

Avi-Yonah, Michael. *The Holy Land.* Grand Rapids: Baker, 1966. 231 pp. As a historical geography, this book covers 536 B.C. to A.D. 640 from a Jewish viewpoint. 24 maps.

Avi-Yonah, Michael, and Emil Kraeling. *Our Living Bible.* New York: McGraw-Hill, 1962. 384 pp. These authors give a lavishly illustrated work on biblical background from the Jewish viewpoint.

Baly, Denis. *Geographical Companion of the Bible.* New York: McGraw-Hill, 1963. 196 pp. This work provides much helpful geographical data; 28 plates, many maps.

Bruin, Paul, and Philipp Giegel. *Jesus Lived Here.* New York: Morrow, 1958. 234 pp. A pictorial study of the places notable in the life of Christ, it is well illustrated with many color and black-and-white plates.

Cannon, William R. *Journeys after St. Paul.* New York: Macmillan, 1963. 276 pp. This resource is a spritely travelogue. Although there are no illustrations, there are maps on the endpapers.

Eichholz, Georg. *Landscapes of the Bible.* New York: Harper, n.d. 152 pp. There are 103 magnificent color plates in this work.

Fulton, John. *The Beautiful Land: Palestine.* 1891. Reprint, New York: T. Whittaker, 1977. 652 pp. A lovely book, deservedly reprinted, it contains drawings of scenes that can no longer be viewed.

Gafni, Shlomo S. *The Glory of the Holy Land.* Cambridge: Cambridge University Press, 1978. 256 pp. Gafni's work contains marvelous color photos of Mount Sinai (pp. 43-44), a Roman road (p. 67), the old city of Jerusalem (p. 85), the caves at Qumran (p. 120), and Montfort (p. 200).

Holley, J. E., and C. F. Holley. *Pictorial Profile of the Holy Land.* Westwood, N.J.: Revell, 1959. 256 pp. There are 248 black-and-white plates illustrating a wide variety of subjects from both the Old and New Testaments.

Leconte, René. *In the Steps of Jesus.* New York: Hastings, 1963. 124 pp. A Roman Catholic portrait of the places in the life of Christ. It contains sixty-eight beautiful plates.

Meistermann, Barnabé. *Guide to the Holy Land.* London: Burns, Oates, and Washbourne, 1923. 744 pp. A Roman Catholic travelogue which, although old, has helpful material, including twenty-three maps and many illustrations.

Morton, H. V. *In Search of the Holy Land.* London: Eyre Methuen, 1979. 159 pp. Reprinted from *In the Steps of the Master* (1937) with the addition of one hundred color photographs by Rene Burri. It is a beautiful portrait of the Holy Land in words and pictures.

————. *In the Steps of St. Paul.* New York: Dodd, Mead, 1936. 499 pp. An old but still useful survey of the lands Paul traversed. There are twenty-five plates in black and white.

Pearlman, Moshe, and Yaacov Yannai. *Historical Sites in Israel.* New York: Vanguard, 1964. 247 pp. Many color and black-and-white plates showing famous places in Israel.

Sanday, William. *Sacred Sites of the Gospels.* Oxford: Clarendon, 1903. 126 pp. An old but still helpful survey of sites famous in the life of Christ.

Terrien, Samuel. *Lands of the Bible.* New York: Simon and Schuster, 1957. A golden historical atlas for young people, this work is a painless means of gaining an amazing quantity of information in full color.

Thomson, W. M. *The Land and the Book.* 1880. Reprint, Grand Rapids: Baker, 1954. Originally three volumes of 592 pages each, this reprint is a helpful survey of the Holy Land and its customs.

Turner, George A. *Historical Geography of the Holy Land.* Grand Rapids: Baker, 1973. 368 pp. There are numerous black-and-white photographs and some color maps in this book. Turner surveys Jerusalem, Galilee, the Maritime Plain, the Hill Country, Judea, and the Negev.

CHAPTER 14
BOOKS ON BIBLICAL NATURAL HISTORY

The expositor will sometimes need help identifying specific animals, birds, or plants mentioned in the Bible. He may wish more information about some than the Bible dictionary can provide for him. Fortunately, there are many such helps available.

Perhaps the finest book on the subject is Michale Zohary's *Plants of the Bible* (London: Cambridge University Press, 1982. 223 pp.). Professor Zohary, an internationally recognized botanist, has held the chair of Botany at the Hebrew University in Jerusalem for years. The two hundred color plates are breathtaking. The introductory subjects are very helpful: "Identification of Biblical Plants," "The Sown Land and the Desert," "Vegetal Landscapes of Biblical Times," "Trade: The Ancient Ways," "Plants in Religion and Worship," and so on. It is the articles on the individual plants, however, that are impressive. In the "Olive" Zohary gives beautiful color photographs of the trees and fruit, lists Scripture passages such as Judges 9:8-9 and Romans 11:17-18, and writes of the four hundred species of olives that currently thrive (pp. 56-57). We learn interesting facts such as every biblical reference to "melon" should be "watermelon" (p. 85). References to "cucumbers" should be "muskmelons," since cucumbers were unknown in biblical times (p. 86). He gives beautiful photos of the Syrian Hyssop, along with Scripture references like Exodus 12:21-22, I Kings 4:33, Psalm 51:7, and John 19:28-30 (pp. 96-97). Other photos cover the cedars of Lebanon (pp. 105-6) and the oak and the terebinth (pp. 108-11). The stone pine is flat-topped instead of pointed (p. 113). He admits that there are no good botanical explanations for the manna (pp. 142-43). He urges caution in identifying the thorns of the Bible because there are twenty different vocabulary words and seventy species of plants in the area to choose from (p. 153). It is gratifying to see what the seeds of the Darnel actually look like (p. 161). He has photos of anemones, including one with the city of Jerusalem in the background (pp. 170-71).

The following is a sample of other helps that are available.

Alon, Azariah. *The Natural History of the Land of the Bible.* London: Hamlyn, 1969. 276 pp. This book is a lavishly illustrated survey by a Jew. She has chapters on and illustrations of animals, birds, reptiles, insects, plants, rocks, and so on. There are beautiful color photos of dates, figs, olives (pp. 10-11), wildflowers (p. 50), sheep (p. 75), basalt pillars (p. 148), fish (p. 186), a tortoise (p. 201), and birds (p. 226).

Anderson, Alexander W. *Plants of the Bible.* New York: Philosophical Library, 1957. 72 pp. The author has a dozen color paintings that illustrate the twenty-four short articles on biblical plants. He is indebted to Moldenke.

Anderson, David A. *All the Trees and Woody Plants of the Bible.* N.p.: Word Books, 1979. 294 pp. Very helpful information on seventy-six different plants from the acacia to wormwood (pp. 75-155). There are also articles on tree gardens (pp. 159 ff.), tree place names (pp. 164 ff.), memorable trees of the Bible (pp. 252 ff.), and other subjects. There are a number of black-and-white photos and drawings.

Cansdale, George. *All the Animals of the Bible Lands.* Grand Rapids: Zondervan, 1970. 272 pp. (British ed. *Animals of Bible Lands.* London: Paternoster, 1970.) The author presents a more thorough discussion of animals but with fewer illustrations than Alon's work. He describes animals, birds, reptiles, fish, insects, and other creatures.

Fauna and Flora of the Bible. N.p.: United Bible Societies, 1972. 207 pp. A book of helps for translating and interpreting the plants and animals in Scripture, it provides scientific names, brief descriptions, and Scripture references for many biblical terms: ant, antelope, ape, arrow snake, ass, bat, bear, bee, behemoth, all the way to vulture, wolf, and worm. The work includes the plant kingdom from acacia, algum, almond, aloes, apricot, balm, barley, all the way to weeds, wheat, and wormwood. There are many drawings of the different plants and animals.

Ferguson, Walter W. *Living Animals of the Bible.* New York: Scribner's Sons, n.d. 95 pp. Ferguson's work is a Jewish survey of Old Testament animals, including an index of Hebrew names (p. 95), but no such New Testament list of Greek names. All illustrations are paintings, some very appealing (Rock Hyrax, p. 21).

Fisher, Jonathan. *Scripture Animals.* 1834. Reprint, Princeton: Pyne Press, 1972. 347 pp. Fisher gives an interesting discussion of Bible animals from adder to wolf. He has some difficulties in identifying lexically what animals were intended by some words.

King, Eleanor Anthony. *Bible Plants for American Gardens.* 1941. Reprint, New York: Dover, 1975. 204 pp. This book gives a very interesting description of the trees, herbs, and flowers that are suitable for planting in American gardens. She gives suggestions for flower arrangements and Bible gardens for home and church (pp. 184 ff.).

Holmgren, Virginia C. *Bird Walk Through the Bible.* New York: Seabury, 1972. 216 pp. Holmgren gives some of the Bible birdlore and a glossary of all the birds mentioned in the Bible (pp. 31-179). She also provides an appendix of the 250 birdlore passages in the Bible (pp. 185 ff.) and a checklist of the birds of Bible lands (pp. 201 ff.).

Moldenke, Harold N., and A. L. Moldenke. *Plants of the Bible.* Waltham, Mass.: Chronica Botanica, 1952, 1986. 328 pp. with plates. Despite some liberal presuppositions, the work is very exact in its classification and a great help in interpreting many biblical passages.

Moller-Christensen, Vilhelm, and K.E.J. Jorgensen. *Encyclopaedia of Bible Creatures.* Philadelphia: Fortress, 1965. 302 pp. The author presents a well-illustrated discussion of biblical mammals, birds, insects, fish, and so on.

Parmelee, Alice. *All the Birds of the Bible.* New York: Harper, 1959. 279 pp. This well-illustrated book includes drawings and some photographs of birds. The author discusses biblical birds from Creation to the flying eagles of Revelation.

Pinney, Roy. *The Animals in the Bible.* New York: Chilton Books, 1964. 227 pp. This is a good discussion with some photographs.

Walker, Winifred. *All the Plants of the Bible.* New York: Harper, 1957. 244 pp. Walker gives a brief discussion and beautiful drawings of biblical plants, from the algum tree and almond to the willow and wormwood. Her work is based in part on the work of Harold N. Moldenke.

Wellborn, Grace Pleasant. *Devotionals on Flowers of the Bible.* Grand Rapids: Baker, 1967. 128 pp. This book is a compilation of warm-hearted meditations on a dozen biblical flowers, from the lily of the valley to the aloe.

———. *Devotionals on Trees of the Bible.* Grand Rapids: Baker, 1966. 109 pp. This book is a compilation of warm-hearted meditations on a dozen trees of the Bible.

Wright, Ruth V., and Robert L. Chadbourne. *Gems and Minerals of the Bible.* New York: Harper, 1970. 148 pp. The authors present a study of sixty-two different gems and minerals mentioned by some translations of the Bible. All the KJV references are given as well as many in the Revised, Moffatt, and Douay versions. They give some Scripture references, literary examples, and a brief description of each specimen.

CHAPTER 15
BOOKS ON ASTRONOMY AND THE BIBLE

Some helpful books are available on astronomy and the Bible. The expositor must take pains to be exact with reference both to the facts of science and to the Bible.

Brackbill, Maurice Thaddeus. *The Heavens Declare.* Chicago: Moody, 1959. 128 pp. In these brief devotional meditations, the author discusses the sun, the stars, and exploding stars. He believes that the stars are billions of years old (pp. 65 ff.) and urges seeing God in nature (pp. 101 ff.).

Custer, Stewart. *The Stars Speak.* Greenville, S.C.: Bob Jones University Press, 1977. 195 pp. This is a treatment of the more than three hundred biblical references to astronomy. There are seventy-four illustrations, including star charts to enable the novice to identify the stars and constellations for himself. The author covers important biblical passages that refer to the star of Bethlehem, modern astrology, the end of the universe, and other subjects.

Lyon, Thoburn C. *Witness in the Sky.* Chicago: Moody, 1961. 128 pp. The author presents brief devotional studies on the stars' beauty, distance, countless number, power, and so on. He holds to theistic evolution (pp. 75-81) and argues that the material universe witnesses to the existence of God (pp. 114 ff.).

Maunder, E. Walter. *The Astronomy of the Bible.* London: Hodder and Stoughton, 1909. 410 pp. Maunder gives professional comments on the references to astronomy in the Bible. He covers Creation, the deep, the firmament, the sun, the moon, stars, comets, constellations, Leviathan, Orion, the Pleiades,

Mazzaroth, time, the cycles of Daniel, Joshua's long day, the dial of Ahaz, and the star of Bethlehem.

Moore, Joan André. *Astronomy in the Bible.* Nashville: Abingdon, 1981. 160 pp. Moore's book gives devotional thoughts from a liberal perspective. She recounts an imaginary conversation between Gabriel and Abraham (p. 22), commends the Apocrypha and the Talmud (p. 27), gives a chart of a three-decker universe as the Bible view (p. 38), and cannot see Messiah in Balaam's prophecy (p. 41).

Unger, Merrill F. *Starlit Paths of Pilgrim Feet.* Findlay, Ohio: Dunham, 1958. 192 pp. Unger has written devotional studies on select biblical references to the stars. He covers angels as morning stars; the darkness of sin and Satan; evening stars; storms and stars; the bright, the morning star; and starlike saints.

CHAPTER 16
BIBLICAL ARCHAEOLOGY

There is a bewildering array of books on the archaeology of Bible lands. The field is so vast that we can select only a few of the more notable and more representative works.

One of the most scholarly and thorough works on this subject is G. Ernest Wright's *Biblical Archaeology* (Philadelphia: Westminster, 1962). It has 288 large pages, 8 maps, 220 illustrations, and a carefully documented text. Although Dr. Wright is moderately liberal in his theology, his work is factual and genuinely helpful.

Another thorough work is Amnon Ben-Tor's *The Archaeology of Ancient Israel* (New Haven: Yale University Press, in conjunction with the Open University of Israel, 1992. 398 pp.). This basic textbook surveys the excavations and findings of the Neolithic, Chalcolithic, Early, Intermediate, Middle, and Late Bronze Periods, and Iron Age I and II-III. There are sharp black-and-white photos of Tel Beersheba (p. 6), the Neolithic tower at Jericho (p. 16), the shrine at En Gedi (p. 63), Megiddo city wall (p. 99), horned altars from Megiddo (p. 326), Jerusalem's broad wall (p. 367), and forty-seven color plates of artifacts (between pp. 168-69).

A more conservative work is *The Biblical World: A Dictionary of Biblical Archaeology* (Grand Rapids: Baker, 1966) edited by Charles F. Pfeiffer. This is a standard reference work of 612 pages with 276 illustrations, many of them strikingly beautiful (e.g., pp. 103, 223, 333). Here the reader can look up subjects such as "Babylon," "Dead Sea Scrolls," "Hittites," "Jerusalem," and "Ur" and find much background material. There is a fine illustration of an archaeological trench and the levels of discovery (pp. 564-65).

Although there are some flaws, such as an upside-down picture (p. 203), most of the work is well done.

Another thoughtful presentation is *The Stones and the Scriptures* (Philadelphia: Lippincott, 1972. 207 pp.) by Edwin M. Yamauchi. He defends the inspiration of the Scriptures (p. 20); discusses the Mari and Nuzi discoveries (pp. 38 f.); explains the lack of evidence for Jericho, Gibeon, and Ai (pp. 57 f.); mentions the finding of the Solomonic gate at Megiddo, Hazor, and Gezer (p. 68); defends the authenticity of Daniel (pp. 87 ff.); describes William Ramsay's defense of Acts (pp. 95 ff.); and discusses Qumran and the Dead Sea Scrolls (pp. 126 ff.).

Two works by F. F. Bruce are useful. First, *Abraham and David: Places They Knew* (Nashville: Thomas Nelson, 1984. 128 pp.) is filled with historical and archaeological background for the lives of Abraham and David in Scripture. There are diagrams of the Ziggurat at Ur (p. 10), the water system at Gibeon (p. 101), and Solomon's temple (p. 107); there are magnificent photographs of Shechem, Mount Gerizim, and Mount Ebal (pp. 24-25), a Bedouin encampment (pp. 28-29), the Sphinx and Pyramid (pp. 34-35), Hebron (pp. 58-59), Jericho excavations (pp. 116-17), and numerous other subjects. Although Bruce opts for the more recent date for the Exodus (p. 37), his treatment of the material is conservative and helpful. Some of his information would be known only by travelers (pp. 61, 83, etc.). The pastor will find this work a rich source of background for biblical interpretation. Second, *Jesus and Paul: Places They Knew* (Nashville: Thomas Nelson, 1981. 128 pp.) provides historical and archaeological background for the lives of the Lord Jesus and the apostle Paul. There are diagrams of the synagogue at Capernaum (p. 29), a first-century house (p. 44), the city of Jerusalem (p. 53), Herod's temple (pp. 58-59), the city of Corinth (p. 104), and Caesarea (p. 113). There are also beautiful photographs of the Mount of Precipitation at Nazareth (pp. 12-13), the Sea of Galilee (pp. 20-21), Jerusalem (pp. 48-49), Neapolis (pp. 88-89), the Acropolis of Athens (pp. 98-99), the temple of Apollo at Corinth (p. 101), the harbor at Caesarea (pp. 112-13), the Roman Forum (pp. 116-17), and numerous other locations.

For the conservative, the best introduction to the field of archaeology is *Biblical Archaeology in Focus* by Keith N. Schoville (Grand Rapids: Baker, 1978. 511 pp.). In Part I he discusses the developing ideas in the Holy Land (pp. 79-93). He has a very practical chapter on "Money, Men, Methods, and Materials" (pp. 95-126). He also describes the development of writing (pp. 127 ff.). In Part II he surveys the major sites in Mesopotamia, Asia Minor, Syria, Lebanon, and Egypt. In Part III he gives a very careful survey of sites within the Holy Land, city-by-city: Ai, Arad, Ashdod, Beersheba, Beit Mirsim, Beth-shan, Caesarea, Dan, Gezer, Gibeon, Hazor, Jaffa, Jericho, Jerusalem, Lachish, Masada, Megiddo, Samaria, Shechem. He also describes the Qumran and Bar Kochba discoveries and concludes with a chapter on the sites in Trans-jordan. Although he gives a liberal date for the Exodus (p. 262) and a liberal date for Daniel (p. 452), he does provide a wealth of factual information and background for the Scriptures. There are multitudes of photographic illustrations in the text. The thorough bibliographies after each site are an especially valuable part of the book. This work will remain a most valuable contribution to the study of biblical archaeology.

Digging Up the Bible by Moshe Pearlman (New York: William Morrow, 1980. 240 pp.) is a popularization of the many archaeological discoveries of the Holy Land. Pearlman recounts the pioneering survey of Edward Robinson ("the Devout Sceptic") in the land of Palestine. Robinson did not believe the myths and stories that travelers were circulating about the places in Palestine, but his faith in Scripture was profound. His survey of the land confirmed the locations of dozens of places (pp. 21 ff.). Pearlman also describes the brilliant work of Sir Flinders Petrie (pp. 51 ff.), who worked out the sequence of pottery dating that is still the standard for the Holy Land. There are beautiful photographs of the shrine over the cave of Machpelah at Hebron (pp. 26-27), Robinson's arch (p. 39), the Dead Sea (p. 88), the hill of Ophel (p. 104), the city of Samaria (p. 136), the Neolithic tower at Jericho (pp. 160-61), Masada (p. 164), the Dome of the Rock (p. 184), the Solomonic gate at Gezer (p. 199), and numerous others.

There are five conservative works on this subject that will provide great help for the Bible expositor.

Free, Joseph P. *Archaeology and Bible History.* Wheaton, Ill.: Van Kampen, 1950. 398 pp., 19 illus., 11 maps. Contains a helpful survey of biblical history.

Thompson, John Arthur. *The Bible and Archaeology.* Grand Rapids: Eerdmans, 1962. 468 pp., 175 illus., 9 maps, 5 charts. The text was originally in three smaller volumes: *Archaeology and the Old Testament,* 1967; *Archaeology and the Pre-Christian Centuries,* 1958; and *Archaeology and the New Testament,* 1959.

Unger, Merrill F. *Archaeology and the New Testament.* Grand Rapids: Zondervan, 1962. 350 pp., 141 illus., maps.

————. *Archaeology and the Old Testament.* Grand Rapids: Zondervan, 1954. 339 pp., 103 illus., 5 maps, 5 diagrams of ground plans.

Wight, Fred H. *Highlights of Archaeology in Bible Lands.* Chicago: Moody, 1955. 243 pp., 17 plates. A survey of the important biblical sites.

The following are recommended not necessarily for their theology but for their factual presentation of archaeological evidence and background.

Albright, William F. *The Archaeology of Palestine.* Rev. ed. London: Penguin Books, 1954. 271 pp., 30 plates, and 63 other illus. A short, technical introduction by the dean of American archaeologists.

Archaeological Institute of America. *Archaeological Discoveries in the Holy Land.* New York: Thomas Y. Crowell, 1967. 220 pp. A useful anthology, this work contains the articles "Jericho: Oldest Walled Town" by Kenyon (pp. 19 f.), "The Rise and Fall of Hazor" by Yadin (pp. 57 ff.), and "Arad" by Amiran and Aharoni (pp. 89 ff.).

Banks, E. J. *The Bible and the Spade.* New York: Association Press, 1913. 193 pp., no illus., some maps.

Barton, George A. *Archaeology and the Bible.* Philadelphia: American Sunday School Union, 1916. 461 pp., 114 plates. An old standby.

Bass, George F. *Archaeology Beneath the Sea.* New York: Walker and Co., 1975. 238 pp. Description of actual marine excavations in the Mediterranean; color photos follow p. 116.

Berkhof, Louis. *Biblical Archaeology.* Grand Rapids: Smitter, 1928. 182 pp., no illus. A conservative text.

Bermant, Chaim, and Michael Weitzman. *Ebla.* New York: Times Books, 1979. 244 pp. The authors give the history of the dispute over the Ebla tablets.

Blaiklock, E. M. *Out of the Earth.* 2nd ed. Grand Rapids: Eerdmans, 1961, 92 pp., 1 plate.

Boyd, Robert T. *A Pictorial Guide to Biblical Archaeology.* Eugene, Ore.: Harvest House, 1969, 1981. 222 pp. A well-illustrated introduction.

———. *Tells, Tombs and Treasure.* Grand Rapids: Baker, 1969. 222 pp. A pictorial guide to biblical archaeology.

Burrows, Millar. *What Mean These Stones?* New Haven, Conn.: American Schools of Oriental Research, 1941. 306 pp., 58 illus. Rather technical.

Caiger, Stephen L. *Archaeology and the New Testament.* London: Oxford University Press, 1936. 218 pp., 24 plates, 2 maps.

Cornfeld, Gaalyahu. *Archaeology of the Bible: Book by Book.* New York: Harper and Row, 1976. 334 pp. Provides archaeological background for each book of the Bible.

Davies, Philip R. *Qumran.* Grand Rapids: Eerdmans, 1982. 128 pp. Provides a good overview of the background of Qumran.

Eisenberg, Azriel, and Dov Elkins. *Treasures from the Dust.* New York: Abelard-Schuman, 1972. 149 pp. Stories recounting the adventure of archaeological discoveries (e.g., "Hazor,

A Dig That Will Take 800 Years" and "The Chocolate-Covered Dead Sea Scroll").

Finnegan, Jack. *Light from the Ancient Past.* 3rd ed. Princeton: Princeton University Press, 1969. 500 pp., 204 illus., 6 maps, 4 diagrams of ground plans. A good reference work.

Frank, Harry Thomas. *Bible, Archaeology, and Faith.* New York: Abingdon, 1971. 352 pp. A liberal survey.

Frost, Honor. *Under the Mediterranean.* Englewood Cliffs, N.J.: Prentice-Hall, 1963. 278 pp. A survey of marine archaeology.

Garstang, John, and J.B.E. Garstang. *The Story of Jericho.* Rev. ed. London: Marshall, Morgan, and Scott, 1948. 200 pp., 20 plates, 2 maps, 24 other illus. A highly interesting account.

Gilbertson, Merrill T. *Uncovering Bible Times.* Minneapolis: Augsburg, 1968. 137 pp., 20 illus.

Gray, John. *Archaeology and the Old Testament World.* London: Nelson, 1962. 256 pp., 25 plates.

Harrison, R. K. *Archaeology of the New Testament.* New York: Association Press, 1964. 138 pp., 24 illus., and maps.

Jerusalem City Museum. *Finds from the Archaeological Excavations near the Temple Mount.* Jerusalem: Israel Exploration Society, n.d. 62 pp. Drawings and photos in color and black and white.

Kelso, James L. *An Archaeologist Follows the Apostle Paul.* Waco, Tex.: Word Books, 1970, 1975. 142 pp. A popular survey of the archaeological background of Paul's journeys, but with some liberal presuppositions.

Kennedy, David, and Derrick Riley. *Rome's Desert Frontier.* Austin: University of Texas, 1990. 256 pp. An aerial survey of Rome's forts in the Middle East.

Kenyon, Frederic G. *The Bible and Archaeology.* New York: Harper, 1940. 310 pp., 31 plates.

Kenyon, Kathleen. *Archaeology in the Holy Land.* New York: Praeger, 1970. 326 pp., 56 plates, 66 other illus., and maps.

Kyle, Melvin Grove. *The Deciding Voice of the Monuments in Biblical Criticism.* Oberlin, Ohio: Bibliotheca Sacra, 1924. 364 pp., no illus. A classic text by a learned scholar. See also Kyle's article "Archaeology" in the *International Bible Encyclopaedia*, I, 226.

———. *Moses and the Monuments.* Oberlin, Ohio: Bibliotheca Sacra, 1920. 278 pp., 16 plates.

Landay, Jerry M. *Silent Cities, Sacred Stones.* New York: McCall Books, 1971. 272 pp. Archaeological discoveries in Israel.

Mazar, Benjamin. *The Mountain of the Lord.* New York: Doubleday, 1975. 303 pp. The author presents the results of his own excavations.

Millard, Alan. *Treasures from Bible Times.* Tring, Herts, England: Lion Publications, 1985. 189 pp. Beautiful photos of the ruins of Palmyra (p. 15), Ur (p. 50), Jericho (pp. 96-97), Persepolis (p. 143), Petra (p. 159), Qumran (p. 164), and Masada (p. 177).

Moorey, P.R.S. *Biblical Lands.* Oxford: Elsevir-Phaidon, 1975. 151 pp. An introduction that includes a glossary of terms.

Moorey, Roger. *Excavation in Palestine.* Grand Rapids: Eerdmans, 1981. 128 pp. A beginning survey.

Negev, Avraham. *Archaeology in the Land of the Bible.* New York: Schocken, 1976. 132 pp.

Owen, George F. *Archaeology and the Bible.* Westwood, N.J.: Revell, 1961. 384 pp., 32 illus.

Prescott, William W. *The Spade and the Bible.* New York: Revell, 1933. 216 pp.

Price, Ira Maurice. *The Monuments and the Old Testament.* Revised by Ovid Sellers and Leslie Carlson. Chicago: Christian Culture Press, 1958. 321 pp., 44 maps and illustrations.

Pritchard, James B. *Archaeology and the Old Testament.* Princeton: Princeton University Press, 1958. 263 pp., 77 illustrations and maps.

Schiller, Ely. *The First Photographs of Jerusalem and the Holy Land.* Jerusalem: Ariel Publishing House, 1980. 239 pp.

Thomas, David Winston. *Archaeology and Old Testament Studies.* Oxford: Claredon, 1967. 493 pp., 19 plates, 12 maps, and other illus.

Time-Life. *The Holy Land.* Alexandria, Va.: Time-Life, 1992. 168 pp. It is a popular interesting presentation. There are photographs of the pool of Siloam (p. 23), Hazor (pp. 50 ff.), Jericho (pp. 60 ff.), Ashkelon (pp. 75 ff.), Jerusalem (pp. 86 ff.), Qumran with its scrolls (pp. 109 ff.), and the pottery shards from Masada (p. 133).

Urquhart, John. *Modern Discoveries and the Bible.* London: Marshall, 1898. 400 pp., some drawings.

Vardaman, E. J. *Archaeology and the Living Word.* Nashville: Broadman, 1965. 128 pp., some maps and illustrations.

Vos, Howard F. *Introduction to Bible Archaeology.* Chicago: Moody, 1956. 127 pp.

Williams, Walter G. *Archaeology in Biblical Research.* New York: Abingdon, 1965. 223 pp., 19 plates, and other maps and drawings.

There are also some fascinating descriptions of the excavation of specific sites, with lavish illustrations.

Kenyon, Kathleen. *Digging Up Jerusalem.* New York: Praeger, 1974. 288 pp.

Pritchard, James B. *Gibeon: Where the Sun Stood Still.* Princeton: Princeton University Press, 1973. 176 pp.

Wright, G. Ernest. *Shechem.* New York: McGraw-Hill, 1964. 288 pp. Wright's description of the archaeological excavations at Shechem contains a table of the archaeological periods vii-ix and a number of photos.

Yadin, Yigael. *Hazor.* New York: Random House, 1975. 280 pp.

———. *Masada.* New York: Random House, 1966. 272 pp.

There are two lavish reference works that will acquaint the reader with the whole field of worldwide archaeology.

Charles-Picard, Gilbert, ed. *The Larousse Encyclopedia of Archaeology.* New York: Hamlyn, 1972. 432 pp. This work contains photos of Masada (pp. 36, 77), Petra (pp. 40-41), Jerash (pp. 44-45), and a dig in Munhatta, Israel (p. 89). Chapters cover "Western Asia before Alexander" (pp. 161 ff.), the "Nile Valley" (pp. 207 ff.), the "Aegean World" (pp. 245 ff.), "Classical Greece" (pp. 267 ff.), and "The Romans" (pp. 307 ff.).

Sherratt, Andrew, ed. *The Cambridge Encyclopedia of Archaeology.* New York: Cambridge, 1980. 495 pp. In this grand survey, Sherratt discusses the beginnings of agriculture in the Near East (pp. 102-11), and other contributors cover the Levant in the early first millennium B.C. (pp. 196-99) with a ground plan of Megiddo (p. 199) and other studies from the Americas to China.

There are three encyclopedias of biblical archaeology that cover the whole subject.

Avi-Yonah, Michael, ed. *Encyclopedia of Archaeological Excavations in the Holy Land.* 4 vols. Englewood Cliffs, N.J.: Prentice-Hall, 1975, 1976, 1977, 1978. 1,237 pp. The contents of the four volumes are as follows: Volume 1, Abu Ghosh–Dothan; Volume 2, Eboda–Jerusalem; Volume 3, Jisr Banat Ya'aqub–Nessana; and Volume 4, Or Ha-Ner–Zeror, tel.

Blaiklock, E. M., and R. K. Harrison. *New International Dictionary of Biblical Archaeology.* Grand Rapids: Zondervan, 1983. 485 pp. An exhaustive work covering "Aaron's Tomb" to "Ziusudra," this reference work contains numerous photos, including twenty-eight color plates located between pages 226 and 227.

Negev, Avraham. *The Archaeological Encyclopedia of the Holy Land.* 3rd ed. New York: Prentice-Hall, 1986, 1990. 419 pp. An exhaustive reference work, the book contains articles ranging from "Abarim" to "Zuzim." Negev's work contains many photographs, gives a list of the twenty-one levels found at Hazor, and has excellent maps of the biblical road system.

Two periodicals will keep the interested layman posted on current excavations and discoveries in biblical lands.

The Biblical Archaeologist. American Schools of Oriental Research, 126 Inman Street, Cambridge, MA 02139.

The Biblical Archaeology Review. Biblical Archaeology Society, 1819 "H" Street, NW, Washington, D.C. 20006.

CHAPTER 17
BOOKS ON JERUSALEM

The Holy City is a center of interest for Jews, Muslims, and Christians. The expositor will find himself preaching on texts over and over again that have Jerusalem as their background. It is good for him to study the city carefully and to avail himself of some of the new works that are now being provided for study of the city. The literature on the subject is so vast that the present bibliography can include only some of the best material available.

Nahman Avigad's *Discovering Jerusalem* (New York: Thomas Nelson, 1980, 1983. 270 pp.) is a record of the archaeological discoveries in the old city of Jerusalem by the archaeologist who supervised most of the digging. He has a fine writing style and gives a thrilling account of these excavations. He discusses the period of the first temple, giving the evidence for the settlement of the western hill (Mt. Zion) by the Jews (pp. 31 f.), showing by ground plans the exact structures that have been found (pp. 32 f.). He demonstrates the resettlement by the Hasmoneans in the period of the second temple (pp. 64 ff.). He has photos of the Herodian residence and other structures from that time (pp. 91 ff.). From the period of the destruction of Jerusalem by Titus, he describes the "burnt house" (pp. 120 ff.) and has photos of the ruins and the human arm found in the rubble (pp. 133-34). He gives a fascinating account of the discovery of Justinian's "Nea" church (pp. 230 ff.), with photos of the corner projecting outside the walls of the city (p. 232). He concludes with a brief chronology of the history of Jerusalem (p. 262). There is a great deal of valuable historical background in this work.

Jerusalem the Holy (New York: Schocken, 1976. 130 pp.), by Michael Avi-Yonah, contains a brief history of Jerusalem (pp. 3-22) and beautiful photographs of the city. Photographs include an aerial view of the Dome of the Rock (p. 1), the Jaffa Gate at night (p. 5), the Golden Gate (p. 7), the tomb of the kings (p. 15), the citadel of David (p. 36), the Wailing Wall (p. 39), Chagall's windows (p. 56), rabbinic students (p. 58), a panorama of Jerusalem (p. 73), the Cathedral of St. James (p. 88), the Hebrew University synagogue (p. 110), and the Shrine of the Book and the Knesset (p. 120).

A brief but careful study of the biblical teaching on the Holy City is David Clifford's *Two Jerusalems in Prophecy* (Neptune, N.J.: Loizeaux, 1978. 192 pp.). The author clearly holds to the coming millennial reign of the Lord (p. 19) as well as the pretribulation rapture of the church (pp. 68, 84); he defends the deity of Christ and His resurrection (pp. 36, 41); he attacks amillennial views (p. 67) and the World Council of Churches (p. 80). He gives a brief survey of earthly Jerusalem's checkered history (pp. 25 ff.), arguing that the Jews have now returned in unbelief but must one day be restored in faith (pp. 73 ff.), interpreting Daniel's seventieth week and the judgments of Revelation literally (pp. 86, 98-104); he holds that the second beast of Revelation 13 is the antichrist (p. 93) and that memorial sacrifices will be offered in the millennial temple (p. 127); he also sets forth the biblical teaching on the heavenly Jerusalem (pp. 130 ff.), interpreting it literally, although admitting symbols in the Book of Revelation (pp. 137-38). It is a fine contribution to the literature on Jerusalem and a real blessing to read.

Joan Comay's *Temple of Jerusalem* (New York: Holt, Rinehart, and Winston, 1975. 279 pp.) is a Jewish historical study of the site, lavishly illustrated with photographs, paintings, diagrams, ground plans, and so on. The author includes a chronology of the site (pp. 269 ff.).

The Glory of Jerusalem (Jerusalem: Jerusalem Publishing House, 1978. 128 pp.), by Shlomo S. Gafni, is a work of magnificent color photographs. There are not only the standard aerial views of the Dome of the Rock (p. 5) but also views of rarely seen Roman milestones (p. 11), the triple Hulda gate (p. 19), the newly discovered stairway south of the temple area (p. 37), the tomb of the kings (p. 38), the bells of Bethlehem (pp. 46-47), details of the interior of the Dome of the Rock (pp. 92-93), Solomon's stables (p. 95), the tower of the ascension (p. 105), the markets and bazaars (pp. 108-11), and the windows of Jerusalem (pp. 112-17).

Martin Gilbert's *Jerusalem: Rebirth of a City* (New York: Viking-Penguin, 1985. 238 pp.) is a history of the expansion of Jerusalem during the 1800s. For every decade there is a map of the city showing the additions and buildings added as well as illustrations of archaeological finds and many antique photographs.

Another interesting work is *Jerusalem in the Time of Jesus* (Philadelphia: Fortress, 1969. 405 pp.) by Joachim Jeremias. Although Jeremias is a liberal form critic, he is also a great authority on the literature and customs of the Jews. He provides material that cannot be found elsewhere on the industries and commerce of ancient Jerusalem, the economic and social status of its inhabitants, and the status of slaves, women, and so on. He includes a thorough index to the Talmud and other Jewish writings.

Jerusalem: City of the Ages (New York: University Press of America, 1987. 407 pp.), edited by Alice Eckardt, contains many useful articles about Jerusalem, including the archaeological history of Jerusalem by Dan Bahat (pp. 32 ff.), the first Americans in Jerusalem (pp. 104 ff.), the economic history of the city (pp. 161 ff.), and the Christians of Jerusalem (pp. 199 ff.). Pinchas Peli writes on what Jerusalem means to his faith (pp. 272 ff.), and Georgina Young writes on what Jerusalem means to her (pp. 316 ff.). Appendix C deals with attempts to establish Jerusalem as the capital of Israel in 1980 and observes, "Jerusalem united in its entirety is the capital of Israel. Jerusalem is the seat of the President of the State, the Knesset, the Government, and the Supreme Court" (p. 376).

Jerusalem (New York: Random House, 1968. 287 pp.), by Teddy Kollek and Moshe Pearlman, contains a four-thousand-year history and is beautifully illustrated: hills of Jerusalem (p. 9), valley of Hinnom (p. 29), map of David's city (p. 37), Hezekiah's tunnel (p. 63), temple and city walls (p. 66), model of Herod's palace (p. 94), citadel of David (pp. 97, 133), Antonia fortress (p. 144), Jerusalem from Russian tower (pp. 158-59), fountain in the street of the valley (p. 188), Lion gate (p. 198), Damascus gate (p. 200), convent of the flagellation (p. 207), Russian church of Mary Magdalene (p. 241), and Hebrew University Synagogue (p. 271).

Jerry M. Landay's *Dome of the Rock* (New York: Newsweek, 1972. 172 pp.) provides a history of the holy place that is in effect a history of the whole city. It is illustrated with magnificent color photographs, the subjects of many of which the tourist is not allowed to photograph (pp. 94, 105, 122-23). Especially striking is the wide-angle photograph from high in the dome (pp. 72-73). He includes a ground plan of and guide to old Jerusalem (pp. 164 ff.).

The Walls of Jerusalem (New York: Bobbs-Merrill, 1976. 125 pp.), by Sandy Lesberg, is a photographic essay on the city of Jerusalem. There are unforgettable views of the citadel of David (p. 7), Jaffa gate (p. 15), the temple area (pp. 24-25), Jews praying at the western wall (pp. 30-33), the people of the city (pp. 64-75), the children (pp. 76-78), the streets (pp. 75-85), goats (p. 114), and the churches (pp. 116-19).

G. Frederick Owen's *Jerusalem* (Grand Rapids: Baker, 1972. 180 pp.) is a book of beautiful description, illustrated by professional black-and-white photographs of the Holy City. The author surveys the valleys, hills, walls, city gates and streets, and historic sites.

The Jerusalem Guide (Jerusalem: Abraham Marcus, 1973. 172 pp.), by Giora Shamis and Diane Shalem, is a detailed guidebook for a walking tour of the city. The authors describe the gates (pp. 8-14), the citadel of David (pp. 17-19), the Church of the Holy Sepulcher (pp. 20-33), the Armenian quarter (pp. 41-46), Mount Zion (pp. 47-53), the Jewish quarter (pp. 54-66), the temple area (pp. 67-92), the Moslem quarter (pp. 93-105), the Mount of Olives (pp. 114-25), the Kidron valley (pp. 126-32), and the new city (pp. 145-70); they also have detailed maps of the old city (pp. 133-39) and the new city (pp. 140-43).

The City of David (Washington, D. C.: Biblical Archaeology Society, 1973, 1975. 128 pp.), by Hershel Shanks, is a fascinating guide to biblical Jerusalem.This book gives descriptions and photographs of archaeological discoveries: the Jebusite wall and shaft, Hezekiah's tunnel and the spring Gihon, and Nehemiah's wall; it also gives a tour of the sites.

Solomon H. Steckoll's *Gates of Jerusalem* (New York: Praeger, 1968. 55 pp. interspersed with 31 photographic plates, many in color) provides photographs of many places the tourist overlooks: the Huldah gate (pl. II), the inside of the Golden Gate (pl. IV), the triple gate (pl. XVI), the gate of mercy (pl. XVIII), the cotton merchant's gate (pl. VI), the Damascus gate (pl. I), St. Stephen's gate (pl. III), and others.

A book that conveys the real flavor of the ancient city is *Jerusalem.* The Great Cities. (Amsterdam: Time-Life Books, 1976. 200 pp.) by Colin Thubron. This book has interesting descriptions and spectacular illustrations of subjects the tourist cannot photograph: Arabs (pp. 20-21, 24-25), Jews (pp. 32, 50-51), the sheep market (pp. 64-65), the inside of the Dome of the Rock (pp. 130-31, 132-35), and Mea Shearim (p. 164).

Jerusalem As Jesus Knew It (London: Thames and Hudson, 1978. 208 pp.), by John Wilkinson, is a survey of the archaeological evidence for the city of Jesus' day that still survives. The author discusses the city plan (pp. 53 ff.), showing the site of Herod's palace (p. 55), the pavement of Herod the Great (p. 61), the steps by the church of St. Peter in Gallicantu (p. 62), Solomon's stables (p. 71), Robinson's arch (p. 78), Wilson's arch (p. 79), the southeast corner of the temple area (p. 93), the pool of Bethesda (p. 99), the road from Bethany to Jerusalem (p. 115), Gordon's Calvary (p. 147), and the rock under the Church of the Holy Sepulchre (p. 149).

Jerusalem Revealed (Jerusalem: Israel Exploration Society, 1975, 136 pp.), edited by Yigael Yadin, is an account of the archaeological excavations in Jerusalem from 1968-74 by the scholars directing it. This book provides many photographs of the sites (pp. 34, 36, 39, etc.), ground plans (pp. 10, 23, 30, etc.), reconstructions of the newly discovered places (pp. 26-27, 88, 93, etc.), aerial views (pp. 92, 98), and other helps.

There are a few older works that are still valuable.

Avi-Yonah, Michael. *Jerusalem.* New York: Orion, 1960. 200 pp. There are hundreds of photographs in this strongly Jewish account.

Join-Lambert, Michael. *Jerusalem.* New York: Putnam's, 1958. 223 pp. This work is a thorough history of the Holy City up to the time of writing. It includes 135 photographs and maps.

Kenyon, Kathleen. *Jerusalem.* New York: McGraw-Hill, 1967. 211 pp. Kenyon's work, an archaeological survey of the history of Jerusalem, contains good ground plans of the whole city (p. 17), the Jebusite city (p. 29), the Solomonic city (p. 57), Nehemiah's city (p. 109), Herod's city (p. 145), and Herod Agrippa's city (p. 157).

CHAPTER 18
BOOKS ON
BIBLICAL POETRY

Poetry is difficult to interpret in any language. In Hebrew it is further complicated by the feature known as *parallelism*. Instead of ending lines with rhyme, Hebrew poetry arranges thoughts in parallel lines. The older scholars distinguished several types of parallelism. The repetition of the same thought in separate lines is *synonymous parallelism*.

Wash me throughly from mine iniquity,
And cleanse me from my sin. (Ps. 51:2)

A contrast in thought between lines is *antithetic parallelism*.

For the Lord knoweth the way of the righteous:
But the way of the ungodly shall perish. (Ps. 1:6)

An advance in the thought in which the second line builds on the first is *synthetic parallelism*.

The Lord is my shepherd;
I shall not want. (Ps. 23:1)

There are even more complex forms of Hebrew parallelism. Obviously, the expositor needs all the help he can get in interpreting the poetry of the Bible.

Perhaps the most helpful of the older works on poetry is Sanford Calvin Yoder's ***Poetry of the Old Testament*** (Scottdale, Pa.: Herald, 1952). Yoder is not extremely technical; he deals primarily with the King James translation of the poetry. A conservative, he holds to the inspiration of the entire Bible (p. xiii). His discussion of Hebrew poetry includes the types of parallelism, the poetic units, and the characteristics of the Hebrew people. He explains the shorter poems in the historical books and treats the major poetical books with great care. He provides a helpful classification of the Psalms (penitential, messianic, nature, imprecatory, national, historical, and so on). The expositor will find an immense amount of help in the 426 pages of this book.

Among the other older works significant for the expositor, four deserve special mention. They are listed in descending order of technicality and difficulty.

Gray, George Buchanan. *The Forms of Hebrew Poetry.* London: Hodder and Stoughton, 1915. 303 pp. A considerable amount of Hebrew.

King, E. G. *Early Religious Poetry of the Hebrews.* Cambridge: Cambridge University Press, 1911. 171 pp. Very little Hebrew, but still technical.

Robinson, Theodore H. *The Poetry of the Old Testament.* London: Duckworth, 1947. 231 pp. Greatly helpful on parallelism but weak in theology.

Gordon, Alex R. *The Poets of the Old Testament.* London: Hodder and Stoughton, 1912. 381 pp. Brief comments on parallelism. A popular explanation of the poems.

Among the newer works there are some that contain great help on the understanding of biblical poetry as literature. Although there are severe limitations to such a study, it is exciting to learn why many literary critics regard biblical poetry as among the greatest poetry in the world's literature. No longer is there a simple classification of three kinds of parallelism; now it is complex beyond words—with perhaps hundreds of varieties.

Alter, Robert. *The Art of Biblical Poetry.* New York: Basic Books, 1985. 228 pp. The author starts with the second poem in the Bible (Lamech, Gen. 4:23-24; pp. 5 f.) and goes on to give brilliant analyses of II Samuel 22 (pp. 29 ff.), Joel 2 (pp. 41 ff.), Deborah's Song in Judges 5 (pp. 43 ff.), the Song of the Sea in Exodus 15 (pp. 50 ff.), and Proverbs 7 (pp. 55 ff.). He discusses the structures of intensification, with illustrations from

Psalms 13 and 39 (pp. 63-67) and Amos 8 and 9 (pp. 73-74). Although he does not hold to the unity of Job (p. 87), he does give a careful explanation of the voice of God in Job (pp. 88-110). He examines the parallelism in Psalms 1, 8, 30, 48, 72, 90, and so on (pp. 114 ff.) and in examples of prophecy (Jer. 36, Isa. 1, 14, 5, etc.; pp. 138 ff.). He also deals with Proverbs ("The Poetry of Wit," pp. 163 ff.) and the Song of Solomon ("The Garden of Metaphor," pp. 185 ff.).

Berlin, Adele. *The Dynamics of Biblical Parallelism.* Bloomington: Indiana University Press, 1985. 179 pp. The author brings the science of linguistics to bear on the study of parallelism, criticizing Kugel's idea that parallelism is not really poetry (pp. 4-5). She contrasts Jael's reception of Sisera in prose with the account in poetry (Judg. 4:19; 5:25; pp. 12 f.). She discusses biblical parallelism in detail (pp. 18 ff.) and covers morphological pairs (different parts of speech, pp. 33 f.), syntactic pairs (pp. 53 f.), word pairs (pp. 65 f.), lexical pairs (pp. 80 f.), and sound pairs (pp. 103 f.)—all of which may show up in biblical poetry. She concludes that there is an "enormous linguistic complexity" in parallelism (pp. 129 f.).

Kugel, James L. *The Idea of Biblical Poetry: Parallelism and Its History.* New Haven: Yale University Press, 1981. 339 pp. Kugel sees the whole idea of Hebrew poetry as parallelism and proceeds to illustrate its complexity (pp. 2 ff.). He urges a pattern: "A and what's more B" (p. 42). Kugel gives an analysis of Psalm 23 (pp. 50 ff.), holds that all parallelism is really "synthetic" (p. 57), charges the rabbis with forgetting parallelism (pp. 96 ff.) and Christians with misreading parallelism to the present day (pp. 140 ff.), and concludes with a solemn warning against treating the Bible merely as literature. Kugel shudders to hear of Joseph being called a "character"; to him Joseph is an ancestor (pp. 303-4).

After reading such works, the expositor will be able to "see" much more in Scripture than he could before. The technical knowledge such books impart on the structure and nature of Hebrew poetry will add greatly to the expositor's grasp of the meaning of the psalms and of other poems in the Bible. Although he must never allow technical analysis to diminish the fire and spiritual impact of the poetry, neither should he allow the lack of such analysis to permit him to misunderstand it. The expositor must strive for both spiritual intensity and factual accuracy.

CHAPTER 19
BOOKS ON
INTERPRETATION

One of the most important books in the expositor's library is a book that will preserve him from making wrong interpretations of given passages in Scripture. If the preacher knows and applies correct principles of hermeneutics (interpretation), he will not interpret a passage contrary to its context or contrary to the historical background of its period. Every expositor should have in his library a book that defines these principles of interpretation.

Perhaps the two most helpful older books in this field are Bernard Ramm's *Protestant Biblical Interpretation* (Grand Rapids: Baker, 1956) and Louis Berkhof's *Principles of Biblical Interpretation* (Grand Rapids: Baker, 1950). Ramm lists the principles of interpretation (pp. 107-43) and discusses major topics such as "The Doctrinal Use of the Bible" (pp. 144-65); "The Interpretation of Prophecy" (pp. 220-53), which favors the premillennial system; and "The Interpretation of Parables" (pp. 254-66). In his later editions, Ramm has deleted the material that is recommended and has changed his views. His later editions are not recommended. Berkhof's work contains the especially helpful articles "Historical Interpretation" (pp. 113-32) and "Theological Interpretation" (pp. 133-66). These two books supplement one another.

Many other books are helpful also. The best of the old classics in this field is Milton Spenser Terry's *Biblical Hermeneutics* (1890; reprint, Grand Rapids: Zondervan, n.d.). Terry is valuable on synonyms (p. 91), parallel passages (p. 221), and the interpretation of types (p. 334); and he strongly refutes the alleged discrepancies (p. 514).

Another good book is J. Edwin Hartill's *Biblical Hermeneutics* (Grand Rapids: Zondervan, 1947). It is strongly dispensationalist (p. 13) and has interesting comments in "The First Mention Principle" (p. 70), "The Progressive Mention Principle" (p. 73), and other subjects not often treated so carefully.

A. Berkeley Mickelsen's *Interpreting the Bible* (Grand Rapids: Eerdmans, 1963) provides special help on figures of speech (p. 179) and the interpretation of poetry (p. 323) and gives a solemn warning in "Distortion through Artificial Assumptions" (p. 396).

A more highly specialized work is *How to Interpret the New Testament* (Philadelphia: Westminster, 1966) by Fred L. Fisher. Although some of the comments can be termed *neo-orthodox,* the author does prove to be a real help in the chapters "Tools of Interpretation" (the use of commentaries, Bible dictionaries, and atlases, p. 23) and "Seek a General Understanding of the Book" (urging a study of a book as a whole before analyzing the paragraphs and verses).

The question of interpretation is a constantly shifting one, however. Any list of the new discussion on hermeneutics would include works such as the following.

Robert Alter's *World of Biblical Literature* (New York: Basic Books, 1992) is a careful study of the Hebrew Bible as literature by a Jew. He holds that the Hebrew Bible portrays human behavior in the foreground, against a background of forces that cannot be grasped or controlled by man (p. 22). He maintains that the Bible demands intellectual humility from readers (p. 23). Alter defends literary style in the Bible (pp. 26 ff.), traces themes in Esther (pp. 30ff.), examines the Deborah story with care (pp. 41 ff.), and gives a liberal date for Daniel (second century B.C., p. 49). The author admits the possible existence of E, J, and P but stresses the beautiful unity of the finished product (pp. 68 ff.). He refers to "a new, subtle appreciation of the density of the literal in the Bible" (p. 87) and shows the importance of biblical allusion (pp. 107 ff.). Alter warns that criticism has undercut the belief in Scripture as the Word of the living God (p. 193): "Given the twin erosion of plain knowledge of the Bible and of belief in the Bible as divinely revealed truth, the notion that the Bible has real prescriptive authority in governing our moral and political lives would seem to be restricted to fundamentalist groups" (p. 196).

James Barr's *Old and New in Interpretation* (New York: Harper, 1966) is a liberal and highly philosophical survey of the theological relationship between the Old Testament and the New Testament. He discusses the multiplex nature of the Old Testament, history and revelation, typology and allegory, and so on. He gives a biased attack on the Fundamentalist movement, referring to "the irrationality and anti-intellectualism of the movement" (p. 201). He dismisses Fundamentalists as traditionalists (p. 203).

Dispensationalism, Israel and the Church (Grand Rapids: Zondervan, 1992. 402 pp.) by Craig A. Blaising and Darrell L. Bock is a presentation of progressive dispensationalism (pp. 380 ff.). The authors discuss literal interpretation (pp. 31ff.) and argue for present and future forms of the kingdom (invisible and visible, pp. 45-46). They contend that the kingdom is not postponed but always coming in two phases (p. 60), hold that the idea of two new covenants is a defenseless position (p. 91), and defend the idea of a universal church (p. 124). On Romans 11 they argue that national Israel must be converted (p. 229), and they hold that the Sermon on the Mount is applicable to all ages (p. 263). Blaising and Bock give an Old Testament allusion in Revelation 21-22 (pp. 278-80) and see three stages of fulfillment in that passage: (1) preliminary blessing brought by the first advent, (2) millennial blessing brought by the second advent, and (3) the ultimate golden age of eternal blessing (pp. 290-92).

F. F. Bruce's *The Hard Sayings of Jesus* (Downers Grove, Ill.: InterVarsity Press, 1983. 266 pp.) gives background to interpret difficult sayings of the Lord, such as, eating His flesh (p. 21), saltless salt (p. 37), one jot (p. 42), the phrase "you fool" meriting hell (p. 49), turning the other cheek (p. 68), sin against the Holy Spirit (p. 88), being greater than John the Baptist (p. 112), violence and the kingdom (p. 115), fall of Satan (p. 133), "you are Peter" (p. 139), and looking back (p. 164).

Hermeneutics, Authority, and Canon (Grand Rapids: Zonder-van, 1986. 468 pp.), edited by D. A. Carson and John D. Wood-bridge, is a New Evangelical view of Scripture. The contributors think along traditional lines but press beyond tradition on new points (p. ix). Carson describes recent developments in teaching concerning the doctrine of Scripture (pp. 5 ff.), recognizes that Hodge and Warfield did not invent inerrancy (p. 11), admits Scrip-ture's claim of inerrancy is very important (p. 23), and is fearful of the diminishing authority of the Bible in churches (pp. 46 f.). Moises Silva writes on "Historical Reconstructionism in New Testament criticism" (pp. 105 ff.); he urges uncertainty because of incomplete information (p. 111) and covers Jesus' treatment of the Pharisees (pp. 114 ff.). Blomberg writes on the legitimacy and limits of harmonization (pp. 139 ff.). Moo writes on the problem of *Sensus plenior* (pp. 175 ff.). Woodbridge discusses misconcep-tions of the impact of the Enlightenment on the doctrine of Scripture (pp. 237 ff.). Bromiley describes Barth's view on the authority of Scripture (pp. 271 ff.), commending Barth's idea that authority is more important than inerrancy (p. 293). Dunbar writes on the biblical canon (pp. 299 ff.).

Robert L. Cate's *How to Interpret the Bible* (Nashville: Broad-man, 1983) discusses the different theories of interpretation, hold-ing that none of them are fully satisfactory (p. 28), and examines the literary style of the Old Testament and the New Testament (pp. 33 ff.). Cate gives a liberal date (167 B.C.) for the last Old Testament writing (p. 39) and commends using the RSV, the *Inter-preter's Dictionary of the Bible,* and others (pp. 70 ff.). He discusses the value of Hebrew grammar and Greek grammar (pp. 105 f.,144 f.) and distinguishes between what the text meant (pp. 161 ff.) and what it means (pp. 183 ff.).

David S. Dockery's *Biblical Interpretation Then and Now* (Grand Rapids: Baker, 1992. 247 pp.) is a study of early church interpretation and its application to current hermeneutics. He shows how Jesus interpreted Scripture of Himself (p. 24), gives five Jewish methods of interpretation (pp. 27 f.), and describes the apostles' interpretation (pp. 34 f.). He goes on to cover the early church, describing the apostolic fathers and the battles over heresy (pp. 45 ff.), the Alexandrian School and its allegorical interpretation (pp. 75 ff.), and the Antiochian School with its literal-historical-typological interpretation (pp. 103 ff.). Dockery mentions that Chrysostom referred to Scripture eighteen thousand times in his writings (p. 115), and he discusses the hermeneutics of Jerome and Augustine (pp. 129 ff.), quoting Augustine's famous maxim "I believe in order that I may understand" (p. 140). He concludes with a summary and synthesis (pp. 155-83), explaining the author-oriented view (pp. 170 f.), the reader-oriented view (Fuchs and Ebeling, pp. 173 f.), and the text-oriented view (pp. 174 f.). He recommends some principles of interpretation (pp. 176 ff.) and gives an exhaustive bibliography (pp. 193-233).

Foundations for Biblical Interpretation (Nashville: Broadman and Holman, 1994. 614 pp.), edited by David S. Dockery, Kenneth Matthews, and Robert Sloan, is a massive anthology of interpretive resources. Erickson explains revelation (pp. 3 ff.); White defends inerrancy (pp. 24 ff.), answering objections and stressing the authority of the Bible (pp. 27 ff.); Dockery gives an overview of biblical interpretation (pp. 36 ff.); Ryken shows that the Bible is literature but not merely literature (pp. 55 ff.), for there is a unifying plot (p. 70); Schoville surveys the influence of geography on the contexts (pp. 73 ff.); Bock holds that Old Testament texts may have a short-term meaning and a long-term one (p. 105) and that New Testament texts show a progressive development of meaning (pp. 107 ff.); Thompson discusses archaeology and the Old Testament (pp. 117 ff.); House treats the Old Testament canon (pp. 134 ff.); Waltke covers Old Testament textual criticism (pp. 156 ff.); Garrett surveys Old Testament historical criticism (pp. 187 ff.) and defends the early date for the fall of Jericho (pp. 198 ff.); Mathews examines the literary criticism of the Old Testament (pp. 205 ff.), showing the chiastic nature of the Flood narrative (pp. 228 ff.); Fowler covers Old Testament history and chronology (pp. 232 ff.); Walton discusses Old Testament cultural background (pp. 255 ff.); Clendenen surveys Old Testament religious background (pp. 274 ff.); Yamauchi treats Old Testament political background (pp. 306 ff.); Kaiser explains Old Testament biblical theology (pp. 328 ff.); Smith discusses New Testament archaeology (pp. 355 ff.); Belleville covers New Testament canon (pp. 374 ff.), referring respectfully to "Q" (p. 379); Black explores New Testament textual criticism (pp. 396 ff.); Blomberg examines New Testament historical criticism (pp. 414 ff.); Melick covers New Testament literary criticism (pp. 434 ff.); Hoehner discusses New Testament history and chronology (pp. 454ff.); Seifrid covers New Testament cultural background (pp. 489 ff.); Church presents New Testament religious background (pp. 509 ff.); Polhill examines New Testament political background (pp. 525 ff.); Corley expounds New Testament theology (pp. 545 ff.); and Sloan concludes with canonical theology (pp. 565 ff.).

Millard J. Erickson's *Evangelical Interpretation* (Grand Rapids: Baker, 1993. 132 pp.) describes and criticizes Kaiser's authorial intent view (pp. 14-30). The author refers to Daniel Fuller's view that agnostics and believers can work side by side on the Bible (p. 36). He examines the problem of making the text contemporary (pp. 55 ff.) and advocates a "dynamic equivalent" (p. 63). He thinks that preachers should exegete the contemporary situation as carefully as the biblical context (p. 75). He discusses philosophical verification (pp. 86 ff.); urges cross-cultural studies (pp. 95 f.), and discusses and criticizes postmodernism (pp. 99 ff.). He recommends a postmodern evangelical interpretation (pp. 114-25).

Michael Fishbane's *Biblical Interpretation in Ancient Israel* (Oxford: Clarendon Press, 1985. 613 pp.) is a very careful Jewish study of scribal comments and corrections (pp. 23 ff.) with discussions of legal exegesis (pp. 91 ff.), Aggadic exegesis (pp. 281 ff.), and Mantological exegesis (pp. 443 ff.). (*Mantological* refers to dreams, visions, omens, etc.) Fishbane refers to "the royal valley" in Genesis 14:17 (p. 45), discusses the case of a pregnant woman being hit in Exodus 21:22 (pp. 92-94), speaks of demythologizing trends in Deuter-Isaiah (p. 322), and holds that Daniel 9 applies to Antiochus Epiphanes (p. 485).

Interpreting God's Word Today (Grand Rapids: Baker, 1970. 313 pp.), edited by Simon Kistemaker, is a Reformed anthology. Groningen discusses the interpretation of Genesis, defending Mosaic authorship against the documentary hypothesis (pp. 9-48). Woudstra surveys the Old Testament, defending against the opinions of von Rad and others (pp. 49-72). Kistemaker writes on the interpretation of the Gospels, providing internal and external evidence for each (pp. 73-124). DeYoung defends Christ's resurrection against Bultmann, Pannenberg, and others (pp. 125-75). Arntzen defends the inspiration and trustworthiness of Scripture, using the term *infallible,* not *inerrant* (pp. 177-212). Praamsma discusses confessional standards (pp. 213-38). Smith writes on the defense of the Faith (pp. 239-90), quoting Packer, who does defend "inerrancy" (p. 265).

Roger Ludin, Anthony Thiselton, and Clarence Walhout in *The Responsibility of Hermeneutics* (Grand Rapids: Eerdmans, 1985. 129 pp.) outline the new ideas on hermeneutics from Calvin College. The authors contrast Cartesian and Baconian logic (pp. 4 ff.); document Emerson's rejection of Scripture (p. 18) and Hodge's inductive method (p. 21); and cover Derrida's deconstruction carefully (pp. 34-40), noting that Derrida abandoned absolute truth or falsity (p. 39). Thiselton advocates "reader-response hermeneutics" (pp. 79 ff.) and commends the ideas of Julicher (p. 96), C. H. Dodd (p. 97), and Jeremias (p. 98) on the parables of Jesus. He expresses his debt to four New Testament scholars for his views: Fuchs, Funk, Dan Otto Via, and John D. Crossan (p. 101).

New Testament Interpretation (Exeter: Paternoster, 1977. 406 pp.), edited by I. Howard Marshall, is an anthology on exegesis. Marshall describes what Professor Hromadka did to I Thessalonians 3 for him (p. 17). The book contains articles by F. F. Bruce, Guthrie, Ellis, and others and contains some very critical chapters on source criticism, form criticism, tradition history, redaction criticism, demythologizing, and so on. Ralph P. Martin on New Testament exegesis quotes Jeremias on *ipsissima verba* and *vox* of Jesus (p. 228) and speaks of the testimony of early Christians woven into the narrative (p. 229).

Robert Morgan with John Barton in *Biblical Interpretation* (Oxford: Oxford University Press, 1988. 342 pp.) examines the nature of biblical interpretation with the intention of bridging the gulf between critical scholarship and faith (p. 25). They admit that scholars study "religion," but believers study "the God we worship" (p. 19). They state that "fundamentalism is one striking attempt to use the Bible religiously" (p. 36) but think that the central problem is relating believers' interests in hearing the Word of God with rational methods that make no such assumptions (p. 38). They hold that a Christology "from below" cannot say what Christians have to say about Jesus (p. 123). They suggest that liberal evangelical scholars try to enlarge the boundaries of their constituency's tolerance (p. 194). They charge that today's secular culture no longer thinks of the Bible as the Word of God (pp. 278 f.). They urge that liberals and conservatives work together theologically (p. 289). They regard Karl Barth as the greatest theologian of the century (p. 299).

Leland Ryken's *New Testament in Literary Criticism* (New York: Ungar, 1984. 349 pp.) is an anthology of quotations on literary aspects of Scripture by a professor of English at Wheaton. He contrasts literary critics with biblical critics: the former accept the New Testament as it stands and treat it as a unified whole; the latter try to get behind the text and deal largely with fragments. He gives quotations for and against the idea of the New Testament as literature (pp. 16 ff.); he gives opinions on the structure of Acts by liberals (Dibelius, Goodspeed, etc.) and by conservatives (F. F. Bruce, A. T. Robertson, etc., pp. 42 ff.); he has brief comments on I Corinthians 13 (pp. 62 ff.). He discusses the epistle as a literary form (pp. 66 ff.), the gospel as a literary form (pp. 84 ff.), humor (pp. 136 ff.), hymn (pp. 142 ff.), Jesus as a poet (pp. 152 ff.), the four Gospels (pp. 164 ff.), parable (pp. 255 ff.), proverb as a literary form (pp. 295 ff.), and Revelation (pp. 302 ff.).

Interpreting the Word of God (Chicago: Moody, 1976. 281 pp.), edited by Samuel J. Schultz and Morris A. Inch, is a festschrift in honor of Steven Barabas. Jennings deals with ancient Near Eastern religion and biblical interpretation, covering subjects such as "tree of life" and "blood sacrifice" (pp. 11-30). Hoerth treats archaeology, urging that it is now used to illuminate, not prove (pp. 31-45). Schultz defends the Old Testament prophets, attacking liberal views (pp. 46-59). Bulluck argues that the prophets used the

Pentateuch to teach about God (pp. 60-77). Hagner examines the New Testament quotations of the Old Testament (pp. 78-104). Fee deals with the genre of New Testament literature (pp. 105-27). Johnson covers history and culture in New Testament interpretation, urging a bicultural approach (pp. 128-61). Inch treats the place of the incarnation, arguing for a Christocentric view of Scripture (pp. 162-77). Lake discusses the Reformers' views of the Bible, holding that "Calvin and Luther stand with the doctrine of verbal inspiration and theological inerrancy" (pp. 178-98). Webber covers the authority of the Bible (pp. 199-216), with critical words toward "the pietists and revivalists" (p. 214). Jacobsen writes on the limitations of hermeneutics (pp. 217-37), and Barabas concludes with lists of recommended books, including many liberal works (pp. 238-72).

Henry A. Virkler's *Hermeneutics: Principles and Processes of Biblical Interpretation* (Grand Rapids: Baker, 1981. 255 pp.) gives a history of interpretation (pp. 15-74); stresses that variant readings do not affect facts, faith, or practice (pp. 39); recommends commentaries by Keil and Delitzsch, Lange, Godet, Alford, Lightfoot, Westcott, Hort, Hodge, and Broadus and manuals by Bairbairn, Terry, Berkhof, Michelson, and Ramm (pp. 72-73). He then covers Historical-Cultural and Contextual Analysis (pp. 75-92); covers six steps to interpreting any biblical text (pp. 76-77); recommends C. K. Barrett, Edersheim, W. C. Kaiser, and others (p. 89). In his Lexical-Syntactical Analysis (pp. 93-115), he covers figures of speech: "His eyes were bigger than his stomach" (p. 107). Theological Analysis (pp. 117-56) covers four biblical concepts—grace, law, salvation, Holy Spirit—that shed light on the continuity-discontinuity continuum (p. 153); covers figures of speech, parables, types, prophecy, and so on (pp. 157-210). He concludes with bibliographies.

Roy B. Zuck's *Basic Bible Interpretation* (Wheaton, Ill.: Victor, 1991. 324 pp.) demonstrates the need for interpretation (pp. 9 ff.), gives a brief history of Bible interpretation (pp. 27-58), provides some principles for interpreting the Bible (pp. 59-75), and in the process defends inerrancy (pp. 70-71). He shows how to bridge the cultural gap, giving helpful guidelines (pp. 76-97); urges the value of grammatical studies (pp. 98-122); and shows how literary categories such as genre and structure are important (pp. 123-42). Zuck discusses figures of speech (pp. 143-68), types and symbols (pp. 169-93), parables and allegories (pp. 194-226), and prophecy, urging a premillennial interpretation (pp. 227-49). He concludes with a discussion of New Testament quotations of the Old Testament (pp. 250-78) and the application of the Word today (pp. 279-92).

For help on the special subject of interpreting the alleged errors and difficulties in the Bible, the following works should prove valuable.

Gleason L. Archer's *Encyclopedia of Biblical Difficulties* (Grand Rapids: Zondervan, 1982. 480 pp.) is a book-by-book survey of Bible difficulties. The author gives longer answers than most. Archer has a section on how to resolve difficulties (pp. 15 ff.) and another on the importance of biblical inerrancy (pp. 19 ff.). The book also has several good bibliographies. However, Archer seems to permit some form of theistic evolution.

W. Arndt in *Does the Bible Contradict Itself?* (St. Louis: Concordia, 1951. 172 pp.) answers alleged contradictions. The author covers both passages of a historical nature (Old Testament, pp. 1 ff; New Testament, pp. 54 ff.) and passages of a doctrinal nature (Old Testament, pp. 96 ff.; New Testament, pp. 163 ff.). He includes a Scripture index (pp. 168 ff.).

F. F. Bruce's *Answers to Questions* (Grand Rapids: Zondervan, 1972. 264 pp.) contains good answers on Scripture texts and on the topics of baptism, Christ, church, Fundamentalism, inspiration (attacking the dictation view), kingdom, ministry, modernism, and so on.

Norman Geisler and Thomas Howe in *When Critics Ask* (Wheaton: Victor Books, 1992. 604 pp.) answer Bible difficulties from Genesis to Revelation. For example, the authors harmonize the three versions of Peter's confession into one (p. 347). They defend an imminent coming of the Lord and have very thorough indexes.

Heinrich Giesen's **When You Are Asked** (Philadelphia: Fortress Press, 1963. 190 pp.) contains questions and answers about faith and life. Giesen thinks that Christians should be able to give answers to the following questions: Are Creation accounts in the Bible reliable? (p. 8); Aren't atheists happy too? (p. 11); Is the Bible actually right? (p. 3); What does 'Born of the Virgin Mary' mean? (p. 37); At what altitude does heaven begin? (p. 45); When does marriage really begin? (p. 94); How do we come to faith? (p. 110); and What does the Bible have against the Roman Catholic Church? (p. 162). He claims that Jesus commanded infant baptism (p. 118) and teaches baptismal regeneration (p. 119).

Cliffe Knechtle in **Give Me an Answer** (Downers Grover, Ill.: InterVarsity, 1986. 165 pp.) asks the following questions: Aren't there many ways to God? Why is Jesus the only way? (pp. 17 f.); Isn't a good life enough? What if someone is sincere? Will heaven be boring? Does God really send people to hell? (pp. 35 ff.); What about those who never heard the gospel? Isn't the Old Testament God a God of wrath and the New Testament God a God of love? Why is there so much evil in the world? (pp. 48 ff.); Why do innocent people suffer? Isn't God responsible? How can one say that Christianity is rational? (pp. 65 ff.); Isn't faith in Jesus irrational? Can one prove that God exists? Why are there so many hypocrites in the church? (pp. 94 ff.); Why denominations? Isn't faith a crutch? Isn't the Bible full of myths? (pp. 105 ff.); Is there a resurrection? Why always quote the Bible? What's wrong with having a good time? (pp. 119 ff.); and Why should I believe in Christ? (pp. 140 ff.).

Josh McDowell and Don Stewart in **Answers to Tough Questions** (San Bernardino, Calif.: Here's Life Publishers, 1980. 198 pp.) reply to matters such as "what makes the Bible so special" (p. 1), the Dead Sea Scrolls (p. 25), whether Jesus claimed to be God (p. 39), how miracles can be possible (p. 79), dinosaurs (p. 94), the differences between Islam and Christianity (pp. 116-17), and the shroud of Turin (pp. 155 ff.).

Two older works that are still useful (and often reprinted) are the following:

George W. H. DeHoff. *Alleged Bible Contradictions.* (1949; reprint, Grand Rapids: Baker, 1951.)

John W. Haley. *Alleged Discrepancies in the Bible.* (1874; reprint, Grand Rapids: Baker, 1951. 473 pp.)

The better the expositor knows the principles of interpretation, the less likely he is to err on the meaning of any given passage of Scripture. No expositor should ever take a verse out of context or force his doctrinal bias into the meaning of a passage of the Bible. His obligation is to unfold what is truly there. The books on interpretation are a real help to one who undertakes this sacred task. See Chapter 3 for a summary of important principles of interpretation.

CHAPTER 20
BOOKS ON THEOLOGY

The expositor needs good reference works on theology to give him the definitions of terms, the summaries of Scripture references, and the leading theological ideas on important doctrines that he encounters in the Bible. The following books are chosen because of their precision and practicality.

Systematic Theology

Among recent works Millard J. Erickson's *Christian Theology* (Grand Rapids: Baker, 1983, 1984, 1985. 1,302 pp.) is a strong contribution. He urges that eclecticism in theology is possible and desirable (p. 65). He holds that the central motif of theology is the magnificence of God (p. 78). He quotes II Timothy 3:16 with the comment that "one cannot really determine what Paul intended to convey" (p. 210). He adopts Harrison's "moderate harmonization" view of inerrancy (pp. 231-32). Erickson warns against the Fundamentalists' opinion that the Bible alone is our authority (pp. 251-52). He defends the orthodox doctrine of the Trinity (pp. 337 f.) and a mild Calvinism (p. 359). He opts for the "day-age" view of Creation (p. 382), choosing progressive Creationism over theistic evolution (pp. 482-84). He does not think that Scripture demonstrates that a fetus is human in God's sight (p. 556). He defends the deity, humanity, and virgin birth of Christ (pp. 683-722, 754). He is neither for nor against the Charismatics (p. 882). He denies universalism (p. 1022). He argues for the Baptist view of church government and baptism by immersion only (pp. 1086, 1102 ff.). He urges that millennial and tribulation views ought not be made a test of orthodoxy (p. 1165), giving a cautious vote for Premillennialism (p. 1217) but arguing zealously for the posttribulation rapture (p. 1224).

He is a New Evangelical who dedicates his book to Ramm, Hordern, and Pannenberg.

Another major work is Alister E. McGrath's *Christian Theology: An Introduction* (Oxford: Blackwell, 1994. 510 pp.). It is a beginning theology supplemented by history of doctrine, church history, and current theological debates. He holds that Barth offers us a vision of Christian theology at its finest (p. xiv). He terms liberal Protestantism one of the most important movements to arise within modern Christian thought (p. 92). He distinguishes Fundamentalism from Evangelicalism, making clear that his sympathy is on the side of Evangelicalism (pp. 112-13). McGrath wishes "to bring the full critical resources of Christian theology to the sphere of pastoral ministry" (p. 122). He considers whether commitment or neutrality should govern theological study and decides that there are virtues on both sides (pp. 143-45). He raises the question "Is God male?" (pp. 205 f.) He thinks that Philippians 2:10-11 is "pre-Pauline" (p. 279). He notes that Jesus is called God three times in the NT (p. 280). He sets forth the Baptist view on infant baptism without comment (pp. 446-47). In evaluating Christianity and other world religions, he sets forth three views (all universalist) without identifying his own view (pp. 458-64). He mentions the current lack of enthusiasm for the doctrine of hell and explains "conditional immortality," again without comment (pp. 474-75). He concludes with a glossary of theological terms (pp. 492-503).

McGrath has expanded his contribution by another volume, *The Christian Theology Reader* (Oxford: Blackwell, 1995. 422 pp.). This is an anthology of quotations on doctrinal subjects: God, Christ, salvation, sin, the church, last things, and so on. He covers a very wide span of opinions from the orthodox creeds (p. 7) to Origen, Augustine, Jerome (pp. 46-49); Luther, Calvin (pp. 54-57); Barth, Brunner, Bultmann (pp. 68-71); liberation theology: Gutierrez, Boff (pp. 31, 121); feminist: Tribble, Carr (pp. 75, 130); Greek Orthodox: Zizioulas (p. 279); Karl Marx (p. 321); Vatican II (p. 328); and so on. There is an overwhelming coverage of trivial and mistaken interpretations as well as biblical ones.

One of the most helpful older works is Archibald Alexander Hodge's *Outlines of Theology* (1860, 1878; reprint, Grand Rapids: Eerdmans, 1949. 678 pp.). He is strongly conservative and maintains a Reformed position. He provides marvelously clear and concise definitions. Unabridged dictionaries will often quote him for the technical theological definition of a word. One need not agree with all his interpretations to perceive the great usefulness of his work for the busy expositor.

Another valuable work is Louis Berkhof's *Systematic Theology* (Grand Rapids: Eerdmans, 1941. 784 pp.). Although this work is more abreast of the modern problems in theology, it is less concise and harder to use. His dogmatic presentation of the Reformed position will offend some (p. 463).

For the Baptist position, the expositor may consult Augustus Hopkins Strong's *Systematic Theology* (Philadelphia: Judson, 1907. 1,166 pp.). He has an amazing quantity of interesting quotations in the fine print. Some of his summaries of theological ideas are of great value. See his treatment of the corroborative evidences of God's existence (pp. 71-89). The expositor should beware of his weaknesses on inspiration and theistic evolution.

An anthology of wonderfully clear, short articles can be found in *The Fundamentals for Today* (Grand Rapids: Kregel, 1958. 657 pp.) edited by Charles L. Feinberg. Great defenders of the faith contributed these articles, many of which are still of the highest value: James M. Gray on inspiration, A. C. Gaebelein on fulfilled prophecy, B. B. Warfield on the deity of Christ, R. A. Torrey on Christ's bodily resurrection, C. I. Scofield on the grace of God, and H.C.G. Moule on justification by faith.

Old Testament Theology

The most useful and practical work is J. Barton Payne's *Theology of the Older Testament* (Grand Rapids: Zondervan, 1962, 554 pp.). Payne provides a conservative, Reformed interpretation. There is a thorough index. Although he stresses the major topics rather than the chronological development of doctrine, it is still a most helpful work.

A much more difficult work to use is Geerhardus Vos's *Biblical Theology* (Grand Rapids: Eerdmans, 1948. 453 pp.). Although there are great treasures in this work, it is very slow and hard reading. It was not designed for easy reference, but there are indexes.

An old classic work is Gustave Friedrich Oehler's *Theology of the Old Testament.* (1873, 1883; reprint, Grand Rapids: Zondervan, n.d. 592 pp.). It is well organized and careful in its discussions and contains good indexes.

New Testament Theology

The most practical recent work is Leon Morris's *New Testament Theology* (Grand Rapids: Zondervan, 1986. 368 pp.). He comes to the study with faith in the traditional canon and seeks to present the teaching of the whole New Testament (pp. 12-15.) He begins with the Pauline Epistles, seeing Paul's center of interest as God (p. 25). He defends the doctrine of propitiation against the attacks of Dodd and others (pp. 34-35). Morris emphasizes Paul's presentation of the deity of Christ (pp. 42-49). He seems to link baptism with justification (p. 81). He teaches an imminent amillennialism (p. 87). He surveys the Synoptic Gospels, stressing their presentation of Christ as the Son of God (pp. 99 ff.). He shows that Luke emphasizes the lovingkindness of God (p. 155). He portrays John's teaching on Christ the Son of God and makes much of the "I am" statements (pp. 232-37). He refuses to discuss the millennium (p. 297). On Hebrews he stresses that Christ the great High Priest is the way to God (p. 306). He concludes that although there are individual differences between the NT writers, "there is impressive agreement on certain fundamental truths" (p. 330).

A most useful work is Chester K. Lehman's *Biblical Theology, New Testament* (Scottdale, Penn.: Herald Press, 1974. 567 pp.). It is a thorough, conservative work that shows the chronological revelation of New Testament doctrine. He has a careful discussion of the virgin birth (pp. 75 ff.); combines his treatment of Acts and

James (pp. 245 ff.); contrasts the punctiliar and linear aspects of sanctification (pp. 362 ff.); but does defend an amillennial view (pp. 529 ff.). There are good indexes.

Another interesting work is *New Testament Theology* by Donald Guthrie (Downers Grove, Ill.: InterVarsity Press, 1981. 1,064 pp.). He begins with an introduction into the theory behind New Testament theology (pp. 1-74). He declares that he comes to New Testament theology with faith (p. 33). He questions the idea of a "canon within the canon" (p. 41), arguing for unity of doctrine (p. 42). He holds that the basic unity of the New Testament is the person of the Lord Jesus Christ (pp. 54-55). He then discusses the doctrine of God (pp. 75-115) and the doctrine of man (pp. 116-218), tracing them through the New Testament in chronological order. He denies the liberal idea that God is the Father of all men (p. 152), and he has an interesting treatment of Paul's anthropological terms (pp. 163-76). He traces Christology through the New Testament (pp. 219-407), discussing the titles applied to our Lord: Messiah, Son of David, Servant, Prophet, Teacher, Son of man, Lord, Son of God, Logos, and so on (pp. 235-43). He covers also the doctrine of the virgin birth (pp. 365-74), Christ's resurrection (pp. 375-91), and the meaning of the ascension (pp. 398-401). He defends both the humanity and deity of Christ (pp. 401-7).

He also has sections on the doctrine of the Holy Spirit (pp. 510-72) and the Christian life (pp. 573-700) in which he discusses repentance, faith, forgiveness (pp. 573-602), and grace (pp. 602-40). He argues for predestination and perseverance (pp. 614 ff.). He traces the doctrine of the church through the New Testament (pp. 701- 89). He groups a number of doctrines under *the future* (pp. 790- 892). He admits that Paul held to an imminent parousia (pp. 804-6). He thinks that Revelation has parallel, not consecutive, visions (p. 814). He attacks the idea of a secret, pretribulational rapture (pp. 845-57), suggesting a posttribulationist (Gundry) as a good example of the premillenial view (p. 869). He argues for a general judgment (pp. 862 f.) and a spiritual millennium as preferable to a literal one (pp. 871 f.). In his treatment of heaven (pp. 874-87) and hell (pp. 887-92), he seems to argue that it is not important whether either heaven or hell is actually a place (p. 892). He concludes with a thorough bibliography (pp. 983-1019).

Another New Evangelical work is George Eldon Ladd's *Theology of the New Testament* (Grand Rapids: Eerdmans, 1974. 661 pp.). It is exhaustive, but deeply flawed: the author considers himself an outstanding theologian (p. 5); gives extensive coverage to every liberal opinion, no matter how unjustifiable, while relegating conservatives to the footnotes (p. 25); omits major doctrines like the virgin birth; defends a posttribulation rapture view (pp. 550ff.); fails to include a subject index.

Another work of some value is Charles Caldwell Ryrie's *Biblical Theology of the New Testament* (Chicago: Moody, 1959. 384 pp.). He has a good survey of the chronological revelation of New Testament doctrine, but he ignores the literature on the subject and skirts many problems. Still, his discussion of some subjects (the theology of James, pp. 131 ff.) is very well done.

A massive reference work that traces words and expressions through the literature is *The New International Dictionary of New Testament Theology,* 3 vols. (Grand Rapids: Zondervan, 1975, 1976, 1978. 822, 1,023, 1,481 pp.), edited by Colin Brown. Unfortunately, it is largely a sounding board for liberal opinion. Brown begins with a glossary of technical terms that lists the favorite liberal words: apocalyptic, chiliasm, demythologization, deutero-Isaiah, elohist, existentialism, heilsgeschichte, kerygma, yahwist, and more.

In the article "Abomination of Desolation," Beasley-Murray gives some typically tepid comments from an amillennial view: "To Jesus the term 'abomination' would probably connote idolatry of some sort" (1:75). In "Antichrist," E. Kauder thinks that Revelation 13 is "neither clear nor unambiguous" and suggests that 666 refers to Nero or Domitian (1:124-26). After "Apostle," by E. von Eicken, H. Linder, and D. Muller, there is an added note by C. Brown admitting that the article is biased by "German scholarship" in advocating a contradiction between Lucan and Pauline doctrine (1:135). Under "Baptism, wash" Beasley-Murray argues that the

Greek words "indicate (mostly total) immersion" but admits figurative uses (1:143); he also thinks that I Corinthians 15:29 teaches that the church baptized the living for the dead (1:147). R. T. Beckwith adds a note advocating infant baptism (1:154-61). In "Blood," F. Laubach gives some very careful teaching on the blood of Christ (1:222-24), as he also does on "Conversion" (1:353-62). In "Cross, Wood, Tree," C. Brown objects to the form critical contention that sayings about the cross in the Gospels are by some "prophets" other than Jesus (1:403). In "Explain," A. C. Thiselton is deeply indebted to the hermeneutics of Bultmann, Fuchs, and Ebeling (1:583-84). In "Father," O. Hofius admits that Jesus did not teach that God is the Father of all men (1:620).

In the second volume under "God, gods, Emmanuel," J. Schneider, C. Brown, and J. S. Wright discuss the meaning of Yahweh (2:67 ff.). They deny that Romans 9:5 calls Christ God (2:80) but admit His deity in John 1:1, I John 5:20, and Titus 2:13. In "Grace," H. H. Esser gives no hint to any end to the spiritual gifts (2:121). In "Heaven," B. Siede, C. Brown, and H. Bietenhard hear echoes in the Old Testament in poetical language of ancient mythological ideas (2:189). "God is said to dwell in 'heaven,' " but there is never any evidence of reflection on the difficulties inherent in this statement" (2:193). In "Hell," H. Bietenhard teaches universalism: "The saving work of Jesus Christ embraces the dead, and nothing is beyond the grace of Christ" (2:208). In "King, Kingdom," B. Klappert claims, "For Jesus the advent of the kingdom was so imminent that he vowed not to 'drink of the fruit of the vine until the kingdom of God comes' " (2:382). In "Miracle," W. Mundle, O. Hofius, and C. Brown suggest that either the tale of the fiery furnace had no historical significance or else the clothing helped them survive (2:628). In "Myth," F. F. Bruce holds that the New Testament uses myth "always in a disparaging sense" (2:644). In "Present, Day, Maranatha, Parousia," G. Braumann, C. Brown, and W. Mundle deny that Paul had in mind a millennial kingdom or any systematic chronological sequence of eschatological events (2:901).

In the third volume under "Punishment," C. Brown denies that eternal punishment is to be taken literally (3:99). In "Resurrection,"

C. Brown has a special note on the resurrection in contemporary theology in which he covers the views of Bultmann, Marxsen, Ulrich Wilckens, Richardson, Ladd, Pannenberg, and others and includes a four-page bibliography (3:281-309). In "Righteousness," H. Seebass and C. Brown object to Bultmann's idea that δικαιόω means to "make righteous" (3:372). In "Scripture" R. Mayer and C. Brown argue that all Scripture is inspired in the sense that it is "expressive of the mind of God" (3:491). In "Shepherd" E. Beyreuther shows that the New Testament did not share the contemporary Jewish view of shepherds (3:566). In "Son, Son of God, Son of Man, Servant of God, Son of David," Otto Michel and I. H. Marshall argue against Bultmann's idea that Jesus did not use the term "Son of Man" (3:621). They also attack Bultmann's idea that the "Son of God" refers to Gnostic Mythology (3:645). In "Woman" H. Vorlander, C. Brown, E. Beyreuther, O. Becker, and S. Solle argue for women deacons (3:1065) and suggest that women have gifts that should be used in the ministry (3:1067). The work concludes with an appendix on prepositions and theology in the Greek New Testament (3:1171-1215).

In the opinion of the reviewer, this work represents three barrels of unbelief with a few handfuls of historical research thrown in to sweeten the mix. Admittedly, there is information on the usage of words in the literature, but the conservative who consults this work should come to it with his guard up and a package of Maalox handy.

CHAPTER 21
BOOKS ON INSPIRATION

A chief area of conflict today is the doctrine of the Scriptures. Many scholars who style themselves as New Evangelicals profess faith in the doctrine concerning the person of Christ and claim to be orthodox while abandoning the traditional conservative view that the Scriptures are verbally inspired and perfectly infallible. They affirm a belief in the authority and inspiration of the Bible while neglecting to stress or sometimes even to mention its inerrancy and its verbal inspiration. Because they speak of orthodoxy and conservatism, they confuse and deceive many. The Bible expositor must have a firm foundation for his ministry. He must be sure of the inspiration and inerrancy of that sacred Book he purposes to expound.

Perhaps the most useful older work on this subject is Edward Young's *Thy Word Is Truth* (Grand Rapids: Eerdmans, 1957). It is both readable and scholarly in its defense of the verbal infallibility of the Scriptures.

Another work that defends inerrancy is Robert P. Lightner's *Saviour and the Scriptures* (Nutley, N.J.: Craig, 1966). Lightner's work, originally a doctoral dissertation presented to Dallas Theological Seminary, makes a detailed study of all the material in the Gospels that throws light on the attitude and teaching of Christ concerning the Scriptures. It has several chapters on contemporary views of inspiration. The author's conclusion is that Christ taught the same doctrine of Scripture the church has taught: "To Christ the Old Testament was true, authoritative, inspired. To Him the God of the Old Testament was the living God, and the teaching of the Old Testament was the teaching of the living God. To Him, what Scripture said, God said" (p. 163).

Stewart Custer, in *Does Inspiration Demand Inerrancy?* (Nutley, N. J.: Craig, 1968), demonstrates from Scripture that inerrancy is the only view compatible with the biblical evidence. Custer cites passage after passage from Scripture in proving that the Bible teaches its own inerrancy. He provides a clear comparison of the teaching of various theological opinions on inspiration. Custer concludes that the inerrancy of the Scriptures is the view traditionally taught by the church and by Scripture. The book closes with a short discussion of a few typical problem passages commonly pointed out as "errors." "Although no attempt is made to list all possible explanations, enough have been given to show that even the most difficult passages do have good solutions to their problems. Most of these difficulties are simply illustrations of the flaws in the thinking of the critics; relatively few of them are actual problems in the text" (p. 93).

The most scholarly defense of verbal inspiration is undoubtedly B. B. Warfield's *Inspiration and Authority of the Bible* (Philadelphia: Presbyterian and Reformed, 1948). It is difficult for the layman to follow the technical arguments as well as the references to Greek, Hebrew, and other languages that Warfield uses. For the scholar, it remains an impressive contribution.

Other books helpful in defending this doctrine are T. E. Engelder's *Scripture Cannot Be Broken* (St. Louis: Concordia, 1944), L. Gaussen's *Inspiration of the Holy Scripture* (Chicago: Moody, 1949), and J. C. Wenger's *God's Word Written* (Scottdale, Pa.: Herald, 1966). The late Ned Stonehouse edited an anthology, *The Infallible Word* (Grand Rapids: Eerdmans, 1953), that provides additional help.

These books not only provide excellent expositions of individual passages in Scripture but also lay a foundation of assurance for the use of the "sword of the Spirit." We have an infallible weapon. Let us use it mightily to honor the Lord Jesus Christ and to build up His people in the Faith.

One of the most interesting and important books on the inspiration of the Bible comes from a New Evangelical who has had enough of the drift to the left in his own movement. Harold Lindsell has set forth a formal defense of biblical inerrancy in his book *The Battle for the Bible* (Grand Rapids: Zondervan, 1976. 218 pp.). He describes the bitter theological wars in the Missouri Synod (pp. 72 ff.), and the Southern Baptist Convention (pp. 89 ff.); he recounts the "Strange Case of Fuller Theological Seminary" (pp. 106 ff.); and he warns that once inerrancy is denied, other concessions must follow: "I am saying that whether it takes five or fifty years any denomination or parachurch group that forsakes inerrancy will end up shipwrecked" (p. 142).

The reviews of *The Battle for the Bible* led Lindsell to write a response, *The Bible in the Balance* (Grand Rapids: Zondervan, 1979). He gives Carl Henry's view that the whole dispute is merely unnecessary "squabbling" (p. 32); shows how Clark Pinnock changed from complete inerrancy to his present denial (pp. 36-43); demonstrates the drift of the N.A.E. (pp. 71-77); discusses the whole position of the Southern Baptist Convention again (pp. 113 ff.); presents B. H. Carroll's defense of inerrancy (pp. 129-37); gives a table showing the percentage of unbelief presently in the students at Louisville Seminary and at Southwestern (p. 173); surveys Fuller Seminary's position, "A Seminary at Bay" (pp. 183-243); recounts Hubbard's whitewash attempt (pp. 285-93); outlines the positions of Jewett, Jack Rogers, Daniel Fuller, and so on (pp. 193 f., 195 ff., 219 ff.); documents Ralph Martin's denial of Pauline authorship of Ephesians (pp. 228-33); gives the position of some of Fuller's graduates, such as Gerald Sheppard at Union Seminary in New York (p. 236); attacks the liberal Historical-Critical method of study (pp. 303-21); denies that men like Jewett, Stagg, and R. Martin ought to be called evangelical (pp. 308 ff.); distinguishes himself from the Fundamentalist position but admits that the term *Fundamentalist* is clear and unambiguous (pp. 319 ff.); and thinks that Falwell's school and Pat Robertson's 700 Club are encouraging signs (pp. 346 ff.)! Conservatives would do well to heed the dire warnings of Dr. Lindsell. Lindsell's book is well documented and is a *must* for Fundamentalist reading.

The new debate on the meaning of *inerrancy* has produced some very helpful literature. Some shorter works have come forth that strongly defend traditional inerrancy. *What the Bible Teaches About the Bible* (Wheaton, Ill.: Tyndale House, 1979) by H. D. McDonald argues for verbal inspiration (pp. 6l f.) and inerrancy (pp. 74-83). He grounds inerrancy in the authority of Jesus (pp. 105 ff.) and the inspiration of the Spirit (pp. 123 f.). Charles C. Ryrie's *What You Should Know About Inerrancy* (Chicago: Moody, 1981) attacks the idea that there are scientific errors in Scripture but not religious errors (pp. 29 f.). He stresses the "God-breathed" nature of inspiration (pp. 38-41). He concludes that God did not permit sinful man to "erroneously record his message" (p. 47). He argues that Christ treated the Scriptures as inerrant (pp. 58-72). James Montgomery Boice's *Standing on the Rock* (Wheaton, Ill.: Tyndale House, 1984) holds that the Bible is God's inerrant Word (p. 46). The most important evidence is the teaching of Christ (pp. 47 ff.). He provides solutions for alleged problems in the Bible (pp. 87-106). He argues that the Bible is the most useful book in the world (pp. 107-23).

There are a number of major anthologies on the inerrancy issue. Perhaps the best of them all is *Inerrancy* (Grand Rapids: Zondervan, 1979, 1980) edited by Norman L. Geisler. Wenham defends Christ's endorsement of the OT Scriptures (pp. 3-36). Blum gives the apostles' teaching on the inerrancy of the Bible (pp. 39-53). Archer provides careful answers to alleged errors (pp. 57-82). Payne criticizes negative higher criticism for prejudging the Scripture (pp. 85-113). Kaiser explains legitimate hermeneutics (pp. 117-47). Bahnsen argues for the inerrancy of the autographs (pp. 151-93). Packer evaluates the adequacy of human language (pp. 197-226). Lewis criticizes Berkouwer as "unorthodox" (p. 240) and explains the human authorship of Scripture (pp. 229-64). Feinberg carefully defines inerrancy and attacks lesser terms such as "indeceivability" (pp. 267-304). Geisler criticizes the presuppositions of biblical errancy, showing the influence of Hobbes, Spinosa, Hume, and Kant (pp. 307-34). Sproul treats the internal witness of the Spirit (pp. 337-54). Preus defends inerrancy as the view of the church from the early fathers to Luther (pp. 357-82). Gerstner gives the views of Calvin, the Westminster divines, Hodge, and Warfield (pp. 385-410). Krabbendam contrasts Warfield with Berkouwer to summarize the doctrine (pp. 413-46).

Another important work is *Inerrancy and the Church* (Chicago: Moody, 1984) edited by John D. Hannah. The first part of the book surveys traditional infallibility of Scripture in European Christianity; Part 2 covers American views, concluding with Davis's commendation of the Princeton scholars who defended inerrancy (pp. 359 ff.). Part 3 is a formal contrast between the teaching of Berkouwer and Lindsell. Bogue argues that Berkouwer stands in the heritage of Briggs and Barth among those who have given up the "authoritative bedrock of God's inerrant Word" (p. 410). Still another work is *Challenges to Inerrancy: A Theological Response* (Chicago: Moody, 1984) edited by Gordon Lewis and Bruce Demarest. They discuss the inerrancy debate in the light of liberalism, Neo-Orthodoxy, Roman Catholic theology, Process theology, and so on. Another anthology is *The Foundation of Biblical Authority* (Grand Rapids: Zondervan, 1978) edited by James Montgomery Boice. Some articles are strong: Archer gives the witness of the Bible to its own inerrancy (pp. 85 ff.); others are weak: Kantzer argues that inerrancy should not be made a test of Christian fellowship (pp. 147 ff.). Another work is *Inerrancy and Common Sense* (Grand Rapids: Baker, 1980), edited by Roger Nicole and Ramsey Michaels. It has less common sense than most. Lovelace urges compromise between inerrantists and limited inerrantists (pp. 37-39). Michaels argues for the term "verbal inspiration" rather than "inerrancy" (pp. 57-70). Davis argues for a symbolic interpretation of Genesis (pp. 150-59). Fee warns about cultural conditioning in biblical words (pp. 169 f.).

A warning is in order against the fountainhead of this unbelief. We do not recommend G. C. Berkouwer's *Holy Scripture* (Grand Rapids: Eerdmans, 1975), the work that has influenced many to abandon the doctrine of inerrancy. He argues that "the gospel did not come to us as a timeless or 'eternal' truth" (p. 184). He stresses that Paul's words on women illustrate the "time-boundness" of

Scripture (pp. 186-87). He commends the idea of "innocent inaccuracies" (p. 245). He mentions the idea that the Evangelists put words into Jesus' mouth and admits that "at first this may give one the feeling of fiction or falsification" (p. 250). Jack B. Rogers was the translator of Berkouwer's book into English. Rogers, along with Donald McKim, wrote *The Authority and Interpretation of the Bible* (New York: Harper and Row, 1979), a work that gives its own view of the history of the doctrine and endorses Berkouwer's work (pp. 426-37).

CHAPTER 22
BOOKS ON
THE HOLY SPIRIT

The doctrine of the Holy Spirit is a subject of critical importance in today's world. There are dangers and abuses of the doctrine in many quarters. Since we should submit to the guidance of the Spirit (I Thess. 5:19; I John 4:6), we should seek to know the biblical teaching on this vital doctrine. Although there is an immense amount of literature on the Holy Spirit, the following works are at least a fair sampling of help for the pastor.

Biederwolf, William E. *A Help to the Study of the Holy Spirit.* New York: Revell, 1904. 222 pp. The author argues for the personality and deity of the Holy Spirit and holds that every believer is "sealed" (which he says is the anointing and baptism of the Spirit) when regenerated. Biederwolf lists fifty-seven fruits of the Spirit (some not valid) and claims that the filling of the Spirit is a continual process of manifestation and power.

Blackwood, Andrew W. *The Holy Spirit in Your Life.* Grand Rapids: Baker, 1957. 169 pp. This collection of sermons on the Holy Spirit by a famous teacher of preachers maintains that the Bible is both human and divine (p. 30), has a good illustration of philosopher Russell's despair (p. 81), argues that the Holy Spirit often works by outward means (police, etc.) (p. 114), and has a good illustration of Matthew Maury, who could not go to sea but discovered the currents in the ocean (pp. 120 ff.).

Broomall, Wick. *The Holy Spirit.* Grand Rapids: Baker, 1963. 211 pp. Broomall defends the personality and deity of the Spirit, attacks liberal views, holds that only an unbeliever can commit blasphemy against the Holy Spirit (p. 156), and includes a helpful chapter on "Spirit-filled Life."

Bruner, Frederick Dale. *A Theology of the Holy Spirit.* Grand Rapids: Eerdmans, 1970. 390 pp. Bruner presents a critical study of the Pentecostal interpretation of the Holy Spirit and the actual scriptural evidence. He holds that Paul's Corinthian opponents were the closest correspondence to Pentecostalism (p. 183) and shows that Paul did not follow the Pentecostal interpretation in dealing with the believers in Acts 9 (pp. 208-11). He says, "Pentecostalism builds its doctrine of a necessary second entry of the Holy Spirit on texts that teach his one entry" (p. 214); he attacks the Pentecostal doctrine of sin (pp. 234 f.); he argues that the Spirit is received by faith, not by conditions (pp. 238 f.), and that the true work of the Spirit evidences the fruit of the Spirit (faith, hope, etc. [Gal. 5:22-23], p. 268).

Carson, D. A. *Showing the Spirit.* Grand Rapids: Baker, 1987. 229 pp. In a theological exposition of I Corinthians 12-14, Carson attempts to be exhaustive and very impartial. He compares the New Testament lists of gifts (pp. 33 ff.), attacks using tongues as the test of the Spirit's baptism (p. 50), and holds that spiritual gifts can be duplicated by pagans but that love cannot (p. 65). He argues that biblical tongues are real languages (pp. 84-85) and holds that some modern tongues are invalid (pp. 87-88). Carson stresses that New Testament prophecy must be distinguished from Old Testament examples (p. 94), shows that Paul put tongues beneath prophecy (pp. 100 f.), and argues that "the assembled church is a place for intelligibility" (p. 106). He attacks the idea that Paul's restrictions on women are not genuine (p. 124) but holds that women keeping silent refers only to the weighing of prophecies (pp. 129 f.). He summarizes the teaching of I Corinthians 14 as "prophecy is heartily encouraged; tongues are not to be forbidden" (p. 134). He thinks that the Lord manifests Himself to believers only by His Spirit (leaving out the influence of the Word, p. 156). He rejects Second Blessing theology but urges continued spiritual growth (pp. 158-60) and distinguishes between infallible biblical revelation and revelation to believers throughout history (pp. 160 ff.). He attacks the idea of tongues as a criterion for anything, as a unifying gift, and as a source of authority (pp. 170 ff.). But he thinks that the Charismatic movement at its best has been a blessing to the church (p. 180). He concludes with his pastoral experiences with the tongues movement: he would not foster public tongues speaking but would not oppose the practice either (p. 187).

Criswell, W. A. *Great Doctrines of the Bible: Pneumatology.* Grand Rapids: Zondervan, 1984. 102 pp. In these doctrinal sermons on the Holy Spirit, the author lists the marvelous works of the Spirit: He works, searches, has knowledge, divides gifts to people, makes intercession, can be resisted, can be vexed, can be grieved, guides believers, convicts the world, points men to Jesus, and pleads for our salvation (p. 21). Criswell gives an illustration of the city of the dead, Cairo (p. 34); endorses Billy Graham (p. 56); and gives an illustration of two men at a symphony concert, one enraptured, the other bored to tears, and contends that musical discernment is like spiritual discernment (p. 67).

Fitch, William. *The Ministry of the Holy Spirit.* Grand Rapids: Zondervan, 1974. 304 pp. The author argues that the Scriptures are inerrant (p. 9), that the Spirit glorifies the Son (p. 21), that all should have fruit of the Spirit (pp. 26 ff.), and that baptism is incorporation into Christ (p. 43). He covers the subject of tongues (pp. 48-87), giving examples of dangers in the use of tongues (pp. 60 f.). In summary, he believes that every believer has some gift and that no one has all gifts. No one gift is possessed by every believer, Fitch contends, and to seek a "baptism" is to be blind to what Christ did for us at adoption. He says tongues are lesser gifts, stresses the difference between tongues in Acts and Corinth, believes the subconscious can influence tongues, and states that tongues do not automatically result in church renewal (pp. 77-83). He gives four reasons for viewing tongues as a modern heresy (pp. 84-87).

(1) To say that the only certain sign of the presence of the Holy Spirit is glossolalia is contrary to the Word of God (I Cor. 12:13, 29-30). (2) To say that after regeneration we need a further baptism of the Holy Spirit is heresy. (3) To say that tongues speaking is essential to a full Christian life denies the teaching of our Lord and the history of the early church. (4) Anything that diverts our focus of vision from Jesus Christ is clearly heretical.

Kuyper, Abraham. *The Work of the Holy Spirit.* 1900. Reprint, Grand Rapids: Eerdmans, 1941. 649 pp. Kuyper, former professor of Systematic Theology at the University of Amsterdam, presents an exhaustive discussion of the Holy Spirit in relation to the whole range of Reformed doctrine. He holds that we cannot have compassion for Satan (p. 11); that the Father brings forth, the Son arranges, and the Spirit perfects (p. 19); and that we have no good in ourselves that we cannot lose (p. 103). He says that the Holy Spirit may work outwardly in bestowing gifts and talents or inwardly in imparting grace, regeneration, and so on (p. 119) and that tongues were a miracle in the hearers (p. 136). He argues for infant salvation (p. 308), that "it" in Ephesians 2:8 means *faith* (pp. 407 ff.), and that no Christian can commit the sin against the Holy Spirit (p. 609).

Lehman, Chester K. *The Holy Spirit and the Holy Life.* Scottdale, Pa.: Herald Press, 1959. 220 pp. Lehman presents a study of the relation of the Holy Spirit to the sanctification of the believer. He covers the Old Testament teaching, the teachings of Jesus and the Epistles, and the interpretation of the church (including the church fathers, Augustine, Luther, the Anabaptists and Mennonites, and Wesley and the perfection movement—which he opposes). The author concludes with "Unto a Holy Life." He treats the punctiliar aspect of sanctification (pp. 109-12) and the linear aspect of sanctification (pp. 113-16).

McConkey, James H. *The Three-Fold Secret of the Holy Spirit.* Pittsburgh: Silver Publishing Society, 1918. 123 pp. The "three-fold secret" of which the author speaks in his title is (1) the secret of His incoming: Union with Christ; (2) the secret of

His fullness: Yielding to Christ; and (3) the secret of His constant manifestation: Abiding in Christ. The responsibility for this fullness of the Spirit is in the believer's hands (p. 53).

Marsh, F. E. *Emblems of the Holy Spirit.* n.d. Reprint, Grand Rapids: Kregel, 1957. 257 pp. Marsh presents a warm devotional study of the symbols of the Holy Spirit in Scripture. He treats the dove, the seal, holy anointing oil, anointing, oil, fire, rain, atmosphere, wind, rivers, dew, water, clothing, and the earnest.

Morgan, G. Campbell. *The Spirit of God.* New York: Revell, 1900. 246 pp. In this practical devotional study, the author covers the personality and relation of the Spirit to the Trinity and the Spirit in Creation, in relation to Old Testament man, and in relation to the Messiah. He discusses Christ's teaching about the Spirit, Pentecost, and the baptism of the Spirit (baptism into the body of Christ, almost all references to Spirit baptism). He distinguishes the filling of the Spirit from baptism and discusses regeneration and phrases such as "resist not," "grieve not," and "quench not the spirit."

Moule, Handley C. G. *Veni Creator.* London: Hodder and Stoughton, 1900. 253 pp. Moule has written remarkable devotional meditations on profound doctrines concerning the Holy Spirit. He maintains that the Holy Spirit is the author of the Bible (p. 52) and offers thorough studies of Johannine doctrine (pp. 63-162) and Pauline doctrine (pp. 163-247). The author says, "The Fruit of the Spirit is a divinely given and developed Character, drawn out of the fulness of Christ" (p. 200). He connects baptism of the Spirit with the birth of the church but says we may seek fillings of the Spirit (pp. 222-25).

Murray, Andrew. *The Spirit of Christ.* London: James Nisbet and Co., 1907. 394 pp. Murray gives thirty-one rich devotional messages on the Spirit. There are extended notes on the baptism of the Spirit, the Spirit as a person, and more.

Pache, René. *The Person and Work of the Holy Spirit.* Chicago: Moody, 1954. 223 pp. The author covers the personality, deity, and symbols of the Holy Spirit and the Holy Spirit in the Old Testament, in the Gospels, in Jesus Christ, and in inspiration. He discusses the dispensation of the Spirit, regeneration and baptism of the Holy Spirit (Spirit baptism into the body of Christ is the same as regeneration to him), the indwelling of the Holy Spirit, not grieving the Spirit, the fullness of the Spirit, sanctification, guidance, the anointing, gifts (pp. 180 ff.), witness, prayer, worship, and the eschatology of the Spirit.

Packer, J. I. *Keep in Step with the Spirit.* Old Tappan, N.J.: Revell, 1984. 299 pp. Although men often desire power from the Spirit, Packer says (p. 21), the most important thing is the presence of the Lord (pp. 47 f.). Packer urges that God's presence in the Spirit should produce personal fellowship with Jesus, personal transformation of character, and Spirit-given assurance (p. 49). He surveys the biblical teaching in the Old Testament (p. 58) but stresses the personality and deity of the Spirit in the New Testament (pp. 61 ff.). He mentions men such as Alexander Whyte and A. W. Tozer who made no bones about their personal devotion to the Lord Jesus (p. 75) and refers to the experiences of Blaise Pascal and John Wesley (p. 78). Packer warns that Evangelicals are insensitive to the holiness of God Himself (p. 101). Believers must allow themselves to be led by the Holy Spirit (pp. 118 f.). He criticizes Wesley's holiness teaching (pp. 136 ff.) and the Keswick teaching (pp. 150 ff.), presenting a Christ-centered way of love and faith instead (pp. 164 ff.). He is very generous toward the Charismatics (pp. 176 ff.), but he does criticize them (pp. 191 ff.). He argues that every true believer is Spirit baptized (pp. 202 ff.). He concludes that Charismatics are essentially regenerate believers (p. 222) and that tongues are good for some people.

Pentecost, J. Dwight. *The Divine Comforter.* Westwood, N.J.: Revell, 1963. 256 pp. In this topical survey, Pentecost defends the personality of the Spirit and inspiration by the Spirit (but denies dictation, p. 45). He holds that the church became God's temple at Pentecost (pp. 114 ff.); that "water" in John 3:5 means cleansing (p. 132); and that the Spirit baptizes only in this age

(p. 136), which is baptism into the body of Christ (p. 142). God offered gifts to the church, he says, not to individuals (p. 170). The author classes miracles (p. 186) and tongues (pp. 187 ff.) as temporary gifts and attacks the idea of a second work of grace (pp. 233-48).

Ridout, Samuel. *The Person and Work of the Holy Spirit.* New York: Loizeaux, 1945. The author offers seven practical and devotional sermons on the Spirit: in dispensation, salvation, sanctification, church, power, Scriptures, and Christ. He defends the infallible Scripture (p. 172) and takes the incorporation view of the baptism of the Spirit (p. 23).

Ryrie, Charles Caldwell. *The Holy Spirit.* Chicago: Moody, 1965. 126 pp. Ryrie gives a series of brief studies in the doctrine of the Spirit. He covers the personality and deity of the Holy Spirit, the Spirit's work in Creation and in relation to man in the Old Testament, and His relation to Jesus Christ. He discusses the sin against the Holy Spirit; common grace and efficacious grace; regeneration; and indwelling, baptizing, sealing, and filling with the Spirit. He offers a bibliography with brief annotations (pp. 121-22).

Sanders, J. Oswald. *The Holy Spirit and His Gifts.* Grand Rapids: Zondervan, 1940, 1970. 155 pp. The author presents a careful study of the doctrine of the Holy Spirit. He discusses His deity, personality, names, and emblems. On the baptism of the Spirit (pp. 61 ff.), the author gives the two views and advocates incorporation on the basis of I Corinthians 12:13. He covers sins against the Spirit, gifts of the Spirit, and tongues. On the last topic, Sanders makes a distinction between Acts and I Corinthians (p. 125). He does not want to rule out the possibility of tongues today but admits the possibility of abuse and counterfeit (p. 127). He ends with the filling of the Spirit and the fruit of the Spirit.

Scofield, C. I. *Plain Papers on the Doctrine of the Holy Spirit.* 1899. Reprint, Grand Rapids: Baker, n.d. 80 pp. Scofield holds that Old Testaments saints were born again but not indwelt by the Holy Spirit (p. 31), that at Pentecost the Spirit baptized believers into Christ (p. 40), and that after the conversion of Cornelius all believers are baptized and indwelt at their conversion (pp. 42-43). He attacks the second work of grace (p. 46), urges necessity of "many fillings" (pp. 48-49), and gives conditions for filling (pp. 54-67; negative—grieve not, quench not; positive—yieldedness, faith, prayer).

Strauss, Lehman. *The Third Person.* New York: Loizeaux, 1954. 190 pp. Strauss writes alliterative devotional messages on the person and work of the Holy Spirit. He has a strong chapter on the leading of the Spirit (pp. 53-72) and provides moving illustrations of Mendelssohn and the church organist (pp. 144-45) and other topics.

Swete, Henry Barclay. *The Holy Spirit in the New Testament.* London: Macmillan, 1910. Reprint, Grand Rapids: Baker, 1964. The author gives an exhaustive exposition of all the New Testament references to the Holy Spirit. He sidesteps some theological problems, such as tongues, but he really attempts to present what the New Testament writers taught and believed. He believes in the virgin birth (or "virgin conception," pp. 26-29). The book provides an excellent summary of the New Testament doctrine of the Holy Spirit (pp. 282-360).

Thomas, W. H. Griffith.*The Holy Spirit of God.* 1913. Reprint, Grand Rapids: Eerdmans, n.d. 319 pp. In Part I, Griffith Thomas covers the biblical revelation: the Holy Spirit in the Old Testament, in the Apocrypha, in Paul's epistles, in Acts, in the Synoptic Gospels, in John, and in other New Testament books. In Part II he gives the history of interpretation. In Part III he gives the theological doctrine: the Spirit of God, of Christ, and of truth; and God's relation to the individual, the church, and the world. In Part IV he surveys modern applications: divine immanence, modernism, mysticism, intellectualism, church problems, and so on.

Unger, Merrill F. *The Baptizing Work of the Holy Spirit.* Wheaton, Ill.: Van Kampen Press, 1953. 147 pp. The author sets forth the doctrine of the baptism of the believer into the body of Christ by the Holy Spirit. He makes distinctions between this and the indwelling and filling. He tends to make all references mean Spirit baptism (pp. 23 ff.) and holds that Old Testament believers (before Pentecost) were not saved (pp. 58 f.) and that the Samaritans were not saved until Peter came and they received the Spirit (p. 66). He also gives the conditions for filling (p. 19) and for power (pp. 125-31).

Walvoord, John F. *The Holy Spirit.* Wheaton, Ill.: Van Kampen Press, 1954. 294 pp. In this study of the person and work of the Holy Spirit, the author covers the personality, deity, and typology of the Spirit. He discusses the Holy Spirit in relation to Christ and in the work of salvation, grace, and regeneration. Walvoord surveys the baptism of the Holy Spirit (Spirit baptism into the body of Christ), the indwelling of the Spirit, the spiritual gifts, filling with the Holy Spirit, and the eschatology of the Spirit.

Williams, John. *The Holy Spirit Lord and Life-Giver.* Neptune, N.J.: Loizeaux, 1980. 320 pp. Williams gives an introduction to the doctrine of the Spirit. He argues that the Holy Spirit is God (pp. 29 f.); gives biblical pictures of the Spirit (pp. 40 f.); holds to inspiration by the Spirit of both the Old Testament and the New Testament (pp. 65 f.); gives a chart of the lists of gifts in the New Testament (p. 93); discusses oral ministry gifts (pp. 105 f.), practical service gifts (pp. 114 f.), and miraculous manifestations (pp. 122 f.); argues that the baptism of the Spirit was universal (p. 183); warns against introspection (p. 199); discusses tongues at length (pp. 205-35); and concludes by saying, "Tongues are only of comparative value and are not to be sought or cultivated by mature Christians" (p. 231). He gives a list of Scriptures on the Spirit (pp. 261-79).

CHAPTER 23
BOOKS ON PROPHECY

There is great interest today in the study of prophetic future. The following books are just a sampling of the most helpful works in a vast field of prophetic literature. A fine reference Bible such as Scofield or Ryrie can also be a great help in understanding the prophetic Word. The books that follow largely reflect the pretribulational premillennial view of prophecy. A second list is added for the benefit of those who wish to investigate other prophetic interpretations.

The Second Coming Bible by William E. Biederwolf (1924 [entitled *The Millennium Bible*]; reprint, Grand Rapids: Baker, 1964) is an impartial study of the prophetic passages in the Bible. Students of all prophetic persuasions can study this word with profit because Biederwolf has quoted a great array of biblical authorities without slanting his work toward premillennialism, amillennialism, or postmillennialism. It is an invaluable reference work for any pastor who wishes to speak on prophetic subjects.

Pretribulational Premillennial Views

Three works are of great significance. First, a particularly useful and unusual volume is *Premillennial Essays of the Prophetic Conference: 1878,* Nathaniel West, ed., (1879; reprint, Minneapolis: Klock and Klock, 1981. 528 pp.). Klock and Klock have done a great service in reprinting these messages from the powerful conference of 1878. One cannot read these messages without getting the feeling that today's preaching is weak and tepid. Many of the sermons in this anthology are so detailed that they must have taken over an hour to preach! There are messages by A. J. Gordon on the first resurrection (pp. 78 ff.) and by Bishop Nicholson on the gathering of Israel (pp. 222 ff.). Henry Parson has a helpful comparison of passages on the antichrist (pp. 215-17); Nathaniel West himself makes comparisons between the Books of Daniel and Revelation (pp. 361 ff.). James Brookes has a great message on the one hundred doctrines influenced by the teaching on the Second Coming of Christ (pp. 270 ff.). John Duffield marshalls powerful arguments to crush the postmillennial position (pp. 408 ff.). When the conference concluded, Mackay summed it up by saying, "Who are Presbyterians I cannot tell, and who are Episcopalians, or Baptists, or Congregationalists, I know not. But I know that every speaker's deepest thought was 'let us exalt His name together' " (p. 470). This book is a gold mine of material for the premillennialist.

A second useful work is by Paul Lee Tan, *The Interpretation of Prophecy* (Winona Lake, Ind.: BMH Books, 1974. 435 pp.). This work is a formal proof that the literal method of interpretation is the only proper one for the study of prophecy as well as of all of the Scriptures. He defends the literal interpretation of prophecy at length (pp. 29-39), gives arguments for the literal interpretation (pp. 59-74), and gives principles for the interpretation of prophecy (pp. 96-130). He has a very careful discussion of the meaning of Acts 15 to show that it does not refer to fulfillment but to agreement with prophecy (pp. 128-30). He also covers the interpretation of symbols and types in prophecy (pp. 152-74). He argues for literal bows and arrows in the last battle (pp. 220-24). He concludes with ten appendixes on such important subjects as the millennial sacrifices (pp. 293 ff.), Jesus' offer of the Kingdom (pp. 299 f.), the temple vision of Ezekiel (pp. 318 ff.), the pretribulation rapture doctrine (pp. 337-43), the uniqueness of the tribulation period (pp. 344 ff.), and other vital subjects. Altogether, the book is a very valuable help to the student of prophecy.

A third valuable work is the *Dictionary of Premillennial Theology* (Grand Rapids: Kregel, 1996. 442 pp.), edited by Mal Couch. There are articles entitled "Amillennialism (p. 37 ff.); "Antichrist" (pp. 43 ff); "Brooks, James Hall" (pp. 64-65); "Daniel, Eschatology of" (pp. 81 ff.); "Day of the Lord" (pp. 87-88); "Dispensationalism" (pp. 96 ff.); "Dispensationalism, Progressive" (pp. 98-99);

"Gog and Magog" (pp. 124 f.); "Hell" (pp. 141-42); "Kingdom of God, of Heaven" used synonymously (pp. 230-31); "Millennium, Doctrine of the" (pp. 259 ff.); "Rapture, Biblical Study of the" (pp. 332-44); a special refutation of "Rapture, the Prewrath" (p. 359); "Revelation, Structure of the Book of" (pp. 372 ff.); "Scofield, Cyrus Ingerson" (pp. 389 ff.); "Wrath" (p. 425); "Zechariah, Eschatology of" (pp. 426 ff.). Contributors include Robert Lightner, Charles Ryrie, Gerald Stanton, and many others.

Other helpful works include the following:

Andrews, Samuel J. *Christianity and Antichristianity in Their Final Conflict.* 1898. Reprint, Greenville, S.C.: Bob Jones University Press, 1971. 358 pp.

Blackstone, William E. *Jesus Is Coming.* Chicago: Revell, 1916. 252 pp.

Clouse, Robert G. *The Meaning of the Millennium: Four Views.* Downers Grove, Ill.: InterVarsity, 1977. 223 pp.

Feinberg, Charles L. *Millennialism: The Two Major Views.* (formerly *Premillennialism or Amillennialism,* 1954) 3rd ed. Chicago: Moody, 1980. 354 pp.

Griffin, William. *Endtime: The Doomsday Catalog.* New York: Collier, 1979. 346 pp.

Haldeman, I. M. *The Coming of Christ.* Atlanta: The Granary, n.d. 325 pp.

Hoyt, Herman A. *The End Times.* Chicago: Moody, 1969. 256 pp.

Ludwigson, R. *A Survey of Bible Prophecy.* Grand Rapids: Zondervan, 1951, 1973. 187 pp.

McClain, Alva J. *The Greatness of the Kingdom.* Grand Rapids: Zondervan, 1959, 1974. 556 pp.

Pache, René. *The Future Life.* Chicago: Moody, 1962. 376 pp.

Pentecost, J. Dwight. *Things to Come.* Findlay, Ohio: Dunham, 1958. 633 pp.

Phillips, John. *Exploring the Future.* Nashville: Nelson, 1983. 342 pp.

Ryrie, Charles C. *What You Should Know About the Rapture.* Chicago: Moody, 1981. 118 pp.

Sproule, John A. *In Defense of Pre-Tribulationism.* Winona Lake, Ind.: BMH Books, 1980. 64 pp.

Stanton, Gerald B. *Kept from the Hour.* Miami Springs, Fla.: Schoettle Publishing Co., 1991. 423 pp. The best work on the pretribulation rapture.

Unger, Merrill F. *Great Neglected Bible Prophecies.* Chicago: Scripture Press, 1955. 167 pp.

Walvoord, John F. *The Church in Prophecy.* Grand Rapids: Zondervan, 1964. 183 pp.

———. *Major Bible Prophecies.* Grand Rapids: Zondervan, 1991. 450 pp.

———. *The Prophecy Knowledge Handbook.* Wheaton, Ill.: Victor Books, 1990. 809 pp.

———. *The Rapture Question.* Grand Rapids: Zondervan, 1957. 204 pp.

———. *The Return of the Lord.* Findlay, Ohio: Dunham, 1955. 160 pp.

Other Prophetic Views

Postmillennial

Boettner, Loraine. *The Millennium.* Philadelphia: Presbyterian and Reformed Publishing Co., 1957. 391 pp.

Hodge, A. A. *Outlines of Theology.* 1860, 1878. Reprint, Grand Rapids: Eerdmans, 1949. 678 pp.

Amillennial

Berkhof, Louis. *Systematic Theology.* Grand Rapids: Eerdmans, 1941. 784 pp.

Vos, Geerhardus. *Pauline Eschatology.* Grand Rapids: Baker, 1979. 374 pp.

Partial Rapture

Lang, G. H. *The Revelation of Jesus Christ,* 2nd ed. London: Paternoster Press, 1948. 420 pp.

Midtribulation Rapture

Gordon, S. D. *Quiet Talks About Our Lord's Return.* New York: Revell, 1912. 226 pp.

Harrison, Norman B. *The End: Re-Thinking the Revelation.* Minneapolis: Harrison Service, 1941. 239 pp.

Posttribulation Rapture

Gundry, Robert H. *The Church and the Tribulation.* Grand Rapids: Zondervan, 1973. 224 pp.

Ladd, George E. *The Blessed Hope.* Grand Rapids: Eerdmans, 1973. 167 pp.

Independent Opinions

Rosenthal, Marvin. *The Pre-Wrath Rapture of the Church.* Nashville: Thomas Nelson, 1990. 319 pp. (For a clear critique of such opinion, see Karleen, Paul S. *The Pre-Wrath Rapture of the Church: Is It Biblical?* Langhoren, Pa.: BF Press, 1991. 102 pp.)

Strauss, Lehman. *Prophetic Mysteries Revealed.* Neptune, N.J.: Loizeaux, 1980. 255 pp. A comparison between the seven parables in Matthew 13 and the letters to the seven churches in Revelation 2–3 is a highly interesting study but one that is nearly impossible to establish to everyone's satisfaction. Strauss holds that both the parables and the churches refer to the church age; he argues for the postponement of the kingdom (pp. 25 ff.) and for the idea of seven successive church ages in Revelation 2–3 (pp. 132 ff.); he does not comment on the difficulty that this interpretation poses for the imminency of Christ's return.

CHAPTER 24
BOOKS ON
INTRODUCTION

When the Bible student needs to know the date, authorship, and background of a book of the Bible, there are books on introduction to provide answers to his questions. Of the books on introduction on the market, most have such destructive and radical presuppositions that the student is better without them. The following list omits liberal introductions such as Werner Kuemmel's revision of the Old Feine-Behm work that raises questions about almost everything in the New Testament.

Biblical Introduction

The Books and the Parchments (Old Tappan, N.J.: Revell, 1950, 1984. 289 pp.) by Frederick Fyvie Bruce is a revised and updated edition of a classic work. This work is probably the most practical book the average pastor can get to answer the question "How did we get our Bible?" F. F. Bruce is certainly at home in the subject. He discusses how books were made in the ancient world (pp. 1 ff.); has a fascinating section on the origin of the alphabet (pp. 7 ff.); and gives the outstanding characteristics of the Hebrew language (pp. 24ff.), the Aramaic language (pp. 39 ff.), and the Greek language (pp. 49 ff.). He carefully defends the unity and authority of both the Old Testament and the New Testament (pp. 72 f.). He discusses the canon of Scripture, defending all sixty-six books of the Bible (pp. 86 ff.), the Samaritan Pentateuch (pp. 116 ff.), the Targums (pp. 123 ff.), and the Greek Old Testament, the Septuagint (pp. 136 ff.). He provides much helpful material on the text of the New Testament, describing the different text types (Alexandrian, Byzantine, etc.) and giving a careful evaluation of their characteristics (pp. 166 ff.). He has a clear history of the English Bible, including the King James Version (pp. 211 ff.). He even extends the history to include the Living Bible (pp. 248 f.), the New International Version (pp. 250 f.), and the New King James Version (pp. 251 f.). There is an excellent bibliography (pp. 265-72) and very thorough indexes (pp. 273 ff.). One need not agree with all of Bruce's interpretations to recognize that there is an immense amount of information here that the pastor would be hard-pressed to find anywhere else.

Old Testament Introductions

The most helpful and practical introduction for the Old Testament is *A Survey of Old Testament Introduction* (Chicago: Moody, 1964. 507 pp.) by Gleason L. Archer Jr. He faces problems honestly and gives helpful answers. He defends the inerrancy of the Bible (pp. 16 ff.), the Mosaic authorship of the Pentateuch (pp. 108 ff.), the unity of Isaiah (pp. 318 ff.), the early date for Daniel (pp. 368 ff.), and so on. He provides good indexes of authors, subjects, and Scripture.

Another helpful work is Edward J. Young's *Introduction to the Old Testament* (Grand Rapids: Eerdmans, 1949. 414 pp.). He also defends the Mosaic authorship of the Pentateuch (pp. 48 ff.), the unity of Isaiah (pp. 199 ff.), and the early date for Daniel (pp. 351 ff.).

Merrill F. Unger has also written a very helpful book on this subject, *Introductory Guide to the Old Testament* (Grand Rapids: Zondervan, 1951. 420 pp.). He defends the absolute inerrancy of Scripture (pp. 37 ff.), the Mosaic authorship of the Pentateuch (pp. 213 ff.), the unity of Isaiah (pp. 315 ff.), and the early date for Daniel (pp. 396-99).

New Testament Introductions

The best recent work is *An Introduction to the New Testament* (Grand Rapids: Zondervan, 1992. 537 pp.) by D. A. Carson, Douglas J. Moo, and Leon Morris. Although there is a tremendous amount of liberal opinion cited, they do defend without equivocation the traditional authorship and dates for every New Testament book.

They defend form criticism but warn against the antihistorical views of Bultmann and so on (pp. 23-24). They manifest an overregard for "Q" (p. 36). On the Book of Revelation, they say that "it is the futurist approach that comes closest to doing justice to the nature and purpose of Revelation" (p. 483). They conclude with a chapter on the New Testament canon (pp. 487-500).

A most useful and practical older work is Henry C. Thiessen's *Introduction to the New Testament* (Grand Rapids: Eerdmans, 1943. 347 pp.). Thiessen defends the verbal inspiration of Scripture (pp. 78 ff.), discusses the Synoptic problem (pp. 101 ff.), and defends the traditional authorship and a conservative date for each of the New Testament books (pp. 130 ff.).

Another work, not quite as easy to use as Thiessen's but filled with excellent material, is Donald Guthrie's *New Testament Introduction,* 3 vols. (London: Tyndale Press, 1961, 1962, 1965. 380, 319, 320 pp.). He discusses the Synoptic problem (I, 114 ff.) and form criticism (I, 178 ff.), defends at length the Pauline authorship of the pastoral Epistles (II, 198-236) and the Petrine authorship of II Peter (III, 143-72), and holds that John the Apostle wrote Revelation (III, 254-69).

D. Edmond Hiebert's *Introduction to the New Testament,* 3 vols. (Chicago: Moody, 1954, 1962, 1977. 300, 383, 300 pp.), is a less technical work than the preceding book, but it does provide helpful background and defends the conservative view of the authorship and dates of the New Testament books.

A less valuable work is Everett F. Harrison's *Introduction to the New Testament* (Grand Rapids: Eerdmans, 1964. 481 pp.). Although he defends the traditional dates and authorship for most of the New Testament, he seems to express hesitancy on some books. For example, on Matthew he comments, "The evidence on authorship is hardly enough to warrant a confident decision" (p. 167). In Revelation he thinks the series of seals, trumpets, and bowls run simultaneously (p. 433) and considers the authorship "difficult to attain with anything like certainty" (p. 444).

The old classic in the field is Theodor Zahn's *Introduction to the New Testament,* 3 vols. (1909; reprint, Grand Rapids: Kregel, 1953. 564, 617, 539 pp.). He is well known for defending an early date for Galatians as the earliest of Paul's epistles (I, 193 ff.).

CHAPTER 25
BIBLE BIOGRAPHY

One of the most interesting kinds of Bible study is the study of the personalities of the Bible. The grand master of biblical biography was Alexander Whyte, whose six-volume *Bible Characters* (London: Oliphants, n.d. Reprint, Kregel, 1990) remains a classic. No one can read his gripping portrayals of Noah, Ham, Lot, and scores of others and forget them. The expositor needs a good concordance (such as Young's) in order to trace out all the references to a Bible character so that his portrait will be accurate and complete. He also can benefit from reference works on Bible characters. Perhaps the most thorough is *Who's Who in the Bible* (Pleasantville, N.Y.: Reader's Digest Association, 1994). It has 480 pages of biographical information. By and large it is a reverent presentation of the biblical facts. There are, however, a few liberal opinions expressed, such as the route of the Exodus through Bitter Lakes (p. 304) and the guess that Romans 16 belongs to Ephesians (p. 362). The major articles extend from Aaron to Zophar, leaving genealogical names to the index (Zuph, Zur, etc.; p. 470). A fascinating part of the work is the numerous artistic illustrations drawn from paintings, sculpture, stained glass, and so on. Many of them are thought-provoking interpretations. Other helpful works include the following:

Alexander, George M. *The Handbook of Biblical Personalities.* Greenwich, Conn.: Seabury, 1962.

Deen, Edith. *All the Women of the Bible.* New York: Harper, 1955.

Hastings, James. *The Greater Men and Women of the Bible.* 6 vols. New York: Clark, 1913-1916.

Lockyer, Herbert. *All the Men of the Bible.* Grand Rapids: Zondervan, 1958.

Meyer, F. B. *Great Men of the Bible.* 2 vols. n.d. Reprint, Grand Rapids: Zondervan, 1981.

One of the best how-to-do-it books on biblical biographical preaching is Faris Daniel Whitesell's *Preaching on Bible Characters* (Grand Rapids: Baker, 1955). Whitesell has an excellent bibliography on Bible characters.

A book much narrower in scope but useful is D. Edmond Hiebert's *In Paul's Shadow* (Greenville, S.C.: Bob Jones University Press, 1992. 269 pp.). The work is subtitled "Friends and Foes of the Great Apostle." It is a careful portrait of the personalities that surrounded the apostle Paul. Each study begins with a list of the Scripture references to the person, such as Apollos (p. 11) and Aquila and Priscilla (p. 23). Then follows a thorough and thoughtful exposition of the biblical picture of the person. Hiebert provides many interesting facts about the persons: he discusses the Roman background of Priscilla (pp. 24- 26), the meaning of Barnabas's name (pp. 37-38), and the education and culture of Luke (p. 57). He carefully traces the "we" passages in Acts (pp. 58 ff.), shows Mark's family connections (pp. 68 f.); describes Silas's place in the Jerusalem church (p. 80), praises Timothy's character as Paul manifests it in his epistles to him (pp. 99-103), and recounts Titus's service all the way to Dalmatia (pp. 105 ff.). He then provides brief descriptions of those persons he calls "lesser lights." He covers Ananias of Damascus (pp. 117 ff.), Andronicus and Junias (pp. 123 ff.), Trophimus (pp. 207 ff.), and Tychicus (pp. 213 ff.). He also includes an alphabetical list of all other named persons in the New Testament whose lives touched Paul's (pp. 223-30). He concludes the book with a strong bibliography (pp. 239-55) and thorough indexes (pp. 257-61).

Some preachers were famous for their studies of individual Bible characters. A. T. Robertson was well known for his *Epochs in the Life of Jesus* (New York: Scribner's, 1929) and *Epochs in the Life of Paul* (New York: Scribner's, 1933). F. B. Meyer authored profound devotional studies on *Abraham* (London: Morgan and Scott, n.d.), *Elijah* (London: Morgan and Scott, n.d.), *Peter* (New York: Revell, 1920), and others. A. B. Davidson's *Called of God* (Edinburgh: Clark, 1903) is a study of God's call on the lives of biblical characters. Other well-known books of wider scope are these:

Ayer, William Ward. *These Men Live.* Grand Rapids: Zondervan, 1939.

Baxter, J. Sidlow. *Mark These Men.* Grand Rapids: Zondervan, 1960.

Bounds, Edward M. *Bible Men of Prayer.* n.d. Reprint, Grand Rapids: Zondervan, 1964.

Chappell, Clovis G. *Sermons on Biblical Characters.* New York: Doran, 1922.

Cumming, James Elder. *Scripture Photographs: Men in the Sunlight of the Word.* Salem, Ohio: Schmul Publishers, n.d.

Macartney, Clarence E. N. *The Greatest Men of the Bible.* New York: Abingdon-Cokesbury, 1941.

Stevenson, Herbert F. *A Galaxy of Saints: Lesser-known Bible Men and Women.* Westwood, N.J.: Revell, 1958.

Every expositor should plan his own series of studies in Bible personalities and work on them until they come alive in his thinking. There is always rich blessing and great insight for the Christian life in the lives of Bible characters.

CHAPTER 26
BOOKS ON
THE LIFE OF CHRIST

The great life task of the expositor is to proclaim the Lord Jesus Christ to men. A godly congregation will echo the desire of those Greeks at the feast: "Sir, we would see Jesus" (John 12:21). The expositor must be prepared to present Christ again and again with endless variety to men. The expositor should be thoroughly acquainted with the life of his Lord. Since the literature on this subject is vast and often skeptical, he must choose his tools carefully. The old books by Renan, S. J. Case, and Goguel will pervert the truth and destroy faith rather than help. The more recent unbelievers do no better: Bornkamm, Fuchs, and Kaesemann set forth an existential Jesus, not the Lord Jesus Christ of the Bible. The following works are of special value for the reverent exposition of the life of Christ.

Andrews, Samuel J. *The Life of Our Lord.* 1862, 1891. Reprint, Grand Rapids: Zondervan, 1954. 690 pp. Andrews writes a very reverent and scholarly life of Christ with special attention to chronology. He has a chronological harmony of the Gospels (pp. xxxiii ff.) and an essay discussing the date of the Lord's birth, baptism, and death (pp. 1-51). Every paragraph in his work is exactly dated; his discussions are genuinely helpful.

Blaikie, William Garden. *The Inner Life of Christ*, and Robert Law. *The Emotions of Christ.* 1876. Reprint, Minneapolis: Klock and Klock, 1982. These are rich devotional works. The author unfolds the Lord's character in the events of His life, showing His delight in His Father's will, and His constant service. Law treats His joy, compassion, anger, and so on.

Bruce, Alexander Balmain. *The Training of the Twelve.* 1894. Reprint, Grand Rapids: Kregel, 1971. 552 pp. Bruce's work is a unique study of the Lord's instruction of His apostles in preparation for their coming ministry for Him. This work not only helps the expositor to instruct his people, but also helps him to see his own responsibility before his Lord.

Culver, Robert D. *The Life of Christ.* Grand Rapids: Baker, 1976. 304 pp. A brief, popular life of the Lord, illustrated with a number of black-and-white photographs of biblical sites. He has lists of the miracles (pp. 83-84), the parables (pp. 153-54), and references to local culture in Jesus' teaching (pp. 190-91). There are thorough indexes.

Edersheim, Alfred. *The Life of Jesus the Messiah.* 2 vols. 1883. Reprint, Grand Rapids: Eerdmans, 1953. 695, 828 pp. This book is perhaps the best and most helpful life of Christ that we may ever have. Because Edersheim was a converted Jew, he has a unique insight into the customs and literature of the Jews. With fervent faith he discusses all the problems and differing interpretations exhaustively. It is well worth prolonged study.

Fairbairn, Andrew M. *Studies in the Life of Christ.* London: Hodder and Stoughton, 1880. 359 pp. Fairbairn's book contains scholarly messages that provide much help on the life of Christ.

Guthrie, Donald. *Jesus the Messiah.* Grand Rapids: Zondervan, 1972. 386 pp. A popular life of our Lord, this book is illustrated by numerous black-and-white photographs. The author quotes the RSV, favors a nonmiraculous interpretation of the star of Bethlehem (p. 27), defends the reality of Jesus' temptations (p. 43), and holds that the paragraph of the woman taken in adultery is genuine but that it was not written by John (p. 234).

Machen, J. Gresham. *The Virgin Birth of Christ.* New York: Harper, 1930. 415 pp. Machen's book is the most powerful defense of the virgin birth of Christ ever written. Every expositor should be aware of his masterful treatment of the birth narratives in Matthew and Luke.

McQuaid, Elwood. *The Outpouring: Jesus in the Feasts of Israel.* Chicago: Moody Press, 1986. 160 pp. This book is a fresh interpretation of the Gospel of John, organizing it on the basis of the feasts of Israel. It is not a commentary, but a thorough discussion of the background and interpretation of John. McQuaid explains the Old Testament background of the Israelite going up to Jerusalem for three festive pilgrimages during the year (pp. 13 f.). He argues that the Old Testament prophecies, types, and ceremonies are first in evidential value. The words of the Messiah are second in importance, and the sign miracles in John are the third confirmation of Messiah (p. 24). He discusses the first Passover (John 2:13–3:21) with considerable background on the temple and its ministries (pp. 28 ff.). He explains the meaning of the Lamb (pp. 52 ff.). He describes the Feast of Trumpets (pp. 57 ff.). There is an interesting reconstruction of the temple mount in A.D. 70 (pp. 74-75). He describes the second Passover (John 6; pp. 76 ff.). He shows the meaning of the Feast of Tabernacles (John 7:2–10:21; pp. 90 ff.). There is a helpful map of Jerusalem (p. 100). He explains the Feast of the Dedication, Hanukkah (John 10:22-39; pp. 111 ff.). The final section of the book deals with the third Passover (John 12:1–20:31; pp. 123 ff.). There are brief discussions of the raising of Lazarus (pp. 124 ff.) and the upper room discourse (pp. 134 ff.). He concludes that Jesus of Nazareth is the King of the Jews and the Savior of the world (p. 158). The book would be a real help to any pastor thinking of expounding the Gospel of John.

Morgan, G. Campbell. *The Crises of the Christ.* New York: Revell, 1903, 1936. 477 pp. This work is a thorough and thought-provoking exposition of the high points in the life of Christ: His birth, baptism, temptation, transfiguration, crucifixion, resurrection, and ascension. The individual expositions are better than those in most commentaries.

Patterson, Alexander. *The Greater Life and Work of Christ.* Chicago: Moody, n.d. 408 pp. Patterson traces the person of Christ from eternity past, His work in Creation, the Old Testament age,

His incarnation, His present work, the Day of the Lord, and all the way to eternity future. The work has a thrilling sweep to it.

Pentecost, J. Dwight. *The Words and Works of Jesus Christ.* Grand Rapids: Zondervan, 1981. 629 pp. He organizes the life on the basis of the offer and rejection of the kingdom. He regularly quotes the NIV (p.10). He defends the inerrancy and authenticity of the Scriptures (p. 24), the preexistence of Christ (p. 28), the virgin birth (p.55), and so on. He includes much historical background, postponement of the kingdom (p. 218), and the premillennial interpretation of Matthew 24-25 (pp. 400 ff.).

Sanders, J. Oswald. *The Incomparable Christ.* Chicago: Moody, 1952, 1971. 256 pp. Sander's book is a compilation of meditations on the person and work of Christ. It is filled with useful homiletic material and breathes a devotional spirit.

Shepard, J. W. *The Christ of the Gospels.* Grand Rapids: Eerdmans, 1939, 1952. This book presents a conservative life of Christ that provides significant historical background (pp. 1 ff.). Shepard defends the virgin birth (p. 19), the personality of the devil (p. 74), and the reality of hell (p. 529). His bibliography is still valuable (pp. 639-42).

Stalker, James. *The Life of Jesus Christ.* New York: Revell, 1891, 1949. 162 pp. One of the clearest and most concise surveys of the life of Christ. This book is a useful tool for organizing and memorizing the events.

————. *The Trial and Death of Jesus Christ.* 1894. Reprint, Grand Rapids: Zondervan, n.d. 185 pp. This book contains powerful and moving studies that will stir the expositor to preach on these subjects himself. It includes studies on the words spoken from the cross.

Torrey, Reuben Archer. *Studies in the Life and Teachings of our Lord.* n.d. Reprint, Grand Rapids: Baker, 1966. 346 pp. There are 149 paragraph studies organized as a harmony of the gospels. In each paragraph Torrey explains the facts of the passage and then draws up the doctrines found in them. On the ministry of John the Baptist in Luke 3:1-18, he classifies the teachings under "Jesus Christ," "The Model Preacher," "The Scriptures," and "The Holy Spirit" (pp. 16-18).

Westcott, Brooke Foss. *The Revelation of the Risen Lord.* London: Macmillan, 1882. 235 pp. Westcott writes rich expositions of the Lord's appearances after His resurrection. Every appearance fits the person or persons who were present. This is a good work to study before Easter.

Whyte, Alexander. *The Walk, Conversation and Character of Jesus Christ Our Lord.* 1905. Reprint, Grand Rapids: Baker, 1975. 340 pp. This book contains powerful messages setting forth the matchless character of the Lord. These are memorable portraits of the eternal Son, incarnate for sinners.

CHAPTER 27
HARMONIES
OF THE GOSPELS

Any careful study of the life and teachings of the Lord Jesus Christ must consider the parallel passages in the Gospels. These passages can be found easily in a harmony of the Gospels. Although some of the following works are by liberals, they usually arrange the Gospel material without comment and have done a significant service for students of the Bible.

Burton, Ernest DeWitt, and Edgar J. Goodspeed. *A Harmony of the Synoptic Gospels in Greek.* Chicago: University of Chicago Press, 1920. 346 pp. This book is especially helpful to those who can read Greek, showing parallels in the exact wording.

Carter, John F. *A Layman's Harmony of the Gospels.* Nashville: Broadman, 1961. 364 pp. Based on the American Standard Version of 1901.

Davies, Benjamin. *Harmony of the Gospels.* Greenville, S.C.: Bob Jones University Press, 1976. 184 pp. Based on the King James Version.

Kerr, John H. *A Harmony of the Gospels.* New York: Revell, 1924. 236 pp. Based on the American Standard Version of 1901.

MacKnight, James. *A Harmony of the Four Gospels.* 2 vols. Grand Rapids: Baker, 1950. 627, 520 pp.

Robertson, Archibald Thomas. *A Harmony of the Gospels.* Nashville: Broadman, 1922, 1950. 305 pp. Based on the English Revised Version of 1881. Robertson includes a number of helpful notes.

Roney, Charles P. *Commentary on the Harmony of the Gospels.* Grand Rapids: Eerdmans, 1948. 573 pp.

Stevens, William Arnold, and Ernest DeWitt Burton. *A Harmony of the Gospels for Historical Study.* New York: Scribner's, 1893, 1907. 283 pp. Based on the English Revised Version of 1881 and includes some liberal notes.

Swanson, Reuben J. *The Horizontal Line Synopsis of the Gospels.* Dillsboro, N.C.: Western North Carolina Press, 1977. 620 pp. Instead of arranging the text in parallel columns, Swanson arranged the text line by line so that differences in wording may be seen at a glance. It is a unique and very helpful contribution to New Testament studies.

Thomas, Robert L., and Stanley Gundry. *A Harmony of the Gospels.* Chicago: Moody Press, 1978. 350 pp. Based on the New American Standard Bible; includes a dozen technical essays on harmonistic studies.

CHAPTER 28
BOOKS ON CREATION AND EVOLUTION

The expositor dare not be ignorant of the long-standing conflict between exponents of evolution and belief in Creation. If the expositor knows some area of science well, he has a source of illustration that can be very effective in his messages. The better his background in the Creationist literature, the better he will be able to set forth his position to his congregation and especially to his young people. The following list will acquaint the expositor with some of the forceful literature published recently. One need not agree with every interpretation in these works to recognize that they set forth a thoughtful and logical alternative to the theory of evolution. After reading these works, the expositor will be ready to take the offensive the next time he expounds Genesis.

Custance, Arthur C. *Genesis and Early Man.* Vol. II, *The Doorway Papers.* Grand Rapids: Zondervan, 1975. 331 pp. All nine volumes of *The Doorway Papers* are worth reading, but this one is especially good. The author, a Christian anthropologist, slaughters a number of sacred cows, charging evolutionists with needing faith in their theory (pp. 12 ff.), holding that the cavemen are examples of degeneration, not evolution (pp. 81 ff.), arguing that early man had high intelligence (pp. 145 ff.), and maintaining that evolutionists have failed to account for the origin of human speech (pp. 250-77).

Daly, Reginald. *Earth's Most Challenging Mysteries.* Grand Rapids: Baker, 1972. 403 pp. The author propounds seven principal "mysteries" that evolutionists have trouble explaining and provides Creationist answers. He details the many contradictory explanations by evolutionists of the extinction of mammoths and dinosaurs (pp. 29 ff.), argues that dinosaurs and mammals were contemporaneous (pp. 89 ff.), collapses the evolutionists' millions of years into thousands (p. 140), and holds that the human race began five thousand or ten thousand years ago (pp. 147-48).

Davidheiser, Bolton. *Evolution and Christian Faith.* Grand Rapids: Baker, 1969. 372 pp. The author presents a thorough refutation of evolutionary theories. He gives a brief history of evolutionary opinions (pp. 38-137); discusses evolutionary theories: atheistic (pp. 164 ff.), theistic (pp. 168 ff.), threshold (pp. 173 ff.), and so on; attacks the suggested mechanisms of evolution: natural selection (pp. 189 ff.), mutations (pp. 208 ff.), hybridization (pp. 216 ff.); demonstrates that the evidences for evolution do not prove it: comparative anatomy (pp. 231 ff.), vestigial structures (pp. 23 ff.), embryonic recapitulation (pp. 240 ff.), taxonomy (pp. 255 ff.); and attacks the idea of the evolution of life (pp. 302 ff.). His book is well documented.

Gish, Duane T. *Evolution: The Fossils Say No!* San Diego: Creation-Life Publishers, 1973, 1979. 129 pp. This book gives a popular presentation of the evidence in the fossil record against evolution. Gish maintains that the theory of evolution is a philosophy, not a science (pp. 1-14); shows how the geologic column favors catastrophism rather than uniformitarianism (pp. 36-44); shows that the fossil record has bursts of new forms rather than slow development (pp. 45-52) and manifests completely developed forms rather than partially developed ones (pp. 53-71); argues that there is always a sharp difference between ape forms and human forms; and charges evolutionists with trying to blur distinctions (pp. 72-111).

Ham, Ken, Andrew Snelling, and Carl Wieland. *The Answers Book.* El Cajon, Calif.: Master Books, 1992. 206 pp. The authors provide conservative answers to twelve commonly asked questions about Creation-evolution controversies. They cover dinosaurs (pp. 21 ff.), continental drift (pp. 41 ff.), carbon-14 (pp. 65 ff.), ice ages (pp. 71 ff.), why God took six days (pp. 89 ff.), the origin of evil (pp. 103 ff.), Noah's Flood (pp. 117 ff.), who was Cain's wife (pp. 177 ff.), how did different races arise (pp. 177 ff.), and so on.

Lammerts, Walter E., ed. *Scientific Studies in Special Creation.* Grand Rapids: Baker, 1971. 343 pp. Contains 31 brief articles. R. J. Rushdoony evaluates the premises of evolutionary thought (pp. 1-8); Robert Reymond defends biblical Creation out of nothing (pp. 9-21) as does John Whitcomb (pp. 22 ff.); Henry Morris discusses the first two laws of thermodynamics (pp. 60-71); Melvin Cook questions the validity of radiological dating methods (pp. 79-97); Frank Marsh discusses the meaning of the Genesis kinds (pp. 136-55); George Howe attacks the idea of the origin of man by evolution (pp. 206-28), and so on.

————. *Why Not Creation?* Grand Rapids: Baker, 1970. 388 pp. In this anthology presenting an alternative to evolution, John Klotz contrasts the ideas of Creation and evolution and presents some of the problems (pp. 5-23); George Mulfinger points out the weaknesses of the various evolutionary theories of the origin of the universe (pp. 39-66); Emmett Williams argues that the second law of thermodynamics makes evolution nearly impossible (pp. 67-79); Robert Whitelaw holds that radiocarbon confirms the biblical Creation (pp. 90-100); Henry Morris presents the geological evidence for a catastrophic flood (pp. 114-37); Melvin Cook presents evidence of fossil trilobites in human footprints (pp. 185-93); and Arthur Custance presents the evidence for fossil men being examples of degeneration (pp. 194-229).

Morris, Henry M. *Evolution in Turmoil.* San Diego: Creation-Life Publishers, 1982. 190 pp. A hard-hitting criticism of evolutionary theories. The author discusses the mystery of the origin of life (pp. 15 ff.), mutations and chaotic genetics (pp. 37 ff.), the total absence of transition fossils (pp. 61 ff.), punctuationism and naturalistic catastrophism (pp. 91 ff.), the war against Creationism (pp. 113 ff.), the compromising Christian and evolution (pp. 141 ff.), and so on.

————. *The Long War Against God.* Grand Rapids: Baker, 1989. 344 pp. A history of the age-long war between Creationist and naturalistic views of origins. The author demonstrates the evolutionary basis of modern thought (pp. 17 ff.), shows the influence of evolution on Hitler (pp. 75 ff.) and on communism (pp. 82 ff.), records Darwin's antibiblical attitudes (pp. 94-95), demonstrates Wheaton College's compromise (pp. 102-3), and laments the demise of Christian morality (pp. 132 ff.). He holds that world religion has always been an evolutionary pantheism (p. 257) and sees evidence for the Trinity in both theology and the material universe (pp. 275 ff.). He thinks that pantheism and polytheism are degenerations from an earlier monotheism (p. 292).

————. *Studies in the Bible and Science.* Grand Rapids: Baker, 1966. 186 pp. The author has written brief articles discussing reason and Christian hope (pp. 13 ff.), arguing for Creation in six literal days (p. 39) and contending that the Flood explains much in the geologic record (pp. 58 ff.). He sets forth the scriptural doctrine for water (pp. 78 ff.), attacks theistic evolution (pp. 89 ff.), argues that the Bible is a textbook of science (pp. 108 ff.), gives seven reasons for opposing evolution (pp. 136 ff.), and contrasts science and scientism (pp. 150 ff.).

Morris, Henry M., ed. *Scientific Creationism.* San Diego: Creation-Life Publishers, 1974. 277 pp. In this defense of Creationism against evolutionary theories, Morris maintains that space exploration has increased the evidence for Creationism (pp. 30-31), argues for purpose in Creation (pp. 32 ff.), holds that the first two laws of thermodynamics destroy the theory of evolution (pp. 37 ff.), thinks that the fossil record teaches catastrophism rather than uniformitarianism (pp. 91 ff.) and that the earth is young rather than old (pp. 131 ff.), and defends the biblical Creation account (pp. 203 ff.).

Morris, Henry M., and Donald Rohrer. *Creation: The Cutting Edge.* San Diego: Creation-Life Publishers, 1982. 240 pp. An anthology of articles on Creation vs. evolution, covering such subjects as the origin of limestone caves (pp. 13 ff.), theistic evolution (pp. 32 ff.), the tenets of Creationism (pp. 59 ff.), the origin of mammals (pp. 75 ff.), an answer for Asimov (pp. 149 ff.), mammal-like reptiles (pp. 165 ff.), and so on.

Morris, Henry M., William Boardman, and Robert Koontz. *Science and Creation.* San Diego: Creation-Science Research Center, 1971. 99 pp. The authors have produced a handbook to enable teachers to present the Creationist view in the classroom. They contrast scientific Creationism and evolutionary uniformitarianism (pp. 11-15); evaluate the conflicting views in physical sciences (pp. 22-24), earth sciences (pp. 24-27), life sciences (pp. 27 ff.), and so on; set forth the classical arguments for evolution and attack them (pp. 35-59); and discuss the origin of life (pp. 60-69) and the age of the universe (pp. 70 ff.).

Smith, A. E. Wilder. *Man's Origin, Man's Destiny.* Wheaton, Ill.: Harold Shaw, 1968. 320 pp. Smith critically questions the principles of evolution. He attacks the idea that man is merely an intelligent animal (pp. 31-51); questions the scientific value of evolutionary arguments and ideas (pp. 52-109); although placing too much value on Velikovsky's ideas (pp. 122-26), defends God's Creation out of nothing (pp. 151-52); shows that evolutionists have not accounted for *plan* in the universe (pp. 161-62); and argues that man's true destiny is to be in the presence of the Lord Jesus Christ (pp. 267 ff.).

Whitcomb, John C. *The Early Earth.* Grand Rapids: Baker, 1972. 144 pp. In this positive defense of the biblical Creation account, Whitcomb argues for a supernatural Creation (pp. 21 ff.); holds to a superficial appearance of age in Creation (pp. 29 ff.); maintains that God created the Sun, Moon, and stars on the fourth day (pp. 58-59); defines the biblical "kind" (p. 81) and argues for the adequacy of the ark (pp. 82-83); defends the direct Creation of man (pp. 103-4); and attacks the gap theory (pp. 115 ff.).

————. *The World That Perished.* Grand Rapids: Baker, 1973. 155 pp. The author presents defense of the biblical Flood as an explanation for many geological phenomena. He discusses the design of the ark (pp. 19 ff.), argues for a universal flood (pp. 43 ff.), describes the formation of fossil beds (pp. 76 ff.), and defends the Bible as the Word of God (pp. 93 ff.).

Whitcomb, John C., and Henry M. Morris. *The Genesis Flood.* Grand Rapids: Baker, 1961. 518 pp. This book is the best study available of the biblical Flood and its geological implications. The authors provide a formal defense of the universal Flood (pp. 1 ff.), answer arguments against a universal Flood (pp. 55 ff.), show the inadequacies of uniformitarian explanations (pp. 130 ff.), carefully recount the scriptural teaching about the Flood (pp. 212-330), answer problems raised against biblical geology (pp. 331 ff.), and provide appendixes on paleontology and the Edenic curse and on Genesis 11 and the date of the Flood (pp. 454 ff.). They include some fascinating photographic evidence (pp. 161, 167, 182, 183, 190, 192, etc.).

CHAPTER 29
BOOKS ON CULTS

We have seen an explosion of cults in the past few years. They have sprung up everywhere, like mushrooms, overnight. These cults range from the weird and foolish to the violent and dangerous. Perhaps the best resources on cults are those by Walter Martin, but there are many others that provide help also.

Martin, Walter R. *The Kingdom of the Cults.* Rev. ed. Grand Rapids: Zondervan, 1977. 443 pp. This work is probably the most thorough and helpful of the books on cults. The author covers a vast number of cults and gives advice on techniques of cult evangelism. The book treats Jehovah's Witnesses (pp. 34 ff.), Mormonism (pp. 147 ff.), spiritism (pp. 199 ff.), Zen Buddhism (pp. 234 ff.), the Bahai (pp. 252 ff.), Armstrongism (pp. 295 ff.), and more. The author gives advice on techniques of cult evangelism, stressing the need for training believers in biblical doctrine (pp. 340-43): (1) Remember that cultists are lost souls who need to be saved; show them the folly of trying to justify themselves. (2) Try to find some common ground on which to begin; avoid argument. (3) Use subliminal seeding; refer to the truths of salvation. If this is difficult, pray and thank God for Christ's sacrifice and blood that saves us. (4) Remember that they have no security and do not now have eternal life; talk and pray as one who does. (5) Persevere: the cults never give up; neither should we!

Martin, Walter R. *The New Cults.* Santa Ana, Calif.: Vision House, 1980. 419 pp. The author covers The Way International (pp. 37 ff.), Hare Krishna, TM (pp. 79 ff.), EST: Erhard Seminars Training (pp. 105 ff.), the Children of God (pp. 143 ff.), the "I AM" Ascended Masters (pp. 203 ff.), Silva Mind Control (pp. 237 ff.),

Church of the Living Word (pp. 269 ff.), Roy Masters (pp. 297 ff.), Reincarnation (pp. 351 ff.), and The Local Church of Witness Lee (pp. 379 ff.).

Walter Martin's Cults Reference Bible. Santa Ana, Calif.: Vision House, 1981. 1,236 pp. This work is another tool for combating the heresies of cults. Martin provides a brief introduction outlining the beliefs of these cults: Baha'i, Christian Science, Hare Krishna, Jehovah's Witnesses, Mormonism, transcendental meditation (TM), the Unification Church, Unity, The Way International, and The Worldwide Church of God. He also gives a chart giving their basic views on major doctrines (pp. 88-95). All through this Bible he has footnotes giving the twisted teachings of the various cults and then providing the Christian response. He makes no attempt to be comprehensive; thus many cults are left out and many passages are not treated, but what he does give is genuinely helpful. Good examples of such texts include Genesis 3:5, which the Mormons twist to mean that men can become gods (Martin notes that "one should not build one's theology on the words of a liar [Satan]"); John 1:1, which the Jehovah's Witnesses twist to mean Christ was not truly God (Martin concludes, "The Word [Jesus Christ] must be Jehovah God"); and many other passages such as Romans 3:20, 8:3-4, and Ephesians 2:1-3, all of which The Worldwide Church of God twists in various directions. The work concludes with suggestions on witnessing to cults. Altogether, there is a great deal of help in this edition of the Bible.

Bjornstad, James. *Counterfeits at Your Door.* Glendale, Calif.: C/L Publications, 1979. 160 pp. This work stresses the truths of Jesus' deity, humanity, death, saving sacrifice, and resurrection (pp. 15-55). It speaks of meeting Jehovah's Witnesses at the door, contrasting their teaching with Scripture (pp. 58 f.) about Jesus (pp. 65 ff.), about God (pp. 77 ff.), and about salvation (pp. 84 ff.). It also includes a discussion about meeting Mormons at your door (pp. 99 ff.), showing teachings about Jesus (pp. 110 ff.) and God (pp. 117 ff.), and salvation (pp. 131 ff.). Finally it warns about the language game (pp. 145 f.).

Breese, Dave. *Know the Marks of Cults.* Wheaton, Ill.: Victor Books, 1975, 1986. 119 pp. In this brief survey, the author explains why the cults prosper (pp. 15 ff.), documents their extrabiblical revelation (pp. 26 ff.), shows their false basis of salvation (pp. 32 ff.), reveals their doctrinal ambiguity (pp. 55 ff.), demonstrates their defective Christology (pp. 71 ff.), and lists the marks of a cult.

Bromley, David, and Anson Shupe. *Strange Gods.* Boston: Beacon Press, 1981. 249 pp. Bromley identifies some of the cults: Children of God, Unification Church, Hare Krishna, Divine Light Mission, Church of Scientology, the People's Temple (Jonestown) (pp. 21 ff.). He discusses brainwashing versus conversion (pp. 92f.) and reviews the leaders (pp. 128 ff.), fundraising techniques (pp. 157 ff.), and deprogramming (pp. 177 ff.). He urges moderation in dealing with the cults.

Burrell, Maurice C. *The Challenge of the Cults.* Grand Rapids: Baker, 1981. 160 pp. In this brief introduction, the author gives some general characteristics of cults: zeal, charismatic leadership, and so on (pp. 9 ff.). He discusses the Worldwide Church of God (pp. 21 ff.), the Unification Church (pp. 52 ff.), the Divine Light Mission (pp. 73 ff.), transcendental meditation (pp. 92 ff.), the Hare Krishna movement (pp. 108 ff.), and Scientology (pp. 125 ff.).

Enroth, Ronald. *The Lure of the Cults.* Chappaqua, N.Y.: Christian Herald Books, 1979. 139 pp. A survey of cults, this book includes discussions of (1) eastern mystical groups: Hare Krishna, Zen Buddhism, Divine Light Mission, Healthy-Happy-Holy (3 HO), Soka Gakkai, Ananda Marga, Meher Baba; (2) aberrational Christian groups: Family of Love (Children of God), Alamo Christian Foundation, Church of Bible Understanding, Love Family, Glory Barn, the Walk, The Way, the Local Church; (3) self-improvement groups: Synanon, Arica Training, Erhard Seminars Training, transcendental meditation, Scientology; (4) eclectic-syncretistic groups: Unification Church, Church Universal and Triumphant (Guru Ma), Eckankar, Sunburst Communities; and (5) Psychic-Occult-Astral groups: Aetherius Society, UFO cults, M-5000 (pp. 17-35). He shows that cults stress that they have the key to the new age (pp. 37 ff.), follow their leader blindly (pp. 47 ff.), believe they have the truth (pp. 55 ff.), control their followers (pp. 63 ff.), depart from biblical teaching (pp. 75 ff.), stress occult and sexual ideas (pp. 83 ff.), and capitalize on the need for family (pp. 93 ff.). He urges resistence to cultic teaching (pp. 101 ff.).

Larsen, Egon [Egon Lehrburger]. *Strange Sects and Cults.* New York: Hart Publishing Co., 1971. 245 pp. Lehrburger discusses Joanna Southcott, British Israelites, Amish, Father Divine, Soka Gakkai, Russian Castrators, Thugs, snake handlers, The Process, the Church of the Final Judgment (p. 208), and Point Loma Theosophical Community (California: Sectual Breeding Ground). He covers Rosicrucians carefully; discusses the alchemist Rosenkreutz and their relation; Robert Fludd; and goes into subdivisions such as Rudolf Steiner's Anthroposophy (pp. 106 ff.).

Passantino, Robert and Gretchen Passantino. *Answers to the Cultist at Your Door.* Eugene, Ore.: Harvest House, 1981. 206 pp. The authors explain why cultists come knocking (pp. 9 ff.), give answers to Jehovah's Witnesses (pp. 47 ff.) and The Way International (pp. 159 ff.), suggest help for a loved one caught in a cult (pp. 183 ff.), and list some recommended reading (pp. 195 ff.).

Petersen, William J. "Scientology and L. Ron Hubbard." In *Those Curious New Cults.* New Canaan, Conn.: Keats, 1973. Pp. 87-96. Hubbard's book is *Dianetics: The Modern Science of Mental Health.* Petersen points out that Hubbard gets 10 percent of all collected by Scientology centers and sails around on his 320-foot yacht while the Food and Drug Administration gives him trouble (p. 89). Hubbard teaches that engrams are problems that haunt your mind and that getting rid of them is becoming "clear" (p. 91). At $175 for a five-hour session, he helps followers trace their engrams back before they were born (p. 92). God does matter to Scientology (p. 95). Hubbard's philosophy teaches: "Never fear to hurt another in a just cause" (p. 95). Scientologists use "E-meters," which are crude lie detectors

(p. 91). They think Thetans, immortal spirits, have been around for seventy-four trillion years (p. 92).

Sire, James W. *Scripture Twisting.* Downers Grove, Ill.: Inter-Varsity, 1980. 180 pp. The author argues that false teachers wish to pick and choose what to believe in the Bible (p. 10). The book gives twenty ways the cults misread the Bible: (1) inaccurate quotation (p. 32); (2) twisted translation (Jehovah's Witnesses; p. 34); (3) biblical hook (p. 41); (4) ignoring immediate context (p. 52); (5) collapsing contexts (Mormons; p. 58); (6) overspecification (Mormons; p. 62); (7) word play (Eddy; p. 64); (8) figurative fallacy (Eddy; p. 66); (9) speculative readings of prophecy (p. 7); (10) saying but not citing (Daniken; p. 76); (11) selective citing (Jehovah's Witnesses; p. 80); (12) inadequate evidence (p. 82); (13) confused definition (Cayce; p. 90); (14) ignoring alternative explanations (Mormons; p. 96); (15) the obvious fallacy (*Obviously;* p. 99); (16) virtue by association (p. 101); (17) esoteric interpretation (Eddy; p. 107); (18) supplementing biblical authority (Mormons; p. 115); (19) rejecting biblical authority (Renan; p. 118); (20) world-view confusion (Moon; p. 128).

Spittler, Russell P. *Cults and Isms.* Grand Rapids: Baker, 1962. 143 pp. The book discusses twenty alternatives to evangelical Christianity: Mormonism, Seventh Day Adventists, Spiritualism, Christian Science, Jehovah's Witnesses, Unity, Moral Rearmament, Theosophy, Bahaism, Zen Buddhism, Anglo-Israelism, Astrology, Father Divine, Rosicrucianism, Swedenborgianism, Roman Catholicism, Humanism, Unitarianism, Liberalism, and so on.

Van Baalen, Jan Karel. *The Chaos of Cults.* Grand Rapids: Eerdmans, 1938, 1962. 414 pp. An old classic but still valuable, the book covers Mormonism (pp. 188 ff.), Seventh Day Adventism (pp. 228 ff.), Jehovah's Witnesses (pp. 257 ff.), and so on.

CHAPTER 30
BOOKS ON
CONTEMPORARY ISSUES

David O. Beale's *In Pursuit of Purity: American Fundamentalism Since 1850* (Greenville, S.C.: Unusual Publications, 1986. 457 pp.) traces the history of American Fundamentalism with great care. He defines the essence of Fundamentalism as the unqualified acceptance of and obedience to the Scriptures (p. 3). He also distinguishes between the periods of nonconformist Fundamentalism (1857-1930) and separatist Fundamentalism (1930 to the present, pp. 5-6). It is heartwarming to read of the old warriors who established the Niagara Bible Conference (pp. 24 ff.) and contributed to *The Fundamentals* (pp. 41-44). Dr. Beale describes in detail the Prophetic Bible Conference held at Holy Trinity Church in New York City in 1878 (pp. 48-54).

An important feature of the book is the sketches of important Christian leaders such as A. T. Pierson and A. J. Gordon (pp. 61-63), W. B. Riley (p. 106), Charles Hodge (pp. 136 f.), and J. Gresham Machen (pp. 156 f.). It is a surprise to see an old photograph of John Roach Straton preaching from a portable automobile pulpit (p. 213).

Dr. Beale portrays the rise of American liberalism (pp. 69 ff.) and the answering voice of the World's Christian Fundamentals Association (pp. 97 ff.). It is a thrill to see photographs of leaders such as Scofield, Torrey, Gray, Rader, Munhall, and Haldeman (p. 101). Dr. Beale recounts both the good and the bad of the battles among the Presbyterians (pp. 113 ff.), the Baptists (pp. 173 ff.), and the Methodists (pp. 303 ff.); and he includes sections on famous heresy trials (pp. 143 ff.), the fall of Princeton Seminary (pp. 165 ff.), and the adventures of J. Frank Norris (pp. 232 ff.). There is also a section on Ian Paisley's Free Presbyterian Church of Ulster (pp. 331 ff.).

Dr. Beale evaluates Fundamentalism today and in the future (pp. 341 ff.). He includes a list of the most significant Fundamentalist leaders (pp. 354-55), which will surely provoke discussion. There is a grand bibliography (pp. 401-30) and a thorough index (pp. 431-57). This is a book that belongs in every pastor's library. There is no way of understanding where we are unless we look back to see the path we have traveled.

Another valuable work from the same author is David O. Beale's *S.B.C.: House on the Sand?* (Greenville, S.C.: Unusual Publications, 1985. 232 pp.). It is refreshing to find a book on a controversial subject that presents an amazing variety of facts with both calmness and kindness. This book contains none of the usual sensationalism and bitterness that is often found in controversy. Dr. Beale documents the drift of the Southern Baptist Convention into liberalism. He gives no rash charges; he simply quotes from the preachers and teachers themselves to prove beyond doubt the exact position they advocate. After documenting the position of the early leaders of the Southern Baptist Theological Seminary (John Broadus, E. Y. Mullins, A. T. Robertson, etc.), he shows that it was Ellis A. Fuller who brought Nels F. S. Ferré to Southern in 1947 (p. 32). Dr. Beale then goes on to quote Ferré's opinions: "outworn morality of parts of the Old Testament" (p. 33), "the use of the Bible as the final authority for Christian Truth is idolatry" (p. 34), "Jesus never was nor became God" (p. 34). Dr. Beale describes Dr. Roy Lee Honeycutt's declaration of war against the conservative elements within the convention (pp. 43-44). He also documents the Hollyfield Thesis that describes the loss of faith in the students at Southern Seminary (pp. 44-46).

Dr. Beale also covers Southwestern Seminary (pp. 50-58), documenting President Russell H. Dilday's attack on inerrancy of Scripture (p. 56). He shows the drift of New Orleans Baptist Theological Seminary (pp. 59-64), Golden Gate Baptist Theological Seminary (pp. 65-69), Southeastern Baptist Theological Seminary (pp. 70-75), and Midwestern Baptist Theological Seminary (pp. 76-83). He also treats the Southern Baptist colleges such as Baylor and Furman (pp. 91 ff.), the liberalism in the Broadman Bible Commentary (pp. 111-19), the Training Union materials (pp. 120 ff.), and others. This is the kind of book that should be put into the hands of Southern Baptist pastors and lay people everywhere.

The thesis of Philip Wesley Comfort's *Quest for the Original Text of the New Testament* (Grand Rapids: Baker, 1992. 200 pp.) is that the "earliest extant manuscripts are the closest copies we have to the N.T. autographs, and they are the documents from which we can recover the original text of the N.T." (p. 17). He argues that the Alexandrian text preserves readings closest to the original text (p. 23). The name *Textus Receptus* was first applied to Elzevir's Greek N.T. (2nd ed., 1633; p. 25). He recounts the history of the search for the oldest manuscripts: Lachmann, Tregelles, Henry Alford, Tischendorf, Westcott and Hort (pp. 27 ff.). He commends Aland's attempt to find the original readings in his Greek N.T. (pp. 29 f.). But he warns that Aland has failed to accept the early dates of some of these manuscripts and hence does not give them the weight they deserve (pp. 30 f.). Comfort evaluates P45, P46, P47 (pp. 75-81), and P66, P72, P75 (pp. 92-97). He shows patterns of descent for Matthew, Mark, Luke, John, and Acts (pp. 106-12). He gives a list of readings from ancient manuscripts adopted by NA 26 (p. 124). Comfort gives a list of manuscripts that should be considered for the original wording (pp. 130-33) and suggests some ancient revisions (pp. 134-56). He concludes with a select bibliography (pp. 167-77) and photographs of some of the manuscripts.

Valuable insight is offered in Edward E. Ericson's *Solzhenitsyn: The Moral Vision* (Grand Rapids: Eerdmans, 1980. 239 pp.). When the courageous Russian writer Solzhenitsyn was exiled to the West, the media lionized him, but now he is being given the silent treatment. The reason is that he is far too conservative and too religious for the liberals in the media. Ericson traces through Solzhenitsyn's writings his ideas on religious and moral questions. He describes the religious basis for all of Solzhenitsyn's writings (pp. 6-7); recounts his famous prayer (p. 10); shows his courage in maintaining unpopular views (p. 13); warns against people who raise a godless generation (p. 22); describes his beautiful portrait of the old Christian Matryona (pp. 26-27); charges that Communism uses religious phraseology because it makes religious demands on its followers (p. 28); stresses the value of the persecuted soul (p. 40); gives a remarkable description of Alyosha the Baptist, the only one in the prison camp who could be cheerful and positive no matter what the conditions (pp. 41-43); shows how Alyosha as well as Solzhenitsyn himself could use the Scriptures powerfully (p. 54); makes comparisons between Dante's *Inferno* and the Communist prison camp system (pp. 55-56); gives apt illustrations of temptation in Russia (pp. 68-69); pictures Stalin in the lowest hell (pp. 70-71); holds that when you lose everything in this life, you are free (pp. 74-75); attacks secular humanist values, specifically Mrs. Roosevelt's visit to Russian prisons (pp. 82 ff.); and recounts Solzhenitsyn's joining of the Russian Orthodox Church (p. 120), his religious and moral principles (pp. 160 ff.), and his high regard for Christians in Soviet prison camps (pp. 169 f.). Also important are the descriptions of Solzhenitsyn's encounters with Christians in prison (pp. 174 f.).

Michael Horton's anthology *The Agony of Deceit* (Chicago: Moody Press, 1990. 284 pp.) is a powerful rebuke to television preachers who are discrediting the ministry by their false teaching and arrogant conduct. The contributors range from well-known conservatives such as R. C. Sproul, to the former Surgeon General C. Everett Koop, to Charismatics such as Walter Martin, and a liberal, John Dart. Horton argues that the basis of unity is the ecumenical creeds (p. 23). It is strange that he does not suggest the Bible. R. C. Sproul maintains that the right of private interpretation does not mean the "Christian is free to find in Scripture something that is not there" (p. 35). He goes on to document many heretical statements of television preachers (pp. 39-45).

Lindsley attacks the "health and wealth" evangelists (pp. 50 ff.). Krabbendam writes on Scripture twisting (pp. 63 ff.), showing that Pat Robertson denies that the Bible is perfect (p. 65). Krabbendam urges the study of theology (pp. 66 f.) and gives examples of the interpretation of Scripture (pp. 73f.). Walter Martin attacks the idea that man can become God (pp. 89 ff.), disagreeing with the Mormons, Armstrongism, Gary North's Reconstructionism, and so on (pp. 90-103). Rosenbladt warns against those who make a magical Christ and believe in magical powers for Christians (pp. 107 ff.). Horton demonstrates that Robert Schuller and Pat Robertson deny the sinfulness of man (pp. 135-37). Godfrey criticizes the television church (pp. 153 ff.), holding that the local church is necessary for teaching, fellowship, the sacraments, and prayer (pp. 158-61). C. Everett Koop attacks faith healers (pp. 169 ff.). Schultze questions the link between television and evangelism (pp. 185 ff.), holding that television is not a communicator but a performer (p. 192). He gives some serious guidelines for controlling television ministries (pp. 201-2). Dart criticizes the whole conservative movement, charging it with alienation from the world (pp. 205 ff.). Nederhood condemns the linking of religion and appeals for money (pp. 233 ff.). He suggests that the Reformation was powerful because it separated religion from money raising (p. 235). This is surely one of the most thought-provoking (and disturbing) books written in recent years.

The false religious teaching that is seducing Christianity is the subject of Dave Hunt and T. A. McMahon's *Seduction of Christianity* (Eugene, Ore.: Harvest House, 1985. 239 pp.). He notes Robert Schuller's teaching of Christianity as success (p. 15) and Peale's urging positive thinking as the solution (p. 24). John Denver popularized the idea of worshiping yourself as god (p. 58); the trend is to worship Lucifer (pp. 60 f.); and Mother Teresa is an ecumenist (p. 71). The authors hold that the Lord quoted Psalm 82:6 to show the rebellion of man (p. 87), attack Yonggi Cho's fourth dimension (pp. 111, 139), show how C. S. Lovett uses the mind sciences (pp. 115, 173), attack the use of the Ouija board (pp. 176 ff.), point out the errors of Freud (pp. 184 f.), reveal Dobson's evangelical humanism (pp. 192 f.), demonstrate that self-esteem is a nonbiblical idea (p. 195), attack the Positive Mental Attitude movement (pp. 217 ff.), and appeal to believers to guard themselves from idols (p. 225).

A thoughtful explanation of the current militant actions of the Arab world is Ishak Ibraham's *Black Gold and Holy War* (Nashville:

Thomas Nelson, 1983. 129 pp.). Ibraham sees the explanation in a resurgence of Islam: "For all its followers, whether moderate or zealot, young or old, religious or secular, Islam carries the harsh, intolerant imperative to convert or conquer unbelievers. To the Muslim idealist there is no room for moderation" (p. 9). He argues that Muslims in Lebanon will not tolerate Christian leadership of an Arab country (p. 10). He holds that the Islamic concept of "community of believers" (Ummah) will lead to increased pressure by the Arab bloc against the West (pp. 18-19). He documents the growth of Islam in America (pp. 21 ff.). He thinks that the Arab world will use oil to gain superiority over the West (pp. 32-33). Under Islamic law non-Muslims must be either converted, subjugated, or eliminated (p. 35). Mohammed advocated "warring against non-Muslims to bring them under control" (pp. 53-54). Whether it is military or economic holy war (jihad), it is a major strategy of Islamic states (p. 57). Christianity knows a loving God who saves; Islam teaches a stern god who judges (pp. 63-64). To a Muslim, love is a weakness; God cannot be weak (p. 73). Therefore, when Sadat negotiated the peace treaty with Israel, he sealed his death warrant in the Arab world (pp. 92-93). Ibraham documents the lack of religious freedom in the Islamic world (pp. 98-106). Islam and communism can agree to being anti-Western (pp. 114 f.). The present economic conflict is only a foretaste of a much greater religious conflict that the future of Islam will bring to the western world.

In a day in which people tend to settle biblical interpretations by experience and "case histories," Alex Konya's *Demons* (Schaumburg, Ill.: Regular Baptist Press, 1990. 151 pp.) is a refreshing work that looks to the Scriptures for all the answers. Konya examines the biblical teaching on demon possession (pp. 19 ff.). He argues that the biblical examples were so obvious that even unspiritual people could recognize the possession (p. 31). He denies that the Lord Jesus Christ was an exorcist; He was the divine Son of God with infinite authority (pp. 36 ff.). He holds that the apostles were authorized by the Lord Jesus and given the power to work miracles, including casting out demons, to manifest God's approval (pp. 51 ff.). He denies that Christians can be demon possessed (pp. 89 ff.). He defends the Bible as our all-sufficient help; we need no other help from case histories or other experiences to prove doctrine (pp. 93 ff.). He concludes with a strong bibliography (pp. 137-51).

John F. MacArthur's *The Charismatics* (Grand Rapids: Zondervan, 1978. 224 pp.) presents a kindly but clear criticism of the Charismatic movement. One need not agree with all the author's interpretations to recognize the force of his argument. He attacks the idea that the Bible is still being written (pp. 15 ff.); shows how a slight deviation from revelation can lead to extremes of misinterpretation (pp. 37 f.); gives five principles of sound biblical interpretation (pp. 44 ff.); provides good answers to the verses the Charismatics advance (pp. 49 ff.); shows that the Charismatics start with experience, not the Bible (pp. 62 f.); brings this line of reasoning down to the question "Is authority in God's Word or in experience?" (pp. 71 ff.); holds that the Book of Acts is a narrative, not a norm to be followed (p. 102); charges that the Charismatics confuse the baptism and the filling (p. 128); criticizes the false healings of the Charismatics (pp. 130-55), especially those of Kuhlman (pp. 136 f.); shows that non-Christians speak in tongues (pp. 175 ff.); argues that gifts cannot guarantee spirituality (pp. 184 ff.); contrasts true spirituality in a difficult life with the "get zapped by the jolly Spirit" kind of life (p. 188); describes the true filling with the Spirit (pp. 189 ff.); and discusses what we can learn from the Charismatics (pp. 200 ff.), warning against dead orthodoxy, suppressing emotion, lack of participation in worship, lack of commitment, and so forth. This is a book that is not only a help to the pastor but also one that can be put into the hands of the Charismatic to recover him from such an error.

Neil Postman's *Amusing Ourselves to Death* (New York: Penguin Books, 1985. 184 pp.) discusses public discourse in the age of show business. The author mentions that the Lincoln-Douglas debates were seven hours long (p. 44); contrasts such intellectual efforts with the style of Graham, Falwell, and others today (p. 56); and notes that pictures took over advertising in the 1890s (p. 60). Postman points out that the age of exposition was when the printing press ruled (p. 63), that the telegraph began the change toward unconnected facts (p. 65), and that all public understanding is now shaped by television (p. 78). Television stages the world (p. 92). The credibility of the speaker, the author says, is now the test of truth (p. 102). He criticizes religious television (pp. 114 f.); contends Robert Schuller's purpose is the same as the A-Team (pp. 120 f.); and charges the religious television leaders with blasphemy (p. 123). Television commercials, he contends, make the viewers feel valuable (p. 128). Television has emptied discourse of content and history (p. 136), is teaching by amusement (pp. 145 f.), and is forming American culture into a show-business entertainment (pp. 157 ff.). Postman urges that we criticize television, teach people what television is doing, and learn how to be critical in our thinking (pp. 161 ff.).

Jacob van Bruggen's *Future of the Bible* (New York: Nelson, 1978. 192 pp.) gives a thorough indictment of the dynamic equivalence theory. The author discusses the principles behind the theory (pp. 67 ff.); gives four reasons that the theory must be rejected (p. 84); and then provides numerous examples of the mistranslations of the dynamic equivalence theory as seen in the TEV (pp. 85-96, 151-68). Some of the poor translations in the TEV that he criticizes include Gen. 1:26 (p. 86); Gen. 15:6 (p. 87); Ps. 110:4 (p. 89); Rom. 5:10 (p. 91); Rev. 5:5 (p. 92); and Isa. 52:13–53:12 (pp. 93 ff.). He also faults the New International Version (pp. 171, 175, 182, 185). Although he favors the majority text, he criticizes modern translations fairly and carefully. He openly urges that the KJV be updated and renewed (p. 148). He does not hesitate to criticize all modern translations when they fail to follow a strong reading (pp. 191-92).

Herbert Weiner's *Wild Goats of Ein Gedi* (Garden City, N.Y.: Doubleday, 1961.) remains one of the most thought-provoking appraisals of the national culture of Israel. The author is a Reform (liberal) rabbi with a wide experience in reading and travel. He charges that although there is great diversity of religious belief in Israel, the level of spirituality is nearly zero (pp. 7 ff.). The Muslim peasant is superstitious; the educated worship Arab nationalism; few abstain from liquor (p. 9). The established Christian movements (Roman and Greek Catholic) want the status quo maintained because they can control their own populace (p. 32). Newer groups (Baptists) feel discriminated against (pp. 36 f.). He describes how some Jews have converted to Catholicism but retain much Jewish influence (pp. 105-6); he describes the ultra-Orthodox Jews ("Guardians of the Wall") who regard the state of Israel as an atheistic abomination and will spit at women who peek at their synagogue (pp. 129-44). He describes the famous Ben Gurion as admitting that most Jewish people do not have God in their hearts and that he could not believe in God either (pp. 222-23). The Orthodox hold that the only proper knowledge of the Bible "must involve the post-biblical interpretations of the rabbis" (p. 234). The young people of the land are very materialistic.

CHAPTER 31
BOOKS ON
BIBLICAL ETHICS

The best-organized work on this topic is T. B. Maston, *Biblical Ethics* (New York: World, 1967. 300 pp.), a survey by a former professor at Southwestern Baptist Theological Seminary. It is organized according to the divisions of the Old and New Testaments and apocryphal Jewish-Christian writings. Under the Law (the five books of Moses), the author sees five central concepts: the character of God (what He commands is good, etc.), the nature of man (unity of race, image of God), the law, God's control of history, and didactic narratives (the character of Abraham, Joseph). In dealing with the Covenant Code, he sees the Ten Commandments as "an epitome of the covenant" (p. 18). The two tables of the law show man's relation to God balanced with man's relation to man.

Chapter 2 deals with the Prophets, seeing in them stern opposition to all that violates morality (p. 41) and noting how they exalt righteousness above ritual (p. 49). Amos is the prophet of justice (p. 52); Hosea, the prophet of love (p. 53); Isaiah, the prophet of divine transcendence (p. 55); and Micah, the preacher against the sins of the cities (p. 57). Chapter 3 outlines the Writings. Chronicles is didactic history (e.g., "turn from their wicked ways" in II Chron. 7:14; p. 72). Ezra and Nehemiah focus on moral and social problems. Psalms reveals the moral character of God—His steadfast love and wrath (pp. 74 ff.). Proverbs explains wisdom and righteousness, covering topics such as the tongue, the strange woman, the family, and bribery. Job, the world's greatest poem, asks why the innocent suffer. One answer is that suffering may enrich one's fellowship with God (p. 99). Chapter 4 deals with ethics as revealed in the Apocrypha, the Pseudepigrapha, and the Dead Sea Scrolls.

Chapter 5, on the Synoptic Gospels, begins Maston's treatment of the New Testament. He says the kingdom of God is central to ethical teaching (p. 152) and describes the way of the disciple as one of humility, forgiveness, service, fruit-bearing, and the cross. He notes six comparisons that Jesus makes concerning the law (Matt. 5:21-48): no murder—no anger; no adultery—no adulterous thought; divorce for "some indecency"—no divorce (except 5:32); no false oaths—no oaths; an eye for an eye—no retaliation; love for neighbor—love for enemy. Jesus filled the law with added meaning.

Chapter 6 covers the Pauline Epistles. Paul used the teachings of Jesus but was more specific and more negative (pp. 177 ff.). Paul balanced doctrine and practice (Rom. 1-11; 12-16). Paul's basic ethic is the moral character of God (p. 185). Major concepts in Paul's ethics include law, union with Christ, work of the Spirit, freedom, and submission. A list of vices and virtues gives the crowning virtue as love (p. 207).

Chapter 7 deals with the Johannine literature. John's ethic is theocentric (p. 216): God is light, love, and so on. The main thoughts in John's Gospel are eternal life, fruitful life, new commandment, and the will of God. The other New Testament writings are the subject of Chapter 8. Maston concludes, "God is as central in the ethics of the Bible as He is in its theology. . . . The dominant ethical appeal in the Bible is for the people of God to be like Him" (p. 282).

Other helpful treatments of biblical ethics include the following works.

Clifford E. Bajema's *Abortion and the Meaning of Personhood* (Grand Rapids: Baker, 1974. 114 pp.) presents the Christian argument that abortion is the killing of an innocent human being (p. 1). Bajema shows that the world is questioning absolute moral values (pp. 7 f.) and unconditional love (pp. 10 f.); argues that the zygote-embryo-fetus is alive, human, and a human being (pp. 15 ff.); shows that brain waves are detected at forty-three days (p. 27); argues that the image of God in man weighs against abortion (pp. 30 ff.); discusses Exodus 21:22 ff. (pp. 50 ff.); argues that there are no grounds for abortion except to save the life of the mother (pp. 61 ff.); and discusses the social problems of the woman (pp. 75 ff.).

Wesley C. Baker's *Open End of Christian Morals.* (Philadelphia: Westminster, 1967. 170 pp.) offers a liberal discussion. Concerning the church's teaching people to be good, he says, "I send my child up there to learn the difference between right and wrong, and for some reason the teaching doesn't come through. You're falling down on your real job!" (p. 17). Further, he holds that the moral code is really a relationship (p. 21), attacks the idea of morality being a duty (p. 26), and changes the statement "I don't care what happens to me; I want to do the *right* things" into "Whatever the eventual justice of the situation, I want to feel morally adequate" (p. 31). Baker admits he was a pacifist during World War II in order to have a morally proper position, but now he questions his decision (pp. 32-33). The author shows that Jesus was not thinking defensively but lovingly (pp. 35-36). He criticizes the American service clubs with their mottos: "Service Above Self," "Service to Mankind," "We Help Others," and "If one tilts his head a little to one side he can almost hear the blast of the trumpets over the alms box" (p. 38). Baker holds that it was loving for David to wrest the kingdom from Saul and that love sent Schweitzer to the Congo, Eugene V. Debs into politics, and so on (p. 64).

In the careful survey *Ethics in a Permissive Society* (New York: Harper and Row, 1971. 223 pp.) by William Barclay, a liberal, sets forth the Old Testament teaching on ethics (pp. 13 ff.) and the teachings of Jesus (pp. 27 ff.) and Paul (pp. 43 ff.). The author sets forth Fletcher's situation ethics and then answers it (pp. 69 ff.). Barclay gives the New Testament teaching on work (pp. 92 ff.): Man has a right (1) to work, (2) to a living wage, and (3) to reasonable working conditions. The author offers a Christian view of pleasure (in which he attacks gambling, drugs, alcoholism, pp. 109 ff.). He discusses the Christian and his money (pp. 143 ff.) and the Christian and the community (pp. 172 ff.). Barclay attacks racialism, urges Christian's to get into politics, urges pacifism, calls for Person-to- Person Ethics, permits divorce for incompatibility (p. 204), and urges sex education (p. 212). He includes a bibliography.

A brief survey is Henlee H. Barnette's *Introducing Christian Ethics* (Nashville: Broadman, 1961. 176 pp.). The author, using the Revised Standard Version, traces the ethics of the Decalogue, of prophets, of sages, of Christ (especially in the Sermon on the Mount), of Paul, of other New Testament writers, and of the Holy Spirit (Acts). Part II discusses problems: duties to self, marriage, and family; race relations (it urges integration, p. 142); economic life; and political life. The work argues against the saving clause in Matthew 5 and the remarriage right in I Corinthians 7:15 (p. 116). The author teaches ethics at Southern Baptist Theological Seminary.

In this thorough survey, *Lying: Moral Choice in Public and Private Life* (N.Y.: Pantheon, 1978. 326 pp.), by Sissela Bok, lying is advocated only in a crisis when all alternatives have been exhausted (pp. 108 ff.). The author portrays Augustine, Wesley, and others as teaching never to lie (pp. 32 ff.). She gives common excuses for lying: denial, lack of responsibility, "virtuous" reasons (avoiding harm, producing benefits, to be fair, to be truthful[!], pp. 74-89). Bok quotes Augustine: "If any lies, like other sins, steal upon us, they should seek not to be justified but to be pardoned" (p. 73). Along with lying to liars, she gives Augustine's example of refusing to deceive Priscilla (pp. 123 ff.) and gives Johnson's lies about Goldwater and the war (pp. 170 ff.). The author reproduces results of a poll: 69 percent of Americans think politicians have consistently lied in the past 10 years; 40 percent hold that politicians are so much alike that it does not matter whom you vote for (pp. 174 ff.). She gives concrete examples of lying in the medical profession (pp. 222 ff.). A liar takes the excuse for lying more seriously than others and magnifies his lack of alternatives (pp. 86 f.). The author teaches ethics at Harvard Medical School and is on the Ethics Advisory Board of HEW.

A well-read newspaperman's evaluation of LSD and religion is *The Private Sea* (Chicago: Quadrangle Books, 1967. 255 pp.) by William Braden. The author holds that LSD provides an experience akin to religious mysticism. Eastern religions stress the immanence of God; LSD, according to Braden, gives an experience like this (pp. 118-19). Thomas J. J. Altizer is similar in holding that the Incarnation and Crucifixion happened but not the Resurrection! Braden says that the transcendent God died; all that is left is immanent God, who became part of the universe (pp. 158 f.). He concludes that LSD leads to quietism, which is dangerous to society (pp. 213 f.). He says that we need the fiction of a divine law to hold society together (pp. 216 ff.). He describes his own experiences on LSD (pp. 229 ff.).

Practical Christian Ethics (Grand Rapids: Zondervan, 1959. 240 pp.), by C. B. Eavey, presents a practical application of ethical principles. He organizes material on duties to God (love, work, worship, etc.; pp. 33 f.), duties to others (love, compassion, justice, truth, etc.; pp. 55 f.), duties to self (mind, body, etc.; p. 76), duties to nature (animals, etc., p. 102), duties of sex life, duties to married and family life, duties in the community (pp. 148 f.), duties to the church (pp. 165 f.), duties of economic and industrial life (p. 179), duties of political life (p. 195), and duties of leisure time. On sex and marriage Eavey observes that sex is more than merely repro-ducing the race (p. 116) and urges duty to marry (p. 125). He says, "Though marriage may fail on physical grounds, unhappy mar-riages are caused almost always by lack of mutual respect and lack of mutual consideration" (p. 135). He states that Jesus does not command divorce but permits it (p. 143) and that when an unbe-liever deserts, the Christian partner is free (p. 144). The author says, "There is no evidence of [Jesus'] ever refusing an invitation to a social gathering" (p. 155). The book urges athletics, reading, and music as leisure time activities and warns against radio and television (pp. 207-30). There is also an extended bibliography (pp. 233-37).

Millard J. Erickson's *Relativism in Contemporary Christian Ethics* (Grand Rapids: Baker, 1964. 170 pp.) is a criticism of situation ethics. The author gives the background for present rela-tivism (pp. 1-33). He criticizes Fletcher for criticizing Jesus (pp. 54-55) and objects to *Situation Ethics,* particularly (1) its arbitrari-ness: the same act being right or wrong depending on the way it is done (pp. 99 f.); (2) its vagueness: anything done in love is right, and love does not help to decide action (p. 102); (3) its tendency to legalism: "No unwanted and unintended baby should ever be born" (p. 103; quoting Fletcher's *Situation Ethics*, p. 39); (4) its inaccuracy of description or analysis in moral discourse (pp. 104-13); (5) its failure to face moral difficulties (pp. 113 f.). Erickson also points up Fletcher's lack of needed information, neglect of long-range factors, ignoring of unresolved problems, lack of ultimate criteria, naiveté regarding the goodness of man, oversight of other alternatives, neglect of binding relationships, excessive individualism, and the problem of moral instruction. The author stresses the need of love of God above all (p. 121); holds that good is what God wills (p. 130); says goodness is an expression of His nature (p. 131); classes ethical methodologies as subjective or objective, distinguishing his view as principled rather than legalistic (p. 137); and suggests that either normative principles do not conflict or that there is a hierarchy of principles (pp. 141 f.).

Norman L. Geisler's *Ethics: Alternatives and Issues* (Grand Rapids: Zondervan, 1971. 270 pp.) is an appeal for normative ethics. He holds to hierarchically ordered universal norms (p. 114-36) and discusses the Christian and war, social responsibility, sex, abortion, mercy killing, capital punishment, and so on. His work *The Roots of Evil* (Grand Rapids: Zondervan, 1978. 96 pp.) is a philosophical survey of the apparent contradictions between the existence of evil and God. The author discusses illusionism, dualism, finitism, sadism, impossiblism, atheism, and theism. He argues against atheism. An all powerful God *can* defeat evil without destroying free choice. An all-loving God *will* defeat evil without destroying free choice. Evil is not yet fully defeated; therefore, God will fully defeat evil in the future (p. 39). Thomas Aquinas argued that this is not the best possible world; rather it is the best possible *way* to the best world (p. 45). God has given man the ability to choose his eternal destiny. Good men are frustrated by evil; bad men by good. Heaven is a place where there is no more evil to frustrate good men; hell is a place where there will be no more good to frustrate evil men (p. 61). Against universalism he argues that evil men should not be able to veto the highest good that good men can attain (p. 62).

In *The Electronic Golden Calf* (Cambridge, Mass.: Cowley, 1990. 225 pp.), by Gregor T. Goethals, the author discusses religion and images. Goethals describes the position of Bernard against images in the church (pp. 30-31), shows the same position in Calvin and Zwingli (who were opposed to any "strange gods") (pp. 48-49), notes Jonathan Edwards's love of nature (p. 59), shows how Protestant artists lack religious opportunity (p. 61), and discusses the artist Cole and his paintings on the "voyage of life" (pp. 62-65). The author believes that America is saturated with images (p. 107); that television provides values, reality, and authority (p. 109); that heroes are selfish (p. 110); and that television news gives us a selective, fabricated view of reality (p. 124), suppressing some stories and pushing others (p. 130). Goethals gives four meanings for American society and culture (pp. 46 ff.); believes that the high arts do not shape public values but that pop art and culture do (p. 156); holds that the mass media makes a huge canopy of fabrication (p. 161); and gives four points of convergence between liberal and conservative faiths: charismatic leadership, polarization of belief, conversion, and sacramentalism (p. 170).

From the standpoint of liberal Democratic politics and liberal theology, Kent Greenawalt's *Religious Convictions and Political Choice* (Oxford: Oxford University Press, 1988. 266 pp.) examines the influence religion should have on politics. He mentions that the New England Federalists of the 1790s held that some religion is essential to morality and that government may support religion for secular reasons (p. 17); argues for total avoidance of religious support in government (p. 20); states that liberal religion emphasizes rationality and downgrades scriptural revelation (p. 21); admits that before the American Revolution, and in all intervening periods, great numbers of people believed in religious principles and held that Christian revelation bears on political choices (p. 25); sees obvious guidance in the Ten Commandments and the Golden Rule (p. 31); and recognizes that a person who believes in inerrant Scripture may believe that adultery is always wrong, but others, more skeptical, may doubt their ability to ascertain ethical truth (p. 33). The author holds that government has no business interfering with sexual acts of consenting adults, even in view of AIDS (p. 90); thinks that *Roe* v. *Wade* was wrong but that legislatures should protect abortion; yet he is closer to pro-life than pro-choice (pp. 120 ff.), arguing that if children under age two have protection of law, so should those yet unborn (pp. 136 f.). He also discusses school prayer and a moment of silence (pp. 196 ff.).

In Nolan B. Harmon's *Ministerial Ethics and Etiquette* (1928; reprint, Nashville: Abingdon, 1987. 187 pp.), the author writes of the "little ways of gentleness that endear preachers to people" (p. 15). He warns against any conduct unbecoming an officer and a gentleman (and a preacher, p. 20); holds that "all the preaching a man may do will not atone for unpaid bills" (p. 46); urges pastoral calling for the sick and the bereaved, for the elderly and the shut-ins, and for new contacts (p. 83); and warns ministers to be careful visiting women, recommending that the pastor take his wife along at such times.

According to Anthony E. Hartle's *Moral Issues in Military Decision Making* (Lawrence, Kan.: University Press of Kansas, 1989. 180 pp.), war is the hardest place for making ethical decisions (p. 1). The author shows how Lord Kitchener put Boers in concentration camps where they starved, claims that the press turned against the war (pp. 13 f.), and gives the elements of a military profession (p. 19). He states that professional ethics does three things—protects society from exploitation, enhances the image of the professional, and may articulate warrant for certain actions morally wrong for a nonprofessional (p. 27). Likewise, he says three elements shape military ethics—values of society, exigencies of the profession, and the laws of war (p. 29). Hartle argues that the laws of war were formed by the Hague-Geneva conventions (p. 61); holds that war should not begin without previous warning by declaration or ultimatum (p. 64); lists as forbidden in warfare poison, treacherous killing, killing men who have surrendered, declaring no quarter, using weapons that cause unnecessary suffering (p. 66); and lists as forbidden behind the lines prison torture, taking hostage, degrading treatment, and executing people without standard court guarantees (pp. 68-70). Among war crimes he includes use of poison, firing on places undefended and without military value, abuse of or firing on truce flags, abuse of Red Cross, use of civilian clothing, pillage, killing without trial, and so on (p. 70). The author gives case histories of Major Blue (pp. 78 ff.), gives many case studies (pp. 129 ff.), and has a thorough bibliography (pp. 171-76).

Carl F. H. Henry's *Baker's Dictionary of Christian Ethics* (Grand Rapids: Baker, 1973. 726 pp.) gives up-to-date, although short, discussions on "relevant" subjects, from "Abandonment" and "Abortion" to "Zoroastrian Ethics." Roger R. Nicole on "Divorce" (pp. 189-90) holds that the Matthean exception permits divorce for the innocent party but is unsure on the Pauline privilege in I Corinthians 7:15. The article "Euthanasia" attacks all types as a violation of the fifth commandment (pp. 22-23). In his *Christian Personal Ethics* (Grand Rapids: Eerdmans, 1957. 615 pp.), he discusses naturalism (pp. 21 ff.), idealism (pp. 97 ff.), and existentialism (pp. 120 ff.). He then turns to Christianity and the moral revelation: the image of God (pp. 145 ff.), the superiority of Christian ethics to speculative morality (pp. 161 ff.), fallen morality (pp. 172 ff.), the good as the will of God (pp. 209 ff.), and love, the divine imperative (pp. 219 ff.). The author reviews Old Testament teaching (pp. 264 ff.), the Sermon on the Mount (pp. 278 ff.), New Testament teaching (pp. 327 ff.), Christian ethics and the morality of the regenerate man (pp. 383 ff.), Jesus as the ideal (pp. 398 ff.), principles of conduct (pp. 419 ff.), empowering of the Holy Spirit (pp. 437 ff.), distinctive New Testament virtues (pp. 472 ff.), and conscience (pp. 509 ff.).

Arthur F. Holmes's *War and Christian Ethics* (Grand Rapids: Baker, 1975. 356 pp.) is an anthology from Plato and Cicero to the present. He offers good quotations from Luther's works on the soldier and his conscience (pp. 140 ff.) and from Calvin on civil authority and the use of force from the *Institutes* (pp. 165 ff.). He winds up weakly with Catholic Drinan advocating pacifism (pp. 318 ff.) and Paul Ramsey advocating limited war in justice but not a nuclear war in any terms ("The Just War and Nuclear Deterrence," pp. 341 ff.).

Law, Morality, and the Bible (Downer's Grove, Ill.: InterVarsity, 1978. 252 pp.), by Bruce Kaye and Gordon Wenham, records a symposium. Gordon Wenham writes on grace and law in the Old Testament, stressing covenant relations to God (pp. 5 ff.) and the Ten Commandments (pp. 27 ff.); Robin Nixon writes on fulfilling law in the Gospels and Acts (pp. 53 ff.); Kaye writes on law and morals in the Epistles (pp. 72 ff.) and on social order and Romans 13 (pp. 104 ff.); Oliver Barclay writes on the nature of Christian morality (pp. 125 ff.); James Packer attacks situation ethics (pp. 151 ff.) and discusses conscience (pp. 175 ff.); Dennis Winter writes on motivation in Christian behavior (pp. 193 ff.); Bronnert discusses social ethics (pp. 216 ff.); Norman Anderson writes on public law and legislation (pp. 230 ff.), dividing law into ceremonial, civil, and moral (p. 231).

A criticism of unethical practices in journalism by a journalist is Stephen Klaidman and Tom Beauchamp's *Virtuous Journalist* (New York: Oxford University Press, 1987. 246 pp.). The authors assert that a free press serves the public interest better than any system of press control (p. 10). But there are rules and principles (p. 15): virtues and character (p. 17), fairness (pp. 20 f.), and so on. They hold that the truth is a standard (pp. 30 ff.), describe the "reasonable person" (pp. 32 f.), urge completeness of truth (p. 34), and list aids to proper understanding of truth (p. 40), including objectivity (p. 44) and accuracy (p. 50). They counsel avoiding bias (pp. 59 ff.); contrast distortion and objectivity (p. 62); warn against selectivity, subjectivity (p. 66), and so on. Klaidman's goals include avoiding harm (pp. 93 ff.), maintaining trust (pp. 154 ff.), and escaping manipulation (pp. 180 ff.).

Albert C. Knudson's *Principles of Christian Ethics* (New York: Abingdon-Cokesbury, 1943. 314 pp.) is an Arminian, personalist view of ethics. The author gives a brief survey of history and sets forth his presuppositions: freedom, moral nature, sin, conversion, moral ideal. The author is against the idea of demons (p. 99); warns that there are no moral holidays (p. 139); holds that neither Jesus' teaching nor example is an infallible moral guide for us today (p. 158); holds there is no conflict of duties, only conflicting evidence as to what our duty is (p. 184); warns that there are no rights for the immoral (prisoners, etc.) (p. 190); holds that the human family is primarily a moral institution (p. 195). Knudson says that the New Testament allowed two grounds for divorce (p. 206) and argues, against the pacifists, that both army and police are valid and necessary (pp. 230-31). He describes Wesley, having gone through British Museum, as saying "What account will a man give to the Judge of the quick and the dead for a life spent in collecting all these!" (p. 258). He says that the Reformation released "work" from the curse of the Fall (p. 272) and objects to the divine will as the ground of Christian ethics (pp. 282 ff.).

C. S. Lewis's *The Problem of Pain* (New York: Macmillan, 1962. 160 pp.) argues that if God is all-wise, He has created the best possible world to attain His purpose. When men say, "Why doesn't God leave me alone?" it is not a manifestation of love but of indifference. A man who loves cares a great deal whether his wife or son is clean, moral, and so on. Pain is sometimes the only thing that breaks a man's self-satisfied absorption with this world. Hell is destruction, but nothing is ever destroyed without leaving a trace: a burning log produces ash, heat, gases, and so on. Lewis was a fellow of Magdalen College, Oxford.

Criticizing the American search for pleasure, Norman M. Lobsenz's *Is Anybody Happy?* (New York: Doubleday, 1962. 190 pp.) says that we have lost the power to enjoy and to have fun but that this is all some people are trying to do. We think we should be continually busy and full of activities and hobbies, so we work harder at our play than at real work! Millions watch television, go to movies, and go driving—whether they enjoy it or not. A child does not have fun; he is given educational "toys" to teach him to get ahead. The shah of Iran revealed his disdain for Western pleasure-seeking when he declined an invitation to the Ascot races, saying, "I am well aware that some horses run faster than others" (p. 151). People travel for place-dropping and can't enjoy it, the author says. Relaxation has died.

A book of very short articles on pertinent subjects is John Macquarrie's *Dictionary of Christian Ethics* (Philadelphia: Westminster Press, 1967. 366 pp.). Subjects range from "Abandonment," "Abelard," and "Abortion" to "Zoroastrian Ethics" and "Zwingli."

The article "Divorce" states that most Protestant churches have permitted divorce and remarriage for the innocent party in view of Matthew 5:32; but in discussion of "Pauline privilege," he refers only to Roman Catholic views. The author admits that Catholics permit a converted Catholic to divorce a person who resists his joining the Roman Catholic Church. The article "Euthanasia" attacks both compulsory and voluntary euthanasia (pp. 119-20).

Roger J. Magnuson's *Are Gay Rights Right?* (Portland, Ore.: Multnomah, 1990. 149 pp.) is a critique of gay rights. The author shows how gays use propaganda (pp. 25 ff.) and intimidation (pp. 27 f.). Magnuson explicitly describes what homosexuals do (anal and oral sodomy, p. 40). He gives statistics of the disease gays spread (pp. 48 f.): 70 percent of the occurrence of AIDS is among gays (p. 53). Magnuson argues that gays are not born that way; they learn it (pp. 55 ff.). He charges that gays really want protection to commit criminal acts (pp. 77 ff.), that they already have all the rights any of us do; that they want to be immune from scrutiny (p. 78), and that they want full social acceptance (p. 89). They want the right to teach children (pp. 91 ff.) and the right to coerce churches to hire them (pp. 98 ff.). The author gives the biblical teaching concerning homosexuality (pp. 115 ff.).

Mary Midgley's *Can't We Make Moral Judgments?* (New York: St. Martin's Press, 1991. 177 pp.) is a study of thinking about moral problems. She attacks the attitude "But surely it's always wrong to make moral judgments" (pp. 3 ff.), holds that the question is a moral judgment, denies that ignorance is a true basis for making moral judgments (pp. 10 f.), states that the stress on human freedom is also a moral judgment (p. 17), argues that doubt and skepticism are not foundations for our life (pp. 19-27), shows that the Lord Jesus urged correct judgments (p. 31), attacks the idea that right to privacy controls all (pp. 66-67), criticizes varieties of subjectivism (pp. 97-110), and ends with Margrave of Brandenburg failing to open packet of J. S. Bach (p. 173).

Another work on ethics is Bernard L. Ramm's *The Right, the Good, and the Happy: The Christian in a World of Distorted Values* (Waco, Tex.: Word Books, 1971. 188 pp.). The first three chapters deal with general ethical principles; the last three deal with specific topics, such as birth control, divorce, abortion, alcohol, drugs, homosexuality, and suicide. He has sections dealing with the Ten Commandments, the Sermon on the Mount, love, justice, and so on. He has an interesting section on the revolution in values (pp. 143-55).

Another survey work is Milton L. Rudnick's *Christian Ethics for Today: An Evangelical Approach* (Grand Rapids: Baker, 1979. 150 pp.). This book is a survey of ethics based on a high view of Scripture (pp. 15 f.). The author holds that man's problem is sin (pp. 23 ff.); teaches that God's grace can overcome sin through Christ (pp. 35 ff.); gives definite principles that should govern the believer (pp. 45 ff.); urges that believers should have a God-centered, people-oriented life (pp. 60 ff.); does not attack reason, but holds that reason should submit to the revelation of Scripture (pp. 75 ff.); argues that God can forgive failure (pp. 101 ff.); and urges that believers must continually improve (pp. 111 ff.).

Thomas A. Shannon's *Bioethics* (New York: Paulist Press, 1976. 513 pp.) is a Roman Catholic anthology covering abortion (pp. 13 ff.), severely handicapped children (pp. 75 ff.), death and dying (pp. 137 ff.), human experimentation (pp. 209 ff.), genetic engineering (pp. 295 ff.), allocation of scarce resources (pp. 373 ff.), and behavior modification (pp. 435 ff.).

Alexander Solzhenitsyn's *Warning to the West* (New York: Farrar, Straus and Giroux, 1975, 1976. 146 pp.) contains five speeches of Solzhenitsyn's after his release and exile. The first head of the Communist Party was Alexander Shliapnikov, later shot because he objected to the Communist clique that ran things for its benefit rather than the workers (pp. 8-9). Solzhenitsyn stresses that morality is higher than law (p. 45); says that "Marxism has always opposed freedom," citing the comment of Marx and Engels that "it will be necessary to repeat the year 1793. After achieving power, we'll be considered monsters, but we couldn't care less" (p. 57); and says that communism holds that good and evil are relative (p. 58) and that communism is really against humanity (p. 59). Now Communism wants dialog with Christianity, the author says, but after being in power, the dialog is carried on with bullets (p. 66). He quotes Bertrand Russell—"Better Red than dead"—and says that instead his generation says, "Better to be dead than a scoundrel" (p. 119). He calls socialism "a kind of worldly religion" and says that socialism is defended "with a passionate lack of reason" (p. 142).

A book for those in the ministry is Joe E. Trull and James E. Carter's *Ministerial Ethics: Being a Good Minister in a Not-so-good World* (Nashville: Broadman and Holman, 1993. 256 pp.). The book urges that the minister should have a calling, not just a career (pp. 18 ff.). The authors recommend having good character, good conduct, and integrity (pp. 44 ff.). They urge self-esteem (p. 68), call for a pastoral image of authority (pp. 98 ff.), and encourage a relationship of trust with colleagues (pp. 129 ff.). They also recommend a ministerial code of ethics (pp. 182 ff.), give specific denominational examples (pp. 226 ff.), and offer a sample code for pastors (pp. 253 ff.).

Gerald R. Winslow's *Triage and Justice* (Berkeley: University of California Press, 1982. 228 pp.) discusses triage, the medical screening of patients in a military or other extreme situation to determine priority of treatment. It involves the separation of patients into three groups: those who cannot survive even with treatment, those who will recover without treatment, and those who need treatment to survive. Winslow discusses questions such as whether the priority should be treatment first of those who need the most help; treatment of the greatest number before the most difficult; and treatment of the least injured so that they can return to battle quickly. He discusses planning for the San Francisco earthquake (pp. 25 ff.) and discusses dire scarcity (pp. 39 ff.). Among the utilitarian arguments used are priority (1) for those who have highest probability of recovery (p. 63), (2) for those who are most useful (p. 70), (3) for those who require smaller amounts of resources (p. 73), (4) for those who have the largest number of dependents (p. 77), and (5) for those believed to have greatest social worth (p. 81). He then traces egalitarian principles: none saved if not all (p. 88); neediest helped first (p. 91); most helpless helped first—women and children (p. 95); first come, first served (p. 98); lottery (p. 101). He lists principles for decision making (pp. 105-6).

CHAPTER 32
BOOKS ON EXPOSITION AND PREACHING

In order not to be buried by an avalanche of books on preaching, the Bible expositor needs to distinguish the most valuable of works in this important area of study. A great many books on this subject have some value, but certain ones are vital.

Blackwood, Andrew W. *Preaching from the Bible.* New York: Abingdon-Cokesbury, 1941. 247 pp. Blackwood's work is a manual of biblical preaching. Although the author was not an example of theological separation, he was an example of effective preaching. He has chapters on series of biographical messages (pp. 74 ff.), series of paragraph messages (pp. 111 ff.), exposition (pp. 126 ff.), chapter sermons (pp. 135 ff.), and book sermons (pp. 169 ff.).

Broadus, John A. *On the Preparation and Delivery of Sermons.* New York: Harper, 1870, 1944. 392 pp. This book is the best single work in the area of preaching and homiletics. Broadus offers exhaustive help on the selection of a text; the formal organization of introduction, body, and conclusion; illustrations; application; style; delivery, including voice and gestures; and so on. Every preacher should have and use this work.

Brown, H. C., Gordon Clinard, Jesse Northcutt, and Al Fasol. *Steps to the Sermon: An Eight Step Plan for Preaching with Confidence.* rev. ed. Nashville: Broadman and Holman, 1963, 1996. 229 pp. The authors give sources for the idea of the sermon (pp. 27 ff.), methods of interpretation (pp. 47 ff.), explanation, application, argumentation (pp. 79 ff.), and strengthening the title (pp. 113 ff.). References to liberals such as Fosdick and Buttrick diminish the value of the work.

Bryson, Harold T. *Expository Preaching.* Nashville: Broadman and Holman, 1995. 437 pp. It is subtitled by its theme: "The art of preaching through a book of the Bible." Bryson declines to treat other methods, concentrating on a series in a single book. He gives helpful advice on studying the background, analyzing the book, following careful exegesis and interpretation, plotting the series of sermons, and so on (pp. 41 ff.). His practice of regularly referring to liberals (Fosdick, Dibelius, Bultmann, etc.) weakens his appeal. He has useful advice on sharpening introductions and conclusions (pp. 334, 337). He concludes with a very thorough bibliography (pp. 407-18).

Chapell, Bryan. *Christ-Centered Preaching.* Grand Rapids: Baker, 1994. 375 pp. He urges the power of the Word in preaching (p. 22). He also stresses the fallen condition of mankind and warns against urging people to "be" and "do" what they cannot (pp. 40 f.). He argues that only by the redemptive power of Christ can anyone be enabled to respond to the message (p. 73). He recommends a balance of explanation, illustration, and application in the sermon (pp. 85 f.). He has advice on strengthening outlines (pp. 150 f.). He warns against sub-Christian messages (p. 267). He includes a number of appendixes covering such topics as methods (pp. 331 ff.), wedding and funeral messages (pp. 340 ff.), bibliographic helps (pp. 351 ff.), and so on.

Faw, Chalmer E. *A Guide to Biblical Preaching.* Nashville: Broadman, 1962. 207 pp. Although the author has some liberal presuppositions, he does provide helpful methods of sermon preparation. He urges beginning with book studies and working down to sections, paragraphs, sentences, and words ("Biblical Atoms"). He is especially helpful on book sermons (pp. 53 ff.).

Jeffs, H. *The Art of Exposition.* London: Clarke, 1910. 253 pp. This work is an old but thought-provoking presentation of the art. In a section on methods of exposition (pp. 102 ff.), Jeffs discusses what he terms "continuous exposition." He interestingly describes Chrysostom, G. Campbell Morgan, Alexander Maclaren, and Joseph Parker as men who always intended to be expositors.

Jones, Bob, Jr. *How to Improve Your Preaching.* Greenville, S.C.: Bob Jones University Press, 1960. 156 pp. Jones offers short but valuable helps. He provides unique help on some subjects: "Improving the Literary Quality of a Sermon" (pp. 43 ff.), "Holding the Interest of an Audience" (pp. 51 ff.), and "Radio Preaching" (pp. 114 ff.).

Lenski, Richard Charles Henry. *The Sermon.* 1927. Reprint, Grand Rapids: Baker, 1968. 314 pp. Lenski organizes the book beautifully on the text (pp. 7 ff.), the division (pp. 61 ff.), the theme (pp. 131 ff.), and the elaboration (pp. 219 ff.) and provides real help in "Mastering the Text" (pp. 44 ff.), analysis (pp. 90 ff.), synthesis (pp. 101 ff.), eliminating faults in outlining (pp. 118 ff.), dividing the theme (pp. 140 ff.), and other subjects.

Lloyd-Jones, D. Martyn. *Preaching and Preachers.* Grand Rapids: Zondervan, 1971. 325 pp. He holds that preaching ought to be central in the church (pp. 11 ff.) and mourns the loss of belief in the authority of Scripture (p. 13). He warns against mere entertainment in church (pp. 17 f.). He stresses that the distinctive part of church service is that Christ is present (p. 43). He argues that a sermon should have form, content, an artistic element, warmth, and urgency (pp. 70-91). He holds that the chief end of preaching is to give people "a sense of God and His presence" (p. 97). He urges a study of Bible, theology, church history, and sermons of preachers before 1900 (pp. 115 ff.). He recommends preaching an evangelistic sermon every week (p. 151). He preaches special sermons at Christmas and Easter, but for the rest of the year he preaches both series and isolated text (pp. 190-201). He argues against giving an invitation (pp. 269-82). See also Tony Sargent, *The Sacred Anointing.* Wheaton, Ill.: Crossway Books, 1994. It is a loving study of the preaching of D. M. Lloyd-Jones, highly profitable for all preachers.

Macartney, Clarence Edward. *Preaching Without Notes.* New York: Abingdon, 1946. 186 pp. The title theme is dealt with in only one chapter (pp. 144-72), but Macartney also has helpful comments on illustrations, biographical preaching, and so on.

Mawhinney, Bruce. *Preaching with Freshness.* Eugene, Ore.: Harvest House, 1991. 259 pp. In the manner of a Christian novel, Mawhinney describes the deadness of a preacher and the steps by which he regains the freshness of his preaching. His chance encounter with his old seminary teacher provides solid help in improving his preaching. He concludes with a "Preaching with Freshness Checklist" that is a helpful summary (pp. 245 ff.).

Morgan, G. Campbell. *Preaching.* 1937. Reprint, Grand Rapids: Baker, 1974. 90 pp. Morgan offers a marvelous treatment of the essentials of a sermon: truth, clarity, and passion. He discusses the selection of a text, the central message, introduction, and conclusion. "I would rather have on my study shelf one book of scholarly exegesis than 40 volumes of devotional exposition" (p. 64).

———. *The Ministry of the Word.* 1919. Reprint, Grand Rapids: Baker, 1970. 252 pp. Morgan defines the Word as the truth of the apostle, the burden of the prophet, the gospel of the evangelist, and the wisdom of the pastor-teacher. He urges that preparation for the ministry be academic, theological, practical, and spiritual (p. 210).

Moule, Handley Carr Glyn. *To My Younger Brethren.* London: Hodder and Stoughton, 1892. This work offers good advice from a veteran expositor. Moule has helpful chapters on walking with God, Scripture, and preaching. He answers the question of how one can attain spiritual power in preaching (pp. 297 ff.).

Quayle, William A. *The Pastor-Preacher.* New York: Eaton and Mains, 1910. 411 pp. Quayle argues for balance in the ministry: the minister must be both a good preacher and a good pastor; maintains that if a minister has studied for six hours in the morning as he should, he needs to get out and visit—actively serve—in the afternoon (p. 28); attacks both riding a hobby and digressing from the Bible (pp. 58-59); has an interesting chapter called "The Sin of Being Uninteresting," which says that it "is in a preacher an exceedingly mortal sin. It hath no forgiveness" (p. 124).

Robinson, Haddon W. *Biblical Preaching.* Grand Rapids: Baker, 1980. 230 pp. Robinson gives a brief survey of method for biblical exposition. He urges getting a theme first (pp. 33-37). He suggests ten stages of sermon preparation: (1) selecting the passage, (2) studying the passage, (3) discovering the exegetical idea, (4) analyzing the exegetical idea, (5) formulating the homiletical idea, (6) determining the sermon's purpose, (7) deciding how to accomplish this purpose, (8) outlining the sermon, (9) filling in the sermon outline, and (10) preparing the introduction and conclusion.

Sangster, W. E. *The Craft of the Sermon.* Philadelphia: Westminster, 1950, 1951. 333 pp. Sangster presents a discussion of both sermon construction and sermon illustration. He classifies sermons by their structural type, has good material on Bible books (pp. 74-75) and Bible biographies (pp. 75 ff.), and gives warnings against common mistakes in the pulpit (pp. 191 ff.).

Skinner, Craig. *The Teaching Ministry of the Pulpit.* Grand Rapids: Baker, 1973. 255 pp. Skinner surveys the history, theology, psychology, and practice of preaching; gives a list of significant preachers (pp. 35-38); discusses the thesis or proposition (p. 163) and the seven interrogative words (how, when, where, why, who, which, what) that lead to the key word to organize a message (pp. 164 ff.); and has a two-page list of suggested key words (pp. 166-67).

Spurgeon, Charles H. *Spurgeon's Lectures to His Students.* Grand Rapids: Zondervan, 1945. 422 pp. This work contains Spurgeon's powerful messages entitled "The Minister's Self-Watch," "The Call to the Ministry," "To Workers with Slender Apparatus," "The Holy Spirit in Connection with Our Ministry," "The Necessity of Ministerial Progress," and so on. "I cannot too earnestly assure you that if your ministries are to be lastingly useful you must be expositors" (p. 196).

Stalker, James. *The Preacher and His Models.* 1891. Reprint, Grand Rapids: Baker, 1967. 284 pp. Stalker gives vivid portraits of the preacher as a man of God (pp. 29 ff.), the preacher as a man of the Word (pp. 91 ff.), the preacher as a Christian (pp. 179 ff.), and the preacher as a thinker (pp. 237 ff.). "Unless God has first spoken to a man, it is vain for a man to attempt to speak for God" (p. 50).

Thomas, W. H. Griffith. *The Work of the Ministry.* London: Hodder and Stoughton, n.d. 432 pp. Thomas's section on preaching (pp. 200 ff.) has helpful advice. He discusses the structure of a sermon (pp. 216-22), warns against using a text as a peg on which to hang one's own thoughts (p. 223), describes the characteristics of good expository sermons, and stresses the importance of biographical sermons (pp. 231-32).

Turnbull, Ralph G. *A Minister's Obstacles.* Westwood, N.J.: Revell, 1963, 1964. 192 pp. This book offers messages and warnings from a minister's heart. Turnbull writes "The Specter of Professionalism," "The Vice of Sloth," "Evasions of Preaching," "The Snare of Substitutes," "The Peril of Privilege," and so on. "How few ministers preach with all their might" (p. 83).

Unger, Merrill F. *Principles of Expository Preaching.* Grand Rapids: Zondervan, 1955. 267 pp. Unger provides illustrations of expository method (pp. 39 ff.), laws of logic (pp. 85 ff.), inductive and deductive reasoning (pp. 97 ff.), grammatical interpretation (pp. 118 ff.), doctrinal interpretation (pp. 154 ff.), and so on. There are special chapters on biblical types (pp. 201 ff.) and prophecy (pp. 217 ff.).

Wagner, Charles U. *The Pastor: His Life and Work.* Schaumburg, Ill.: Regular Baptist Press, 1976, 1988. 404 pp. The book stresses the necessity of a divine call to the ministry (p. 17) and urges the pastor to be a leader, not a dictator (p. 47). He recommends that the pastor study five hours a day five days a week (p. 74). He urges the pastor to get a good library (p. 77) and gives a considerable list of books to help the pastor in biblical and theological areas (pp. 83-134). He gives suggestions for being a good administrator (pp. 137-61) and recommends time management skills (pp. 163-70), and using a computer in the ministry (pp. 171-74). He has a long chapter on "The Pastor and Evangelism" (pp. 187-252). In it he urges visitation campaigns and busing, with a strong emphasis on numbers (pp. 193 ff.). He gives advice on visitation—house-to-house, in hospitals, for new visitors in church, and so on (pp. 253-62). He argues that a Regular Baptist church should support only Regular Baptist missionaries (p. 323). He discusses the pastor and his family (pp. 329 ff.). He dispatches pastoral ethics in a mere three pages (pp. 345-47). Although one will not agree with everything in this book, there are genuinely helpful sections in it.

Westcott, Brooke Foss. *Lessons from Work.* London: Macmillan, 1901. 451 pp. This book offers helpful advice from a master expositor. Westcott has thought-provoking chapters entitled "Christian Doctrine: The Method and Spirit of Studying It" (pp. 63-90), "How to Study the Bible" (pp. 127-41), and so on. "A Psalm thought out daily will leave us marvelously richer at the end of the year" (p. 129).

Whitesell, Faris D., and Lloyd M. Perry. *Variety in Your Preaching.* Westwood, N.J.: Revell, 1954. 219 pp. The authors urge and demonstrate variety in sermon content, subjects, themes, propositions, key words, supporting material, illustrations, conclusions, introductions, and even in the whole year's preaching program (pp. 181 ff.).

CHAPTER 33
BOOKS FOR THE STUDY
OF BIBLICAL GREEK

The expositor who can use Greek in his study of the Bible has an immense advantage. God inspired the New Testament in Greek. It is a sacred task to unfold the treasures of the Greek Testament and to make it live in the minds and hearts of the people.

Texts

Aland, Kurt, Matthew Black, Carlo Martini, Bruce Metzger, and Allen Wikgren. *The Greek New Testament.* 4th ed. New York: United Bible Societies, 1966, 1968, 1975, 1983, 1993. 989 pp. This work uses very readable type. It contains footnotes on the major textual variants.

Nestle, Eberhard. *Novum Testamentum Graece.* 26th ed. Stuttgart: Wurtembergische Bibelanstalt, 1898, 1927, 1963, 1975, 1979. 781 pp. This pocket-sized book contains systematic footnotes on textual variants and places the best cross-references in the margin.

Rahlfs, Alfred. *Septuaginta.* 2 vols. Stuttgart: Wurtembergische Bibelanstalt, 1935. 1,184 and 941 pp. This is a helpful edition of the Old Testament in Greek.

Swete, Henry Barclay. *The Old Testament in Greek, According to the Septuagint.* 3 vols. 4th ed. Cambridge: University Press, 1934. This book is a very technical edition.

Westcott, Brooke Foss, and Fenton John Anthony Hort. *The New Testament in the Original Greek.* New York: Macmillan, 1948. 619 pp. This is the old classic edition which uses large type but prints Old Testament quotations in uncials.

Grammars

Black, David Alan. *Learn to Read New Testament Greek.* Nashville: Broadman and Holman, 1994. 236 pp. This is perhaps the best of the modern elementary grammars.

Blass, Friedrich Wilhelm, and Albert Debrunner. *A Greek Grammar of the New Testament.* Trans. Robert W. Funk. Chicago: University of Chicago Press, 1961. 325 pp. This book is a scholarly edition that preserves pre-Deissmannian opinions and often gives inferior help.

Crosby, Henry, and John Schaeffer. *An Introduction to Greek.* New York: Allyn and Bacon, 1928. 378 pp. This work is a good introduction to classical Greek.

Dana, H. E., and Julius R. Mantey. *A Manual Grammar of the Greek New Testament.* New York: Macmillan, 1927. 368 pp. This manual is a good intermediate grammar.

Machen, J. Gresham. *New Testament Greek for Beginners.* New York: Macmillan, 1958. 287 pp. Machen's work is a good elementary grammar.

Moulton, James Hope. *A Grammar of New Testament Greek.* 4 vols. Edinburgh: Clark, 1906, 1919, 1963, 1976. 274, 543, 417, 174 pp. (Vols. III and IV by Nigel Turner.) Moulton provides the most thorough and helpful grammar available; the best part is Vol. III, *Syntax,* by Nigel Turner.

Robertson, Archibald Thomas. *A Grammar of the Greek New Testament in the Light of Historical Research.* Nashville: Broadman, 1934. 1,454 pp. This work is a rather poorly organized encyclopedia of grammatical information.

Thackeray, Henry St. John. *A Grammar of the Old Testament in Greek According to the Septuagint.* Cambridge: Cambridge University Press, 1909. 325 pp.

Young, Richard A. *Intermediate New Testament Greek: A Linguistic and Exegetical Approach.* Nashville: Broadman and Holman, 1994. 308 pp. This is a strong approach.

Concordances

Hatch, Edwin, and Henry A. Redpath. *A Concordance to the Septuagint.* 3 vols. Oxford: Clarendon, 1897-1906. 1,504 pp., (supplement—272 pp.).

Morrish, George. *A Concordance to the Septuagint Version.* Grand Rapids: Zondervan, 1976.

Moulton, W. F., and A. S. Geden. *A Concordance to the Greek Testament.* Edinburgh: Clark, 1953. 1,033 pp. Moulton's work is the best concordance of the Greek New Testament.

Lexicons

Abbott-Smith, G. *Manual Lexicon of the New Testament.* Edinburgh: Clark, 1921. 512 pp. This book is a generally inferior work, but it is helpful in Old Testament references.

Arndt, William F., and F. Wilbur Gingrich. *A Greek-English Lexicon of the New Testament and Other Early Christian Literature.* Chicago: University of Chicago Press, 1957. 946 pp. This work is the most helpful and up-to-date lexicon available. It contains strongly conservative definitions.

Kittel, Gerhard. *Theological Dictionary of the New Testament.* 10 vols. Grand Rapids: Eerdmans, 1964-76. Kittel's work is an exhaustive historical study of select words. Its conclusions are voiced with rampant liberalism. The set has unequal value.

Liddell, Henry, and Robert Scott. *A Greek-English Lexicon.* 9th ed. Oxford: Clarendon, 1940, 1973. 2,195 pp. This work is the standard lexicon for classical Greek.

Moulton, James Hope, and George Milligan. *The Vocabulary of the Greek New Testament.* Grand Rapids: Eerdmans, 1949. 705 pp. This book gives illustrations from the papyri that shed light on the meaning of New Testament words.

Thayer, Joseph Henry. *A Greek-English Lexicon of the New Testament.* New York: American Book Company, 1889. 727 pp. The

definitions in this old, but still helpful, work contain some
Unitarian opinions.

Greek Reference Sets

Alford, Henry. *The Greek Testament.* 2 vols. 1874. Reprint, Chicago: Moody, n.d. Alford provides a concise and helpful explanation of the Greek.

Nicoll, W. Robertson, ed. *The Expositor's Greek Testament.* 5 vols. Grand Rapids: Eerdmans, 1951. Nicoll's work contains comments of unequal value; part is very valuable (Knowling on Acts); part is nearly worthless (Moffatt on Revelation).

Robertson, Archibald Thomas. *Word Pictures in the New Testament.* 6 vols. Nashville: Broadman, 1930. Robertson's book is valuable on the location and meaning of Greek words.

Vincent, Marvin R. *Word Studies in the New Testament.* 4 vols. Grand Rapids: Eerdmans, 1887. Vincent provides studies on selected words throughout the New Testament.

Other Monographs

Chapman, Benjamin. *New Testament Greek Notebook.* Grand Rapids: Baker, 1977. 131 pp. Chapman provides practical help in grammar, exegesis, and vocabulary. He has a good list of difficult principal parts (pp. 109 ff.).

Deissmann, Adolf. *Light from the Ancient East.* New York: Harper, 1909, 1922. 567 pp. Deissmann proves that New Testament Greek was the common written language of the first-century world. He offers liberal opinions, but the book is still helpful.

Moule, Charles Francis Digby. *An Idiom Book of New Testament Greek.* 2nd ed. Cambridge: Cambridge University Press, 1953, 1959. 246 pp. Moule's work is an incipient grammar.

Robertson, Archibald Thomas. *The Minister and His Greek New Testament.* New York: Doran, 1923. 139 pp. Robertson is especially helpful on "Pictures in Prepositions," "Grammar and Preaching," "Sermons in Greek Tenses," and so on.

CHAPTER 34
BOOKS FOR THE STUDY
OF BIBLICAL HEBREW

It is much more difficult for the expositor to keep up his Hebrew than his Greek studies, but such studies can be a rich source of blessing for his people.

Texts

Ginsburg, Christian David. *The Old Testament, Diligently Revised According to the Masorah and the Early Editions.* London: British and Foreign Bible Society, 1927. 4 vols.

Kittel, Elliger, and Ruger. *Biblia Hebraica Stuttgartensia.* 4th ed. Stuttgart: Deutsche Bibelgesellschaft, 1937, 1949, 1967, 1990. 1,574 pp. This is the most respected edition of the Hebrew.

Grammars

Kautzsch, E., ed. *Gesenius' Hebrew Grammar.* 2nd ed. Revised by A. E. Cowley. Oxford: Clarendon, 1910. 598 pp. Kautzsch's book is the most helpful grammar available.

Marks, John Henry, and Virgil M. Rogers. *A Beginner's Handbook to Biblical Hebrew.* New York: Abingdon, 1958. 174 pp. This is a good elementary text.

Sperber, Alexander. *A Historical Grammar of Biblical Hebrew.* Leiden: Brill, 1966. 705 pp. Sperber traces the historical development of the Hebrew language.

Stevenson, William B. *Grammar of Palestinian Jewish Aramaic.* Oxford: Clarendon, 1924, 1956. 96 pp. This book is helpful on the Aramaic portions of the Old Testament.

Concordances

Lisowsky, G. *Konkordanz zum Hebraischen Alten Testament.* Stuttgart: Wuerttembergische Bibelanstalt, 1958.

Mandelkern, Solomon. *Veteris Testamenti Concordantiae: Hebraicae atque Chaldaicae.* Tel Aviv: Sumptibus Schocken Hierosolymis, 1967.

Lexicons

Brown, Francis, S. R. Driver, and C. A. Briggs. *A Hebrew and English Lexicon of the Old Testament.* Oxford: Clarendon, 1907, 1955. 1,126 pp. This work is the most helpful lexicon on the Hebrew.

Harkavy, Alexander. *Student's Hebrew and Chaldee Dictionary to the Old Testament.* New York: Hebrew Publishing Company, 1914. Harkavy's work is handy for quick reference.

Holladay, William. *A Concise Hebrew and Aramaic Lexicon of the Old Testament.* Grand Rapids: Eerdmans, 1988. 425 pp. A popular work based on Koehler and Baumgartner.

Koehler, Ludwig, and Walter Baumgartner. *Lexicon in Veteris Testamenti Libros.* Grand Rapids: Eerdmans, 1951, 1953. 1,138 pp.

CHAPTER 35
BOOKS ON BIBLE WORDS AND PHRASES

Real exposition must come to grips with the words and expressions used in a given passage of Scripture. The expositor must bring out of them their meaning for his congregation. There are helpful books for the study of words and phrases.

Barclay, William. *Flesh and Spirit.* Nashville: Abingdon Press, 1962. 127 pp. Barclay covers the vocabulary that Paul uses to describe the works of the flesh (Gal. 5:19-21) and the fruit of the Spirit (Gal. 5:22-23). He treats words such as ἀγάπη, "love" (p. 63); εἰρήνη, "peace" (p. 83); ἔρις, "strife" (p. 42); and μέθη, "drunkenness" (p. 60).

—————. *More New Testament Words.* New York: Harper, 1958. 160 pp. This is a sequel to *A New Testament Wordbook, covering other New Testament words, such as* ἀλαζών, "boasting" (p. 38); ἐλπίς, "hope" (p. 42); and λόγος, "Word" (p. 106).

—————. *A New Testament Wordbook.* London: SCM Press, 1955. 128 pp. The author provides a study of specific New Testament words, applying the evidence of the papyri. He treats words such as ἀγάπη, showing the "paid in full" meaning (p. 17); διαθήκη, the word for "testament" or "covenant" (p. 30); and so on. He is liberal in his theology but very knowledgeable in first-century background.

Custer, Stewart. *A Treasury of New Testament Synonyms.* Greenville, S.C.: Bob Jones University Press, 1975. 143 pp. The author presents a study of words, close in meaning but not identical, that are commonly confused with one another in English translations. Some of the subjects treated are six different words for *power* (pp. 27 ff.), and three words for *righteousness* (pp. 43 ff.), four words for soul (pp. 56 ff.), and three words for *trickery* (pp. 72 ff.). All Greek words are translated so that the reader who does not know Greek may follow the argument.

Earle, Ralph. ***Word Meanings in the New Testament.*** Vol. IV, *Romans.* Grand Rapids: Baker, 1974. 261 pp. The author studies the meaning of different words found in Romans. He gives helpful material on a number of words, defends the deity of Christ in 9:5 (pp. 180-85), makes clear that he writes from an Arminian viewpoint (pp. 166, 175, 188, and so on), and denies the doctrine of predestination (p. 193).

Girdlestone, Robert Baker. ***Synonyms of the Old Testament.*** 1897. Reprint, Grand Rapids: Eerdmans, 1956. 346 pp. In this helpful study of Hebrew words, the author treats the names of God (pp. 18 ff.); the names of man (pp. 45 ff.); the words for soul (pp. 55 ff.), sin (pp. 76 ff.), and atonement (pp. 12 ff.); and so on. Although not as thorough as Trench, he remains the only practical help in the field of Old Testament synonyms.

Hobbs, Herschel L. ***Preaching Values from the Papyri.*** Grand Rapids: Baker, 1964. 123 pp. The author presents practical homiletical studies in Greek words illustrated from the papyri. He treats αἴρω, "Away with Him!" (pp. 11 ff.); ἀποστασία, "Rebellion" (pp. 25 ff.); κοινωνία, "the Tie that Binds" (pp. 72 ff.); and so on.

Leete, Frederick D. ***New Testament Windows.*** New York: Funk and Wagnalls, 1939. 150 pp. This book is a good source of background material and illustrations for sermons. Leete treats "picture words" like *herald,* "Greek compounds" like *help,* "potent particles" like *not so,* "divinity in prepositions" like *upon,* and "sermons in tenses" like *He became poor* (II Cor. 8:9).

Silva, Moises. ***Biblical Words and Their Meanings.*** Grand Rapids: Academie Books, 1983. 201 pp. An introduction to lexical semantics. Silva disagrees with Turner's *Christian Words* (p. 21). He charges that fear of proof texts has moved men to proof words (p. 23) and argues that etymology actually helps understanding ἁμαρτάνω in Romans 3:23 (p. 50). He discusses semantic change, ellipsis (pp. 82 ff.), semantic borrowing, and loan words (pp. 86 ff.). He explains the Ogden-Richards triangle (pp. 102 ff.), principles of phonology and vocabulary (pp. 109 ff.), and varieties of sense relations (pp. 119 ff.). He concludes by applying these principles to New Testament words (pp. 137 ff.).

Trench, Richard Chenevix. *Synonyms of the New Testament.* 1854. Reprint, Grand Rapids: Eerdmans, 1953. 430 pp. This is *the* classic work on New Testament synonyms in English. Although Trench assumed every reader of his work would be a scholar and hence did not always bother to translate Greek, Latin, German, and so on, his work is still a most valuable help to serious preachers. He provides much help on many words such as *life,* ζωή, βίος; *lord,* κύριος, δεσπότης, σαγήνη; *thief,* κλέπτης, ληστής; *net,* δίκτυον, ἀμφίβληστον; and *beast,* ζῷον, θηρίον.

Turner, Nigel. *Christian Words.* Edinburgh: Clark, 1980. 513 pp. Careful word studies by a grammatical authority. He confesses, "Guided by traditional views of inspiration, nevertheless, I cannot believe that the Scriptures enshrine any ultimate or essential error, any defect, any excess, anything except heavenly wisdom" (p. ix). He covers the history and biblical usage of many words: apostasy (pp. 20-21); baptism, discussing water and Spirit baptism (pp. 73-78); church, universal and local (pp. 68-71); the Comforter (pp. 73-78); faith (pp. 153-58); grace (pp. 191-95); hell (pp. 206-11); justification (pp. 239-45); paradise (pp. 308-12); repentance (pp. 374-77); resurrection (pp. 377-81); salvation (pp. 390-98); soul (pp. 417-25); wrath (pp. 503-5); and so on.

―――. *Grammatical Insights into the New Testament.* Edinburgh: Clark, 1965. 198 pp. Turner has written brief grammatical and practical studies on God, Jesus, Paul, John, and so on. He defends the deity of Christ grammatically (pp. 13-17), has an interesting defense of Barnabas and Paul's dispute as tactful (p. 96), defends James and Paul on faith and works (pp. 111-12), and concludes with a discussion on the language that Jesus spoke (pp. 174-88).

Ward, Ronald. *Hidden Meaning in the New Testament.* Old Tappan, N.J.: Revell, 1969. 109 pp. The author gives helpful instruction to preachers on how to use grammar in sermons. He discusses "pinpoints" (the aorist tense), "panoramas" (linear tense), "footprints" (the perfect tense), "self-interest" (the middle voice), "relations" (prepositions), "sunken treasure" (metaphors), and so on.

Wuest, Kenneth S. *The Practical Use of the Greek New Testament.* Chicago: Moody, 1946. 156 pp. Wuest gives helpful advice on turning case (p. 26), tense (p. 39), prepositions (p. 59), synonyms (p. 72), word studies (p. 84), and so on into sermons. He stresses the place of the Holy Spirit in interpretation (pp. 143 ff.).

CHAPTER 36
BOOKS ON
CHURCH HISTORY

Most pastors will take at least some interest in church history, if only for illustrating sermons and for personal edification. There is an astonishing variety of books on the topic. But a few will be of more use than others to the Fundamentalist wanting to read in this field.

Church History Surveys

One could easily collect a whole shelf full of church history surveys, but which are most profitable to the Fundamentalist Christian? Probably Earle Cairns's *Christianity Through the Centuries,* 3rd ed. (Grand Rapids: Zondervan, 1996) is the best conservative survey. A former professor of history at Wheaton College, Cairns is obviously somewhat soft on matters such as the New Evangelicalism, but he is on the whole dependable, if sometimes dry, and he avoids technical discussions. He also has a clearly delineated, biblical philosophy of history. Bruce Shelley's *Church History in Plain Language,* 2nd ed. (Waco, Tex.: Word Books, 1995) is even more of an introductory volume, attempting to explain issues in church history to the uninitiated layman. His work is good and simpler in approach than Cairns's. But on controversial topics such as Roman Catholicism and the ecumenical movement, the Fundamentalist will find even more to object to in Shelley than he does in Cairns. The best-illustrated conservative survey is unquestionably *The History of Christianity*, rev. ed. (Oxford: Lion Publishing, 1990), edited by Tim Dowley; it was originally released in America country as *Eerdmans' Handbook to the History of Christianity* in 1977. Written by a team of evangelical scholars, this handbook contains a large number of excellent maps, charts, diagrams, and photos. The writing varies from the very good to the pedestrian, depending on which author wrote the section under consideration. A major flaw is the book's reflection of the modern evangelical tendency to stress social action over an "other-worldly" proclamation of the gospel that focuses mainly on eternal salvation. Perhaps the most conservative survey is S. M. Houghton's *Sketches from Church History* (Edinburgh: Banner of Truth, 1980). Houghton's main shortcoming is reflected in his title; the coverage is indeed "sketchy" in some periods, notably the nineteenth and twentieth centuries. The book might, however, be the best resource for a lay Christian approaching church history for the first time. An anthology of church history articles from the Fundamentalist viewpoint designed to provide an introduction to and survey of church history for the layman is *Faith of Our Fathers: Scenes from Church History* (Greenville, S.C.: Bob Jones University Press, 1989), edited by Mark Sidwell.

There are many liberal surveys. Most, such as the highly touted but inferior *Oxford Illustrated History of Christianity* (Oxford: Oxford University Press, 1990), are clearly of far less worth to the Fundamentalist Christian than the conservative works mentioned above. At least two, however, are of note, at least as supplements to the conservative works. Kenneth Scott Latourette's *History of Christianity,* 2 vols. (1953; reprint, New York: Harper and Row, 1975) has enjoyed widespread popularity. Latourette, styled an "evangelical liberal" by some, is sometimes stultifying in his mass of detail, but, by the same token, he has provided one of the most thorough surveys available. Unlike many liberal writers, Latourette's is willing to give notice to evangelical leaders and movements. Williston Walker, Richard A. Norris, David W. Lotz, and Robert T. Handy's *History of the Christian Church,* 4th ed. (New York: Scribner's, 1985) has been a standard textbook survey since the first edition was published in 1918. Little of Walker's original work is left except his outline, and it is even more liberal than Latourette, but the readable text is relatively traditional in its approach (focus on Europe, discussion of recognized leaders of influence) and is unmarred by recent historical subservience to multiculturalism and other icons of modern historiography.

In a special niche of its own is Philip Schaff's eight-volume *History of the Christian Church* (1910; reprint, Grand Rapids: Eerdmans, 1981). Schaff, called the Father of American Church History, wrote a set that is smoothly readable and warmly evangelical. Although his bibliography is obviously much out-of-date, his engaging style and genuine sympathy for biblical Christianity (so much in contrast to modern historians) make his work a delight to use.

Reference Works

Few Fundamentalist pastors or laymen will need to burden themselves with the cost of purchasing major reference works in church history. Some are worth noting, however. The standard dictionary is *The Oxford Dictionary of the Christian Church,* 3rd ed. (London: Oxford University Press, 1997). Better perhaps for the conservative Christian (and less expensive) is *New International Dictionary of the Christian Church,* rev. ed. (Grand Rapids: Zondervan, 1978), edited by J. D. Douglas. Although the work is not wholly dependable from a Fundamentalist point of view, some of its articles show a distinct sympathy to the conservative Protestant viewpoint. (See, e.g., "Vatican II.") Another interesting work is Robert C. Walton's *Chronological and Background Charts of Church History* (Grand Rapids: Zondervan, 1986). This collection of the data of church history in chart form fosters greater understanding of the subject by organizing the material in a visually attractive format. This work would be of special use to someone teaching church history. For readings in the original sources, see Henry Bettenson's *Documents of the Christian Church* (New York: Oxford University Press, 1943). Reprinted many times, Bettenson's collection is ubiquitous among used-book dealers and contains a fair sampling of important original documents in the church's history. Also highly useful is Philip Schaff's *Creeds of Christendom* (1931; reprint, Grand Rapids: Baker, 1983). Schaff's first volume is an excellent overall history of creeds, and the second and third volumes contain the texts of the major universal creeds, the Catholic and Orthodox creeds, and the Protestant creeds.

One should also note the periodical *Christian History,* published by *Christianity Today.* Published quarterly, the magazine follows the format of popular yet scholarly historical magazines such as *American Heritage.* Each issue is devoted to a single topic, most often the career of a famous Christian. As one would expect from its publisher, the quality and the usefulness of the magazine vary. Some issues are first-rate and provide as fine an introduction to the topics discussed as a full biography or book-length survey; the issues on William Tyndale, pietism, Augustine, and Christianity in the Civil War are examples of the magazine at its best. Occasionally a few issues are of only marginal value; an uncritical issue on radical German theologian Dietrich Bonhoeffer and one on Francis of Assisi written almost entirely by Roman Catholic authors are examples of the latter.

History of Doctrine

The history of doctrine is one of the essential fields of church history. There are many older works still available which are useful, if sometimes heavy reading, and are dependably conservative. William Cunningham's *Historical Theology* 2 vols. (1862; reprint, Edinburgh: Banner of Truth, 1960) and W.G.T. Shedd's *History of Christian Doctrine,* 3 vols. 9th ed. (1889; reprint, Minneapolis: Klock and Klock, 1978) have long been of service. More compact is Louis Berkhof's *History of Christian Doctrine* (1937; reprint, Grand Rapids: Baker, 1975). Berkhof prepared the volume as a supplement to his magisterial *Systematic Theology,* and it provides a solid introduction. Berkhof's work is probably the best introduction for a layman.

More recent surveys, unfortunately, tend to be more liberal. Typical is Justo L. Gonzalez's *History of Christian Thought,* 3 vols. (Nashville: Abingdon, 1970-75). Although his outlook is liberal, he gives fair coverage to all schools of thought up to the nineteenth century, including a full discussion of post-Reformation Protestant orthodoxy, a topic often scorned by liberals. Gonzalez is surprisingly sketchy in his discussion of the last two hundred years, however, and may need to be supplemented by a survey on contemporary theology. A modern work that is a happy exception to the liberal outlook is Harold O. J. Brown's *Heresies* (Garden City, N.J.: Doubleday, 1984). Brown surveys the history of doctrine as well as the heresies of the title. Unfortunately, Brown detracts from an otherwise helpful work by leveling uncalled-for and inaccurate criticisms at Fundamentalism.

Eras of Church History

Books on the different eras of church history can allow the reader to come "up close" to topics he may be interested in. On the early church, one should consult two works by New Testament scholar F. F. Bruce. *New Testament History* (New York: Doubleday, 1971) is an interesting gathering and analysis of the historical data of the New Testament era. Even more valuable is his *The Spreading Flame* (1958; reprint, Grand Rapids: Eerdmans, 1979). It is a model of readable scholarship that does not shortchange its topic; *The Spreading Flame* is strongly recommended.

The Middle Ages is not a rich period for devotional reading. A fairly evangelical survey is G.S.M. Walker's *Growing Storm: Sketches of Church History from A.D. 600 to A.D. 1350* (Grand Rapids: Eerdmans, 1961), and a standard work is William Cannon's *History of Christianity in the Middle Ages* (1960; reprint, Grand Rapids: Baker, 1983). However, the reader who has Schaff's *History of the Christian Church* would do well simply to consult the three volumes on the medieval church in that set.

The Reformation is a tremendously important topic in church history, second only to the New Testament era. Unfortunately, no single work covers it adequately. Fairly good surveys are James Atkinson's *Great Light: Luther and the Reformation* (Grand Rapids: Eerdmans, 1968); Harold J. Grimm's *Reformation Era, 1500-1650,* 2nd ed. (New York: Macmillan, 1973); and Owen Chadwick's *Reformation* (New York: Penguin, 1964). Many readers might, however, profit more from specific works of a narrower focus. For example, on Martin Luther, the most important figure in the Reformation, one should read Roland Bainton's *Here I Stand: A Life of Martin Luther* (1950; reprint, New York: New American Library, 1978). Also good, and from a broadly evangelical point of view, is Alister E. McGrath's *Life of John Calvin* (1990; reprint, Grand Rapids: Baker, 1994). These works by Bainton and McGrath not only discuss the lives of their subjects but also provide first-rate introductions to the rise of the Reformation itself.

The conservative Christian certainly cannot ignore the work of Swiss church historian J. H. Merle d'Aubigné (1794-1872). His two multivolume sets on the Reformation (a total of thirteen volumes) were best sellers in the nineteenth century among evangelical Christians. Merle's grace in style and strong Protestant faith make his works devotionally edifying as well as historically enriching. His original volumes are sometimes reprinted, but with excruciatingly small type. Some publishers, however, have excerpted his work into smaller, more focused volumes. *The Triumph of Truth: A Life of Martin Luther* (Greenville, S.C.: Bob Jones University Press, 1996) collects Merle's sections on the great reformer into a readable biography, and *The Reformation in England,* 2 vols. (Edinburgh: Banner of Truth, 1962) presents all of his discussion of the English Reformation.

For the era from the end of the Reformation through the French Revolution, Gerald Cragg's *Church and the Age of Reason 1648-1789* (Baltimore: Penguin Books, 1970) is a good survey. For a focus more on the tremendous revivals in this era (Wesley and Whitefield, the Great Awakening, etc.), see A. Skevington Wood's *Inextinguishable Blaze: Spiritual Advance in the Eighteenth Century* (Grand Rapids: Eerdmans, 1960). For a devotional, yet still intellectually respectable study of the period, see J. C. Ryle's *Christian Leaders of the 18th Century* (1885; reprint, Edinburgh: Banner of Truth, 1978).

For the modern period, the pre-eminent survey is Kenneth Scott Latourette's *Christianity in a Revolutionary Age,* 5 vols. (1958; reprint, Grand Rapids: Zondervan, 1969). Like most of Latourette's works, it is detailed to the point of tediousness, but it is undeniably thorough. Much shorter but adequate is Alec R. Vidler's *Church in an Age of Revolution* (Grand Rapids: Eerdmans, 1961). A fairly conservative survey from a Lutheran point of view is Roy A. Suelflow's *Christian Churches in Recent Times* (St. Louis: Concordia, 1980).

American Church History

Without question the standard and authoritative survey of the history of American Christianity is still Sidney Ahlstrom's *A Religious History of the American People* (New Haven: Yale University Press, 1972). Although massive in size, its success in surveying current scholarship and touching the major issues makes it a worthwhile resource. The author's outlook, however, is liberal, and he devotes some space to non-Christian religions. Perhaps more enjoyable for the layman is *Eerdmans Handbook to Christianity in America* (Grand Rapids: Eerdmans, 1983). Edited by Mark Noll, Nathan Hatch, George Marsden, David Wells, and John Woodbridge, the work combines a broadly evangelical viewpoint with colorful illustrations and a fairly consistent readability. Another work with a somewhat conservative outlook is Mark Noll's *History of Christianity in the United States and Canada* (Grand Rapids: Eerdmans, 1992). It has a good chance of becoming the standard evangelical survey. A useful reference work, also from a broadly evangelical point of view, is *Dictionary of Christianity in America* (Downers Grove, Ill.: InterVarsity Press, 1990), edited by Daniel G. Reid, Robert D. Linder, Bruce Shelley, and Harry S. Stout. Its articles are full in content and clear in presentation. For a work on the layman's level, see *Faith of Our Fathers: Scenes from American Church History* (Greenville, S.C.: Bob Jones University Press, 1991), edited by Mark Sidwell.

On denominational history, two useful reference works are Frank S. Mead and Samuel S. Hill's *Handbook of Denominations in the United States,* 9th ed. (Nashville: Abingdon, 1990) and J. Gordon Melton's *Encyclopedia of American Religions,* 4th ed. (Detroit: Gale Research Inc., 1993). Melton's work is much more exhaustive, but it is also much more expensive. Readily available histories of specific denominations today are usually of surprisingly low quality. Baptists, however, benefit from one of the best: H. Leon McBeth's *Baptist Heritage: Four Centuries of Baptist Witness* (Nashville: Broadman, 1987).

There are two volumes by Peter Marshall and David Manuel on early American Christianity that are worthy of notice: *The Light and the Glory* (Grand Rapids: Revell, 1977) and *From Sea to Shining Sea* (Grand Rapids: Revell, 1986). These books are popular surveys, aimed at the general reader and not the professional historian. They provide a highly readable, indeed dramatic introduction to American Christianity. The first volume covers America from its discovery through the Revolution; the second deals with the young nation from the Constitutional Convention (1787) to the Battle of the Alamo (1836). The main shortcoming of the books is their adherence to what has been called the "Christian America" approach to history. They tend to accept uncritically any kind of professed Christianity as sincere (e.g., Christopher Columbus as a Christian evangelist-explorer), to view American origins as almost uniformly Christian, and to verge on insinuating that the United States has a special national relationship with God much as ancient Israel did. Marshall and Manuel are not as extreme as some other proponents of "Christian America," however, and a wary reader can profit from their work.

Special Topics

Citing works on special topics in church history could easily become an endless task. A few areas, however, are of particular interest and use to the Fundamentalist Christian.

On the history of missions, the standard work is still Kenneth Scott Latourette's *History of the Expansion of Christianity,* 7 vols. (1939; reprint, Grand Rapids: Zondervan, 1970). It is simply the most exhaustive work on the subject. Latourette, although a liberal, had planned to go to the mission field himself and had some firsthand understanding of the field. A work often cited on this topic is Stephen Neill's *History of Christian Missions* (Baltimore: Penguin Books, 1964). Much better, however, is Ruth Tucker's *From Jerusalem to Irian Jaya: A Biographical History of Christian Missions*

(Grand Rapids: Zondervan, 1983). A professor at Trinity Evangelical Divinity School, Tucker offers honest portrayals of missionaries, "warts and all," but she has a definite sympathy with the topic and aims to edify the reader.

Works on the history of revival vary. Thorough but disappointingly dull is Earle E. Cairns's *Endless Line of Splendour* (Wheaton, Ill.: Tyndale House, 1986). The many works of J. Edwin Orr are good resources; see especially his *The Light of the Nations* (Grand Rapids: Eerdmans, 1965) on revivals in the nineteenth century and his companion volumes *The Second Evangelical Awakening in Britain* (London: Marshall, Morgan, and Scott, 1949) and *The Second Evangelical Awakening in America* (London: Marshall, Morgan, and Scott, 1952). But Orr often seems undiscerning in many of his works in what he recognizes as "revival" (note, e.g., *Evangelical Awakenings in Latin America, Evangelical Awakenings in the South Seas, Campus Aflame,* etc.). On American revivals in particular, two good surveys by Keith Hardman are *The Spiritual Awakeners* (Chicago: Moody Press, 1983) and *Seasons of Refreshing: Evangelism and Revivals in America* (Grand Rapids: Baker, 1995). A good work, with a strongly Calvinistic slant, is Iain Murray's *Revival and Revivalism* (Edinburgh: Banner of Truth, 1994).

One should also consult biographies of important revival leaders. On Jonathan Edwards, Iain Murray's *Jonathan Edwards: A New Biography* (Edinburgh: Banner of Truth, 1987) is strongly recommended. For studying George Whitefield a well-received though flawed critical study is Harry S. Stout's *Divine Dramatist: George Whitefield and the Rise of Modern Evangelicalism* (Grand Rapids: Eerdmans, 1991). Less critical and more thorough is Arnold Dallimore's *George Whitefield: The Life and Times of the Great Evangelist of the Eighteenth Century,* 2 vols. (Edinburgh: Banner of Truth, 1970, 1980), a massive work of better than twelve hundred pages. Dallimore has also prepared a much shorter, introductory volume, *George Whitefield: God's Anointed Servant in the Great Revival of the Eighteenth Century* (Westchester, Ill.: Crossway Books, 1990). On Charles Finney, Keith Hardman's

Charles Grandison Finney, 1792-1875 (1987; reprint ed., Grand Rapids: Baker, 1990) is a fair and full biography. On D. L. Moody, there is no single satisfactory work. The most authoritative is James F. Findlay's *Dwight L. Moody: American Evangelist, 1837-1899* (Chicago: University of Chicago Press, 1967). Much warmer in devotional emphasis are William Moody's *The Life of Dwight L. Moody* (1900; reprint, Murfreesboro, Tenn.: Sword of the Lord Publishers, n.d.), by his son, and John L. Pollack's *Moody: A Biographical Portrait* (New York: Macmillan, 1963). On the somewhat controversial Billy Sunday, one might try Lyle Dorsett's *Billy Sunday and the Redemption of Urban America* (Grand Rapids: Eerdmans, 1991).

Finally, the history of Fundamentalism has been a topic of special interest in the last few years. The best narrative history is one from within the Fundamentalist ranks: David O. Beale's *In Pursuit of Purity: American Fundamentalism Since 1850* (Greenville, S.C.: Unusual Publications, 1986). It simply does the best job of sorting through and organizing the countless men and movements associated with Fundamentalism's history. For a major interpretative discussion of the movement, see George Marsden's *Fundamentalism and American Culture: The Shaping of Twentieth-Century Evangelicalism, 1870-1925* (New York: Oxford University Press, 1980). For short and sometimes critical biographies of seven major Fundamentalist leaders, see C. Allyn Russell's *Voices of American Fundamentalism* (Philadelphia: Westminster, 1976). On recent developments, particularly the rise of the New Evangelicalism, see George Marsden's *Reforming Fundamentalism: Fuller Seminary and the New Evangelicalism* (Grand Rapids: Eerdmans, 1987); see also his *Understanding Fundamentalism and Evangelicalism* (Grand Rapids: Eerdmans, 1991). For a Fundamentalist counterbalance to these works, see Ernest Pickering's *Tragedy of Compromise: The Origin and Impact of the New Evangelicalism* (Greenville, S.C.: Bob Jones University Press, 1994).

CHAPTER 37
BIBLICAL STUDIES ON COMPUTER

At present computer studies are the fastest growing aspects of all Bible study. The best programs are expanding every year in features and content (and price). This review will show you the relative strengths of software programs. Of necessity it is a select list that will continue growing.

The best bargain for your money is *The Online Bible* 2.5.3, separate CD-ROMs for Macintosh or Windows. Not only do they provide ten different English translations and the Greek and Hebrew, but they also include the Bible in Spanish, French, German, Italian, Dutch, Russian, and so on. There are Bible dictionaries, Thayer's Greek Lexicon; BDB Hebrew Lexicon; topical studies; selections from commentaries by Matthew Henry, John Gill, A. T. Robertson, and John Wesley; the Geneva Bible Notes; and other helps. It is fun to open and tile a dozen of these resources at one time so that you can go through a passage comparing the different translations and comments verse by verse. It is also a great help to run searches through the Bible. They can be single words: "cross," phrases: "Son of God," or different words: "God" and "help" in the same verse, or complex studies of "life," "light," and "love" in I John. Higher priced CD-ROMs provide more of the modern copyrighted translations, such as the NASB, NIV, NRSV, and so on. (Call 908-741-4298.)

The most powerful and sophisticated search engine for biblical words is *Accordance* 2.0 for Macintosh or *Gramcord for Windows* 2.0 from the Gramcord Institute. Not only is it helpful for English word searches, but it is also especially valuable for Greek and

Hebrew (and Septuagint) word searches. It can run down Greek and Hebrew words, phrases, and specific grammatical forms as well. You may be looking for "I have spoken," (λελαληκα) a verb, first pers., sing., Perfect Active Indicative of λαλω; it will trace that exact grammatical form throughout the entire Greek New Testament. That study is a special blessing in John 14-16. The program also has Greek and Hebrew lexicons, Spicq's *Theological Lexicon,* the works of Philo and Josephus, Calvin's *Institutes,* the Historic Creeds, and other valuable helps. It is pleasant to run the cursor over a Greek or Hebrew word and see the location show up in the Parsing Box! (Call 360-576-3000.)

Logos Research Systems uses the same accurate Gramcord search engine, but it does not work as smoothly as in *Accordance.* However, the **Logos Bible Software** is a vast library search engine for PC only. It can not only search the Bible for a given word but also search for that word through a great variety of other books as well. Hence, it is most useful in connection with **Nelson's Electronic Bible Reference Library.** The Logos search engine can open on your screen any of Nelson's electronic books: *The New Treasury of Scripture Knowledge, Vine's Complete Dictionary of OT/NT Words, Nelson's New Illustrated Bible Dictionary, Matthew Henry's Unabridged Commentary* (6 vols.), Nelson's *3-D Bible Maps,* and many others. Logos has invited other publishing houses to use the Logos Library System, so there should be a steadily increasing number of biblical reference books available. It is too bad that this software does not work for the Macintosh. There are four levels of Logos Bible Software available. (Call 1-800-87-LOGOS; for Nelson, call 1-800-933-9673.)

Galaxie Software has added a valuable segment to the Logos Library System. They are producing Folio Views CD-ROMs of important theological journals. They offer a CD-ROM of Dallas Seminary's **Bibliotheca Sacra,** 1955-1995; another of the **Westminster Theological Journal,** 1980-1995; and they project that the **Grace Theological Journal** will follow. These CD-ROMs will work on both Macintosh and Windows. (Call 1-800-GALAXIE.) **The Ages Digital Library** is the economic best buy for a library of over 330 Bibles, commentaries, theologies, and other religious works. The books include Hodge's commentaries on Romans, I Corinthians, II Corinthians, and Ephesians; Calvin on Hebrews, Vincent's NT Word Studies (4 vols.); the *Complete Works of John Wesley* (14 vols.); Foxe's *Book of Martyrs;* Bunyan's *Pilgrim's Progress* and the *Holy War;* Law's *A Serious Call;* Luther's "95 Theses"; Jonathan Edwards's "Sinners in the Hands of an Angry God"; 12 sermons by D. L. Moody; Finney's *Lectures on Revival;* the complete Ante-Nicene and Post-Nicene Fathers (38 vols.); Spurgeon's *Morning and Evening;* Josephus's *Life and Writing;,* and many more. All the material is public domain and can be copied, pasted, and printed. The CD-ROM will work on either Macintosh or PC. (Call 1-800-297-4307.)

Bible Works for Windows is another strong search tool from Hermeneutika. It works more smoothly than the Logos system, but it is only a Bible search for PC. There seem to be a number of errors in the data bank; it will take some time to clean up the entries for the grammatical classifications. It emphasizes dictionaries and lexicons rather than commentaries. Bible Works also has optional extra modules. (Call 406-837-2244.)

Bible Master is a smooth, searchable version of the New American Standard Bible by American Bible Sales. Other translations with it include the KJV, NIV, and NRSV. The CD-ROM will work on either Macintosh or PC. (Call 1-800-535-5131.)

Quickverse 4.0 is a very fast search engine for windows from Parsons Technology. It deals largely with English translations. Since it complies with the STEP system of electronic publication, there will be other electronic books that it can read. For DOS or Windows only. (Call 1-800-223-6925.)

Kirkbride Technology produces the ***Thomson Chain Hyper-Bible,*** the only complete version available. Other companies offer only the elementary 1917 version, which is public domain. The CD-ROM offers a number of English translations, *Strong's Concordance,* and other helps. For Macintosh or Windows. (Call 1-800-428-4385.)

There are other individual CD-ROMs that have highly interesting material for Bible students.

Future Vision Multimedia produces *Pathways Through Jerusalem* on two CD-ROMs. There is a huge quantity of historical information from all periods of the city's history, an interactive main map that opens up photos and explanations of every conceivable tourist attraction, and nine guides that take you through tours that explain the Christian, Jewish, or Islamic significance of the places. Some guides are a distraction: King Herod sounds like a New York City car salesman!

Another very beautiful CD-ROM is *A Walk in the Footsteps of Jesus* that Parsons Technology produces. It is a virtual tour of Palestine with fisheye photographs of historic places and audio of Scripture for each place. One photograph of the Church of the Annunciation at Nazareth places the viewer in the plaza where he can pan around the plaza, coming back to the church; pan down to see pavement patterns; pan up to see the tower against the sky; click on the church door to find himself inside the church with a pan around the four walls to see the great murals. There are panoramas of the baptismal site at Jordan, a night pan of the plaza at the Wailing Wall in Jersusalem, a pan of the city of Capernaum with the synagogue, a pan from the shore of Galilee, a pan from the top of Mount Tabor, a pan of Jerusalem from the Church of All Nations at Gethsemane, many views of the interior of the Church of the Holy Sepulcher, a night pan of Jerusalem from the Seven Arches Hotel, and so on. The CD will work with either PC or Macintosh. (Call 319-395-0115.)

Logos Research Systems distributes *The Dead Sea Scrolls Revealed* by Pixel Multimedia. This is a CD-ROM for Macintosh or Windows that gives the history of their finding, the background and setting, a CAD fly-thru of the Qumran Community, and copies of the actual manuscripts. They can be enlarged to the point that you can actually read them (if you read paleographic Hebrew!). It is impressive to see the great Isaiah scroll. There are photos of the caves in which these were found and discussions by scholars of their significance. (Call 1-800-87-LOGOS.)

Emme Interactive has produced *The Gospels* from the New Jerusalem Bible. It is for Roman Catholics (with the approval of the Italian Bishop's Conference). The text may be searched for words or themes; there are explanations of terms and symbols. You may read the text while church music plays, or you may listen to the text being read while you look at reproductions of great art from the cathedrals and monasteries of Europe. It is different. For Macintosh or Windows. (Call 203-406-4043.)

Oxford University Press has produced a Bible for liberals: *The New Oxford Annotated Bible: Electronic Edition,* with the NRSV as text. There are CD-ROM versions for Macintosh or Windows. They hope to publish separately *The New Oxford Maps,* which may be worth investigating. (Call 1-800-334-4249.)

CHAPTER 38
BOOKS FOR THE PASTOR'S HEART

Academic preparation is not the only need in the expositor's life. His heart, too, needs to be "strangely warmed," his spirituality needs to be deepened, and his courage and faithfulness need to be strengthened. Although the number of so-called devotional books runs into the thousands, most of them are of little help for the expositor. Few pastoral books even give suggestions on this subject. But there are some books that are powerful preparations for preaching. After reading them, the fire burns in the bones.

For this extensive subject we must be extremely selective. The following books are chosen, not for their theology or even for their information, but for their spiritual impact. Although the reader may disagree with some of the biblical interpretations in some of these works, he will surely recognize that these men loved God and had a spiritual devotion and faithfulness that he needs in his own heart.

Biographical Works

Choy, Leona. *Andrew Murray: Apostle of Abiding Love.* Fort Washington, Pa.: Christian Literature Crusade, 1978. 276 pp. Mrs. Choy has given a modern portrait of one of the greatest devotional writers the church has ever had. Most of his books are thirty-one chapters long, designed to be read during a month of devotional meditations. She describes his conversion (pp. 42-43), his fifty-thousand-square-mile parish in South Africa (pp. 55 ff.), and his missionary heart (pp. 198 ff.). Especially valuable is her description of the background of his many devotional books: *Abide in Christ* (pp. 93, 254, etc.), *Absolute Surrender* (p. 245), *Like Christ* (p. 263), *The School of Obedience* (p. 268), *The True Vine* (p. 270), *Waiting on God* (p. 271), *With Christ in the School of Prayer* (p. 272), and many others. Murray introduced into the staid Dutch Reformed Church the custom of giving invitations and holding "after meetings" for the inquirers (pp. 124f., 230f.).

Davidson, Noel I. *First Citizen Smyth.* Belfast, Ireland: Ambassador Press, 1996. 143 pp. The story is a touching account of a dyslexic boy from Northern Ireland, Eric Smyth, who ultimately overcame all his trials and became Lord Mayor of Belfast. It recounts the early influence of Mormons on Smyth (pp. 11 f.), his conversion at a mission hall (pp. 19 f.), the change in his conduct (p. 27), Rev. Ian Paisley's influence on Smyth (pp. 36 f.), his intense struggle to learn to read the Bible (pp. 44, 48, etc.), his election as city councillor (p. 66), Dr. Peter Ng's influence (pp. 78 f.), his ordination (p. 84), his adoption of children with birth defects (pp. 111, 117), his courage when two of his children were arrested for drugs (pp. 126 f.), his welcome of President Clinton, and the lighting of the Christmas tree (pp. 138 f.).

Edwards, Jonathan, ed. *The Life and Diary of David Brainerd.* 1817. Reprint, Chicago: Moody, 1949. 385 pp. Edwards recounts how Brainerd used to walk in the woods and pray while the Indians watched him (p. 69), describes the effects of praying and reading the Bible (pp. 141-42), gives portraits of his preaching to the Indians (pp. 169, 175), records how he baptized his interpreter (p. 207), and describes the revival that occurred among the Indians (pp. 216 ff.).

Gartenhaus, Jacob. *Famous Hebrew Christians.* Grand Rapids: Baker, 1979. 207 pp. The author gives brief sketches of thirty-three converted Jews. These are highly interesting and heart-warming accounts of dedicated believers who often had to sacrifice everything for Christ. Some of these men are almost unknown, such as the first Anglican bishop of Jerusalem, Michael Solomon Alexander (pp. 29 ff.); others are world famous, such as the British prime minister Benjamin Disraeli (pp. 69 ff.) and the composer Felix Mendelssohn (pp. 129 ff.); others are well-known

Bible scholars such as Alfred Edersheim (pp. 75 ff.), David Baron (pp. 37 ff.), and Adolph Saphir (pp. 165 ff.).

Maher, Bill. *Beyond My Dreams.* Greenville, S.C.: Emerald House Group, 1996. 143 pp. This is the story of a triply disabled child who became a preacher with a worldwide ministry to the disabled. He describes the harsh treatment he received from "Christians" (p. 13), his conversion and change of attitude (pp. 27-28), his use of a tape recorder to learn how to speak correctly (p. 43), his first preaching opportunities (p. 48 ff.), his leading his own father to the Lord (p. 53), how he met his wife (pp. 63 ff.), his ministry at Bob Jones University (p 72 ff.), his starting of a weekly radio broadcast (pp. 97-98), his helping found Hidden Treasure Christian School (p. 117), and his mission trips to Brazil and Africa (pp. 119 f., 132 ff.)

Merle d'Aubigné, J. H. *The Triumph of Truth: A Life of Martin Luther.* Greenville, S.C.: Bob Jones University Press, 1996. 427 pp. This book is a powerful portrait of a courageous reformer. His trust in God in the study of Scripture is touching.

Morgan, Jill. *A Man of the Word.* New York: Revell, n.d. 404 pp. This book covers the life of G. Campbell Morgan. The author shows how he reorganized the Sunday school (p. 154) and how his Sunday morning messages were devoted to the continuous exposition of Bible books (p. 158).

Padwich, Constance E. *Henry Martyn: Confessor of the Faith.* Chicago: Moody, 1950. 254 pp. This book tells about the life of a sacrificial missionary and Bible translator.

Pierson, Arthur T. *George Mueller of Bristol.* New York: Revell, 1899. 492 pp. The author describes Mueller's systematic Bible study (p. 49), his habit of praying over the Bible as he studied (pp. 139-40), and the number of times he read the Bible through: two hundred (p. 287).

Wakefield, Gordon. *Bunyan the Christian.* London: HarperCollins, 1992. 143 pp. This is a short evaluation of John Bunyan as a believer. Gordon covers his early life as a preacher and controversialist (pp. 31 ff.), his imprisonment (pp. 53 ff.), his church (pp. 66 ff.), *The Pilgrim's Progress* (pp. 72 ff.), *The Holy War* (pp. 97 ff.), his last years (pp. 110 ff.), and the man: his place in the history of spirituality (pp. 118 ff.).

Wesley, John. *The Journal of John Wesley.* Chicago: Moody, 1951. 438 pp. Wesley describes hearing the preface to Luther's *Epistle to the Romans* read, its effect (p. 64), and his joy at being able to proclaim the love of Christ to sinners (p. 221).

Devotional Works

Augustine. *"The Confessions."* Vol. 1 of *Basic Writings of Saint Augustine.* Edited by Whitney J. Oates. New York: Random House, 1948. Augustine describes his conversion by reading Paul's epistles (pp. 125-27) and prays for understanding as he studies Scripture (pp. 183-85).

Bonar, Andrew A., ed. *Memoirs of M'Cheyne.* Chicago: Moody, 1948. 448 pp. This is a compilation of letters and sermons of a young saint.

Bunyan, John. *Grace Abounding to the Chief of Sinners.* Grand Rapids: Zondervan, 1948. 117 pp. In his spiritual autobiography, Bunyan tells of his conversion and early Christian life.

————. *The Holy War.* Chicago: Moody, 1948. 378 pp. Bunyan has also written another highly instructive allegory that more Christians should read. King Shaddai makes war upon Diabolus to regain the town of Mansoul.

————. *The Pilgrim's Progress.* New York: Rinehart, 1949. 329 pp. This work is known as the greatest Christian classic, second only to the Bible itself. Spurgeon read it a hundred times; Alexander Whyte preached and later published a famous series of sermons on Bunyan's characters *(Bunyan's Characters).* No preacher should be ignorant of this masterpiece.

Drummond, Henry. *The Greatest Thing in the World.* New York: Grosset and Dunlap, n.d. 45 pp. One need not agree with Drummond's theology to realize that he gives a powerful presentation of I Corinthians 13.

Foxe, John. *The Book of Martyrs.* New York: Eaton and Mains, n.d. 413 pp. Although this is not a pleasant book to read, there is no doubt that most of the terrible sufferings Foxe depicted are historically accurate.

Henry, Matthew. *The Quest for Communion with God.* 1712. Reprint, Grand Rapids: Eerdmans, 1954. 110 pp. This book gives deeply spiritual directions for maintaining fellowship with God. Henry covers how to begin every day with God (Ps. 5:3; pp. 9 ff.), how to spend the day with God (Ps. 25:5; pp. 39 ff.), and how to close the day with God (Ps. 4:8; pp. 72 ff.). He also warns against continuing under the power of a carnal mind, living without God in the world (p. 104).

Hiebert, D. Edmond. *Working with God Through Intercessory Prayer.* Greenville, S.C.: Bob Jones University Press, 1991. 129 pp. This work is a study of the ministry of intercession. Hiebert discusses the privilege of working with God (pp. 1 ff.); the power of prayer (pp. 9 ff.); the need for prayer-sent laborers (pp. 25 ff.); the prayer ministry of the church (pp. 35 ff.); examples of O.T. intercession (pp. 47 ff.); Epaphras, man of prayer (pp. 69 ff.); the Divine Astonishment (pp. 81 ff.); and learning to pray from Daniel (pp. 101 ff.).

Krummacher, Friedrich Wilhelm. *The Suffering Saviour.* Chicago: Moody, 1947. 444 pp. The author presents eloquent messages on the last week of the Lord's life on earth, divided into "The Outer Court," "The Holy Place," and "The Most Holy Place."

Murray, Andrew. *Abide in Christ.* New York: Grosset and Dunlap, n.d. 223 pp. Murray gives warm-hearted meditations on living in fellowship with the Son of God, based on John 15:1-12 and other suitable passages.

————. *The Spirit of Christ.* London: Nisbet, 1907. 392 pp. The author has written a month's meditations on the theme of the indwelling presence of the Holy Spirit in the believer, drawn from John 14-16, Romans 8, and other passages.

Newton, John. *Voice of the Heart (Cardiphonia).* Chicago: Moody, 1950. 432 pp. The reader will be inspired by the letters of this famous hymn writer.

Owen, John. *The Glory of Christ.* Chicago: Moody, 1949. 285 pp. The author gives devout meditations on the person of Christ and His glory, based on John 17:24.

Rutherford, Samuel. *The Letters of Samuel Rutherford.* Edited by Frank E. Gaebelein. Chicago: Moody, 1951. 480 pp. This book is a compilation of spiritual letters written by a famous theologian now remembered for his devotion.

Spurgeon, Charles H. *The Soul Winner.* Grand Rapids: Zondervan, 1948. 151 pp. Every pastor should read these impassioned yet practical messages on soulwinning by "the prince of preachers."

Tholuck, Friedrich August. *Light from the Cross.* Chicago: Moody, 1952. 293 pp. This book by a famous preacher and theologian presents messages on the suffering and death of the Lord.

Tozer, A. W. *The Pursuit of God.* Harrisburg, Pa.: Christian Publications, 1948. 128 pp. Tozer exhorts the believer to cultivate the sense of the presence of God in his life.

Wingert, Norman A., ed. *I Was Born Again.* Mechanicsburg, Pa.: Lighthouse Press, 1946. 254 pp. The editor has compiled moving stories of the conversions of Bob Jones Sr., Oswald J. Smith, Charles E. Fuller, Harry Ironside, J. Wilbur Chapman, and many others.

We ought not to neglect the devotional power of the great hymns. There are many books that record the stories behind the hymns; perhaps the best is Kenneth W. Osbeck's, *101 Hymn Stories.* (Grand Rapids: Kregel, 1982). He gives warm-hearted stories giving careful attention to accurate background.

CHAPTER 39
MORE BOOKS
FOR THE PASTOR

There are some books that do not fit exactly any of the categories covered in the chapters of the present work and yet are important for the pastor's notice. Some of the following works will provide many seed thoughts for messages, illustrations, and applications.

Philip Wesley Comfort's *I Am the Way* (Grand Rapids: Baker, 1994. 212 pp.) is a warmly devotional exposition subtitled "A Spiritual Journey Through the Gospel of John." He argues that John the son of Zebedee wrote the Gospel (pp. 28-30). Comfort knows the manuscript evidence (p. 30) and organizes the book as a journey of the Lord Jesus from heaven to earth, to the cross, and back to the Father in heaven; but the Lord intends to take believers with Him to the Father, and so the purpose of John is to lead readers to believe in the Lord Jesus for themselves (John 20:31). Comfort stresses the equality of the Lord Jesus with the Father (p. 66). Jesus is the "I am" (pp. 84 ff.), the Messiah Shepherd (pp. 92 ff.), and the Way to the Father (pp. 119 ff.).

The Eternal Sonship of Christ (Neptune, N.J.: Loizeaux, 1993. 126 pp.) by George W. Zeller and Renald E. Showers is a formal defense of the eternal sonship of Christ. They attack incarnational sonship (pp. 10 ff.). They defend the deity and pre-existence of the Son (pp. 17-22), list numerous Scriptures that teach the eternal sonship (pp. 26 ff., 36 ff.), and criticize those who deny the eternal sonship: F. E. Raven, *Dake's Annotated Reference Bible,* and John MacArthur Jr. (pp. 30 ff.). The authors discuss the meaning of the term "Son of God" (pp. 49 ff.) and the meaning of Psalm 2:7 (pp. 56 ff.).

They deal with the objections (pp. 65 ff.), stress the necessity and importance of the doctrine (pp 78 ff.), and conclude with testimonies to the doctrine by Spurgeon, Ironside, Charles Hodge, Warfield, John Murray, Scofield, John Walvoord, and so on (pp. 110 ff.). This is a refreshing and inspiring book.

Robert A. Peterson's *Hell on Trial: The Case for Eternal Punishment* (Phillipsburg, N.J.: Presbyterian and Reformed, 1995. 258 pp.) tries the reality of hell. As in a courtroom Peterson introduces the witness of the Old Testament (pp. 21 ff.), the witness of the Redeemer (pp. 39 ff.), the witness of the apostles (pp. 77 ff.), and the witness of church history (pp. 97 ff.) and then cross-examines the false witnesses: universalism (pp. 139 ff.), annihilationism (pp. 161 ff.), and so on. He then argues the case for eternal punishment (pp. 183 ff.).

Alan E. Bernstein's *Formation of Hell* (Ithaca, N.Y.: Cornell University Press, 1993. 392 pp.) is a worldly survey of death and retribution in the ancient and early Christian worlds. He covers the netherworlds of Greece and Rome: "If death were a release from everything it would be a boon for the wicked" (Plato, pp. 19 f.). He notes that Plato taught postmortem punishment (p. 52) and that some taught that ghosts could escape death (pp. 84 ff.)He observes, "What pagans attributed to human devising . . . Jews and Christians consider part of the providential working of divine justice" (p. 108). He quotes Daniel on the afterlife in ancient Judaism—"And many of those who sleep in the dust of the earth shall awake, some to everlasting life, and some to shame and everlasting contempt" (Dan. 12:2, p. 131)—but regards Daniel's view as a minority opinion (p. 178). Instead he recounts the views of Enoch (pp. 183 ff.).

On hell in the New Testament, he quotes from Jesus, "Depart from me, you cursed one, into the eternal fire prepared for the devil and his angels" (Matt. 25:41, p. 203), and says that the Christian view of history goes from Creation to Redemption to Resurrection (p. 205). "For the individual there is only one life: no reincarnation, no second chance after death. . . . Thus death become the deadline for conversion and right action" (p. 205). He claims, "There is no certainty concerning the authorship, the dates, or the order of composition of the books of the New Testament" (p. 205) and "Paul did not have a clear idea of hell" (p. 207) On the other hand, he says, "There can be no question about the threat of hellfire here" (Mark 9:43-48; p. 229). He stresses that the parable of the rich man in Sheol-Hades shows a principle of justice: Dives had received good things, Lazarus evil things; now matters are reversed (p. 240). Bernstein sees a "myth" that governs the content of the whole Bible: man is responsible and judgment is coming (pp. 248 ff.). In that regard, he argues that in Revelation the Lamb is not only Redeemer but also avenger (p. 255), that God's vengeance is divine wrath, manifested in fire and brimstone, torments that will endure forever (p. 256); that the good will see the torments of the wicked (p. 257); that the wicked will be tormented day and night forever and forever (this certainly denoting eternity; p. 258); that the lake of fire and sulfur receives the Devil, the Beast, and the False Prophet, and then all the dead. Thus hell finally contains all the authors of evil in the universe (p. 259): "It is eternal, fiery, and contains all whose robes were not made 'white in the blood of the Lamb' (Rev. 7:14)" (p. 259). Bernstein also discusses the opinions of the church fathers (pp. 267 ff.).

Stanley J. Grentz's *Primer on Postmodernism* (Grand Rapids: Eerdmans, 1996. 199 pp.) is an introductory survey on the ideology of postmodernism. He surveys the opinions of Derrida, Foucoult, and Rorty (pp. 6 ff.); sees a point of contact between postmodernism and *Star Trek: The Next Generation* (pp. 8 ff.); and shows that postmodernism denies absolute Truth, a single worldview, and belief in inevitable progress (pp. 8-13). Postmodernists are prepared to mix Christian and non-Christian ideas (p. 15). Grentz charges that postmodernism is a centerless movement (p. 19); that postmodernist architecture puts together elements incompatible in style and form (p. 23); that postmodernist art prefers "impurity" in style (p. 25); that postmodernist theater gives no sense of permanent truth (pp. 27-28); that the postmodernist filmmaking industry blends truth, fiction, reality, and fantasy (pp. 32 f.); that television has now disseminated postmodernism throughout society, bringing together news, storytelling, war, murder, sex, scientific discoveries, sports, advertisements, old movies, the weather, sitcoms, cop shows, soap operas, as all of equal importance, blurring past and present together (pp. 33-35); that postmodernism ends an appeal to any central legitimating "myth"; that it attacks all things that claim universality (p. 45); that postmodernism has killed a unified science; and that there are only shifting areas of inquiry (pp. 46 ff.). Grentz recounts Nietzsche's attack on Modernism (pp. 88 f.), Dilthey's turn to experience (pp. 99 ff.), Heidegger's idea of "being there" (pp. 104 f.), Gadamer's opinion that interpreters cannot discover the meaning of history (pp. 109 ff.), and Foucoult's attraction to homosexuality (p. 125). Grentz concludes that Christians must reject the central postmodernist ideas:there is a universal central truth revealed in Christ—He is the incarnate Son, the Second Person of the Triune God (p. 164). We must admit that the postmodernists were correct in some of their criticisms of "Modernism" (pp. 165 ff.); we need to recognize that the goal of God's program is the establishment of a community, not just salvation of individuals (p. 168).

With *Christian Reflections,* we come to the gleanings of the literary productions of a great man, C. S. Lewis. These essays, published posthumously (Grand Rapids: Eerdmans, 1967), are written in his usual polished style. Many of them provide real help in Christian faith. Lewis was always stressing the "enormous common ground" (p. vii) of true believers in Christ, regardless of their backgrounds. He had nothing to say on divisive doctrines.

One of the essays of particular importance is "Modern Theology and Biblical Criticism." Although Lewis specifically disclaims being a Fundamentalist (p. 163), he brings one of the most crushing attacks against Bultmann and his fellow critics that can be found in any writing. He charges them with a whole array of errors from "lack of literary judgement" (p. 154) to an imaginative reconstruction of ancient documents (p. 158). He states bluntly, "These men ask me to believe they can read between the lines of the old text; the evidence is their obvious inability to read (in any sense worth discussing) the lines themselves. They claim to see fern-seed and can't see an elephant ten yards away in broad daylight" (p. 157). We heartily agree that Bultmann foists his opinions on the text "with shocking lack of perception" (p. 155).

Many of these essays provide good examples of Lewis's memorable thought. In "Christianity and Literature" he says, "The unbeliever is always apt to make a kind of religion of his aesthetic experiences. . . . But the Christian knows from the outset that the salvation of a single soul is more important than the production or preservation of all the epics and tragedies in the world" (p. 10). In "Christianity and Culture" he concludes that "culture is a storehouse of the best (sub-Christian) values. . . . They will save no man" (p. 23). In "Poison of Subjectivism" he advances the idea, "Either the maxims of traditional morality must be accepted as axioms of practical reason which neither admit nor require argument to support them and not to 'see' which is to have lost human status; or else there are no values at all" (p. 75).

In some of these essays there are disturbing elements. In "The Funeral of a Great Myth," Lewis attacks the "myth" of evolution, but he refuses to call the scientific hypotheses of practicing biologists myths. He does emphasize that the general tenor of the process called evolution is degeneration and not improvement (p. 85). In the essay "The Psalms," he gives some poor interpretations of the "imprecatory Psalms" (p. 118). He calls such petitions "wicked" (p. 120), although he admits that Mary's Magnificat and the words of our Lord were steeped in the Psalms (p. 121).

In spite of such errors, this collection as a whole is well worth reading. The concluding essay, "The Seeing Eye," gives some solemn warnings about space travel. "We are not yet fit to visit other worlds. We have filled our own with massacre, torture, syphilis, famine, dust bowls and with all that is hideous to ear or eye. Must we go on to infect new realms?" (p. 173). Such words do provoke thought.

When a new book in the field of Old Testament theology comes from the press, the conservative pastor may find no more of the biblical revelation left than "two legs, or a piece of an ear" (Amos 3:12) that the devouring lion of unbelief has left. It is refreshing, therefore, to come across a little book that does manifest a clear faith on theological subjects. Such a book is F. F. Bruce's *New*

Testament Development of Old Testament Themes (Grand Rapids: Eerdmans, 1968). Although he spends much time quoting opinions of everyone from spokesmen for the Vatican Council II (p. 12) to liberal critics such as Hans Conzelmann (p. 38), Bruce does clearly defend the revelation of God.

Bruce treats seven prominent Old Testament themes found also in the New Testament. On the "Rule of God" he refers to Daniel 2, in which one like a son of man comes to rule (p. 26). He finds a clear connection with our Lord's use of this title, even though he does not make much of the eschatological use of the title. In "Salvation of God" he begins with the Exodus and concludes with the Lucan portrait of redemptive history. In "The Victory of God" he draws material from the imagery of Ugaritic myths (p. 41), concluding with the imagery of the Apocalypse (p. 50). In "The People of God" he works from the covenant in the Old Testament to the new Israel (p. 62). Premillennialists will not be happy that he gives an amillennial interpretation of Acts 15 in "The Son of David" (p. 79). He does give an impressive treatment of the "Servant Messiah," showing the relationship between Isaiah 42 and the following chapters and the New Testament uses of this theme. He concludes with "The Shepherd King." The reader need not agree with everything here to find real help in the interpretation of these great biblical themes.

A truly great book on the New Testament doctrine of salvation is Leon Morris's *Cross in the New Testament* (Grand Rapids: Eerdmans, 1965). It will suggest many ideas for sermons. It is an excellent treatment of soteriology after the method of biblical theology. Morris traces the teaching of the cross through the entire New Testament in chronological order. His knowledge of the literature on the subject is impressive. But his portrayal of Paul's doctrine of "The Plight of Man" will provoke whole series of sermons on sin, death, demonic powers, the flesh, and other subjects. In the same way, the section on "The Salvation of God" will provide rich material on the death of Christ, deliverance, the gospel, justification, and life "in Christ." His last section on the Pauline Epistles, "Man's Response," is equally valuable on repentance, faith, the life of the believer, and other subjects. The church certainly needs a renewed emphasis on the great doctrines of the Faith. This book belongs on every pastor's bookshelf.

An investigation of the documentary evidence for the faith of the first Christian Roman emperor is Thomas George Elliott's *Christianity of Constantine the Great* (Scranton, Pa.: University of Scranton Press, 1996. 366 pp.). Elliott argues that Constanine's father, Constantius, was also a Christian but a compromising one (pp. 22-27); holds that Constantine regarded the war against Maxentius as a Christianizing mission (pp. 48-49); claims that the vision of the cross did not convert him but confirmed his already existent faith and prompted him to have a standard made (pp. 67-69, 71 ff.); gives quotations that show how Constantine argued for correct doctrine against the Donatists (pp. 88 ff.); holds that his broad legislation came from his Christian way of thinking (p. 104); shows that he outlawed crucifixion as a legal punishment (p. 108) but would not legislate people into being "Christians" (p. 114); and shows that in the Edict of Milan Constantine gave religious freedom to all (p. 117). Elliott holds that Constantine was a conscientious Christian who was not part of the Christian community because he was not baptized until at the point of death (p. 214). Elliott also holds that Athanasius was a bitter and unscrupulous adversary of Eusebius of Nicomedia, who himself was not a perfect Arian and could sign the Nicene Creed sincerely (p. 227). He takes Constantine's letter against Arius as genuine and defends its logic (pp. 279 ff.), thinks that Constantine was trying to be "Catholic" and Athanasius was "schismatic" (p. 319), and concludes that Constantine was a better Christian (and ruler) than many modern scholars think (pp. 329 f.). One need not agree with all of Elliott's views to recognize that this is a valuable study in church history.

When a pastor or other Christian worker has finished a long day's work for the Lord, sometimes he feels like sitting back for a few minutes and relaxing with a good book. But where in modern fiction can a Christian find a good book? The late J.R.R. Tolkien wrote a whole series of marvelously entertaining books. His prologue, *The Hobbit,* and the great trilogy *The Lord of the Rings* (*The Fellowship of the Ring, The Two Towers, The Return of the King*) (New York: Ballantine, 1937-65) appear to be delightful fairy stories, but the reader is soon caught up in the cosmic struggle between good and evil that brings the third age of middle earth to an end. Frodo (a three-foot-tall Hobbit) must bear the sinister ring of power to its destruction, although he cannot use it, for it corrupts all who use its power. For pure enjoyment and high adventure, this is the best tale of our times.

CHAPTER 40
THE CRITICS' CORNER

Some books have dangerous misconceptions or outright doctrinal errors in them and yet provide some valuable help on certain important subjects. The following books will provide many helpful ideas and yet must be read with great caution.

The Five Gospels: The Search for the Authentic Words of Jesus (New York: Macmillan, 1993. 553 pp.) by Robert W. Funk, Roy W. Hoover, and the Jesus Seminar is an attempt by men to make a scholarly equivalent of the red-letter New Testament. Their edition, however, is a red, pink, gray, and black edition. These scholars state bluntly that "eighty-two percent of the words ascribed to Jesus in the gospels were not actually spoken by him" (p. 5). In their view the red words alone are authentic; the pink means Jesus probably said something like this; the gray means Jesus did not say this but the idea may go back to Him; the black means Jesus never said anything like this (p. 36).

Most of the Gospels are in black type. They treat the Gospels in the order of Mark, Matthew, Luke, John, and the noncanonical Gospel of Thomas, which is known only from a few Greek fragments and a Coptic translation. The only red-letter statement in Mark is from Mark 12:17: "Pay the emperor what belongs to the emperor, and God what belongs to God" (p. 102). They also list this saying in Matthew 22:21 and Luke 20:25 (pp. 236, 378). They list a half dozen statements in Matthew in red letters, but some are mere fragments. In Matthew 5:44 only the phrase "love your enemies" is in red (p. 145). In the Lord's prayer only "Our Father" is in red (Matt. 6:9, p. 148). In Matthew 13 only the short parable of the leaven is in red (13:33, p. 195). In the Gospel of Luke they list nine passages in red, including the parables of the good Samaritan and the unjust steward (Luke 10:30-35; 16:1-8*a*; pp. 323, 357 f.). They do not list a single word in red in the Gospel of John. They give only a single statement even in pink: John 4:44, which is translated as "A prophet gets no respect on his own turf" (p. 412). On the other hand, they give three passages in the Gospel of Thomas red letters (20:2-3, 54; 100:2-3; pp. 484, 504, 526). In their dictionary of terms. they classify all four canonical Gospels as anonymous works that are not authentic (pp. 545-46).

These men may be scholars, but they are biased against the text of the New Testament. They are unbelievers, seeking the approval of the world. Even in their dating they will not use the traditional A.D and B.C. but use instead the Jewish classifications C.E. and B.C.E. (the Common Era, Before the Common Era; p. 543). They may call the Lord Jesus Christ "common," but we will object to such bitter renunciation. Such teaching may be acceptable at Harvard, Rutgers, Vassar, Notre Dame, and Ball State (p. xiii), but it is not acceptable to believers in the Lord Jesus Christ. Any candid reading of the Gospels gives men a portrait of the Lord that is gripping and powerful. All the scholarly devices of these unbelievers cannot hide the beautiful picture of Christ, the Savior of the world. Heaven and earth may pass away, but His words shall not. Let us read them with faith.

A formal critique of the Jesus Seminar and its publication, *The Five Gospels,* is **The Real Jesus** (San Francisco: HarperCollins, 1996. 182 pp.) by Luke Timothy Johnson, a Catholic scholar at Emory. He charges that the Jesus Seminar is a self-appointed group of about forty participants with perhaps two real scholars among them, who dare to speak for the scholarly world (pp. 2-3). *The Five Gospels* is a color-coded book that throws out the picture of Jesus as the divine Son of God and presents Him as mere man (pp. 20 ff.). It rejects the Gospel of John and replaces it with the Gospel of Thomas (pp. 14, 21). Johnson criticizes the men who discount the Bible: Borg, Crossan, and Mack (pp. 39, 44, 50). He warns that critical university professors fail to meet the needs of students who intend to be pastors (p. 75). He argues that the New Testament is the best historical witness to the origin of Christianity (p. 89). He gives numerous agreements in sources concerning Jesus (pp. 112 ff.) He lists seventeen points of agreement between Paul and the Gospels (pp. 121 ff.). He urges that the real Jesus must be the resurrected Jesus (pp. 135 ff.). He holds that there is profound unity of understanding concerning Jesus throughout the N.T. literature (p. 152). The pursuit of the historical Jesus is really a flight from the image of Jesus in Scripture (p. 166). As a N.T. teacher, he asserts that "Jesus is Son of God made flesh" (p. 170). Although his Catholicism is a problem, he has shot a dangerous movement down in flames.

The Feminist Gospel. (Wheaton, Ill.: Crossway Books, 1992. 287 pp.) by Mary A. Kassian is a history of the feminist liberation movement showing women's desire to name themselves, the world, and God.

Kassian quotes noted feminists, such as Mary Daly, who attacked the character of God and the Bible (pp. 40-41); Letty Russell and Mary Ruether, who chose the liberation of women as the main controlling principle and "interpreted the Bible according to their preconceived definitions" (p. 58); Adrienne Rich, who attacked the institution of motherhood, saying that women should produce as many children as they want, in or out of marriage (pp. 79 f.) and who attempted to make lesbianism "natural" (pp. 83 ff.); and Fiorenza, who advocated a hermeneutic of suspicion, choosing Galatians 3:28 and throwing away other verses (pp. 111-13).

Kassian also points out that the feminists defined doctrines to suit themselves. God exists to serve man, not man to serve God (p. 95). Jesus is not one who saves, but an example of salvation (p. 96). Sin is not a violation of right and wrong, but a situation of no community (p. 96). Salvation is a journey toward freedom from sex-class oppression (pp. 96-97). The church exists to serve the revolution, not God (p. 97). On eschatology, feminism will bring in the new humanity and the new age (p. 97).

In the pursuit of feminism, women's studies have urged no absolutes, no truths (p. 121). Kassian describes the "Feminization of God" (pp. 135 ff.): to refer to God as male is idolatry (pp. 140-41), but feminists have decided to apply feminine titles to God—"She," "Mother," and so on (p. 144). They argue that Father, Ruler, Judge, Master, and King should not be applied to God (p. 145). Mollenkott uses "He/She/It" for the Trinity (p. 145). Bloesch warns that feminists are here to deny who God is: Father/Son/Holy Spirit (p. 146). Rita Brock holds "Jesus Christ need not be the authoritative center of a feminist Christian faith" (p. 147).

Kassian shows the connection between Feminism and witchcraft (pp. 149 ff.). Daly suggests not attacking God but just leaving "Him" behind (p. 153). Charlene Spretnak moves to pantheism, "The Goddess is All" (p. 160). Z. Budapest suggests the goddess "is self worship" (pp. 162, 168). Russell says that "the Word of God is **not** identical with Biblical texts" (p. 169), and authority really lies in community (p. 170). Ruether redefined "conversion" so that it is not a religious experience (pp. 170-71) and gives a new canon: Hebrew and Greek mythology, Christian Science, paganism, goddess worship, and new "post-Christian consciousness" (p. 172). Elaine Pagels advocates Gnosticism: "only one's own experience offers the ultimate criterion of truth" (p. 176). Mollenkott urges changing "God" from a noun to a verb: we all need to go about "godding" (manifesting God's love in human flesh, p. 185). And Ruether commends forming the "Women-Church," the exodus community (pp. 196-97).

To the feminist, all correct interpretation of the Bible starts with women's rights (p. 208). Kassian documents the change in the Feminist Movement: the original "Biblical Feminist Liberation." Mollenkott, Scanzoni, and Hardesty "left evangelicalism to join liberal religious feminism." The EWC became the Evangelical and Ecumenical Women's Caucus in 1990. Their replacements are marching off in the same direction: Margaret Howe, Patricia Gundry, and Mary Stewart VanLeeuwen (p. 216). Kassian quotes the pagan witch Margot Adler as stating, "Feminists and pagans are both coming from the same source without realizing it and heading toward the same goal without realizing it, and the two are now beginning to interlace" (*Drawing Down the Moon: Witches, Druids,*

Goddess-worshippers and other pagans in America today, p. 182 [p. 219]).

In conclusion Kassian warns that the Feminist Liberation movement is on "the slippery slope that leads towards a total alteration or rejection of the Bible" (p. 227). She then gives examples in the changing emphasis of Mary Daly, Rosemary Ruether (pp. 233 f.), and Virginia Mollenkott (pp. 237 ff.). Kassian argues that only God has the right to name Himself (pp. 242 ff.). She wishes to balance a real submission to God's Word with a refusal to submit to abusive male superiority (p. 247). Only the Bible contains the real hope for the liberation of women (p. 253).

Although modern society is critical and sophisticated, it is still faced with the supernatural. This is the thesis of Peter L. Berger's *A Rumor of Angels* (New York: Doubleday, 1969. 129 pp.). Man may talk about the death of God, but man cannot escape Him that easily; man may scoff at the thought of angels and demons, but angels and demons go right on existing despite the inability of modern man to perceive them (p. 52). This book is not written from a conservative viewpoint, but it is certainly thought-provoking to any reader.

Berger is a professional sociologist, and he always argues from that viewpoint. He states that man is strongly influenced by the faith of those about him. Man's beliefs do not exist in a vacuum; his beliefs are affected by other members of a society. Consequently, it is difficult for a member of a minority faith (such as Fundamentalism) to maintain his faith in the face of the universal unbelief surrounding him. Liberal Protestantism has long been open to "dialogue" with the opposing views and quick to embrace those views. Berger thinks that this manifests, at the least, "lack of character" on its part (p. 12). Roman Catholics have maintained a much more closed attitude toward outside thought, and, consequently, they have preserved their faith more fully. A Catholic who does listen to outside thought often goes all the way over to existentialism. "If one once starts to clobber the opposition, one stops clobbering at one's peril" (p. 17). This is the very thing that conservatives have said concerning the New Evangelicals; they have stopped clobbering the opposition, and it is only a matter of time until they join the opposition to orthodoxy.

Another major point that Berger scores is the double standard of modern theology. Modern theologians speak patronizingly of the relative ignorance of the apostle Paul and others of the first century. They wish to make all the teachings of the New Testament relative. These same theologians, however, set forth their own opinions as though they were infallible, as though "every thinking man" would have to agree with them. If people in the past had only a relative grasp of the truth, the present generation of scholars is afflicted with the same malady (as the next generation will be quick to point out). The conservative will not admit that the apostle Paul was mistaken, but he can perceive at once the inconsistency of the liberals' double standard (p. 51).

When Berger sets forth his argument for the existence of the divine world, he makes the mistake that most modern theologians make: he starts with man and ignores divine revelation. This reduces the value of the book precipitously; though he is probably right in his arguments, he does not go far enough. He gives the illustration of the child who wakes up in the middle of the night from a nightmare, crying. His mother comes in and says, typically, "Everything is all right." Berger raises the question, "Is the mother lying to the child?" (p. 68). If the mother is a Christian, she is uttering a profound truth (Rom. 8:28), but if the mother is an unbeliever, everything is not all right. At any rate, this statement presupposes a divine order behind all the events of the universe. Even unsaved men have a consciousness of such an order. In the same manner Berger argues from play (pp. 72-75), hope (p. 75), damnation (p. 81), and humor (p. 86) that there must be a divine world. The conservative will regret that Berger does not show that clear revelation in the Bible concerning the existence of such a world.

Let no one think that Berger is a conservative. He makes it very clear that he does not accept the facts the New Testament sets forth concerning the gospel record as historical (p. 115). Even though his book has limited value, it does expose the illogic of modern society and the inconsistency of modern theology.

Nathan A. Scott Jr., of the University of Chicago Divinity School, has written a book, *The Broken Center* (New Haven: Yale University Press, 1966. 237 pp.), in which he surveys the theological horizon of modern literature. He has put his finger on a sore spot in today's literature. In all earlier periods of literature, God was the center around which man's life, literature, society, and morals revolved. For modern man, God is missing, the center of life is broken, and all of life is in doubt and conflict. Scott refers to the famous saying of Albert Camus that for the human mind only two possible worlds exist: the world of grace and the world of rebellion. Modern man, having rejected the grace of God, finds himself lost in the world of rebellion.

In his chapter "The Bias of Comedy," Scott clearly asserts the reality of the incarnation: "Jesus Christ *is* God Himself incarnate" (p. 113). On this basis Scott urges an attitude of respect for the things of this world, "since for approximately thirty years this was the home of God himself" (p. 115). The hero of tragic literature chooses himself, not God, and is guilty for his choice (pp. 126-27); consequently, his life must end in defeat (p. 131). Scott raises the question of whether there can be a "Christian tragedy" and concludes that, in the light of eternity, the answer must be "No" (pp. 135-38). For modern man, however, this is still Good Friday (p. 141). Today the idea of the "sacred" is gone; there is death of the awareness of God (p. 150). In sharp terms Scott charges that the modern theologian is without anything to say to the world (p. 163). The modern "Christian" has lost the Word, the church, and God Himself. Scott calls the idea that God is dead a myth (p. 186).

Although the conservative would not share some of his presuppositions and although some of the literature he surveys is revolting, Scott still gives a critical appraisal of modern literature, philosophy, and theology that is strikingly accurate and illuminating. This book leaves the conservative Christian profoundly thankful that the center of his life is filled by "the living God."

Wayne A. Meeks's *The First Urban Christians* (New Haven: Yale University Press, 1983. 299 pp.) is a sociological study, subtitled "The Social World of the Apostle Paul." Meeks gives the background for the first-century evangelism of the church; describes the cities in which Paul ministered (pp. 40-50); portrays Paul as a Greek-speaking Jew in a Roman world (p. 50); and has an interesting discussion of "evil and its reversal" (pp. 183 ff.) that includes bondage and liberation, guilt and justification, estrangement and reconciliation, deformity and transformation.

Allan Bloom, a professor at the University of Chicago, has delivered a devastating criticism of higher education in America in his *Closing of the American Mind* (New York: Simon and Schuster, 1987. 392 pp.). He charges that the sole virtue inculcated by the university system is relativism: openness to all ideas without belief in any truth (pp. 25-26). This openness is actually the closing of the mind against all truth (p. 34). Students have lost not only the desire for real knowledge but also any desire for religion. "Real religion and knowledge of the Bible have diminished to the vanishing point" (p. 56). Bloom regularly asks his classes what books really count for them. For the vast majority of his students there is not a single book that means anything to them (p. 62). Such a student could walk through the Louvre with his ignorance of the Bible and classical literature, viewing Raphael, Leonardo, and Michelangelo, seeing nothing more than colors and forms (modern art). He would be totally ignorant of the stories that give meaning to the paintings (p. 63). Bloom charges rock music with destroying the minds of modern youth. The three great themes of rock music are "sex, hate and a smarmy, hypocritical version of brotherly love" (p. 74). He believes that "it ruins the imagination of young people and makes it very difficult for them to have a passionate relationship to the art and thought that are the substance of liberal education" (p. 79). When they finally grow up and leave rock music, they will find that they are deaf to all else (p. 81).

Bloom maintains that modern students are totally self-centered (pp. 82 ff.). They no longer have heroes; they are survivalists (p. 84). All the great ideas that have moved men (country, religion, family, etc.) have been rationalized away and "have lost their compelling force" (p. 85). Female modesty has been phased out (p. 89).

Young people no longer love one another; there is a passionless "relationship" (p. 99). Bloom is shocked to see a young couple live in sin during their college years and then break it all up with a handshake and move out (p. 123). Young people do not have love affairs any more; they have "relationships" (p. 124).

One of the things that most disturbs Bloom is "value relativism" (p. 142). He deplores the idea introduced by German philosophy that "God is dead" (p. 143). "The truth is the one thing most needful" (p. 179). Now men talk about the "dignity of man." It used to be that God had dignity. Now man is the highest of beings (p. 180). Man, who needs God, has now lost "his Father and Savior" (p. 195). Bloom, however, does not write from a Christian viewpoint. He urges seeking authentic values through the great religious leaders. "Moses, Jesus, Homer, Buddha: these are the creators, the men who formed horizons" (p. 201). Bloom sees the seriousness of the problems. Modern man thinks his basic rights are "life, liberty, and the pursuit of property and sex" (p. 233). Bloom quotes Rousseau: "Ancient statesmen spoke endlessly of morals and virtue; ours speak only of commerce and money" (p. 304).

All Bloom can propose for a solution is a return to the study of the great books (p. 344). He would include the Bible as one of them (p. 374). He even deplores the fact that the Bible is treated either under higher criticism or comparative religions. "A teacher who treated the Bible naively, taking it at its word, or Word, would be accused of scientific incompetence and lack of sophistication. Moreover, he might rock the boat and start the religious wars all over again" (p. 374). The best he can recommend is reading Plato and Shakespeare (p. 380).

Bloom's book is valuable because it accurately portrays the evils of the modern, worldly university system and the total collapse of standards and morals in modern society. The believer in Christ knows the real solution to this problem. Faith in Christ and His Word is the solution to all that Bloom deplores in modern life.

Donald E. Knuth in his *3:16 Bible Texts Illuminated* (Madison, Wis.: A-R Editions, Inc., 1991. 268 pp.) studies the Bible using the "stratified sampling" method (p. 5). He samples the Bible by looking at the 3:16 reference in all the different biblical books. He omits the books that are too short to have the 3:16 reference, but for those that have too short a chapter, he counts on into chapter 4 to get a 3:16 (Ps. 4:8, [pp. 82 ff.]). This method gives him fifty-nine verses to use (p. 7). His view is that stratified sampling gives a better grasp of the subject than random sampling would. That leaves open the question of whether a consecutive, verse-by-verse study would give an even better impression of the subject. Knuth refers to the numbering of the Israelites at over six hundred thousand armed men, commenting that "almost every Bible scholar agrees that these numbers are impossibly large" (p. 24). His method of study by sampling has obviously given him tunnel vision. He commends the documentary hypothesis for Genesis (p. 10). The fact that he uses his own translation for the verses leaves something to be desired. The element that makes this work highly interesting is that every verse used is portrayed in calligraphy. Many of these works of art are challenging and thought-provoking: Judges 3:16 (p. 35); I Samuel 3:16 (p. 43); II Samuel 3:16 (p. 47); II Kings 3:16 (p. 55); Job 3:16 (p. 79). At times the calligraphy is a little confusing (I Kings 3:16 [p. 51]; Isaiah 3:16 [p. 99]; Lamentations 3:16 [p. 107]). There are, however, other verses in which the artist manifests genuine insight and real helpfulness in interpretation: Matthew 3:16 (p. 159); Acts 3:16 (p. 174); II Corinthians 3:16 (p. 187); Galatians 3:16 (p. 191); II Thessalonians 3:16 (p. 211); and II Peter 3:16 (p. 235). There are some artistic portraits that must be termed brilliant: John 3:16 (p. 171); Ephesians 3:16 (p. 195); and I John 3:16 (p. 239).

There are some books that deal with a vital subject but manifest such negative overtones that they fail to be of much help. Such a series is *New Testament Theology* published by Cambridge University Press. *The Theology of the Johannine Epistles* (Cambridge: Cambridge University Press, 1991. 130 pp.) by Judith M. Lieu sees multiple authors and editors in the Johannine literature, "yet to none of these figures can we put a name" (p. 17); systematically refers to "the holy spirit" in lower case (pp. 29, 45-49);

stresses the language of religious experience (pp. 31 ff.); and sees a hint of cosmic dualism (p. 82).

Another such work is *The Theology of the Shorter Pauline Letters* (Cambridge: Cambridge University Press. 208 pp.) by Karl Donfried and I. Howard Marshall. On Thessalonians, Donfried argues that "Jesus died and rose again and is undoubtedly a pre-Pauline formula" (p. 33); he holds that Paul was "an ecstatic prophet thoroughly shaped and influenced by the milieu of Jewish mystical-apocalypticism" (p. 39). On Philippians and Philemon Marshall defends Pauline authorship (pp. 118, 177); warns against problems caused by dogs, evil doers, and mutilators (p. 123); defends the Pauline authenticity of the "hymn" section (p. 129); studies the phrase "in Christ" (pp. 138-44); concludes that the theology of Philippians expresses the same thinking that lies behind the other Pauline letters (p. 166); and sees in Philemon the implication that Christian faith is incompatible with ownership of slaves (p. 190). Marshall has produced the best portion of this series.

A negative approach to New Testament Theology is Andrew Chester and Ralph P. Martin's *The Theology of the Letters of James, Peter, and Jude* (Cambridge: The University Press, 1994. 189 pp.). Chester thinks the arguments for James's authorship are not compelling (p. 14); is not certain about the background (p. 15); discusses faith and works, concluding that James contradicted Paul (pp. 20-28, 46); speaks of James's "savage indictment of the rich" (p. 30); attacks the attempts to conform James to the rest of N.T. teaching (p. 39); denies that James has the elevated Christology that is "read into" 2:1 (p. 44); holds that James's theology "may be deficient and inadequate in some respects" (p. 59). Martin summarizes Jude's theology as adherence to the Faith once delivered to the saints (p. 75), holds that God acts through Jesus and that includes judgment (p. 77), sees Jude as a window and a mirror for us today (pp. 81 f.), on I Peter leaves open the question of authorship (p. 92); thinks that there is a growing consensus that I Peter is genuine (p. 98), evaluates the descent into hell (p. 144), on II Peter argues against Petrine authorship (pp. 137-46), lists modern doubts (pp. 148-51),; and sneers at II Peter's "vigorous use of invective" (p. 163).

CHAPTER 41
RECOMMENDED OLD TESTAMENT COMMENTARIES

The expositor should avoid spending money on inferior commentaries. If he takes the time and the trouble to select the best commentaries on the individual books of the Bible, he will have a library of unparalleled helpfulness and value to him all his life. As he uses them, he will notice that the content of his preaching is being greatly strengthened. One never outgrows the best commentaries. The expositor should try to obtain two or three of the best commentaries on each of the New Testament books and as many of the best commentaries as he can on Old Testament books. Good books are much rarer in the Old Testament field.

The following list, like the preceding bibliographies, is selective. Books with an asterisk(*) before their entry should be in every expositor's library; they may never be equaled.

Genesis

Leupold, Herbert Carl. *Exposition of Genesis.* Columbus, Ohio: Warburg, 1942. 1,220 pp. Leupold's work is the most thorough and helpful exposition of Genesis. Leupold defends Mosaic authorship (pp. 6-7), attacks the documentary hypothesis (pp. 13-20), advocates literal Creation days (pp. 56-58), has a rich treatment of 3:15 (pp. 163-70), holds that "sons of God" in Genesis 6 were Sethites (pp. 250-51), argues for a universal Flood (pp. 301-4), and attacks the charge that the patriarchs were legendary (p. 405). He does have a typically Lutheran overemphasis on the sacraments (p. 120).

Candlish, Robert S. *Commentary on Genesis.* 2 vols. 1868. Reprint, Grand Rapids: Zondervan, n.d. 479, 381 pp. This book is a rich devotional and practical exposition. Candlish seems to allow for long ages before the six days of Genesis (I, p. 19), is helpful on "The Fruit of the First Sin" (I, pp. 71-85), holds that the "sons of God" in Genesis 6 were the righteous who married the godless (I, p. 122), and attacks the documentary hypothesis (II, pp. 349-55). The book contains many digressions and cross-references but has a helpful treatment of most passages.

Keil, C. F., and F. Delitzsch *Genesis.* Vol. I, *The Pentateuch.* Grand Rapids: Eerdmans, n.d. Pp. 1-414. This work provides a careful exposition of the Hebrew text. The authors maintain the historical credibility of Genesis, the reality of supernatural revelation from God (p. 28), and the historicity of the Creation account (p. 37); believe that the days of Creation were literal days (p. 51), the serpent was a tool of Satan (p. 92), the "sons of God" were Sethites (p. 128), and the Flood was universal (p. 146); have a helpful exposition of Abraham's call (pp. 192-95) and of 15:6 (pp. 212-21); and hold that Lot's wife did not become salt but was encrusted with it (p. 235).

Exodus

Davis, John J. *Moses and the Gods of Egypt.* Grand Rapids: Baker, 1971. 331 pp. This is the best recent commentary on Exodus and is illustrated by many photos and drawings. The author provides a chronological chart; defends an early date for Exodus (1445 B.C., pp. 14-33); defends Mosaic authorship, the supernatural character of the burning bush, and the plagues (pp. 37 ff., 62, 84 ff.); gives careful explanations of difficulties (pp. 71-72); denies that there were secondary causes in the death of the firstborn (pp. 133-34); has a chart of the Hebrew calendar (p. 142); defends the accuracy of the number 600,000 (pp. 146-47); argues for the miraculous nature of the events in the crossing of the Red Sea (pp. 165-66); suggests the Bitter Lakes region for crossing (pp. 169 ff.); gives Ugaritic parallels of Bitter Lakes region for crossing (pp. 169 ff.); gives Ugaritic parallels of the law (p. 236); defends the reality of the tabernacle as a revelation from God (p. 243); warns against abusing types and numbers (p. 247); argues for a flat-roofed tabernacle (p. 250); charges Jereboam with stealing Aaron's sermon outline on the golden calf (p. 285)!

Keil, C.F., and Franz Delitzsch. *Exodus.* Vols. I and II, Biblical Commentary on the Old Testament. 1859-60. Reprint, Grand Rapids: Eerdmans, 1956. 346 pp. This is a thorough commentary on the Hebrew text. The authors defend Mosaic authorship (I, pp. 17-28); hold that the burning bush was a miracle (I, p. 438) and that the plagues were also miraculous (I, pp. 478-79, 481, 483, etc.), especially the death of the firstborn (II, p. 24); defend the accuracy of the number 600,000 (II, pp. 28-29); stress the miraculous nature of the events at the crossing of the Red Sea (II, pp. 46-48); and hold that the tabernacle was actually built (II, pp. 162, 259).

Leviticus

Bonar, Andrew. *A Commentary on the Book of Leviticus.* Grand Rapids: Zondervan, 1959. 513 pp. Originally published in the nineteenth century, this work is sometimes wordy but always spiritually beneficial. It maintains that the rites of Leviticus were typical, "intended by God to bear resemblance to some spiritual truth" (p. viii). The comments are verse by verse and rich in allusions to the gospel and parallels to Christ and His work.

Wenham, Gordon J. *The Book of Leviticus.* The New International Commentary on the Old Testament. Grand Rapids: Eerdmans, 1979. 361 pp. The author argues against the standard critical view of Levitical sources (p. 7); gives various views of authorship and date but remains noncommittal; he, however, does suggest that the evidence points to an early rather than postexilic date (pp. 8-13). He provides a helpful section on the theology of Leviticus, including a discussion on the book's relevance to the Christian (pp. 15-37); notes that the role of the law was not a means to salvation but a response to salvation "teaching," "how men are to imitate God" (p. 34); gives comments on the text that are thorough, explaining both the general meaning and significant details. There are also helpful discussions of the structural patterns for each section. The book also demonstrates the typical significance for the various sacrifices and claims that Christ is "the only sufficient burnt offering'" and that His blood was the payment of the "'perfect ransom price" (p. 65). Concerning the detailed laws of Chapter 19, he claims that applications may change but the "fundamental principles of holy living remain unaltered" (p.275).

Numbers

Harrison, R. K. *Numbers: An Exegetical Commentary.* Grand Rapids: Baker, 1992. 452 pp. This is a useful commentary that still leaves much to be desired. Harrison defends Mosaic authorship (pp. 21 ff.), but with later editing (p. 24), has a brief section on the theology of Numbers (pp. 25-28), defends the high numbers quoted (pp. 45-48), describes the seriousness of Miriam's attack on Moses' authority (pp. 197 ff.), and holds that Balaam was not a true prophet of the Lord but a self-seeking hireling (p. 331).

Wenham, Gordon J. *Numbers.* The Tyndale Old Testament Commentary. Downers Grove, Ill.: InterVarsity Press, 1981. 240 pp. This is a commentary on the Hebrew text that usually quotes the RSV. He defends Mosaic authorship (pp. 21 ff.), has a careful discussion on the theology of Numbers (pp. 39-49), gives four different solutions to the high numbers without warmly commending any (pp. 62-66), and regards Balaam as a Babylonian diviner (p. 179).

Deuteronomy

Keil, C.F., and F. Delitzsch. "The Fifth Book of Moses (Deuteronomy)," in *The Pentateuch,* trans. James Martin. Grand Rapids: Eerdmans, n.d., V 269-531. This commentary has an eight-page introduction, which divides Deuteronomy chapters 1-30 into three great addresses: Chapters 1-4, Chapters 5-26, and Chapters 27-30. The work is conservative, detailed, and regularly punctuated with references to the Hebrew. It is typically "Keil and Delitzsch." It correctly interprets 6:4 as teaching that Jehovah is "the one absolute God" rather than as teaching His "unity." It properly evaluates love for God under the "new covenant" as "more intensive and cordial" (p. 324) but not otherwise different from love under the "old covenant." It recognizes the generic nature of the word *prophet* in 18:15, referring to "the sending of prophets generally," but also recognizes the messianic nature of "a prophet . . . like unto" Moses (pp. 394-95). It notes the general nature of the dispersion and regathering in Chapter 30, not limiting it to Assyrian and Babylonian captivities (p. 452). This old commentary does not deal specifically with the suzerainty treaty form of Deuteronomy and with matters of form criticism, but it is an excellent aid for the serious student.

Merrill, Eugene H. *Deuteronomy.* Vol. 4, New American Commentary. Nashville: Broadman and Holman, 1994. 477 pp. This is the most helpful present exposition based on the NIV. Merrill argues for Mosaic authorship and a date of c. 1400 B.C. (pp. 22-23, and gives a clear outline (pp. 38-40) and a short theology of Deuteronomy (pp. 47-56). He holds that the purpose of Deuteronomy was to call the people of Israel to covenant renewal (p. 67), harmonizes apparent anachronisms (pp. 94, 98), distinguishes apodictic and casuistic laws (pp. 144 ff.), links the law with Jesus' interpretation of it (p. 157), shows that Jesus emphasized the need for love and obedience to God (pp. 163-64), stresses the need to remember the Lord's words (p. 210), defends the prophecy of the central sanctuary (pp. 222 f.), holds that Deuteronomy 27 is a list of "statutes whose violation brings a curse" (p. 346), argues that Jeremiah used Deuteronomy to describe the Babylonian captivity (p. 365), and defends the Song of Moses (p. 408).

Schneider, Bernard N. *Deuteronomy: A Favored Book of Jesus.* Grand Rapids: Baker, 1970. 163 pp. Schneider is a conservative author laboring under the conviction that God's people in the twentieth century neglect Deuteronomy, failing to recognize that its emphasis on love makes it to the Pentateuch what John's Gospel is to the four Gospels (p. 11). He begins the book with "A Bird's Eye View of Deuteronomy," in which he states the purpose as "reminding Israel for all time of their special relationship to God" (p. 15). He points out clearly that Deuteronomy has much instruction for believers today since it teaches the need for a proper "heart" response to God (p. 20). In the remainder of his book, Schneider considers various aspects of Deuteronomy that have especially rich application to the Christian. His comments on Deuteronomy 6 regarding love and fear for God are insightful (pp. 56-59). He is sensitive to the book's material warning against false prophets and apostasy (pp. 83-90) and has an especially interesting, but rather superficial, section on witchcraft and wizardry (in connection with 18:9-22). He gives proper consideration to the curse material in Chapter 28 (131-37) but leaves Chapter 30 in the realm of the futuristic and fails to integrate it with the development of Deuteronomy's theology (pp. 137-41). In all, however, this little book is very devotional, helpful, and inspirational and is a delightful contribution to the pastor who has never really appreciated Deuteronomy properly.

Joshua

Blaikie, William G. *The Book of Joshua.* 1908. Reprint, Minneapolis: Klock and Klock, 1978. 416 pp. The book begins with a general survey of approaches to Bible history and gives a lengthy biography of Joshua, the man. This commentary is divided into chapters by particular topics that may or may not relate to chapter divisions of Joshua. Comments are general without any technical or direct reference to specifics of the text. It includes some good applications and recognizes the supernatural throughout.

Davis, Dale R. *No Falling Words: Expositions of the Book of Joshua.* Grand Rapids: Baker, 1988. 204 pp. The author's comments are general but full of helpful applications and preaching hints. He notes that the story of Rahab stresses God's sovereignty and the beauty of grace, claims that interpreters get so involved with Rahab's lie that they overlook her truth (p. 26), and stresses the centrality of the ark in the crossing of the Jordan. Davis also notes that although Israel was active, the people were primarily spectators (p. 33) and that crossing the Jordan at flood stage taught them the lesson that only God's grace and power can prevent His people from being overwhelmed in impossible times (pp. 38, 39). The title of his chapter "Joshua did not fight the battle of Jericho" makes a clear point (p. 51). He also says that the extermination of the Canaanites was an expression of God's highest and most patient justices (p. 52). The focus on the "ban" showed that the conquest was a true holy war and not a means for Israel to become rich (p. 55). He notes that the real miracle in Chapter 10 was the issue of prayer. He argues that the long day involved a period of darkness (pp. 84-86).

Judges

Wood, Leon. *Distressing Days of the Judges.* Grand Rapids: Zondervan, 1975. 434 pp. This is the most helpful conservative exposition to date. Wood argues for an early date for the book (pp. 10-17), holds that Judges was written to record Israel's sin (p. 37), gives an extensive introduction (pp. 1-157), includes maps (pp. 138, 142, 164, 170, 190, etc.), holds that God caused the Kishon to overflow and mire Sisera's chariots (p. 192), gives careful distinctions between two kinds of water-lapping by Gideon's men (p. 232, note 26), evaluates the interpretations of Jephthah's daughter, favoring her celibacy rather than sacrifice (pp. 288-95), and concludes with chapters on Eli and Samuel (pp. 341-97).

Ruth

Cox, Samuel. *The Book of Ruth.* London: Religious Tract Society, 1876, 1910. 155 pp. This is a warm-hearted devotional exposition. The author explains the mistake Elimelech made in leaving the Promised Land (pp. 31 ff.); stresses the strength of love Ruth manifested to Naomi (pp. 50-51); shows the compassionate attitude of Boaz (pp. 67 ff.); explains the Muenuchah, "rest" that Ruth found in Boaz (pp. 81 ff.); stresses the kinsman redeemer that Ruth found in Boaz (pp. 91 ff.); and concludes with Christ, the true kinsman redeemer of mankind (pp. 146 ff.).

I and II Samuel

Blaikie, W. G. *The First Book of Samuel.* 1887. Reprint, Minneapolis: Klock and Klock, 1978. 440 pp. In this warm-hearted exposition, the author discusses the problem of seemingly unanswered prayer (pp. 16 f.), teaches human depravity (p. 22), shows parallels between the Song of Hannah and the Song of Mary (pp. 30 ff.), attacks a Romanist attitude toward the sacraments (pp. 65 f.), balances divine predestination and human freedom (p. 122), denies that Saul was regenerated (p. 131), harmonizes alleged errors in Scripture (pp. 241, 268, 373 f.), defends Samuel's silent purpose in visiting Jesse (p. 255), teaches a hierarchy of moral responsibility (p. 334), and attacks the sin of drinking (p. 433).

Davis, John J. *The Birth of a Kingdom.* Grand Rapids: Baker, 1970. Pp. 1-110. In this brief exposition of I and II Samuel, the author gives a short introduction and background (pp. 17-27); discusses Samuel as judge and prophet (pp. 28 ff.), Saul as a rustic warrior and rejected king (pp. 42 ff.), and David as a valiant shepherd (pp. 64 ff.) and fugitive (pp. 75 ff.); attacks situation ethics (p. 81); and includes a number of photographs of biblical subjects (pp. 21, 42, 50, 56, 69, etc.). He holds that the Amalekite who claimed to slay Saul was a mercenary (p. 112); includes photos of Hebron (p. 116), the pool of Gibeon (p. 119), the wilderness of Judah (p. 132), Tekoa (pp. 150-51), and more; gives reasons for God's refusing to let David build the temple (pp. 135-36); and terms Joab a ruthless military leader (p. 159).

Blaikie, W. G. *The Second Book of Samuel.* 1887. Reprint, New York: Armstrong, n.d. 400 pp. In this warm-hearted exposition, the author holds that the Amalekite lied about Saul's death (pp. 2-3); stresses the light that the gospel of Christ has brought to man (p. 60); sees parallels between David and Christ (pp. 65,

246 f.); defends the messianic meaning of the Davidic promise (p. 107); relates David's repentance to Psalm 51 (pp. 182 ff.); describes old age as a crown set with six stones (pp. 312 f.); analyzes David's last song (p. 351); urges men to come to Christ to receive His free grace (p. 375); and summarizes the content of I and II Samuel (pp. 388-400).

I and II Kings

House, Paul R. *1, 2 Kings.* Vol. 8, The New American Commentary. Nashville: Broadman and Holman, 1995. 432 pp. In this reverent and careful exposition based on the NIV, the author recommends a single author for Joshua through II Kings (p. 38); defends the miracles in Scripture (p. 54); contrasts true prophecy with the lying spirits (pp. 78 f.); portrays the strengths and weaknesses of David and Solomon (p. 95); stresses the messianic hope in Jesus Christ (p. 103); shows the complexity of Solomon's kingdom that required skilled organization (p. 116); explains the work force that Solomon used in building (p. 158); notes that Baal was the storm god who brought rain (p. 210); explains Micaiah's prophecy with care (pp. 236-38); warns against a multicultural society (p. 249); defends Elisha's judgment on the forty-two boys (pp. 260 ff.); emphasizes that Israel was divided between the remnant who served God and the rebellious majority who did not (p. 312); and calls the exile God's most important warning (p. 404).

Keil, C. F., and F. Delitzsch. *The Books of the Kings.* 1877. Reprint, Grand Rapids: Eerdmans, 1950. Pp. 1-283. In this thorough commentary on the Hebrew text, the authors date Kings in the last half of the Babylonian exile (p. 11), harmonize differences between Kings and Chronicles (p. 63), list the seven petitions of Solomon's prayer (pp. 128-33), give a chronological chart of the kings of Israel and Judah (pp. 189-90), and defend the miracles of Elijah (pp. 231-32).

Whitcomb, John C. *Solomon to the Exile.* Grand Rapids: Baker, 1971. Pp. 1-66. In these brief studies in Kings and Chronicles, the author argues that God merely permitted the old kings to have multiple wives (p. 17), provides a chronological chart (p. 22), has some illustrations and diagrams of Samaria (pp. 39-41), holds that literal "ravens" fed Elijah (p. 50), has a photo of the horse stables of Ahab at Megiddo (p. 52), and defends the miraculous nature of the fire on Carmel (p. 56) and the obedience of Elijah in executing the prophets of Baal (p. 56). He identifies the lads who mocked Elijah as "irresponsible delinquents" (p. 67); defends Elisha's miracles (pp. 72 f.); has photos of the Moabite stone (p. 70), the Black obelisk (p. 86), Hezekiah's tunnel (p. 113), and other background; defends the miraculous nature of Hezekiah's deliverance (pp. 121 f.); attacks Wallhousen's idea that the Book of the Law is a "pious fraud" (p. 136); and concludes with a helpful bibliography (pp. 159-61).

I and II Chronicles

Selman, Martin J. *I Chronicle* and *II Chronicles.* 2 vols. The Tyndale Old Testament Commentary. Downers Grove, Ill.: Inter-Varsity Press, 1994. 551 pp. This is a helpful commentary that holds that the Chronicler is giving interpretation of the Bible (p. 26). He stress the Davidic Covenant (pp. 45 ff.) and Jerusalem as the proper place of worship (pp. 56 ff.), dates Chronicles in the fourth century B.C. (p. 71), emphasizes David as king (pp. 138 ff.), thinks that the account of Solomon is basically continuing David's history (pp. 285 f.), holds that the NT shows a link between worship and God's glory (p. 316), discusses Solomon's slave labor (pp. 347 f.), and states that the account of Jehoshaphat has a "historical nucleus" but much of the geographical data "cannot be verified" (p. 422).

Ezra and Nehemiah

Kidner, Derek. *Ezra and Nehemiah.* The Tyndale Old Testament Commentaries. Downers Grove: InterVarsity Press, 1979. 174 pp. The author adopts the traditional date for the book (p. 77). He thinks that Hanani may have been either a brother or a kinsman (p. 78); argues from archaeological evidence that Geshem was more powerful than Sanballat or Tobiah (p. 83); emends the text occasionally (e.g., pp. 94, 99) and admits the possibility of copyist errors as an explanation for differences between the various lists of people and places found in Nehemiah and in Ezra and Chronicles (pp. 103, 125); explains Shemaiah's confinement (6:10) as due to ritual defilement (p. 99); and defends Nehemiah's handling of the mixed marriages (13:23-39) compared with the reforms of Ezra.

Esther

Whitcomb, John C. *Esther: The Triumph of God's Sovereignty.* Chicago: Moody, 1979. 128 pp. This is a conservative exposition. The author argues for a Persian date (p. 13) and the historicity of the book (pp. 16-20), supplies a great amount of historical background (pp. 30-36, 38-42, etc.), explains the meaning of "the gate" (p. 60), and argues that prayer is implied in the mention of fasting (p. 79), and that all Scripture is inerrant (p. 105). There are also charts of Old Testament kings and prophets, a ground plan of Persepolis, and maps (pp. 5 ff.). The book concludes with a selected bibliography (pp. 127-28).

Job

Alden, Robert L. *Job.* Vol. 11, The New American Commentary. Nashville: Broadman and Holman, 1993. 432 pp. In this careful exposition based on the NIV, the author takes Job to be an actual person from patriarchal times (pp. 25-26); has a brief survey of the theology of the books (pp. 39-40); holds its purpose is to show that God knows all things and guides them all to His ultimate purpose (p. 41); shows that God limits the power of the Devil (p. 56); says that Eliphaz states the position of the three friends: good comes to the righteous and bad to the wicked (p. 8); notes a chiasmus quoted in I Corinthians 3:19 (p. 94); classifies the constellations carefully (p. 26); holds that Job expresses confidence in God's justice (13:15, p. 158); defends Job's hope in his Redeemer, Jesus Christ (p. 207); thinks that Job was sure that God directed his steps and would make him a better person (p. 242); says that Elihu disagrees with both Job and his friends: God is greater than they have said (pp. 324 f.); shows that Jehovah blitzed Job with questions about the natural creation (p. 368) and challenged Job's idea of divine justice (p. 393); and says that Job confessed that his God had been too small (p. 408).

Barnes, Albert. *Job.* 2 vols. Edited by Robert Frew. Grand Rapids: Baker, n.d. 702 pp. In this thorough conservative exposition, Barnes argues that Job was a real person (pp. ii-viii) and denies critical claims that God's transactions with Satan were fictional (p. vi). He locates Uz in northern Arabia (pp. viii-xiii), dates Job in the patriarchal era (pp. xii-xiv), defends the integrity of the book (pp. xiv-xv), credits Job himself as author (p. xxxvii), denies that "Daysman" is a particular reference to Messiah (I, pp. 224-25), sees no allusion to the Resurrection in 19:26 (I, p. 328), describes "behemoth" as a hippopotamus (II, pp. 242-47) and "leviathan" as a crocodile (II, pp. 253-56).

Davidson, A. B. *The Book of Job.* The Cambridge Bible. Cambridge: University Press, 1908. 296 pp. Davidson claims that the book is not literal history although it is based on historical traditions (pp. xvii, xviii). He says that the Elihu section was not an original part (p. xi), defines Job's fear of God as including both right thinking and conduct (p. 3), identifies the sons of God as angels and suggests that Satan's coming before God indicates God's overall providence (pp. 6, 7), and takes the behemoth as an Egyptian word that has been "Hebraized" (p. 279).

Zuck, Roy. *Job.* Chicago: Moody, 1978. 192 pp. Although the author's comments are over large sections of text, they do include specific interpretations when necessary. The style is popular and practical. The author favors the view that Job himself is the author of the composition (p. 9); lists twelve reasons for dating the events of Job to the patriarchal age (pp. 9-11); argues that the fact that leviathan may be a creature in myth tradition does not mean that Job believed in myths (p. 24); offers a concise summary of the speeches of Job's friends (pp. 29-31); gives a good review of the translation and interpretation options of 19:25-27 (p. 88); and concludes that one of Job's purposes is to show that the motive for worship is not a "give and get bargain with God" (p. 189).

Psalms

Spurgeon, Charles Haddon. *The Treasury of David.* 6 vols. 1882. Reprint, Grand Rapids: Zondervan, 1966. 428, 487, 490, 479, 479, 470 pp. Spurgeon's is the most helpful exposition of the Psalms. He has many pithy statements in his own comments: "Prayer without fervency is like hunting with a dead dog" (I, p. 50) and "Faith derives both light and life from God, and hence she neither dies nor darkens" (II, p. 178). He quotes gems from a vast array of other authors: "Those that lie in jest will (without repentance) go to hell in earnest" (John Trapp, I, p. 58) and "The benefit of life is not in the length, but in the use of it. He sometimes lives the least that lives the longest" (Seneca, II, p. 148).

Leupold, Herbert Carl. *Exposition of the Psalms.* Columbus, Ohio: Warburg, 1959. 1,017 pp. In a most thorough and helpful exposition, Leupold defends the titles giving authorship of some psalms (Psalm 90 by Moses, Psalm 72 by Solomon, p. 7); dates the completion of the psalter c. 400 B.C. (p. 8); attacks Mowinckel's interpretations (pp. 11-12); defends the imprecatory psalms (pp. 18-20); states the doctrines in Psalms (pp. 22-27); defends "kiss the son" in Psalm 2 (pp. 54-55), the messianic meaning of Psalms 16, 22, 45, 72, 110 (pp. 153, 196-97, 351, 516, 770-71), and the Davidic authorship of Psalms 32 (p. 264) and 51 (p. 399); stresses the eternal nature of the Davidic covenant in Psalm 89 (p. 638); and has a most thorough exposition of Psalm 119 (pp. 821-61).

Perowne, J. J. Stewart. *The Book of Psalms.* 2 vols. 1864. Reprint, Grand Rapids: Zondervan, 1966. 614, 523 pp. Perowne provides good translations, outlines, and exhaustive notes. He defends an early date for the psalter (I, 18) and offers help on the messianic psalms (pp. 41-55) and the imprecatory psalms (I, 62-65); defends some, but not all, inscriptions (I, 103); thinks Solomon wrote Psalm 1 (I, 108); defends the messianic meaning of "son" in Psalm 2 (I, 118); often gives helpful outlines of psalms (I, 172, 201-2, 222, 266, 295, 369, 381, 505; II, 438); has illuminating comments on Psalm 51 (I, 411-24); holds that Psalm 90 is by Moses (II, 163); and defends the prophetic character of Psalm 110 (II, 296).

Delitzsch, Franz. *The Psalms.* Keil and Delitzsch Commentaries. 3 vols. 1859-1860. Reprint, Grand Rapids: Eerdmans, n.d. 428, 420, 420 pp. This work is a thorough commentary on the Hebrew text. Delitzsch gives a history of the exposition of the Psalms (I, pp. 47-64); discusses their doctrines (I, pp. 64-78); attacks those who deny the messianic meaning of Psalm 2 (I, p. 91); defends "kiss the son" (I, p. 98); sees a human and messianic meaning in Psalm 8 (I, pp. 156-57); defends the messianic meaning of Psalm 16 (I, p. 230), Psalm 22 (I, p. 305), Psalm 45 (II, p. 74), Psalm 72 (II, p. 299), Psalm 110 (III, pp. 184 ff.), Psalm 118 (III, p. 229); defends the Davidic meaning of Psalm 51 (II, p. 134) and the Mosaic authorship of Psalm 90 (III, p. 48); and has a careful exposition of Psalm 119 (III, pp. 242-68).

Gaebelein, Arno Clemens. *The Book of Psalms.* Neptune, N.J.: Loizeaux, 1939. 509 pp. This book contains premillennial and devotional studies organized according to the five books of Psalms. He explains the imprecatory psalms as cries of the tribulation saints (p. 12); draws extensive parallels between the five books of the Psalms and of the Pentateuch (pp. 12-14); offers many dispensational interpretations (pp. 19, 42, 52, 61, 131, 255, and so on); stresses the eternal sonship of Christ (p. 24); attacks rationalism (p. 97), divine healers (p. 171), Bullinger (p. 202), and evolution (p. 343); foretells the return of the Jews to their land (p. 265); and mentions that the first verse he ever learned was 50:15 (p. 217).

Lloyd-Jones, D. Martyn. *Faith on Trial.* Grand Rapids: Eerdmans, 1965. 125 pp. In an outstanding exposition of Psalm 73, Lloyd-Jones discusses why the righteous must suffer, states that the great periods of Protestantism realized the need of discipline (p. 23), stresses the need of spiritual thinking (p. 38) and understanding (p. 44), charges that idealists fail to take sin into consideration (p. 49), holds that man is not getting better (p. 50), gives powerful illustrations of the death of the wicked (pp. 51-52), urges self-examination and discipline (pp. 70-71), gives a reformed interpretation of Hebrews 6 (p. 92), argues for final perseverance (pp. 100 ff.), and urges preaching heaven and hell (p. 120).

Proverbs

Garrett, Duane A. *Proverbs.* Vol. 14, The New American Commentary. Nashville: Broadman and Holman, 1993. Pp. 1-252. In this strong exposition based on the NIV, the author has a clear discussion of verse patterns (pp. 33 f.) and structure (pp. 39 ff.); gives a date of early monarchy, holding that Solomon's authorship is reasonable (pp. 51-52); has a careful outline of Proverbs (pp. 59-62); points out chiastic structure (pp. 71, 142, etc.); holds that parents have the greatest opportunity of shaping the lives of young people (p. 86); argues that wisdom (Prov. 8) is a powerful personification of Christ but not a reference to Him (p. 112); takes Agur and Lemuel as real persons, not pseudonyms (pp. 235, 245); and thinks that Almah means merely "young woman" (p. 241, n. 21). Included in the same volume are expositions of Ecclesiastes and the Song of Solomon. He thinks that the Song is merely a love song (pp. 365 f.) and commends Karl Barth's interpretation as best (pp. 375 ff.).

Kidner, Derek. *The Proverbs.* London: Tyndale, 1964. 192 pp. In these short technical comments, he gives a brief outline (p. 22); holds that the contents could have been in existence in Solomon's time but not gathered into one book (p. 27); suggests several subject studies: God and man (p. 31), wisdom (p. 36), the fool (p. 39), the sluggard (p. 42), words (p. 46), the family (p. 49), and life and death (p. 53). His comments hold that wisdom is often personified (p. 60); describe the lifelong pilgrimage: seek, choose, concentrate (p. 66); and discuss the praise of wisdom in Proverbs 8 (p. 76), the proverbs of Solomon in Proverbs 10 (p. 84), the way of life in Proverbs 12:28

(p. 100), and the heaven or hell at home (p. 133). He concludes with a short concordance (pp. 185-92).

Ecclesiastes

Garrett, Duane A. *Ecclesiastes.* Vol. 14, The New American Commentary. Nashville: Broadman and Holman, 1993. Pp 253-345. In this careful exposition based on the NIV, Garrett argues for Solomonic authorship (pp. 257-67); gives a thirty-five point outline for the book (pp. 269 f.); holds that the purpose is to drive the reader to God and to help him see life as a gift from God (pp. 275, 278); thinks the key word is *vapid,* "meaningless" (p. 282); stresses that all joys are fleeting (p. 291); stresses that the ability to enjoy life is a gift from God (p. 300); urges the reader to live reverently before God (p. 310); and holds that the final poem exhorts readers to remember the Creator before old age and death come (p. 340). See also Garrett, Proverbs.

Song of Solomon

Burrowes, George. *Commentary on the Song of Solomon.* 1856. Reprint, London: Banner of Truth Trust, 1958. 453 pp. This work is a warm-hearted exposition aimed at the "soul animated with fervent love for the Lord Jesus, and craving the hidden manna which the Holy Spirit has lodged in this precious portion of the Scriptures" (p. 12). He gives an extended analysis of the Song, interpreting it as the relationship between the Lord Jesus and His people (pp. 31-66). His comments stress that Solomon wrote of the consummation of the love of Christ and His church (p. 71). He wishes to claim the promise of "I will love him, and will manifest myself to him" (John 14:21); refers to "O thou whom my soul loveth" and urges that such love far transcends love of power, money, and so on (p. 110); holds that the "rose of Sharon" applies to the bride (2:1, p. 180), as does 2:7 (p. 212); quotes Virgil (p. 305), Homer's *Illiad* (p. 306) and *Odyssey* (p. 405), John Bunyan's *Pilgrim's Progress* (p. 434), and so on; and concludes with Revelation 22:20 (p. 453).

Isaiah

Young, Edward J. *The Book of Isaiah.* 3 vols. Grand Rapids: Eerdmans, 1965-1972. 534, 604, 579 pp. Young's book is a strongly reformed, amillennial exposition. The author defends the authorship and unity of Isaiah (II, 556-65; III, 538-49) and interprets the millennial prophecies as applying to the Christian church in the present age (II, 446 ff.).

Jennings, F. C. *Studies in Isaiah.* New York: Loizeaux, n.d. 784 pp. This book is a thought-provoking premillennial exposition by a Plymouth Brethren expositor. Jennings clearly distinguishes between Israel and the Christian church in prophecy (pp. 417 ff.).

*Delitzsch, Franz. *The Prophecies of Isaiah.* 2 vols. 1877. Reprint, Grand Rapids: Eerdmans, n.d. 461, 524 pp. Delitzsch provides a thorough commentary on the Hebrew text. The author holds to the unity of Isaiah (I, pp. 56-62), applies kingdom predictions to the church (I, p. 116), argues that 7:14 and 9:6 apply to Messiah (I, pp. 218, 248-53), thinks that the Jews will be restored (I, p. 289), denies that *Lucifer* refers to the Devil (I, p. 312), defends Isaiah as author of chapters 40-66 (II, pp. 132-38), argues that the Servant Songs refer to Christ (II, pp. 174 f.), claims that 52:13–53:12 "looks as if it had been written beneath the cross upon Golgotha" (II, p. 303), and seems to admit the possibility of a millennium (II, p. 493).

*Leupold, Herbert Carl. *Exposition of Isaiah.* 2 vols. Grand Rapids: Baker, 1968, 1971. 589, 379 pp. In a thorough, helpful commentary, Leupold criticizes ideas of multiple authorship (I, pp. 19-27); argues that *almah* means virgin in the strictest sense (I, p. 156); thinks that Chapter 24 describes universal judgment (I, pp. 373 ff.); holds that Isaiah 32 refers both to a contemporary of Isaiah and to the Messiah but that Isaiah 35 refers only to the future Messiah (I, pp. 497, 536); maintains that the Servant is the Lord Jesus Christ alone (II, pp. 59 f.); attacks liberal interpretations (II, p. 80); argues that God names Cyrus 150 years before he appeared (II, p. 116); argues for the unity of the book (II, pp. 261-62); refers to the Old Testament church

(II, p. 307); and does not see the millennium in 65:19-25
(II, pp. 366-67).

Jeremiah

Laetsch, Theo. *Jeremiah.* St. Louis: Concordia, 1952. 412 pp. Laetsch's
work is a conservative amillennial Lutheran commentary. The
author denies the premillennial interpretation (p. 57), attacks liberal views (p. 101), defends messianic prophecy (p.
190), and interprets the new covenant as fulfilled in the New
Testament church (pp. 257, 270).

Lamentations

Kaiser, Walter C. *A Biblical Approach to Personal Suffering.*
(Lamentations) Chicago: Moody, 1982. 141 pp. In this brief
exposition of Lamentations, Kaiser lists ten aspects of the disaster that overwhelmed Israel (p. 18), organizes Lamentations
by a chart (p. 24), argues for Jeremiah as the author (pp. 24-
29), holds that Lamentations 3:22-24 is the focal point of the
whole book (p. 35), provides teaching outlines for each chapter (Chapter 1, pp. 46-47, Chapter 2, p. 65, Chapter 3, p. 82,
Chapter 4, p. 101, and Chapter 5, p. 113), and concludes with a
discussion of eight different kinds of suffering (pp. 121 f.).

Ezekiel

Feinberg, Charles Lee. *The Prophecy of Ezekiel.* Chicago: Moody,
1969. 286 pp. This book is a conservative premillennial exposition. Feinberg stresses the unity of the biblical message of
redemption through Jesus Christ (p. 98), teaches the judgment
and restoration of Israel to the land (pp. 114 ff.), holds that the
language of Chapter 28 refers to Satan (pp. 161-62), teaches a
literal conversion of the Jews (p. 205), places the invasion of
Gog and Magog at the end of the Tribulation (pp. 218-19),
argues for a literal millennial fulfillment of Chapters 40-48
(pp. 234-39), and includes a helpful bibliography (pp. 280 ff.).

Daniel

Boutflower, Charles. *In and Around the Book of Daniel.* 1923.
Reprint, Grand Rapids: Zondervan, 1963. 314 pp. This work is

not a connected commentary but a refreshing defense and study of special subjects. Boutflower charges critics with forced interpretations (p. 4), attacks the idea that the fourth kingdom is Greece (pp. 13 ff.) and that the word *Chaldean* proves a late date for Daniel (pp. 35-44), defends messianic interpretation (pp. 55-64) and the reality of Belshazzar (pp. 114 ff.) and of Darius the Mede (pp. 142-67), discusses the meaning of the handwriting on the wall (pp. 136-40), argues that the seventy weeks have messianic meaning but does not perceive the reference to antichrist (pp. 168-205), defends an early date for Daniel by Aramaic words (pp. 226-40) and Old Persian words (pp. 241-67), and explains the force of Christ's testimony to the authenticity of Daniel (pp. 286-93).

Culver, Robert D. *Daniel and the Latter Days.* Chicago: Moody, 1954. 244 pp. Culver's work is a premillennial study of the eschatological portions of Daniel and is the best exposition of the parts of the book it treats. The author sets forth the essentials of premillennialism (pp. 24-25) and discusses at length difficult problems of premillennial interpretation and gives answers (pp. 27-90). He then compares the premillennial view with Daniel 2, 7, 9, 10-12 (pp. 96-176); outlines Daniel by its languages (p. 100); holds that Nebuchadnezzar did not forget his dream (p. 106); attacks liberals who deny that the fourth kingdom is Rome (p. 111); stresses that the seventy weeks cannot be fulfilled by Antiochus (p. 136); and identifies the willful king as antichrist (p. 164).

Gaebelein, Arno Clemens. *The Prophet Daniel.* n.d. Reprint, Grand Rapids: Kregel, 1955. 212 pp. Gaebelein's book is a premillennial commentary on Daniel. The author defines prophecy as "history prewritten" (p. 1); defends the authenticity of Daniel (p. 7), attacks the postmillennial view (p. 33), calls the Bible infallible (p. 33), defends the historicity of Daniel (p. 82), gives parallels between Daniel and Revelation (pp. 85-86), believes the seventy weeks began in 445 B.C. (p. 135), identifies the prince who shall come as the head of the fourth empire

(p. 142), gives a chart of the seventy weeks (p. 151), and attacks the modern cults (p. 191).

Miller, Stephen R. *Daniel.* Vol. 18, The New American Commentary. Nashville: Broadman and Holman, 1994. 348 pp. In this premillennial commentary based on the NIV, Miller defends a conservative date and authorship (pp. 34-42); argues for a premillennial interpretation of the great image in Daniel 2 (pp. 97-100); defends the miracles of deliverance for the three Hebrews and for Daniel in the lion's den (pp. 122 ff., 188); thinks that Nebuchadnezzar had a genuine salvation experience (p. 144); identifies the fourth beast as Rome, the ten toes as a ten nation confederacy, the little horn as antichrist (pp. 202 f.); holds that the $3\frac{1}{2}$ times are the $3\frac{1}{2}$ years of the Great Tribulation (pp. 214-15); defends the premillennial view of the seventy weeks (p. 257); and interprets the willful king of Daniel 11:36 as the Antichrist (p. 30).

Walvoord, John Flipse. *Daniel: The Key to Prophetic Revelation.* Chicago: Moody, 1971. 317 pp. In a very thorough and careful premillennial exposition, Walvoord defends the genuineness of Daniel (pp. 16-25); identifies the four kingdoms as Babylon, Medo-Persia, Greece, and Rome (pp. 64-68, 145 ff.); gives both amillennial and premillennial interpretations (pp. 72 ff.); defends the historicity of Darius the Mede (pp. 132 ff.); identifies the "little horn" of Daniel 7 as antichrist (p. 175) and of Daniel 8 as Antiochus (p. 196); recommends Sir Robert Anderson's chronology of the seventy weeks (p. 228); identifies the willful king as the Roman world ruler, antichrist (pp. 272, 276); and thinks that Old Testament saints are raised after the tribulation period (p. 287).

Young, Edward J. *The Prophecy of Daniel.* Grand Rapids: Eerdmans, 1949. 330 pp. In a thorough amillennial exposition, Young admits his debt to Montgomery and Rowley (p. 5); defends Daniel as author (pp. 19-20); identifies the four kingdoms as Babylon, Medo-Persia, Greece, and Rome (pp. 74-75, 143, 147); attacks the idea that the Greek words in Daniel are an argument for a late date (p. 87); thinks that Nebuchadnezzar was converted (p. 114); cannot identify the ten kingdoms but does identify the "little horn" in Daniel 7 as antichrist (pp. 149-50) and in Daniel 8 as Antiochus (p. 170); defends the deity of Christ (p. 156); holds that the seventy weeks are an indefinite period of time down to the first advent of Christ (pp. 196-201) and that Messiah causes a covenant to prevail (p. 208); identifies the willful king as antichrist (pp. 247 ff.); and teaches a general resurrection (p. 256).

Nahum

Maier, Walter A. *The Book of Nahum.* St. Louis: Concordia, 1959. 386 pp. This work is a famous radio preacher's thorough verse-by-verse exposition of Nahum, giving special attention to the Hebrew text. Maier argues for a date c. 654 B.C. (pp. 27-27), defends Nahum against liberal attacks (pp. 70-87), provides much historical background (pp. 87-139), stresses God's avenging power (p. 156); makes comparisons between the Masoretic Text and the Septuagint (p. 166), brings out messianic meaning (p. 219), describes the cruelties of the Assyrians (pp. 290-92) and their witchcraft (p. 303).

Zechariah

*Baron, David. *The Visions and Prophecies of Zechariah.* 1919. Reprint, Grand Rapids: Kregel, 1972, 554 pp. This book is a thorough premillennial exegesis by a Hebrew Christian, who knows both the language and the customs of his people. The work is warmly devotional and gives a clear portrait of Israel's place in God's prophetic program.

Feinberg, Charles Lee. *God Remembers.* Wheaton, Ill.: Van Kampen, 1950. 283 pp. This work is a thorough premillennial exposition of Zechariah by a Hebrew Christian. The author is especially good on the chronological sequence of prophetic events (p. 219, etc.); and includes a helpful bibliography (pp. 281 ff.).

Unger, Merrill F. *Zechariah.* Grand Rapids: Zondervan, 1963. 275 pp. Unger provides a careful premillennial exposition. He argues for the unity of authorship (pp. 12 ff.), holds to the millennial restoration of Jerusalem (pp. 43-44, 136), stresses the messianic prophecies (pp. 65-66, 114, 161-62), identifies the worthless shepherd as antichrist (p. 207), teaches a national conversion of the Jews (pp. 214 ff.), and holds that literal waters will flow from the restored millennial temple (p. 255).

CHAPTER 42
RECOMMENDED NEW TESTAMENT COMMENTARIES

The following list, like the preceding bibliographies, is selective. The first book listed in each category is the editor's choice as the best book. Books with an asterisk (*) before their entry should be in every expositor's library; they may never be equaled. The New Testament commentaries are divided into *Greek exegesis* (for those who read Greek) and *expositions* (whose authors may well use the Greek but do not usually quote it). Some volumes in the International Critical Commentary are included for their help on the Greek rather than for the reliability of their interpretations.

Matthew

Expositions

*Broadus, John A. *Commentary on the Gospel of Matthew.* Philadelphia: American Baptist Publication Society, 1886. Reprint, Kregel, 1990. 661 pp. Broadus provides the most helpful exposition of Matthew. Although one will not agree with every interpretation, one can turn to almost any verse and find more practical help in understanding it than in any other work. He defends the virgin birth (p. 8) and miracles (pp. 80-81). His explanations of some difficult passages are impressive: "Resist not evil" (pp. 118 ff.) and "The kingdom of Heaven suffereth violence" (pp. 241 ff.). He gives an amillennial interpretation of Matthew 24-25.

Morgan, G. Campbell. *The Gospel According to Matthew.* New York: Revell, 1929. 321 pp. This work consists of seventy-three expository messages that amount to a verse-by-verse commentary on Matthew. The author strongly defends the virgin birth (pp. 10 ff.) and the other miracles (pp. 81 ff.); gives the usual premillennial interpretation of the parables of Matthew 13; and divides the Olivet Discourse so that Matthew 24:1-44 refers to Jews, 24:45–25:30 refers to the church, and 25:31-46 refers to the judgment of the nations (pp. 280-95). On the whole he gives remarkably practical explanations. He is especially helpful on the Sermon on the Mount.

Franzmann, Martin H. *Follow Me: Discipleship According to Saint Matthew.* St. Louis: Concordia, 1961. 249 pp. This work is a reverent exposition of Matthew with the purpose of showing how the Lord molded the disciples for their future service. Not a verse-by-verse commentary, it is rather a careful portrayal of the thought of every part of Matthew. The author's Lutheran background is seen most clearly in his treatment of the sacraments. He holds strongly to the factuality of the virgin birth, miracles, and so on. "The embarrassed fumbling with the miraculous which is characteristic of so much present-day theology is but one of a number of indications that the church's teaching and preaching has become sicklied o'er by the pale cast of thought and can deal only inadequately with the bright and plastic world of divine revelation" (p. 68). He has a marvelous passage on the failure of the disciples: only *"The Son of God"* could go "under the judgment of the God who smites the Shepherd and lays on One the iniquity of all" (pp. 206-7).

Lloyd-Jones, D. Martyn. *Studies in the Sermon on the Mount.* 2 vols. Grand Rapids: Eerdmans, 1959, 1960. 320, 337 pp. This work contains careful and thorough expository messages that still retain their original sermonic form. The author manifests good common sense and a warm heart. He stresses principles, not just actions (I, p. 22); often harmonizes the Sermon on the Mount with Paul's teaching (I, p. 207); and holds that Christ was giving the proper interpretation of the Mosaic law (I, pp. 213-14). The style is British. This is certainly a most helpful work.

Fitch, William. *The Beatitudes of Jesus.* Grand Rapids: Eerdmans, 1961. 132 pp. This book is a warmly devotional exposition of the Beatitudes and is probably the best book on the
subject. The author has a fine sense for choosing the right
hymn or poem to illustrate his points. He takes strong exception to the extreme dispensational interpretation that would
remove the Sermon on the Mount from present relevancy (p. 6).

Dods, Marcus. *The Prayer That Teaches to Pray.* Cincinnati:
Cranston and Curts, 1893. Reprint, New Canaan, Conn.: Keats,
1980. 176 pp. Dods's work is a fervent, eloquent, and powerful
exposition of the Lord's Prayer. Although the reader may not
agree with everything here, he will be struck with more devotional and inspirational thoughts per page than he would think
possible.

Greek Exegesis

Plummer, Alfred. *The Gospel According to St. Matthew.* Grand
Rapids: Eerdmans, 1956. Reprint, Baker, 1982. 497 pp. Plummer's is the most helpful technical and critical commentary on
Matthew even though the author denies Matthaean authorship
(p. x). Plummer holds to a date a little after A.D. 70 (p. xxxii);
has an interesting section on the plan of the gospel (pp. xviii-
xxv); and defends the virgin birth (pp. 3-11) and the reality of the
miracles (pp. 51-53, 122) and of demonic possession (pp. 134 ff.).
Nevertheless, he has a wretched doctrine of inspiration, wishing
to remove the Lord's Prayer from the Sermon on the Mount (p. 93),
and alleges inaccuracies in Scripture (pp. 132-33).

Mark
Expositions

*Hiebert, D. Edmond. *The Gospel of Mark.* Greenville, S.C.:
Bob Jones University Press, 1994. 516 pp. Hiebert's book is a
most thorough and helpful commentary. He defends Markan
authorship (pp. 5 ff.), gives a date of A.D. 64-67 (p. 11),
stresses the high Christology of Mark (pp. 13-14, 22), distinguishes between present and future aspects of the kingdom
(pp. 43-44), analyzes the grouping of the twelve apostles

(pp. 94-96), stresses that Jairus's daughter was actually dead (p. 149), holds that Elijah will be the forerunner of Christ's second coming (p. 251), shows that Jesus recognized one ground for divorce (p. 320), defends two cleansings of the temple (p. 370), gives a premillennial interpretation of the Olivet Discourse (p. 375), holds to a pretribulation rapture (p. 322), and does not decide the textual problem of the ending of Mark (pp. 480, 489).

Alexander, J. A. *Commentary on the Gospel of Mark.* 1864. Reprint, Klock and Klock, 1980. 444 pp. This work is an old but helpful exposition. Alexander stresses that Christ is a divine person (p. 2), holds that Christ taught as one who had the authority to give the Law (p. 20), shows Mark's attention to detail (p. 58), attacks Romanist doctrine (p. 143), denies the doctrine of immersion (pp. 182-83), stresses Christ's love for children (p. 260), advocates infant baptism (p. 278), and interprets the abomination of desolation as the Roman triumph under Titus in A.D. 70 (p. 353).

Lane, William L. *The Gospel According to Mark.* Grand Rapids: Eerdmans, 1974. 652 pp. Lane's work is an exhaustive commentary that attempts to discuss every shade of liberal interpretation; much of it is not fitting for the Bible expositor. He thinks that Mark is the oldest Gospel (pp. xi, 1), acknowledges indebtedness to Marxsen's liberal methods of interpretation (pp. 3-7), thinks that Mark built his Gospel by the use of key-word associations (pp. 39-40), holds that Mark did not portray disciples as winning a victory over temptation (pp. 60-61), claims that there was no unreserved disclosure of the Son of Man until after the Resurrection (p. 97) but that the "Amen" sayings prove Jesus the true witness of God (p. 144), holds that Peter's confession is the theological center of Mark's Gospel (pp. 288-89), thinks that the transfiguration is a "new Sinai" theophany (p. 317) and that John the Baptist was Elijah (p. 326), interprets the abomination of desolation as fulfilled in A.D. 66-70 (p. 466), gives forty pages of amillennial interpretation of the Olivet Discourse without a single reference topremillennial literature (pp. 444-84), and rejects the longer ending of Mark (pp. 591-92).

Greek Exegesis

Swete, Henry Barclay. *The Gospel According to St. Mark.* 1898. Reprint, Grand Rapids: Eerdmans, 1952. 554 pp. This work is the most thorough commentary on the Greek text of Mark. Swete defends the book's authenticity (pp. xii-xxxviii); has special studies on Mark's vocabulary (pp. xliv ff.), relation to the other Synoptics (pp. lxvi ff.), and use of the Old Testament (pp. lxxvi ff.); stresses the divine sonship of Christ (pp. xc-xcv); shows the force of tenses (pp. 4, 5, 8, 10, etc.), cases (p. 7, etc.) and voice (pp. 84, 141, and so on); contrasts Greek synonyms (pp. 20, 147); holds that the Lord claimed the divine prerogative (p. 35); shows Mark's portrait of Christ's characteristic actions (p. 52); holds that any sin is preceded by a deliberation in the sinner's mind (p. 153); lists the characteristics of a loyal disciple (p. 182); claims that "the spirit of service is the passport to eminence in the kingdom of God" (p. 205); and teaches that Christ's death is a supreme act of service to humanity (p. 240).

Luke

Expositions

Geldenhuys, Norval. *Commentary on the Gospel of Luke.* Grand Rapids: Eerdmans, 1951. 685 pp. This work is perhaps the best exposition of Luke. Geldenhuys defends the Lucan authorship (pp. 15-17), the virgin birth (pp. 107-9), the deity of Christ (p. 115), His Resurrection (pp. 628-30), and His miracles (p. 224); and has very helpful comments on the temptation (pp. 156-64), the good Samaritan (pp. 310-14), the prodigal son (pp. 405-13), the rich man and Lazarus (pp. 424-30), the Pharisee and the publican (pp. 450-53), Zacchaeus (pp. 469-72), and the Crucifixion (pp. 607-17). He regularly comments on the Greek text and provides a thorough bibliography (pp. 47-50).

Arndt, William F. *The Gospel According to St. Luke.* St. Louis: Concordia, 1956. 534 pp. Arndt provides one of the finest, most thorough expositions. He believes in an inspired, infallible Bible (p. ix); thinks that Luke may have used Mark (p. 13) and perhaps "Q" (p. 18); defends the existence of angels (p. 44), the virgin birth of Christ (pp. 53-57), and His deity (p. 82); attacks A. T. Robertson on baptism and defends baptismal regeneration (pp. 109, 115); argues the existence of demons (p. 146); opposes allegorical interpretation (p. 172); has a most helpful treatment of the prodigal son (pp. 349-54); defends amillennialism (p. 393); and mightily defends the Resurrection and ascension of Christ (pp. 480-500).

Morgan, G. Campbell. *The Gospel According to Luke.* New York: Revell, 1931. 284 pp. Morgan writes a carefully reasoned exposition. He assumes Lucan authorship (p. 9); defends the deity and virgin birth of Christ (pp. 21-24); often explains the Greek (pp. 36, 120, 129, 199-200); sometimes gives apt illustrations (p. 133); catches minute distinctions ("also," p. 140); gives premillennial interpretations (pp. 165, 217); and holds that the Lord, under oath, confessed that He was the Son of God (p. 257).

Godet, Frederic. *A Commentary on the Gospel of St. Luke.* 2 vols. 1870. Reprint, Edinburgh: Clark, 1976. 441, 462 pp. This work is an exhaustive technical commentary. It defends the deity of Christ (I, p. 91), the virgin birth (I, pp. 93-94, 161), the existence of Satan (I, p. 210) and of demons (I, p. 244); defends miracles (I, p. 253); provides good background (I, p. 354); attacks documentary solutions of the synoptic problems (I, pp. 380, 408-9); offers a thorough exposition of the story of the prodigal son (II, pp. 150-57) and of the Crucifixion (II, pp. 326-32); defends the Resurrection (II, pp. 361-65) and the ascension (II, pp. 367-71); and dates the book A.D. 64-67 (II, p. 416).

Greek Exegesis

Plummer, Alfred. *The Gospel According to St. Luke.* International Critical Commentary. Edinburgh: Clark, 1896. 680 pp. Plummer's book is the most exhaustive and helpful commentary on the Greek text. He defends Lucan authorship (pp. xxiii-xxvii);

dates the book about A.D. 75-80 (p. xxxii); defends the deity and virgin birth of Christ (pp. 25, 27); has helpful theological discussion (p. 106); gives and evaluates a variety of interpretations (p. 202); is most valuable on the Greek, giving fine distinctions between words (pp. 164, 252) and bringing out the exact meaning of words (p. 335); has interesting comments on Hades (p. 383); and defends the Resurrection of Christ (p. 546).

Marshall, I. Howard. *The Gospel of Luke.* NIGTC. Exeter: Paternoster Press, 1978. 928 pp. This work is a thorough commentary on the Greek text. Marshall takes "Q" too seriously (pp. 30 ff., 135); defends Lucan authorship (pp. 33-35) and the virgin birth (pp. 64 f., 105); stresses that Christ was the Son of God (pp. 67, 77, 129); holds that the temptation shows that Jesus is obedient to God's will as revealed in Scripture (p. 166); thinks that Luke 4:16 is the oldest known account of a synagogue service (p. 181); holds that Luke inserted material "with good reason" (p. 244); explains that the term *exodus* refers to Jesus' death, our redemption, and salvation (p. 384); stresses the importance of the journey towards Jerusalem (pp. 400 ff.); holds that the parables of Luke 15 show the joy that God manifests over the recovery of the lost (p. 597); rejects the obvious interpretation of the unjust steward (pp. 614 ff.); holds that *Hades* refers to the intermediate abode of the dead before the final judgment (p. 636); sees the account of Zacchaeus as the climax of Jesus' journey toward Jerusalem (p. 694); thinks that Luke rewrote a paragraph from Mark (p. 771); and stresses that Jesus had the authority to welcome a criminal into paradise (p. 873).

John

Expositions

Morris, Leon. *The Gospel According to John.* Grand Rapids: Eerdmans, 1971. 936 pp. Morris's is a most thorough exposition. He defends the authorship of John the Apostle (pp. 8-30); is uncertain about the date but suggests before A.D. 70 (p. 34); defends the deity of Christ (p. 77) and the incarnation (p. 102); lists seven who witness of the Lord (p. 90); defends the reading "only begotten God" in 1:18 (p. 113); has additional notes on Logos (pp. 115 ff.), the world (pp. 126 ff.), Son of Man (pp. 172-73), Paraclete (pp. 662 ff.), and miracles (pp. 684 ff.); defends the doctrine of the wrath of God (p. 249); stresses that Jesus claimed deity (pp. 466, 473); and defends the Resurrection of Jesus (pp. 830 ff.), linking it with His deity (p. 857).

Godet, Frederic. *A Commentary on the Gospel of John.* 2 vols. 1886. Reprint, Grand Rapids: Zondervan, n.d. 559, 551 pp. In a very thorough exposition, Godet discusses the apostle John (I, pp. 29-53); holds that the ruling idea of John is the incarnate *Logos* (I, p. 66); defends Johannine authorship (I, pp. 167-204); stresses the eternity, personality, and deity of the *Logos* (I, pp. 245-46); argues that Jesus as the Lamb of God fulfills the type of the Servant of Jehovah in Isaiah 53 (I, p. 312); defends the miracles of Christ (I, p. 472); identifies the rivers of living water as streams of new life flowing from the hearts of the believers through gifts of the Spirit (II, p. 78); regards 7:53–8:11 as an interpolation (II, pp. 84-85); argues that Christ exists in an absolute, eternal, divine sense (II, p. 122); stresses the eyewitness nature of John's description of the raising of Lazarus (II, p. 190); thinks the promise "I come again" refers to the coming of the Holy Spirit (II, p. 270); holds that John 17 was spoken on the way to Gethsemane (II, p. 291); calls John 17 the prayer of the High Priest of mankind, "who begins His sacrifice by offering Himself to God" (II, p. 323); and defends the reality of the bodily resurrection of the Lord (II, pp. 426 ff.).

Rainsford, Marcus. *Our Lord Prays for His Own.* 1895. Reprint, Chicago: Moody, 1950. 476 pp. Rainsford writes powerful devotional messages on every verse of John 17. He stresses that Christ prayed as Mediator, for as God He could not pray (p. 38); sets forth the finished work of Christ as prescribed, definite, and complete (pp. 81-82); speaks of the eternal glory of the Son (pp. 89 ff.); lists the seven things the Father gave the Son as Mediator (pp. 137 ff.); stresses that all three Persons of the Trinity are engaged in the sanctification of God's people (p. 397); warns that only those who believe what the apostles

taught are those for whom Christ prayed (p. 371); and meditates on the registered will of the Son (p. 437).

Reith, George. *The Gospel According to Saint John.* 2 vols.
Edinburgh: Clark, 1889. 197, 176 pp. In a warmly devotional
exposition, Reith defends this Gospel's authenticity (pp. xxi ff.);
defines "only begotten" as showing Jesus Christ's eternal, necessary, and essential relation to the Father (I, p. 14); emphasizes that Christ saves "not *from* but *in* life's common paths"
(I, p. 38); makes familiar verses glow (3:16, I, pp. 51-52); teaches
the eternal coexistence of the Father and the Son (I, p. 84) and
the preexistence of the Son (II, p. 22); stresses the divine infallibility of the Scripture (II, pp. 49, 126); teaches Christ's return
for His own (II, p. 90); and defends the doctrine of the Trinity
(II, p. 114).

Greek Exegesis

*Westcott, Brooke Foss. *The Gospel According to St. John.* 1881.
Reprint, Grand Rapids: Eerdmans, 1964. 404 pp. This work is the
best commentary on John. Westcott defends Johannine authorship (pp. v-xxxii); discusses the symbolism of the Gospel (pp. lxxv ff.); stresses that the absolute, eternal, immanent
relations of the Person of the Godhead are the basis for the
revelation of the Word (p. 2); holds that in Christ, eternity and
time, the divine and the human are reconciled (p. 10); thinks that
the water that became wine came from a well, not waterpots
(p. 38); teaches baptismal regeneration (p. 50); stresses that God's
enabling does not destroy man's freedom (p. 104); teaches
Christ's timeless existence (p. 140); does not regard 7:53–8:11 as
genuine (pp. 141 ff.); calls the raising of Lazarus a revelation of
Christ's divine glory (p. 164); thinks that "I come again" refers to
Christ's coming in the Paraclete, His coming at death for the
believer, and His second coming (p. 201); holds that John 17 was
prayed in the temple courts before the crossing of Kidron (p. 237);
thinks the falling of the soldiers showed that the Lord chose to
give Himself up to them (p. 259); and defends the Johannine
authorship of John 21 (p. 299).

Acts

Expositions

Bruce, Frederick Fyvie. *Commentary on the Book of the Acts.* Grand Rapids: Eerdmans, 1954. 555 pp. This book is perhaps the best exposition for the Bible expositor. He offers helpful general comments; provides careful historical background (p. 481); defends Lucan authorship (p. 19) and the Resurrection and ascension (p. 40); attacks baptismal regeneration (p. 77); identifies the famine visit of Acts 11 with Galatians 2 (pp. 244, 300); attacks the premillennial interpretation of Acts 15 (p. 309); holds that Paul's restoration after stoning "has a flavor of miracle about it" (p. 296); and holds to the reality of demon possession (p. 332), of Eutychus's death (p. 408), and of the viper bite (pp. 521-22).

Morgan, G. Campbell. *The Acts of the Apostles.* New York: Revell, 1924. 547 pp. Morgan's work is an expository message on Acts. He has genuinely helpful explanations for "when this sound was heard" (p. 36) and for "despot" (p. 129); defends the deity and humanity of Christ (p. 73); has no comment on the problems in Stephen's speech; gives Arminian interpretations (p. 334); and holds that Paul died when he was stoned (p. 344) and that Eutychus actually died and was raised (p. 470). The book is stronger at the beginning: he covers the first thirteen chapters in 337 pages, the last fifteen in 210 pages.

Rackham, Richard Belward. *The Acts of the Apostles.* London: Methuen, 1901. Reprint, Grand Rapids: Baker, 1978. 636 pp. This book offers a most thorough, helpful exposition by an Anglican. Rackham defends Lucan authorship (p. xvii), a dating before A.D. 64 (p. lii), the ascension (p. 8), and Paul's conversion (p. 131); has helpful comments on the Spirit of Pentecost (pp. 14-15); lists fifteen different problems in Stephen's speech and gives answers for some (pp. 99-102); holds that the Galatian view (pp. 195-98) teaches both predestination and free will (p. 221); identifies Acts 15 with Galatians 2 (pp. 239-47);

has an extensive treatment of Paul at Athens (pp. 301-20); believes that Paul was miraculously restored after stoning (p. 235), that Eutychus was raised from the dead (p. 380), and that a real viper bit Paul (p. 492); and provides a thorough index. He overemphasizes the sacraments and church offices.

Winter, Bruce W. and Andrew D. Clark, eds. *The Book of Acts in Its Ancient Literary Setting.* Vol. 1, *The Book of Acts in Its First Century Setting.* Grand Rapids: Eerdmans, 1993. 479 pp. In this anthology dealing with the literary aspects of Acts, Palmer examines Acts and the ancient historical monograph (pp. 1 ff.). Alexander treats ancient intellectual biography (pp. 31 ff). Rosner covers Acts and biblical history (pp. 65 ff). Peterson investigates the motif of fulfillment in Luke and Acts (pp. 83 ff). Bauckham examines the Acts of Paul as a sequel to Acts (pp. 105 ff.). Nobbs covers subsequent ecclesiastical histories (pp. 153 ff.). I. H. Marshall discusses Acts and the "Former Treatise" (pp. 163 ff.). Hillard, Nobbs, Winter, and Wenham examine ancient literary parallels and the parallels between Acts and Paul (pp. 183 ff.). Gempf covers public speaking and published accounts (pp. 259 ff.). Winter examines official proceedings and the forensic speeches in Acts 24-26 (pp. 305 ff.). Satterwhile treats classical rhetoric (pp. 337 ff.). Spencer surveys the modern literary approaches to Acts (pp. 381 ff.). There is an appendix by Head on the textual problems in Acts (pp. 415 ff.).

Gill, David W. J., and Conrad Gempf, eds. *The Book of Acts in Its Graeco-Roman Setting.* Vol. 2, *The Book of Acts in Its First Century Setting.* Grand Rapids: Eerdmans, 1994. 627 pp. It is a technical anthology of the broader setting of Acts. Rapske treats travel and shipwreck (pp. 1 ff). French discusses Acts and the Roman roads (pp. 49 ff.). Winter examines food shortages (pp. 59 ff.). Gill and Winter cover local Roman religion and the Imperial cult (pp. 79 ff.). Gill investigates Acts and the urban elites (pp. 105 ff.). Blue examines Acts and the house church, with thirty-four figures of archaeological ground plans of structures used as meeting places (pp. 119 ff.). Tracey surveys the Roman province of Syria (pp. 223 ff.); Nobbs, the province of Cyprus (pp. 279 ff.); Trebilco, the province of Asia (pp. 291 ff.); Hansen, the province of Galatia (pp. 377 ff.); and Gill, the provinces of Macedonia (pp. 397 ff.) and Achaia (pp. 433 ff.). Clarke discusses conditions in Rome and Italy in the first century (pp. 455 ff.). Scott examines Luke's geographical horizon (pp. 483 ff.). There is an excursus on the "we" passages in Acts by Porter (pp. 545 ff.). There are also appendixes on the Asiarchs by Kearsley (pp. 363 ff.) and the Politarchs by Horsley (pp. 419 ff.). The work concludes with massive indexes (pp. 575-627).

Rapske, Brian. *The Book of Acts and Paul in Roman Custody.* Vol. 3, *The Book of Acts in Its First Century Setting.* Grand Rapids: Eerdmans, 1994. 512 pp. Technical background on the legal system in the Roman world is given. Rapske shows the influence of status on the magistrates and courts (pp. 46 ff.); examines Paul's status as a citizen of Tarsus and of Rome (pp. 71 ff.); argues that the Lucan evidence shows that Paul was a full member of the Sanhedrin (p. 103); surveys the trials Paul had in Philippi (pp. 115 ff.), Jerusalem (pp. 135 ff.), Caesarea (pp. 151 ff.), and Rome (pp. 173 ff.); gives a grim description of prison conditions in the Roman world (pp. 197 ff.); and discusses the shame of bonds (pp. 283 ff.) and the kind of helpers Paul had in prison (pp. 369 ff.). He concludes that the record in Acts compared with the first century context increases confidence in the historical trustworthiness of the Lucan record (p. 429).

Bauckham, Richard, ed. *The Book of Acts in Its Palestinian Setting.* Vol. 4, *The Book of Acts in Its First Century Setting.* Grand Rapids: Eerdmans, 1995. 526 pp. This is an unequal anthology. Rajak discusses the culture of Jews, Greeks, and foreigners in Palestine (pp. 15-26). Hengel gives a liberal appraisal of the geography of Palestine in Acts (pp. 27-78), suggesting that Luke made mistakes (p. 47), used legends (p. 57), reworked traditions, and shaped them editorially (p. 60); and thinks that Luke exaggerated the number of the soldiers that escorted Paul (p. 65). Williams provides a rather dry discussion of

Jewish personal names in Acts (pp. 79-113). Mason evaluates the chief priests, Sadducees, Pharisees, and Sanhedrin in Acts (pp. 115-177). He thinks that Jesus taught that the Pharisees had the kingdom (p. 142) but the moment Jesus confronted the chief priests, they tried to kill him (p. 144); thinks that the Sadducees are flat characters in Luke (p. 147); and wonders whether Luke knew more when he divided the Sanhedrin into two parties (p. 154). Riesner defends the historicity of the synagogues in Jerusalem in Luke and Acts (pp. 179-210). Fiensy studies the composition of the Jerusalem church (pp. 213-36), concluding that the socioeconomic composition of the Jerusalem church was as pluralistic as that of the population of Jerusalem (p. 230). Reinhardt evaluates the population size of Jerusalem and the numeric growth of the church (pp. 237-65), concluding that the first-century size was 60,000-120,000 (p. 263). Falk examines Jewish prayer literature and the Jerusalem church (pp. 267-301), concluding that Luke portrays Christian prayer as Jewish and authentic to the pre-A.D. 70 period (p. 298). Murphy-O'Connor argues that the Cenacle was the first assembly-place of the church in Jerusalem (pp. 303-21). Capper thinks that the Essene community of goods may have a connection with the early Christian community of goods (pp. 323-56). Bammel documents Jewish activities against Christians (pp. 357-63). Legasse discusses Paul's pre-Christian career (pp. 365-90). He holds that none of the five references in Acts to Paul's being from Tarsus offer a guarantee of historicity (p. 366); refers to Paul's "certainly authentic letters" (p. 375, n. 29); sees Luke as a redactor (p. 379) and wonders what facts Luke embellished (p. 389). Schwartz covers Peter and Ben Stada in Lydda (pp. 391-414), presenting antichristian, Jewish interpretations that are demeaning to Peter, Stephen, and others. Bauckham studies James and the Jerusalem church (pp. 415-480). He gives a sympathetic portrait of James gradually replacing the twelve as the leadership of the church and shows the historical accuracy of Luke's description of the Jerusalem Council.

Levinskaya, Irina. *The Book of Acts in Its Diaspora Setting.* Vol. 5, *The Book of Acts in Its First Century Setting.* Grand Rapids: Eerdmans, 1996. 284 pp. The book provides a technical study of the Jewish conditions and status in the Diaspora. The author discusses the problem of the Jewish identity (pp. 2 ff.), the existence of proselytes among the Jews (pp. 19 ff.), and the evidence for the "God-fearers" (pp. 51 ff.); provides a specific case study from Bosporan Kingdom (pp. 105 ff.); discusses "God-fearers" in the book of Acts (pp. 120 ff.); surveys the Jewish Diaspora communities in Antioch, Asia Minor, Macedonia, Rome (pp. 127 ff.); and concludes that the account in Acts provides excellent testimony for the ancient historian (p. 195).

Vol. 6 in *The Book of Acts in Its First Century Setting* was not published in time to be reviewed.

Greek Exegesis

Knowling, Richard John. *Acts.* Vol. II, The Expositor's Greek Testament. 1907. Reprint, Grand Rapids: Eerdmans, 1951. Pp. 1-554. This book is the best, most thorough commentary on the Greek text of Acts. Knowling defends Lucan authorship (pp. 3-11) and the ascension (p. 57); observes the Greek articles (p. 59) and conjunctions (p. 164); gives an exhaustive treatment to some verses (6:1; 9:2; 17:34; etc.); provides many solutions to the problems in Stephen's speech (pp. 180-96); holds that Paul did not necessarily die when stoned but that his recovery was by God's hand (p. 311); gives an amillennial interpretation of Acts 15 (p. 321); and defends the reality of demon possession (p. 347), of Eutychus's death (p. 425), and of the viper bite (p. 539).

Romans

Expositions

*Moule, Handley Carr Glyn. *Romans.* The Expositor's Bible. 1896. Reprint, Grand Rapids: Eerdmans, n.d. 453 pp. Moule provides probably the finest, most helpful exposition of Romans in print. He is intensely devotional but writes with real scholarship and insight. His sympathy with the thought and phraseology of Paul is remarkable.

Hodge, Charles. *Commentary on the Epistle to the Romans.* Grand Rapids: Eerdmans, 1886. 462 pp. This commentary is an exhaustive exposition from a strongly Calvinistic position. Although not easy reading, it is immensely helpful. He vigorously defends the deity of Christ in 9:5. In an unusually lengthy treatment of 5:12 (pp. 142-55, 178-90), he advocates the federal-headship view.

Bruce, Frederick Fyvie. *The Epistle of Paul to the Romans.* Tyndale Commentaries. Grand Rapids: Eerdmans, 1963. 288 pp. Bruce presents perceptive comments from a Reformed viewpoint, manifesting a wide knowledge of literature and of the theological writers. His writing is occasionally too brief (3:21) and often marvelously full (3:25). He holds that Paul taught the deity of Christ in 9:5 but urges moderation toward those who disagree.

Murray, John. *The Epistle to the Romans.* 2 vols. Grand Rapids: Eerdmans, 1959, 1965. 433, 302 pp. Murray's is a thorough, strongly Reformed commentary. On 5:12, referring to the account in Genesis 3, he says, "The apostle places his imprimatur upon the authenticity of this account" (I, p. 181). He argues for the deity of Christ in 9:5 (II, pp. 245-48).

Lloyd-Jones, D. Martyn. *Romans.* 5 vols. Grand Rapids: Zondervan, 1970-1974. 250, 370, 313, 358, 438 pp. This book contains messages on Romans 3:20–5:21 with much good exposition and many digressions. The author stresses the need for conviction of sin (on 3:21); gives clear word studies (on 3:25-26); dares, though a Reformed expositor, to disagree with John Calvin (on 5:12); and plainly rejects Karl Barth's teaching (on 8:3-4).

Candlish, Robert S. *Studies in Romans 12.* 1867. Reprint, Grand Rapids: Kregel, 1989. 364 pp. This is a classic example of a powerful exposition with beautiful and accurate analysis and loving and faithful application. He bases it all on the Christian's relationship to God (vv. 1-2) and goes on to show how that influences his relationship with the church (vv. 3-13) and to the wicked world (vv. 14-21). He stresses the need of separation from the world (pp. 50 ff.); warns against self-esteem (pp. 99 ff.); brings out the force of the Greek: the need for diligence, fervency, and service (pp. 159 ff.); urges leaving retribution to God alone (pp. 308 ff.); and commends allowing good to overcome evil (pp. 329 ff.).

Greek Exegesis

Sanday, William, and Arthur C. Headlam. *The Epistle to the Romans.* International Critical Commentary. Edinburgh: Clark, 1895. 562 pp. This work is a very thorough commentary on the Greek text from a strongly Arminian view. In an exhaustive discussion of 9:5, the authors defend the deity of Christ (pp. 232-38). On 5:12 they hold that all men sin because they inherited tendencies from Adam: the Fall transmitted the liability to sin (p. 132). This book is probably the most helpful commentary on the Greek.

I Corinthians

Expositions

Hodge, Charles. *An Exposition of the First Epistle to the Corinthians.* Grand Rapids: Eerdmans, n.d. 394 pp. Hodge provides the most thorough exposition of I Corinthians. He stresses the effectual call of the Spirit (pp. 3, 23); holds to the infallible inspiration of the Scriptures (p. 16); often gives different interpretations and then evaluates them (pp. 37-38, 42-43, 55, 78-79, 134, 143, 155, etc.); thinks that "deliver to Satan" includes more than mere excommunication (p. 85); maintains that adultery or willful desertion annuls marriage (p. 113); warns against false security (p. 181); holds that "baptized into one body" refers not to water baptism but to spiritual regeneration (p. 254); and thinks that tongues are foreign languages (p. 278).

Morris, Leon. *The First Epistle of Paul to the Corinthians.* Grand Rapids: Eerdmans, 1958. 249 pp. Morris provides a very accurate and helpful exposition. He defends the authenticity (pp. 26-27); dates the Epistles in the mid-fifties (p. 29); thinks "the princes of this world" means human rulers only (pp. 54-55); defends verbal inspiration (p. 59); distinguishes between Greek synonyms (p. 69); holds that the deserted believer is free to remarry (p. 111); attacks the idea that Paul meant that tongues were ecstatic speech in Corinth, languages in Acts (pp. 172-73); and holds that heavenly beings have heavenly bodies (p. 225).

Grosheide, F. W. *Commentary on the First Epistle to the Corinthians.* Grand Rapids: Eerdmans, 1953. 415 pp. This work presents a thorough commentary from a Reformed view. Grosheide attacks F. C. Burr's idea of a war between Peter and Paul (p. 36); holds that the "rulers of this age" are the "powers who determine the character of this world" (p. 65); thinks that "carnal" means "under the dominion of sinful flesh" (p. 80); holds that desertion by an unbeliever permits divorce for a believer (p. 166); attacks the idea that "virgin" refers to fiancée (p. 182); says that the New Testament canon was closed about A.D. 200 (p. 287); claims that tongues were ecstatic speech (pp. 288-89, 317); gives several interpretations for "baptized for the dead" (pp. 371-74); and takes "maranatha" as a prayer (p. 406).

Greek Exegesis

Robertson, Archibald, and Alfred Plummer. *The First Epistle of St. Paul to the Corinthians.* International Critical Commentary. Edinburgh: Clark, 1911. 494 pp. This work is the most thorough commentary on the Greek text. The authors defend the authenticity (pp. xvi ff.); summarize the doctrine of the epistle (pp. xxxiv–xlvi); list Old Testament quotations (pp. ii ff.) and give a good bibliography of older works (pp. lxvi ff.); regularly bring out fine shades of meaning from the Greek (pp. 10, 21, 26, 30, etc.); hesitate to identify Jehovah with Jesus (p. 28); deny that Paul claimed verbal inspiration (p. 46); hold that "deliver to Satan" implies remedial punishment as well as excommunication (p. 99); stress that Paul believed in the preexistence of Christ (p. 201); think that angels are present in worship services (p. 233); emphasize the blessing of the sacraments (p. 244); hold that tongues are ecstatic speech (pp. 267-68); and stress the reality of the bodily resurrection (p. 334).

II Corinthians

Expositions

*Hughes, Philip Edgcumbe. *Paul's Second Epistle to the Corinthians.* Grand Rapids: Eerdmans, 1962. 544 pp. This book is the most helpful commentary on II Corinthians. Hughes gives an extensive defense of the unity of II Corinthians (pp. xxi-xxxv); defends the deity of Christ (p. 7) and His preexistence (p. 301); often gives many interpretations (pp. 17, 107, 201-8, 217-18, 312, and so on); claims that the doctrine of the Trinity needs no defense (p. 45); identifies the repentant sinner with the one in I Corinthians 5 (p. 63); holds that the "building from God" is the resurrection body (p. 163); stresses that only the redeemed stand before the Judgment Seat of Christ (p. 182); discusses the term "paradise" (p. 436) and Paul's "thorn" (pp. 442-48); and holds that the doctrine of the Trinity "is one of the clearest inferences to be drawn from Scripture" (p. 489).

Hodge, Charles. *An Exposition of the Second Epistle to the Corinthians.* Grand Rapids: Eerdmans, n.d. 314 pp. Hodge provides a very thorough commentary. He explains the earnest of the Spirit (p. 25); stresses the intelligence and power of Satan (p. 41); evaluates different interpretations of "cause to triumph" (p. 44); urges that the "building from God" is heaven itself (pp. 107-13); warns against turning the gospel into a philosophy (p. 235); holds that the "thorn" was some "painful bodily affliction" (p. 285); and maintains that the apostolic benediction is a clear recognition of the doctrine of the Trinity (p. 314).

Greek Exegesis

Plummer, Alfred. *The Second Epistle of St. Paul to the Corinthians.* International Critical Commentary. Edinburgh: Clark, 1915. 462 pp. This book is the most exhaustive commentary on the Greek text. The author considers the genuineness of the entire book beyond question (p. xxiii) but thinks chapters 10-

13 were from a separate letter of Paul (pp. xxvi ff.); gives a list of Greek words peculiar to II Corinthians (pp. xlix ff.); rejects the identification of the forgiven offender with the one in I Corinthians 5 (p. 54); defends the reality of Satan (pp. 114-15); thinks that Paul was near to the substitutionary view of the atonement without accepting it (p. 188); lists many interpretations of Paul's "thorn" but considers them all guesses (pp. 348-51); and holds that the genitives of the apostolic benediction are subjective: grace comes from the Lord Jesus, love from God, fellowship from the Spirit (pp. 383-84).

Galatians

Expositions

Guthrie, Donald. *Galatians.* The New Century Bible, New Series. London: Nelson, 1969. 175 pp. A careful, exegetical commentary based on the RSV. He argues for Pauline authorship (pp. 1-8), cautiously favoring the south Galatian view (p. 27). He includes an annotated bibliography (pp. 50-54). He favors the interpretation that elemental spirits refers to personal spiritual powers (p. 118). He holds that the sending forth of the Son implies His preexistence (p. 119). He claims that Paul classes all other religious systems as "weak and beggarly" (p. 123). He gives very specific identification for the works of the flesh and fruit of the Spirit (pp. 145-49). He concludes with an appendix on the centrality of Christ in the epistle (pp. 164 ff.).

Ridderbos, Herman N. *The Epistle of Paul to the Churches of Galatia.* Grand Rapids: Eerdmans, 1953. 238 pp. This book is a thorough, helpful exposition. The author favors the south Galatian view (pp. 30-31); identifies Galatians 2 with Acts 15 (pp. 76-80); sometimes weighs interpretations at length (pp. 82-83, 113); argues for the substitutionary atonement (p. 127); stresses the one-sided nature of the New Covenant (pp. 130-31); denies that the "elements" were spirits (p. 153); and attacks the idea that Paul's infirmity was a disease (pp. 166-67).

Tenney, Merrill C. *The Charter of Christian Liberty.* Grand Rapids: Eerdmans, 1957. 216 pp. Tenney's work is an example of

Bible study intended to encourage others. Tenney applies ten different methods of Bible study to the book of Galatians: synthetic, critical, biographical, historical, theological, rhetorical, topical, analytical, comparative, and devotional. Although it is not a commentary, this book does provide much help in interpreting Galatians. It is especially valuable as an illustration of techniques that can be used with any book of the Bible.

Greek Exegesis

Bruce, Frederick Fyvie. *The Epistle to the Galatians.* Grand Rapids: Eerdmans, 1982. 305 pp. This is the best conservative exegesis of the Greek text. He gives a history of the Galatian region (pp. 3 ff.), favoring the south Galatian view (p. 18). He commends Lightfoot's view that the Jerusalem apostles agreed with Paul against the Judaizers (pp. 22-23). He draws on the teaching of the Lord (p. 38). In passing he abandons the unity of II Corinthians (p. 52). He dates Galatians as the first of Paul's epistles (p. 55). He provides a select bibliography (pp. 59-69). He calls Galatians 1:4 the earliest written statement in the New Testament about the significance of the death of Christ (p. 77). He holds that Paul refused to acknowledge the Judaizers as genuine believers (p. 112). He explains Paul's allegory carefully (pp. 214-27). He interprets "walk by the Spirit" to mean "Let your conduct be directed by the Spirit" (p. 243). He examines each Greek word in the works of the flesh and the fruits of the Spirit (pp. 247-55). He concludes with thorough indexes (pp. 279-305).

Lightfoot, Joseph Barber. *The Epistle of St. Paul to the Galatians.* 1865. Reprint, Grand Rapids: Zondervan, n.d. 384 pp. Lightfoot's work is the best older Greek commentary. The author describes the character of the Gauls (pp. 14-17); holds the north Galatian view (pp. 18 ff.); accepts a date of A.D. 57-58 (p. 40); gives a brief outline (pp. 65-67); has special notes on Paul's stay in Arabia and so on (pp. 87 ff.); holds that Titus was not circumcised (p. 104); identifies Galatians 2 with Acts 15 (pp. 123-28); holds that Paul's infirmity was a disease but does not decide which (pp. 186-91); and has an extended discussion of the "Brethren of the Lord" and "St. Paul and the Three" (pp. 252 ff.). This book is extremely helpful on historical background (p. 166) and Greek words (p. 217).

Barclay, William. *Flesh and Spirit.* Nashville: Abingdon, 1962. 127 pp. Barclay provides brief comments with historical background. He draws parallels between Paul's letters and the papyri (pp. xv-xvi); explains some Greek words that Paul used (p. 26); illustrates the ancient custom of coming of age (p. 37); suggests that Paul had malaria (p. 42); explains the Jewish method of interpreting the Old Testament (p. 44); and gives careful definitions of the words for the works of the flesh and the fruit of the Spirit (pp. 51-57).

Ephesians

Expositions

Moule, Handley Carr Glyn. *Ephesian Studies.* London: Pickering and Inglis, n.d. 340 pp. Moule's work is a warmly devotional exposition. He defends the genuineness of the book (pp. 13 ff.); stresses the "Trinity of Eternal Love" (p. 38) and the "glory of the Christ of God" (p. 52); warns that the church has become afflicted with "bureaucratic tyranny" (p. 58); teaches the ideal or invisible church (p. 59); calls the indwelling of the Spirit the "sovereign gift of God" (p. 139); stresses the deity of Christ (p. 140); and urges total abstinence from sins of temper and tongue (p. 235).

Hodge, Charles. *A Commentary on the Epistle to the Ephesians.* Grand Rapids: Eerdmans, 1950. 398 pp. Hodge writes a thorough Reformed exposition. He defends the genuineness of the book (pp. xv ff.); holds that Christ is Lord in the sense of being God (p. 25); stresses the sovereign election of God (pp. 29-35, 57); asserts that only those in whom the Spirit dwells are members of the true church (p. 87); states that the entire Trinity is involved in redemption (p. 144); stresses total depravity (p. 182); believes in a general judgment (p. 218); and attacks baptismal regeneration (p. 324).

Bruce, Frederick Fyvie. *The Epistle to the Ephesians.* (NIC bound with Colossians and Philemon) Grand Rapids: Eerdmans, 1984. Pp. 229-442. In this helpful exposition, Bruce defends Pauline authorship (p. 240); mentions parallels with Colossians (p. 268); stresses that the church in Ephesians is the universal church (p. 275); holds that the church is built on the foundation of the Christian prophets and apostles (p. 304); holds that 4:4-6 is a confession of faith (p. 335); urges replacing greed with generosity (p. 362); discusses the "house table" with care (pp. 382 ff.); and warns against the wiles of the devil (pp. 404 ff.).

Simpson, E. K., and F. F. Bruce. *Commentary on the Epistles to the Ephesians and the Colossians.* Grand Rapids: Eerdmans, 1957. Pp. 1-158. This book is a pedantic exposition. Simpson uses many foreign phrases (pp. 26-27, etc.); teaches the reality of Satan (p. 48); stresses grace and the new birth (pp. 54-56); warns that God is not "the almighty Sentimentalist" (p. 62); holds that the Trinity was active in redemption (p. 64); and warns against the sin that was the downfall of Rome (p. 103).

Greek Exegesis

*Eadie, John. *Commentary on the Epistle to the Ephesians.* 1883. Reprint, Grand Rapids: Zondervan, n.d. 547 pp. Eadie offers a thorough commentary on the Greek text. He defends Pauline authorship (pp. xiii-xlv); stresses both that we were chosen in Christ before the commencement of time (p. 21) and that man has a free moral nature (p. 24); argues that the sealing of the Spirit followed believing (p. 66); distinguishes synonyms (pp. 94-95); stresses that Jesus is enthroned above all angelic beings (p. 102); holds that grace and faith are the efficient and modal causes of salvation (p. 149); holds that the universal church has divine energy in it (p. 325); and warns that we contend with spirits of high rank (p. 459).

*Westcott, Brooke Foss. *St. Paul's Epistle to the Ephesians.* 1906. Reprint, Grand Rapids: Eerdmans, n.d. 280 pp. This work is a posthumous but very valuable study. Westcott defends Pauline authorship (p. xxxvi); lists words found only in Ephesians in the New Testament (pp. xxxviii f.); compares Ephesians and Colossians (pp. xlii ff.); holds that Paul speaks to the universal church (p. 3); shows the rhythmical structure of vv. 3-14 (p. 5); thinks Paul's phraseology refers to the "spiritual world" (p. 7); stresses the importance of the blood of Christ, not just His death (p. 11); warns that disobedience lays men open to the working of Satan (p. 30); holds that the phrase "lower parts of the earth" refers to Hades (p. 61); denies that the Lord can be regarded as merely human (p.77); warns against nonhuman principalities and powers that are our enemies (p. 93); and gives an extended note on the theology of Ephesians (pp. 126-50).

Philippians

Expositions

Hawthorne, Gerald F. *Philippians.* Waco: Word Books, 1983. 284 pp. A very thorough New Evangelical commentary, the book quotes and draws upon many liberal commentaries (as well as conservative ones): Barclay, Barth, Beare, Caird, Keck, Kennedy, Scott, Weiss, and so on (pp. xxv-xxvi); defends Pauline authorship and the unity of the book (pp. xxvii-xxxii); suggests Philippians was written in Caesarea in A.D. 59-61 (pp. xliii f.); notes that the plural "bishops" indicates no single officer over the Philippian church (p. 8); explains chiasmus (pp. 36, 145); interprets "to depart" as an army striking camp and moving on (p. 48); provides more than four pages of bibliography on Philippians 2:5-11 (pp. 71-75); explains 2:6-11 as a hymn, but not in specific strophes, which may be by Paul (pp. 76-78, 95); holds that Christ possessed "all the characteristics and qualities belonging to God" (p. 84); claims that at the incarnation "Christ became more than God, if this is conceivable, not less than God" (p. 88); sometimes chooses the majority text reading rather than the older one and at times dissents from both (pp. 129, 194); notes changes in verb tense (p. 136); and even diagrams sentences (p. 186).

Melick, Richard R., Jr. *Philippians.* The New American Commentary. Nashville: Broadman, 1991. Pp. 1-159. This is a solid exposition based on the NIV. The author holds to the inerrancy

(p. 7). He gives the background of Philippi (pp. 22 ff.); and defends Pauline authorship and integrity (pp. 30-32). He does not hesitate to correct the language of the NIV (pp. 55, 64, 222, 242, 354, etc.). He attacks the idea of soul sleep (p. 86 note); defends both the humanity and the deity of Christ (p. 104); and thinks that 2:5-11 is a hymn, but Paul used it and approved it (p. 109). He does like to quote liberals: G. B. Caird (p. 153), H.A.A. Kennedy (p. 157), F. W. Beare (p. 159). The volume includes expositions of Colossians and Philemon as well.

Mueller, Jac. J. *The Epistle of Paul to the Philippians and Philemon.* Grand Rapids: Eerdmans, 1955. 156 pp. Mueller writes a concise but especially helpful exposition. He defends the unity of the epistle (p. 20); has a thorough discussion of 2:5-8, defending the preexistence and deity of Christ (pp. 77-86); offers interesting comments on 3:12-16, the "perfect" passage (pp. 120-27); and provides a number of helpful notes on the Greek text (pp. 96, 145, etc.).

Meyer, Frederick Brotherton. *Devotional Commentary on Philippians.* n.d. Reprint, Grand Rapids: Kregel, 1979, 1984. 261 pp. This warm-hearted exposition is memorable. He urges compassion upon boys and girls whose restless and obstinate natures seem to resist every overture (p. 28); balances the blessings of life and the blessings of death (p. 53); stresses Christ's deity and equality with God the Father (pp. 82 f.); commends a holy discontent with ourselves (p. 107); warns against "cranks" who introduce fads and hobbies, exaggerating the importance of trifles (pp. 144 f.); urges believers to press past secondhand knowledge to stand in the personal presence of the living Savior (p. 162); assures believers that having fellowship with God will involve being driven into the wilderness (p. 167); gives the negative example of the philosopher John Stuart Mill (pp. 173 f.); urges believers to become conscious of the presence of the angel of their pilgrimage (p. 210); and warns against failing to guard and thoughts (p. 232).

Johnstone, Robert. *The Epistle of Paul to the Philippians.* 1875. Reprint, Grand Rapids: Baker, 1955. 490 pp. This work is a very thorough, practical, and homiletical exposition by a strong Presbyterian. Johnstone warns against thinking that church membership, baptism, and adherence to the Westminster Confession are grounds for salvation (pp. 254-55); maintains the preexistence and deity of Christ (pp. 146-48); and includes a considerable number of notes on the Greek text (pp. 429-90).

Greek Exegesis

Lightfoot, Joseph Barber. *Saint Paul's Epistle to the Philippians.* London: Macmillan, 1868. 366 pp. Lightfoot has the most thorough and helpful commentary on the Greek text. He discusses every grammatical and interpretative problem in the book and has extended notes on special subjects (e.g., "bishop" and "presbyter," pp. 95-99); defends the preexistence and deity of Christ; holds that Christ emptied Himself "not of His divine nature, for this was impossible, but of the glories, the prerogatives, of deity. This He did by taking upon Him the form of a servant" (p. 112). He gives extended discussion of "The Christian Ministry" and of "St. Paul and Seneca."

Silva, Moises. *Philippians.* Chicago: Moody, 1988. 255 pp. This is a scholarly exposition based on the Greek text. Silva gives good historical background (pp. 2-5) and defends the integrity of the book (pp. 14-16). He consistently has a careful analysis of textual variations (pp. 22-27). He notes "the ease and naturalness with which Paul appears to regard his Lord as on the same level with the Father" (p. 43). He manifests high regard for Chrysostom (pp. 56-57). At times he criticizes the Majority Text (p. 74). He takes pains to show that the overall thought of a section is borne out by each verse (pp. 99-102). Dr. Silva clearly argues for the divine and preexistent Christ (p. 113). There are a few typographical errors both in Greek and in English (pp. 137, 224). He gives precise distinction between words (p. 180) and notes chiasmus (p. 185). He argues that women were part of the leadership of the Philippian church (p. 221). He concludes with four different indexes (pp. 243-55).

Plummer, Alfred. *A Commentary on St. Paul's Epistle to the Philippians.* London: Robert Scott, 1919. 138 pp. In a brief but thorough commentary, Plummer frequently uses the Greek; draws illustrations from the papyri (p. 7); defends the Pauline authorship and integrity of the epistle (pp. xi-xii); holds that joy is the "dominant note of the epistle" (p. 9); defends the deity and preexistence of Christ (pp. 42-43); and includes helpful grammatical notes (pp. 74-75) and a bibliography of thirty-nine commentaries on Philippians (pp. xxi-xxii).

Colossians

Expositions

*Nicholson, W. R. *Oneness with Christ.* 1903. Reprint, Grand Rapids: Kregel, 1951. 284 pp. Nicholson writes rich devotional expositions. He attacks liberal theology (p. 25) and the papacy (p. 80); stresses the infinite value of the blood of Christ (p. 58); holds that Christ is both the image and the likeness of God (pp. 71-72); defends the deity of Christ (pp. 73, 190) and His sinlessness (p. 125); teaches the premillennial return (p. 149); and emphasizes the resurrection life of believers (pp. 217-18).

Moule, Handley Carr Glyn. *Colossian and Philemon Studies.* London: Pickering and Inglis, n.d. Pp. 1-275. This work contains warmly devotional expositions. The author stresses the central position of Christ in our faith (pp. 13 ff., 78 ff.); shows that Scripture is both human and divine (pp. 34-35); holds that the Bible teaches theology by worship (p. 73); warns against universalism (p. 88); maintains that the Bible tells us how to do what other religions can merely encourage (pp. 111 ff.); teaches Christ's divine fullness (p. 144); holds that baptism is a "sealing ordinance" (p. 153); and urges a strong standard of missionary conduct (p. 202) and holiness at home (p. 232).

Bruce, F. F. *The Epistles to the Colossians, to Philemon, and to the Ephesians.* (NIC) Grand Rapids: Eerdmans, 1984. 442 pp. With this very helpful exposition, Bruce refutes Hooker's ideas of heresy at Colossae (p. 18); believes the "dominion of darkness" refers to angels (p. 51); holds that the doctrine of Christ is the best safeguard against heresy (p. 55); takes Colossians 1:19 as "in him all the fulness of deity was well pleased to take up residence" (p. 72) and states that 2:9 reinforces this interpretation (p. 100); gives examples of free and slave alike who suffered martyrdom for Christ (p. 151); and discusses the "house tables" (pp. 163 ff.). For comments on Ephesians and Philemon, see those books.

Thomas, W. H. Griffith. *Studies in Colossians and Philemon.* Grand Rapids: Baker, 1973. 200 pp. This book contains devotional expositions published posthumously. Thomas stresses the Word of God "revealed, received, reproduced, related" (pp. 28-29); teaches the efficacy of prayer (pp. 41-42); emphasizes the divine sonship of Christ (pp. 47-48, 144); characterizes the Christian ministry (p. 73); cites Spurgeon's remark that Colossians 3 "begins in heaven (vv. 1-4) and ends in the kitchen (vv. 22-25)" (p. 106).

Greek Exegesis

*Eadie, John. *The Epistle of Paul to the Colossians.* 1856. Reprint, Minneapolis: Klock and Klock, 1977. 354 pp. In a very thorough exposition of the Greek text, Eadie defends the genuineness of Colossians (pp. xxii-xxx); holds that the Lord is the radiance of heaven (p. 34); teaches that the one kingdom of God is both earthly and celestial (p. 38); defends the deity and humanity of Christ (pp. 42 ff.); presents Him as universal Creator (pp. 52-53); stresses the universal church as the company of the redeemed (p. 64); warns against the heresies that use biblical phraseology (p. 132); and stresses the divine fullness of Christ (p. 144) and His divine right to forgive sin (p. 243).

*Lightfoot, Joseph Barber. *Saint Paul's Epistles to the Colossians and to Philemon.* 1879. Reprint, Grand Rapids: Zondervan, n.d. 430 pp. Lightfoot offers the best commentary on the Greek text. He has extended introductory notes on "The Churches of the Lycus" (Laodicea, Hierapolis, and Colossae) (pp. 1-72) and on "The Colossian Heresy" (pp. 73-113); gives word studies (pp. 141, 214, etc.); stresses that "firstborn" implies both priority to and sovereignty over all creation (pp. 146-47); holds that there is a celestial hierarchy of angels (pp. 153-54); teaches the divine nature and incarnation of Christ (pp. 181-82); and concludes with an extended note on the Essenes (pp. 349-419).

Philemon

Expositions

Moule, Handley Carr Glyn. *Colossians and Philemon Studies.* London: Pickering and Inglis, n.d. Pp. 277-318. In this warmly devotional exposition, Moule sketches the background of the times and the situation (pp. 279-300), and stresses the sanctity of duty (p. 312), and encourages gentleness of manner (pp. 313-14).

Greek Exegesis

Lightfoot, Joseph Barber. *Saint Paul's Epistles to the Colossians and to Philemon.* 1879. Reprint, Grand Rapids: Zondervan, n.d. Pp. 301-46. Lightfoot has the best commentary on the Greek text. He provides background information (pp. 303-29); stresses the full knowledge of believers (p. 336); holds that Paul wrote the entire letter with his own hand (p. 344).

Thessalonian Epistles

Expositions

*Hiebert, D. Edmond. *The Thessalonian Epistles.* Chicago: Moody, 1971. 383 pp. With this book, Hiebert provides the most thorough premillennial commentary. The author discusses how long Paul was in Thessalonica (pp. 16-17); gives Greek word studies (p. 44); notes the force of the perfect tense (pp. 65); stresses the imminent return of Christ (pp. 70, 219); at times discusses textual variants and translations (pp. 83, 93, 169); emphasizes the rightfulness of prayer to the Lord Jesus (pp. 153-54); and attacks the posttribulation rapture view (p. 205).

Walvoord, John Flipse. *The Thessalonian Epistles.* Findlay, Ohio: Dunham, 1955. 158 pp. This book is a popular premillennial exposition. The author defends election (p. 14); warns about coming judgment (p. 19); urges soulwinning and prayer (pp. 37, 42); holds to the imminent return of Christ (p. 47); discusses the words of *coming* (pp. 48-49); denies a general resurrection (p. 59); defends the pretribulation rapture (pp. 64-65); thinks that only New Testament saints will be resurrected at the rapture, though the Scofield Bible disagrees (p. 72); and holds that the "Day of the Lord" includes the tribulation period and the millennium (pp. 76-78).

Hogg, C. F., and W. E. Vine. *The Epistles to the Thessalonians.* 1914. Reprint, Grand Rapids: Kregel, 1959. 307 pp. This book is a conservative exposition that emphasizes word studies. The authors defend the authenticity of the book (pp. 11-12); list its major doctrines (pp. 14 ff.); show that the Lord Jesus Christ is called Lord (pp. 22 ff.); give special word studies on *Word* (p. 39), *Satan* (pp. 82-83), *sons* (pp. 158-59), *Christian joy* (pp. 186 ff.), *Spirit, soul,* and *body* (pp. 204 ff.); and teach a premillennial return of the Lord (p. 144).

Greek Exegesis

Milligan, George. *St. Paul's Epistles to the Thessalonians.* 1908. Reprint, Grand Rapids: Eerdmans, 1953. 304 pp. Milligan's work is the best commentary on the Greek text. The author has an introduction that gives the background of the city (pp. xxi f.) and the church of Thessalonica (pp. xxvi ff.); discusses the language (pp. li ff.) and the doctrine of the Epistles (pp. lxiii ff.); defends the authenticity (pp. lxxi ff.); teaches that the present aspect of the kingdom is *rule,* the future aspect is *glory* (p. 27); holds that *vessel* in 4:4 means "body" (pp. 48-49); and warns against treating the rapture too literally (p. 60). Milligan also has special notes on Paul as a letter writer (pp. 121 ff.), the divine names in the epistles (pp. 135 ff.), the words for the second coming: *parousia, epiphany, apocalypsis* (pp. 145 ff.), the biblical doctrine of the Antichrist (pp. 158), and other subjects.

Wanamaker, Charles A. *The Epistles to the Thessalonians.* New International Greek Testament Commentary. Grand Rapids: Eerdmans, 1990. 316 pp. This commentary gives some help on the Greek text, but places more emphasis on Pauline Christianity "as a socio-religious movement" (p. xii); argues that II Thessalonians was actually first (pp. xiii, 37-45); describes conversion as a "resocialization" process (p. 14); defends Pauline authorship (pp. 17-28); gives a rhetorical analysis (pp. 48 ff.); holds that Paul believed in a personal evil power but had not developed a clear doctrine of Satan (p. 122); urges that "Evangelical Christianity needs to strive to create a social context or community in which converts may be resocialized into a new and distinctive Christian pattern of behavior and practice. Without this, conversion is not complete and has little chance of being genuinely transformative in the long term" (p. 139). He holds that the assumption was presented in symbolic terms, but probably Paul believed "in some type of historical realization" (p. 173); does not use the term *Rapture;* sees the "Day of the Lord" as a threatening time of judgment (p. 225); argues that Paul does not teach the "final annihilation of the godless" (p. 229); and thinks that Paul took the "defilement of the temple" as part of Old Testament prophecy (p. 247).

Lineberry, John. *Vital Word Studies in I Thessalonians.* Grand Rapids: Zondervan, 1960. 132 pp. In a conservative exposition that provides special Greek word studies, Lineberry maintains the deity and humanity of Christ (p. 25); stresses the imminent return of Christ (pp. 39, 98, 103, etc.); attacks Modernism (p. 64); defends the bodily resurrection of Christ (p. 97); and advocates the pretribulation rapture view and attacks the opposing views (pp. 101, 113).

————. *Vital Word Studies in II Thessalonians.* Grand Rapids: Zondervan, 1960. 93 pp. Lineberry writes a conservative exposition that provides special Greek word studies. He distinguishes between the rapture and the revelation (pp. 7, 26); defends verbal inspiration (pp. 8, 68); gives an expanded translation (pp. 13-15); stresses the deity of Christ (pp. 27-28, 36); holds that *parousia* refers to the rapture and *apokalupsis* to the revelation (p. 37); identifies the falling away with the rapture rather than with the apostasy (p. 42); and interprets the hinderer as the church or the Holy Spirit in the church (pp. 49, 52).

Pastoral Epistles

Expositions

Guthrie, Donald. *The Pastoral Epistles.* Grand Rapids: Eerdmans, 1957. 228 pp. Guthrie makes brief but careful comments. He defends Pauline authorship (pp. 11-53); stresses the necessity of keeping false teachers in check (p. 57); holds that the saying "Christ came to save sinners" is the cardinal fact of Christian truth (p. 65); thinks that "deliver to Satan" means both excommunication and physical disaster (p. 68); holds that Paul forbade women to teach in public (p. 76); defends the inspiration of Scripture (p. 164); and concludes with an appendix answering linguistic arguments against the genuineness of the pastoral epistles (pp. 212-28).

Fairbairn, Patrick. *Commentary on the Pastoral Epistles.* 1874. Reprint, Grand Rapids: Zondervan, n.d. 451 pp. In a thorough exposition, Fairbairn defends Pauline authorship (pp. 1-19); warns against progressive error in false teaching (p. 85); holds that Christ was a substitutionary ransom for sin (p. 117); thinks that "cutting straight" refers to laying out a road (p. 344); warns of the moral evils that come from selfishness (p. 365); stresses the divine inspiration of Scripture (p. 379); and concludes with three appendixes on problem passages (pp. 405 ff.).

Kent, Homer A., Jr. *The Pastoral Epistles.* Chicago: Moody, 1958. 320 pp. This book is a Conservative Plymouth Brethren commentary. Kent defends Pauline authorship (pp. 24-40) and answers liberal attacks (pp. 41-71); stresses that Christ alone is Mediator and excludes angels, the virgin, and so on (p. 105); holds that women are not to teach in public (pp. 112-13); argues that "saved through childbearing" refers to the incarnation (pp. 118 ff.); thinks that the early church had deaconesses (p. 140); holds to the ordinance of footwashing (p. 174); and teaches the inspiration of the Scriptures (p. 290). He treats II Timothy and Titus much more briefly than I Timothy.

Stott, John R. W. *Guard the Gospel.* Downers Grove, Ill.: Inter-Varsity, 1973. 127 pp. Stott's work is a very perceptive and helpful exposition of II Timothy. The author defends Pauline authorship (pp. 13 ff.); shows the greatness of Christ's victory over death (pp. 37 ff.); warns that "some Christians never get down to any serious Bible study" (p. 59); explains "rightly dividing" as *cutting straight* (p. 67); argues that man's basic sin is selfishness (pp. 84 ff.); defends the inspiration of the Bible (pp. 100 ff.); and urges the necessity of study (p. 121).

Greek Exegesis

Knight, George W., III. ***The Pastoral Epistles.*** Vol. 14, New International Greek Testament Commentary. Grand Rapids: Eerdmans, 1992. 514 pp. This is a very careful commentary on the Greek text. He has a thorough bibliography (pp. xxii-xxxiv); formally defends Pauline authorship (pp. 4-52); and gives the date of early A.D. 60s to 68 (p. 54). On I Timothy he urges that the law was given to deal with moral questions, not for speculation (p. 83); holds that continued and unrepentant practice of homosexuality results in exclusion from the kingdom of God (p. 86); holds that Paul objected to excess of adornment in women (p. 138); urges women to silence and submission, yet not as an absolute (pp. 140 ff.); holds that the bishop should be married (as a norm) and should be faithful (pp. 157 ff., 289). On Titus he urges that elders should not be "self-willed" (p. 291); holds that false teachers need to be silenced (p. 297); disagrees with Fee that what is unacceptable to non-Christians is merely cultural (Knight holds that it reflects a transcultural moral standard) (p. 310); and argues for the translation "of our great God and Savior Jesus Christ" (one Person, pp. 322-25). On II Timothy he shows how Paul encouraged Timothy not to be embarrassed by the world's last days (pp. 428 f.); organizes the list of vices (p. 430); and concludes with thorough indexes (pp. 479-514).

Hebrews

Expositions

Bruce, Frederick Fyvie. ***The Epistle to the Hebrews.*** Grand Rapids: Eerdmans, 1964. 511 pp. Bruce provides a thorough, reverent exposition from a reformed viewpoint with many helpful insights.

He maintains that its authorship remains unknown (p. xlii); dates it before A.D. 70 (p. xliv); holds that Hebrews 6 is a real warning against apostasy (p. 123) but does not question the perseverance of the saints ("those who persevere are the true saints") (p. 118); and suggests Simon Magus as an example of this apostasy (p. 122).

Davidson, Andrew Bruce. *The Epistle to the Hebrews.* Grand Rapids: Zondervan, 1950. 260 pp. Though small in size, this book offers a treasure of help and insight. Davidson holds that Christ is addressed as God (p. 49), that He is the Author of salvation in 2:10 (p. 62), and that He was preexistent (p. 74); maintains that the people in 6:1-6 apostatized "against experience and better knowledge" (p. 122) and that the passage is written as a hypothesis to prevent this; and offers helpful notes on the "Rest of God," "Word of God," "Priesthood of Christ," "The Two Covenants," and other phrases.

Hughes, Philip Edgcumbe. *A Commentary on the Epistle to the Hebrews.* Grand Rapids: Eerdmans, 1977. 623 pp. This work is a superior commentary on an inferior text, the RSV. The author sees Hebrews as an answer to those influenced by the Essenes (Dead Sea Scrolls people, pp. 10-15); defends a date before the destruction of Jerusalem (pp. 30-32, 302); defends the deity of Christ (pp. 41-44); identifies Jesus as the OT Lord God (p. 68); notes chiasmus constructions (pp. 90, 409); defends the doctrine of propitiation, not merely expiation (p. 121); refers to Christ as the eternal Son (p. 134); teaches eternal security and personal responsibility (p. 139); warns that the external rite of baptism guarantees nothing (p. 151); attacks "chiliastic" (premillennial) interpretations (p. 161); and identifies those in Hebrews 6 as those who sin against the light but finally show their true colors (pp. 216-18). He has extended notes on Melchizedek (pp. 237 ff.); "the true test" (pp. 283 ff.); the blood of Jesus (pp. 329-49); the doctrine of Creation (pp. 443 ff.); and faith (pp. 438 ff.). He gives many Roman Catholic interpretations, quoting St. Thomas Aquinas eighty-seven times.

Saphir, Adolph. *The Epistle to the Hebrews.* 2 vols. New York: Loizeaux, 1932. 890 pp. This book contains fervent, warm-hearted messages on Hebrews by a converted Jew. Saphir argues for Pauline authorship (p. 18); has a powerful exposition of Hebrews 4:12 (pp. 232 ff.); holds that Hebrews 6 refers to professing Christians (pp. 316-17) and that a true believer can never perish; and states that the elect are perfectly safe (p. 325).

Kent, Homer A. *The Epistle to the Hebrews.* Grand Rapids: Baker, 1972. 303 pp. Illus. In a careful exposition, Kent stresses the full deity of the Son (p. 44); warns against apostasy from Christ to Judaism (p. 73); explains the idea of rest (p. 88); argues that the apostasy of Chapter 6 is a hypothetical case (p. 113); stresses the unique character of the once-for-all offering of Himself for sin (p. 144); holds that the new covenant is for both Israel and the church (pp. 158-59); and includes an extensive bibliography (pp. 297-303).

Schneider, Johannes. *The Letter to the Hebrews.* Grand Rapids: Eerdmans, 1957. 139 pp. This book offers very helpful comments by a European Baptist. Schneider holds that its author is unknown; dates it around A.D. 70 (p. 5); stresses the deity of Christ (p. 12); has a good treatment of the Word of God in 4:12 (pp. 34 ff.); holds that 6:1-6 teaches the impossibility of a second repentance (p. 51); and stresses the "eternally efficacious power" of Christ's blood (p. 83).

Greek Exegesis

Westcott, Brooke Foss. *The Epistle to the Hebrews.* 1889. Reprint, Grand Rapids: Eerdmans, 1955. 584 pp. Westcott offers the best and most thorough commentary on the Greek text. In addition to the exhaustive exegesis, there are valuable notes on special subjects throughout the book: Melchizedek (pp. 199-203), the tabernacle (pp. 233-40), the Christology of Hebrews (pp. 469-95), and many others. He dates it A.D. 64-67 (p. xlii); favors the translation "God is thy throne" in 1:8 (p. 25); holds, concerning 6:1-6, that divine life was given (p. 148) but that all gifts were personal (p. 150), and that it was a past act of apostasy (p. 151), a hypothetical case (p. 165).

Ellingworth, Paul. *The Epistle to the Hebrews.* New International Greek Text Commentary. Grand Rapids: Eerdmans, 1993, 764 pp. This book is a technical commentary on the Greek text that stresses grammar and structure rather than doctrine. Ellingworth gives a huge bibliography (pp. xxiv-xcviii); discusses the authorship (pp. 3-21); suggests a date before A.D. 70 (p. 33); has a brief study of the theology of Hebrews (p. 63-77); lists the manuscript evidence for Hebrews (pp. 81-85); employs a TEV-style translation (pp. 89 ff.); stresses the essential unity between God and His Son (p. 99); holds that Psalm 45 is used to show that the Son is addressed as God and Lord (p. 122); thinks that the author was not a second generation believer (p. 141); argues for "expiation" rather than propitiation in Hebrews (p. 189); denies that Christ has a "house" (p. 195); interacts with the liberal views of Harnack, Bultmann, and others (p. 289); argues that the fear Christ manifested was reverence for God (p. 290); notes chiastic structure (p. 350); gives a table of associations of "covenant" with other terms (pp. 386-88); calls some wording in Scripture "awkward" (p. 436); stresses the substitutionary sacrificial shedding of blood in Christ's death (p. 473); teaches that Christ is coming again for a final triumph (p. 487); sees apostasy resulting in a punishment worse than death (pp. 538 ff.); holds that the Old Testament emphasizes that the fall of Jericho was an act of God (p. 620); and concludes with indexes of subjects, authors, and Greek words (pp. 737-64).

James

Expositions

*Hiebert, D. Edmond. *The Epistle of James.* Chicago: Moody, 1979. 354 pp. This is the most helpful and careful commentary on James that has appeared in our century. Hiebert defends James, the Lord's brother, as author (pp. 11-25); gives a date of A.D. 46-49 (p. 41); at times cites numerous translations to help in giving the interpretation (p. 60); discusses man's blaming

God for sin (pp. 102-3); brings out the force of the Greek constructions (pp. 139-40); harmonizes James and Paul on faith and works (pp. 174 ff.); points out a chiastic construction (p. 186); defends the existence of demons (p. 188); denies the doctrine of synergism (p. 194); discusses difficult interpretations at length (pp. 254-57); distinguishes the meaning of words (p. 275); and concludes with a very thorough bibliography (pp. 339-54).

Adamson, James B. *The Epistle of James.* (NIC, rev) Grand Rapids: Eerdmans, 1976. 227 pp. Adamson provides a very thoughtful exposition. He defends James the brother of the Lord as the author (pp. 18-20, 49); sees the Christ of glory as a reference to the Shekinah (pp. 25, 104); harmonizes James and Paul on faith and works (pp. 34-38); has a strong bibliography (pp. 40-44); maintains that "God gives his wisdom to men not only just for the asking but also without chiding a man for his previous sins" (p. 56); holds that "begot" refers to the new birth (pp. 76-77); thinks that Paul is James's best interpreter (p. 86); has an excursus on "implanted" as the best meaning in 1:21 (pp. 98-100); stresses "the law of the Great King" (p. 115); argues that James means the kind of "faith" that is impotent, unable to save (p. 121); shows that James links faith indissolubly to works, "neither being unduly stressed at the expense of the other" (p. 129); warns against lightly entering the ministry (p. 141); attacks the oppression of the poor and the weak (p. 189); defends the imminence of the *parousia* (p. 191); and sees a beautiful, logical connection in the thought of the epistle (p. 202).

Johnstone, Robert. *The Epistle of James.* 1888. Reprint, Grand Rapids: Baker, 1954. 433 pp. In a strong exposition, Johnstone has brief notes on the Greek text (pp. 7-45), an introduction (pp. 47 ff.), and thirty-one paragraph expositions. He stresses that the Bible *is* the Word of God (p. viii); holds that God's gifts act on the soul of man (p. 114); assumes that Christian principle will bridle the tongue (p. 159); harmonizes Paul and James on faith and works (pp. 214 ff.); warns against earthly wisdom (pp. 269-70) and vain confidence regarding the future (pp. 340 ff.); and urges patience in view of the blessed hope (pp. 364 ff.).

Robertson, Archibald T. *Studies in the Epistle of James.* 1915. Reprint, Nashville: Broadman, n.d. 200 pp. Robertson writes helpful expository messages. He gives a brief life of James (pp. 1-27); has good word studies (pp. 33, 65, and so on); harmonizes the interpretation of Paul and James on works and faith (pp. 91 ff.); stresses that faith is not mere intellectual assent (p. 96); holds that the best preachers build up the saints in the faith as well as win converts (p. 105); urges patient waiting for the *parousia* of the Lord (p. 178); and thinks that prayer and medicine should be combined (p. 189).

Greek Exegesis

Mayor, Joseph B. *The Epistle of James.* 1913. Reprint, Grand Rapids: Zondervan, 1954. 596 pp. Mayor makes careful notes on the Greek text. He defends the authorship of James as the Lord's brother (pp. xi-lxv); has an extensive introduction covering date, style, grammar, and so on (pp. lxvi-ccxci); provides many word studies (pp. 48, 60, 189-90); harmonizes James and Paul on faith and works (pp. 216 ff.); discusses biblical wisdom (pp. 222-23), the world (pp. 224 ff.), divine jealousy (pp. 226-27), swearing (pp. 231-32), healing the sick (pp. 232 ff.); and concludes with special notes on Dr. Hort's writings, the doctrine of Creation according to James, and other topics.

Davids, Peter H. *The Epistle of James.* New International Greek Text Commentary. Grand Rapids: Eerdmans, 1982. 226 pp. This is a commentary on the Greek text. He favors a two-stage authorship: James the Just could have written the first homilies, and then a redactor put them together into present form (pp. 12-13); wonders whether the redaction took place in A.D. 55-65 or A.D. 75-85 (p. 22); gives a structural diagram (p. 29); suggests theological themes in James: suffering/testing, eschatology, Christology, poverty-piety, Law, Grace, Faith, wisdom, and prayer (pp. 34-57); refers to anemones and cyclamen withering in the Palestinian sun (p. 77); stresses the deity of Jesus Christ (pp. 106-7); holds that for James "there is no such thing as a true and living faith which does not produce works" (p. 122); thinks that James does not have Paul in mind at all (p. 127); warns against praying with anger (pp. 155 ff.); stresses the imminence of Christ's coming (p. 185); and thinks the oil was "a sacramental vehicle of divine power" (p. 193).

I Peter

Expositions

Hiebert, D. Edmond. *I Peter: An Expositional Commentary.* Chicago: Moody Press, 1984. 329 pp. This is the most helpful exposition of I Peter. Hiebert sees the main theme as "triumphant faith amid suffering" (p. 1), defends Petrine authorship (pp. 2 ff.), discusses the unity and form of the epistle (pp. 11 ff.), dates it in A.D. 64 (p. 19), provides a thorough outline (pp. 23-28), discusses the geographical locations of the readers (pp. 35 ff.) defends the doctrine of the Trinity (pp. 38-39), stresses that trials benefit believers (p. 57), urges a life of personal holiness (pp. 81 ff.), refers to the power of the precious blood of Christ (p. 93), explains the grammatical structure of the Greek (p. 104), holds that the Word is the means of spiritual growth (p. 115), expounds "Christ the Stone" (pp. 120 ff.), stresses believers as sojourners (pp. 142 ff.), urges submission to the state (pp. 151 ff.) and in marital relations (pp. 181 ff.), recounts the blessedness of suffering for righteousness (p. 209), presents different views on the preaching to the spirits in prison (pp. 268 ff.), stresses the internal presence of the Spirit during suffering (pp. 268 ff.), appeals to the elders to shepherd the flock (pp. 280 ff.), and concludes with a thorough bibliography (pp. 313-25).

Stibbs, Alan M. *The First Epistle General of Peter.* Grand Rapids: Eerdmans, 1959. 192 pp. This work is an unusually helpful exposition with a thorough introduction by Andrew Walls. Stibbs defends Petrine authorship (pp. 15-18); gives a date of A.D. 63-64 (p. 67); provides a brief outline (pp. 69-70); brings out the force of the Greek tense (pp. 86, 89, etc.); rebukes rebellion against society (p. 106); commends the Westminster Confession (p. 113); attacks the pope (p. 122); stresses that only

Christ, not baptism, can impart life and forgiveness (p. 140); holds that Christ proclaimed His victory to evil spirits after His death (pp. 142-43); and concludes by giving the teaching of I Peter on God, Christ, the Holy Spirit, God's people, suffering, and other subjects (pp. 178-92).

Greek Exegesis

Selwyn, Edward Gordon. *The First Epistle of St. Peter.* London: Macmillan, 1946. 517 pp. In an exhaustive commentary on the Greek text, Selwyn gives an extended argument for Silvanus's drafting of the epistle and Peter's adding to it and authorizing it (pp. 7-38); dates the epistle A.D. 63-64 (p. 62); discusses major doctrines in I Peter (Christian life, God, the Church, etc.) (pp. 64-115); refers to "II Isaiah" (p. 152); carefully points out distinctions in tense (p. 181), mode (p. 190), and case (p. 184); holds that the phrase "spirits in prison" refers primarily to supernatural beings but may also include the wicked dead (p. 199); teaches baptismal regeneration (p. 204); and has extended essays on Christ's descent into hell (pp. 313 ff.) and Formgeschichte (pp. 363 ff.).

Hort, Fenton J. A. *The First Epistle of St. Peter.* London: Macmillan, 1898. 188 pp. Hort writes an exhaustive exposition of the Greek text of I Peter 1:1–2:17. He gives careful word studies (pp. 19-20, 26, 36, 98, etc.); stresses the character of the Son as the "Only Begotten" (p. 21); discusses the titles applied to the Lord Jesus (pp. 29-31); emphasizes the new birth (p. 91); and concludes with notes on the names of Peter, the terms for sojourning, and so on (pp. 151-84). The work was cut off by Hort's untimely death.

II Peter and Jude

Expositions

*Hiebert, D. Edmond. *Second Peter and Jude.* Greenville, S.C.: Unusual Publications, 1989. 324 pp. Most of the books written on II Peter and Jude are by liberals and unbelievers. Dr. Hiebert has put Fundamentalism deeply into his debt by writing a very thorough, conservative commentary on these books. On the one hand Dr. Hiebert is always accurate, being careful of the wording of the Greek text; on the other hand he is warm-hearted, applying the truths to the hearts of believers today. He defends the authenticity of II Peter (pp. 1-20) and Jude (pp. 185 ff.); dates II Peter A.D. 65, Jude A.D. 67-68 (pp. 22, 203); gives a helpful outline of each book (pp. 26-29, 206-7); interprets "faith" as referring to the body of apostolic teaching (p. 33); makes a strong point of defending the deity of Christ (pp. 36-37); brings out the rich meaning of Greek words (pp. 51 ff.); characterizes Peter's faith as "Christocentric" (p. 62); contrasts the cunningly devised fables with the revelation to eyewitnesses (pp. 70 ff.); warns against private interpretation of Scripture (pp. 81 ff.); discusses the false prophets and teachers (pp. 86 ff.); emphasizes the arrogance of these false teachers (pp. 110 f.); pictures their doom (pp. 123-24); defends the biblical Flood (pp. 145-46); attacks Universalism (p. 157); shows Peter's consistency with the modern scientific view of atomic structure (p. 160); urges separation and dedication (pp. 162-63); brings out the force of the tense of the verb (p. 168); compares II Peter and Jude (pp. 195-96); brings out the meaning of earnestly contending for the faith (pp. 218-19); and argues that "such a divinely given faith admits no subsequent additions or subtractions such as the false teachers were seeking to introduce" (p. 221). It is refreshing to be able to give an unqualified recommendation to this book. The Bible-believing Christian can find help and inspiration on every page. Dr. Hiebert's commentary is the finest work written on II Peter and Jude in this generation.

Manton, Thomas. *An Exposition of the Epistle of Jude.* Reprint, London: Banner of Truth Trust, 1958. 376 pp. In an exhaustive, wordy Puritan exposition, Manton warns that God's people have always been troubled by persecutors outside and sectaries inside (p. 6); stresses God's election and effectual calling (p. 18) and preservation (p. 43); urges growth in grace (p. 88) and preservation of the truth (p. 110); states "we must bark when we see a wolf, though in a sheep's garment" (p. 124); and attacks ignorance (p. 136) and "popish idolatry" (p. 253).

Greek Exegesis

Bigg, Charles. *The Epistles of St. Peter and St. Jude.* International Critical Commentary. Edinburgh: Clark, 1901. Pp. 199-304 (II Peter). Bigg writes the most thorough commentary on the Greek text. He has extensive introductory notes (pp. 199-247); defends Peter as the author (p. 242); maintains that Peter called Christ *God* (pp. 250-52); stresses that God gives both revelation and its interpretation (p. 270); thinks that Peter refers to fallen angels of Genesis 6 (p. 275); gives no explanation for the elements being loosed (p. 298); and believes that Peter read Paul's epistles within a month or so of their being written (p. 301).

Bigg, Charles. *The Epistles of St. Peter and St. Jude.* International Critical Commentary. Edinburgh: Clark, 1901. Pp. 305-53 (Jude). Bigg's work is the most thorough commentary on the Greek text. The author gives a brief introduction (pp. 305-22); identifies Jude as the brother of the James of Acts 15 (p. 317); holds that he quoted from the book of Enoch (p. 336); and gives a careful comparison of the subjects of II Peter and Jude (p. 221).

Johannine Epistles

Expositions

*Candlish, Robert Smith. *The First Epistle of John.* Reprint, Grand Rapids: Zondervan, n.d. 577 pp. This work is an exhaustive exposition of surprising fervency. Candlish holds that the "Word of life" is personal (p. 4); gives a moving portrait of Christ the Advocate (pp. 65-66) and of the walk of Jesus (pp. 88 ff.); stresses that the atonement meets the needs of all mankind (pp. 75-76); defends the doctrines of the atonement (p. 193) and the virgin birth (p. 355); denies a sacramental interpretation of "abiding" (pp. 197-98); attacks Romanist doctrine (p. 519); has a memorable exposition of "Having Confidence at His Coming" (pp. 204-14); refers to love within the Trinity (pp. 386-91); and warns against the atmosphere produced by the "prince of the power of the air" (pp. 546-47).

*Hiebert, D. Edmond. *The Epistles of John.* Greenville, S.C.: Bob Jones University Press, 1991. 371 pp. Hiebert's work is the best modern exposition, written in full knowledge of the Greek text and the commentary literature. He defends Johannine authorship (pp. 3-16, 281); explains the textual problems of I John 5:7 (pp. 26 f.); provides a careful outline (pp. 29-34); stresses the sacrificial nature of propitiation (p. 75); teaches a premillennial interpretation of antichrist (pp. 109 ff.); urges the imminency of Christ's return (p. 137); stresses the two classes of humanity: those in Christ and those practicing sin (pp. 143 ff.); warns against false teachers of the occult (p. 180); argues that the elect lady refers to an actual lady and her children (p. 282); warns that Christian growth must remain true to the revelation in Christ (p. 307); and concludes with a thorough bibliography (pp. 351-60) and indexes (pp. 361-77).

Ross, Alexander. *The Epistles of James and John.* Grand Rapids: Eerdmans, 1954. Pp. 105-249. In a very helpful, practical exposition, Ross refutes C. H. Dodd's opinions on I John (pp. 110-11); defends Johannine authorship (pp. 207-13); attacks the idea of another "John the Elder" (pp. 125-29); defends the meaning of "propitiation" in 2:2 (pp. 151-52) and the idea of a personal Antichrist (pp. 169-70); argues from the meaning of the present tense in Greek (p. 183); attacks the false cults (p. 197); and holds that the phrase "water and blood" refers to Christ's baptism and death (p. 213).

Marshall, I. Howard. *The Epistles of John.* NIC. Grand Rapids: Eerdmans, 1978. 274 pp. A careful exposition of the NIV by a well-known British conservative. He explains the views of the false teachers (pp. 14 f.); and gives eight different outlines for I John (pp. 22-26). Although he thinks it is improbable that the author of the epistles also composed Revelation (p. 42), he concludes "so far no convincing alternative has been suggested" (p. 46). Following Brooke in the ICC, Marshall takes "elect lady" as a metaphor for a church (p. 60); urges sympathy for those who differ on doctrine: "Today's heresy may well become tomorrow's orthodoxy" (p. 74); holds III John to be a true personal letter (p. 81); admits that there cannot be unity between those who accept and those who do not accept Jesus Christ as Savior (p. 107); defends the translation "propitiation" (I John 2:2, p. 118); distinguishes between the visible church and the invisible church (p. 152); argues that "to reduce Jesus to the status of mere man . . . is to strike at the root of Christianity" (p. 159); criticizes the NIV translation of I John 3:1 (p. 170); admits that conservatives regularly solve 3:6 ff. by stressing present tense verbs, but Marshall thinks it refers to the ideal character of Christians (pp. 180-83); defends the ancient text of I John 5:7 (pp. 235-36); and stresses that Jesus is the true God and eternal life (pp. 254-55).

Bruce, Frederick Fyvie. *The Epistle of John.* Old Tappan, N.J.: Revell, 1970. 160 pp. Bruce provides a brief, popular exposition. He defends the apostle John as author (pp. 1, 5); gives a short introduction (pp. 25-33); holds that the words *world* and *life* are key words of John (p. 36); stresses the role of Christ as Advocate (p. 49); warns Christians against placing their eggs in such a perishable basket as the world (pp. 63-64); teaches the coming of a future Antichrist (pp. 67 ff.); holds that a sinful life marks one as not being a child of God (p. 90); and has a note rejecting the authenticity of the passage on the three heavenly witnesses (pp. 129-30).

Law, Robert. *The Tests of Life.* Edinburgh: Clark, 1909. 422 pp. This work is not a verse-by-verse commentary but a study of major topics in I John. Law centers most of his thoughts on three great tests—of righteousness, of love, and of belief—found in I John; but he also discusses the doctrines of Christ, sin, propitiation, eternal life, and so on. He stresses that Jesus is "God's only-begotten Son" (p. 73), the eternal Son (p. 100); defends the doctrine of the Trinity (pp. 78-80) but admits that the full doctrine may not be found in I John (p. 98); thinks that John teaches the impeccability of the righteous man and that this is puzzling rather than instructive (p. 70); and appropriately asserts that "individual sins are like islets, which appear as separate and casual specks on the surface of the ocean, but are, in reality, the mountain-peaks of a submerged continent" (p. 133).

Greek Exegesis

Westcott, Brooke Foss. *The Epistles of St. John.* 1883. Reprint, Grand Rapids: Eerdmans, 1955. 436 pp. This book is the best, most thorough commentary on the Greek text. Westcott defends John's authorship (pp. xxx ff.); holds that the "word of life" refers to the revelation, not the Person (p. 4); stresses that the threefold revelation of God's nature leads to practical living (p. 17); has extended notes on special subjects: fatherhood of God (pp. 27-34), blood of Christ (pp. 34-37), sin (pp. 37-40), Antichrist (pp. 92-93), love (pp. 130-34), names of Christ (pp. 136-38); and has exhaustive comments on the text of 5:7 (pp. 202-9).

Revelation

Expositions

Smith, Jacob Brubaker. *A Revelation of Jesus Christ.* Scottdale, Penn.: Herald Press, 1961. 369 pp. Chart. In a very thorough futurist interpretation, Smith discusses the names of the Lord (pp. 1 ff.); lists many symbols that are interpreted (pp. 18-19); draws an outline from 1:19 (p. 56); interprets the judgments literally (pp. 139 ff.); identifies Abaddon with Satan (p. 145); regards Revelation 10 and 11 as the midpoint of the tribulation (p. 149); identifies the two witnesses as Moses and Elijah (p. 169); thinks the 666 refers to Nero (p. 207); stresses that the one thousand years are literal (p. 269); holds that the unity of believers is seen in the foundations and gates (p. 293); stresses imminency (p. 301); and concludes with a number of appendixes (pp. 309-63).

Seiss, Joseph A. *The Apocalypse.* 1865. Reprint, Grand Rapids: Zondervan, n.d. 536 pp. Seiss writes powerful messages from Revelation. He stresses the deity of Christ (p. 46); warns against Laodicean lukewarmness (p. 64); teaches a partial rapture: holds that the twenty-four elders are the senior company of raptured saints (pp. 104-5); interprets the judgments literally (pp. 191 ff.); attacks spiritualism (p. 214); identifies the two hundred million horsemen as infernal cavalry (p. 219); errs on Chapter 12; holds that the woman is the visible church and the man child the true church (pp. 297, 300); stresses the literal nature of the binding of Satan (p. 446) and the literal one-thousand-year reign (p. 474); and thinks that the New Jerusalem will be suspended over the earth (p. 497).

Walvoord, John Flipse. *The Revelation of Jesus Christ.* Chicago: Moody, 1966. 347 pp. In a careful futurist commentary, Walvoord stresses that Christ is the main theme of the book (p. 7); defends the authorship of the apostle John (pp. 11 ff.); surveys the theology of Revelation (pp. 30 ff.); often gives different opinions without deciding which one is most accurate (pp. 42, 52, 58-59); holds that the twenty-four elders represent the church (p. 107); teaches a pretribulation rapture (p. 139); argues for a literal interpretation (pp. 153-54); holds that the scorpion locusts are demons (p. 16); thinks that the two witnesses are unknown future prophets (p. 179); does not think that the false prophet is a Jew (p. 205); holds that the everlasting gospel is not the gospel of grace (p. 217); and argues for premillennialism (pp. 300 ff.).

Ironside, H. A. *Lectures on the Book of Revelation.* New York: Loizeaux, 1920. 366 pp. Ironside offers a premillennial interpretation. He defends the doctrine of the Trinity (pp. 15, 44); attacks Romanism (pp. 56-57), Christian Science (pp. 1, 53); and so on; teaches a pretribulation rapture (p. 80); interprets the scorpion locusts as false cults, Spiritism, and so on (pp. 158-59); holds that the entire millennium is a period of judgment (p. 198) and that the woman clothed with the sun is Israel (p. 21); thinks that the second beast of Revelation 13 is the Antichrist (p. 236); argues for premillennialism (pp. 333 ff.); and denies a general judgment (p. 345).

Tenney, Merrill C. *Interpreting Revelation.* Grand Rapids: Eerdmans, 1957. 220 pp. This book is not a commentary but a study of special topics. Tenney defends John, an early disciple, as author (p. 15); gives background in history (pp. 20-21), society (pp. 22-23), religion (pp. 23-24), and the Old Testament (pp. 101-2); examines the structure of the book (pp. 32 ff.); has a chart of the "sevens" (p. 38); gives a brief survey of the contents (pp. 42 ff.); has a thorough study of the seven churches (pp. 50-69); contrasts Babylon and the New Jerusalem (p. 91); discusses the Christology of Revelation (pp. 117 ff.), the chronology (pp. 135 ff.), and the different millennial views (pp. 174 ff.); provides help on the symbolism (pp. 186 ff.); and gives an extensive bibliography (pp. 207-11).

*Neal, Marshall. *Seven Churches: God's Revelation to the Church Today.* Greenville, S.C.: Bob Jones University Press, 1977. 102 pp. Neal writes a very helpful exposition of the messages to the seven churches. He gives the general characteristics of each letter (pp. 5-6); attacks the idea that they refer to consecutive church ages (p. 10); provides interesting historical sidelights (p. 16); warns against the dangers of compromise (p. 49); identifies the morning star as Christ (p. 62); warns against overconfidence (p. 69); and shows the need for real repentance (pp. 97-98). The work is especially valuable because Dr. Neal has visited each location himself and can describe the circumstances of each place (pp. 92-93). There are beautiful color photos of each city following.

Greek Exegesis

Swete, Henry Barclay. *The Apocalypse of St. John.* 1906. Reprint, Grand Rapids: Eerdmans, 1951. 557 pp. This work is a strong analysis of the Greek text but weak in interpretation and theology. Swete lists the forty-two Greek paragraphs with headings (pp. xxxvii ff.); discusses the unity of Revelation (pp. xlvi ff.), the Antichrist in Asia (pp. lxxviii ff.), the vocabulary, style, and so on (pp. cxx ff.), and the symbolism (pp. cxxxi ff.); distinguishes between Greek words and gives their history (pp. 24, 39, etc.); thinks that there may be an inconsistency in the writer's thought (p. 113); holds that the two witnesses represent the church (p. 134); teaches a general judgment (pp. 146, 270); and does not believe in a literal reign on the earth (p. 265).

CHAPTER 43
THE PASTOR'S FIVE-FOOT BOOKSHELF

What reference works should be purchased first and always kept within arm's reach? The five-foot shelf of great books has been a popular idea in the educational and literary worlds for some time.

Let us assume that the pastor will have the biblical text before him, good reference Bibles, and, if he can use them, the Greek and Hebrew texts as well. Let us also assume that he will acquire, as he is able to, the best commentaries on the Bible that he can get.

The Absolute Essentials

1. Young, Robert. *Analytical Concordance to the Bible.* Grand Rapids: Eerdmans, n.d. There is no excuse for a pastor's wasting hours paging through the Bible looking for a reference when he can find it in a few seconds by using a good concordance. Some may prefer to use Strong's *Exhaustive Concordance.*

2. Orr, James, ed. *The International Standard Bible Encyclopaedia,* 5 vols. Grand Rapids: Eerdmans, 1939. Rev. ed. 1979-88, 4 vols. Whether it is a biblical person, place, thing, or doctrine, it can be found in this work with very helpful discussion and Scripture summaries. Some will prefer the *Zondervan Pictorial Encyclopedia of the Bible,* also in five volumes. It has up-to-date information and excellent photographic illustrations. Some pastors will prefer to have both and to use them to supplement one another.

3. Wright, George E., and Floyd V. Filson. *Westminster Historical Atlas to the Bible.* Philadelphia: Westminster, 1956. The

pastor must be able to find out where biblical sites are in relation to one another. The excellent maps and thorough indexes will be a great help to him. The text of the work is liberal, however.

4. Aharoni, Yohanan, and Michael Avi-Yonah. *Macmillan Bible Atlas.* New York: Macmillan, 1968. The format of this book is so different that it does not duplicate the previous work. Every page has a map and text that illustrate a specific biblical event. The authors are Jewish.

5. Pfeiffer, Charles F., and Howard F. Vos. *The Wycliffe Historical Geography of Bible Lands.* The student needs not only Bible atlases but also a work that describes the terrain and physical surroundings of different sites. The thorough descriptions of biblical sites, the historical background, and other helps make this a very useful book. If the student has been able to travel to Israel, he has probably obtained one of the great traveler's guides: Zev Vilnay's *Guide to Israel* (Jerusalem: Vilnay, 1955, 1970. 720 pp. An excellent Jewish guide.) or Eugene Hoade's *Guide to the Holy Land.* (Jerusalem: Franciscan Press, 1974. 993 pp. A Catholic guide.). Both are not usually available outside of Israel. They provide an incredible amount of background information.

6. *The American Heritage College Dictionary,* 3rd ed. New York: Houghton Mifflin, 1993. It is essential for the pastor to know the meaning of every word in his English Bible. Some may prefer to use an unabridged dictionary. An economical work that provides great help in finding alliterative words for outlines is Richard Soule's *Dictionary of English Synonyms* (New York: Bantam, 1930, 1960) *Roget's Pocket Thesaurus* (New York: Pocket Books, 1923, 1946) also is helpful.

If the pastor can use Greek, he should have the best Greek tools at hand as well.

Arndt, William F., and Wilbur Gingrich. *A Greek-English Lexicon of the New Testament.* Chicago: University of Chicago, 1957. The best.

Moulton, William F., and Alfred S. Geden. *A Concordance to the Greek Testament.* Edinburgh: Clark, 1897. An equally excellent resource.

If the pastor can use Hebrew, he should have

Brown, Francis, S. R. Driver, and Charles A. Briggs. *A Hebrew and English Lexicon of the Old Testament.* Oxford: Clarendon, 1907, 1955.

The Most Useful Helps

7. *The New Topical Text Book.* New York: Revell, 1897, 1935. This anonymous work has been a blessing to generations. It sometimes provides verses in which the idea, but not the word, is found so that it gives help in addition to what concordances can provide.

8. Smith, Jerome H. *The New Treasury of Scripture Knowledge,* revised and expanded. Nashville: Nelson, 1992. 1,660 pp. This is the best and most complete source for cross-references and marginal notes. (The cross-references on Genesis 1 fill three pages!) Symbols increase its help: * means an especially clear reference; + means that verse has a fuller list of references on that word.

9. Trench, Richard C. *Synonyms of the New Testament.* Grand Rapids: Eerdmans, 1880, 1953. The pastor should always try to make a clear distinction between words that may be confusing. Trench gives much help in distinguishing a number of words.

10. Carson, D. A., Douglass J. Moo, and Leon Morris. *An Introduction to the New Testament.* Grand Rapids: Zondervan, 1992. This is the best recent work. The authors defend traditional authorship and dates for every New Testament book.

11. Archer, Gleason L. *A Survey of Old Testament Introduction,* revised and expanded. Chicago: Moody, 1964, 1994. Archer gives conservative answers to questions of Old Testament authorship, dates, and so on.

12. Erickson, Millard J. *Christian Theology.* Grand Rapids: Baker, 1983, 1984, 1985. This is the best recent work on systematic theology. He is New Evangelical and a cautious premillennialist.

The Special Topics

When studying a difficult subject, the pastor should have the best books on that subject at hand. Again and again these books will provide answers; and even after using them for years, the pastor will discover new things in them.

13. Morgan, G. Campbell. *The Parables and Metaphors of Our Lord.* New York: Revell, 1943. The author presents a good discussion of the parabolic method (pp. 13 ff.) with genuinely helpful explanations of the parables.

14. Fairbairn, Patrick. *The Typology of Scripture.* Grand Rapids: Zondervan, n.d. 904 pp. This exhaustive work discusses the tabernacle, the sacrifices, the feasts, the meaning of the law, the prophetic types, and so on.

15. Pentecost, J. Dwight. *Things to Come.* Findlay, Ohio: Dunham, 1958. 663 pp. In this thorough, premillennial study of biblical eschatology, the author defends the pretribulation rapture view (pp. 193-218) and discusses Daniel's seventy weeks (pp. 239 ff.), the campaign of Armageddon (pp. 340 ff.), and so on. Another thorough work is the *Dictionary of Premillennial Theology,* edited by Mal Crouch (Grand Rapids: Kregel, 1996).

16. Morris, Leon. *The Cross in the New Testament.* Grand Rapids: Eerdmans, 1965. 454 pp. This is a thorough and reverent study of the doctrine of salvation as it unfolds in the New Testament. Morris defends the vicarious, substitutionary atonement (pp. 32 ff.) and stresses that all salvation depends on the death of Christ (pp. 216-17).

17. Edersheim, Alfred. *The Life and Times of Jesus the Messiah.* 2 vols. Grand Rapids: Eerdmans, 1953. 695, 828 pp. This is the most thorough and helpful work available on the

life of Christ. Edersheim is a converted Jew who has real insight into Jewish customs and interpretations.

18. Scroggie, W. Graham. *Guide to the Gospels.* London: Pickering and Inglis, 1948. 664 pp. In this rich study guide to the Gospels, the author provides much unique material on each Gospel and studies the parables, miracles, use of the Old Testament, and so on. He defends "Q" (p. 254).

19. Conybeare, W. J., and J. S. Howson. *The Life and Epistles of St. Paul.* Grand Rapids: Eerdmans, 1953. 850 pp. The authors have prepared a careful study of the life of Paul with paraphrases of his epistles inserted at the time during his life when they were written. It is very valuable for historical background.

20. Ben-Tor, Amnon. *The Archaeology of Ancient Israel.* New Haven: Yale University Press, 1992. This is the best work on Old Testament archaeology. The best New Evangelical introduction to the whole field is *Biblical Archaeology in Focus* by Keith N. Schoville.

21. Whyte, Alexander. *Bible Characters.* 6 vols. London: Oliphants, n.d. This is the greatest series of messages ever preached on Bible biography. The studies are powerful and moving.

22. Alter, Robert. *The Art of Biblical Poetry.* New York: Basic Books, 1985. This is the most helpful single work. Another is James L. Jugel's *Idea of Biblical Poetry: Parallelism and Its History* (New Haven: Yale University Press, 1981). Both men are Jews who speak the language.

23. Morris, Leon. *New Testament Theology.* Grand Rapids: Zondervan, 1986. This is the most practical recent work that defends the traditional canon and doctrine. The most exhaustive is Donald Guthrie's *New Testament Theology* (Downers Grove, Ill.: InterVarsity Press, 1981).

24. Hasel, Gerhard. *Old Testament Theology,* 4th ed. Grand Rapids: Eerdmans, 1972, 1991. This is the most practical in Old Testament theology.

25. Feinberg, Charles L., ed. *The Fundamentals for Today.* Grand Rapids: Kregel, 1958. 657 pp. The editor has compiled an anthology of articles defending the great doctrines of the Faith. This work will provide ideas for many messages.

26. Swete, Henry Barclay. *The Holy Spirit in the New Testament.* 1910. Reprint, Grand Rapids: Baker, 1964. 417 pp. Swete presents a thorough and thought-provoking study of the doctrine of the Holy Spirit as it is unfolded in the New Testament.

27. Unger, Merrill F. *Biblical Demonology.* Wheaton, Ill.: Van Kampen, 1952. 250 pp. Unger has set forth the most sensible and balanced presentation of the doctrine of the powers of evil in Scripture. He also covers current evil influence in the world.

28. Bruce, Frederick Fyvie. *The Books and the Parchments.* London: Pickering and Inglis, 1950. 257 pp. This book covers the Greek, Hebrew, and Aramaic languages, the canon of Scripture, and the transmission of the text all the way to the English Bibles.

29. Broadus, John A. *On the Preparation and Delivery of Sermons.* New York: Harper, 1870, 1944. 392 pp. It is good for the pastor to keep returning to a great classic in homiletics. If he stops trying to improve, he will deteriorate; if he keeps trying to improve, he will improve as long as he preaches.

30. Martin, Walter R. *The Kingdom of the Cults.* Rev. ed. Grand Rapids: Zondervan, 1977. This is the best and most helpful of the books on the cults. Believers run into them so frequently that it is vital to have help close at hand.

INDEX